19TH EDITION
2019-2020

by Simon Scott

A Complete Guide
for Yachtsmen, Divers
and Watersports Enthusiasts

D1557722

THE CRUISING GUIDE
TO THE
VIRGIN ISLANDS

Cruising Guide Publications, Inc. is a special-interest publisher of sailing guides to cruising in various areas around the world and other publications of nautical interest. CGP endeavors to provide comprehensive and invaluable materials to both inveterate sailors and less experienced seafarers seeking vital vacationing tips and navigational information relative to the journey to and the enjoyment of their destinations.

The Cruising Guide to the Virgin Islands is intended for use in conjunction with either U.S. National Ocean Survey charts, U.S. Hydrographic Office charts, N.V. Charts, or British Admiralty charts. Every effort has been made to describe conditions accurately. However, the publisher makes no warranty, express or implied, for any errors or omissions in this publication. Skippers should use this guide only in conjunction with the above charts and/or other navigational aids and not place undue credence in the accuracy of this guide. **The Cruising Guide to the Virgin Islands** is not intended for use for navigational purposes.

For regular V.I. information updates see our website: www.CruisingGuides.com

Published by
Cruising Guide Publications, Inc.

PO Box 1017
Dunedin, FL 34697-1017
Telephone: 727-733-5322

Email: info@cruisingguides.com
www.CruisingGuides.com

Publisher/ Managing Editor: Simon Scott
Senior Editor: Bonnie Harrison

Art Dir./Graphics/Layout
Julie L. Johnston

Graphic Design
Carol Design, Inc.
Affinity Design
A.E. Sabo

Advertising /Mktg Director
Maureen Larroux

Production Mgr/Distribution
Ashley Scott

Public Relations/Media
Sharon Friedes

Editor
Chelsea Scott

Illustrations
Roger Burnett
Roger Bansemer

Photography
A.J. Blake
Diane Butler
Nancy & Steve Cooper
Aragorn Dick-Read
Marc Downing
Walker Mangum
Jeff Monuszko
Babette Rittmeyer
Mark Robinson
Jim Scheiner
Simon Scott
Chris Simmons
Brett Szematowicz
Dougal Thornton
Bitter End
Nanny Cay Marine Center
USVI Tourist Board
VI National Park
Virgin Island Charters
Yacht Haven Grande
Yacht Shots BVI

Contributing Writers
Carol Bareuther
Julian Putley
William Stelzer
Neil Whitehead, PhD

Cruising Guide Publications would like to extend our thanks to the following people for their ongoing support, input and endless requests for information:
• Colene Penn, *Head of Communications BVI RDA*
• Matthew Wakefield, *Deputy Dir. Project Strategy BVI RDA*
• Richard Stein, *GM Lighthouse Marina/Admiral Management*
• Vivian Wheatley, *Proprietor/ Owner Anegada Reef Hotel*
• Claire Shefchik, *Business Editor BVI Beacon*
• Tessa Callwood, *Foxy's, Jost Van Dyke*
• Tom Warner, *GM Foxy's Bar and Restaurant*
• Keith Dawson, *Marketing Manager, BVI Tourist Board*
• Nadia Penn, *Island Birds (Charter)*
• Susan Zaluski, *Dir. of the Van Dyke Preservation Society*
• Jacek Wierzbicki & Maya Soueidi, *Crew/Catamaran Sta Ana- Wave 58*
• Tyler Clendenin, *aerial drone surveyor*

Copyright © Maritime Ventures, Ltd. 2019
Nineteenth Edition
Printed in China

Front Cover Photography:
Yacht Shots BVI/Jim Scheiner

ISBN: 978-1-7333053-2-7

THE
CRUISING
GUIDE
TO THE
VIRGIN ISLANDS

Dedicated to "THE VI STRONG"
for rebuilding Paradise

"The storm is over, you won't remember how
you made it through, how you managed to survive.
You won't even be sure, whether the storm is really over.
But one thing is certain. When you come out of the storm,
you won't be the same person who walked in.
That's what this storm's all about."

Haruki Murakami

19TH EDITION

2019-2020

by Simon Scott

A Complete Guide
for Yachtsmen, Divers and Watersports Enthusiasts

BRITISH VIRGIN ISLANDS

ROAD HARBOUR

EASTERN TORTOLA

WESTERN TORTOLA

THE CHANNEL ISLANDS

VIRGIN GORDA SOUTH

GORDA SOUND

ANEGADA

JOST VAN DYKE

U.S. VIRGIN ISLANDS

ST. JOHN NORTH/WEST

ST. JOHN EAST

ST. JOHN SOUTH

CHARLOTTE AMALIE/WEST

ST. THOMAS SOUTH/EAST

ST. THOMAS N. COAST

ST. CROIX

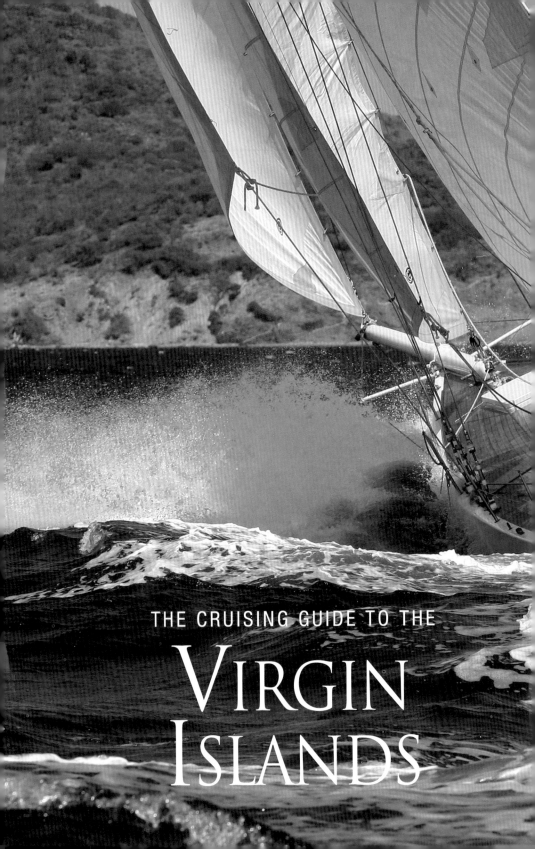

THE CRUISING GUIDE TO THE

VIRGIN
ISLANDS

INTRODUCTION

AFTER THE STORM

It has now been two years since the islands of the Caribbean were dealt a double blow from the passage of Hurricanes Irma & Maria; both carving a path of devastation and destruction from Dominica in the lower Leeward Islands, north to The Virgin Islands before setting a course to Puerto Rico to the west.

We are all familiar with the horrific scenes of destruction and suffering that were posted all over the internet and media worldwide. For those of us who are familiar with the islands, it was staggering to contemplate the extent of the damage, communities, houses, businesses, churches, marinas, trees, foliage and communications infrastructure, for the most part they were either severely damaged or just gone! There were in all over 300 wrecked, sunk or derelict vessels around the islands, the beaches and the hillsides surrounding them all strewn with the debris of broken dreams.

Now, two years after this mammoth tragedy of nature's betrayal, we are, in the simplest of terms, amazed! They say "it takes a village" and this much loved island chain became a village with the common goal of recovery. It was, without doubt, in the interest of everyone, to stand up, clean up and start up all over again. Tales of community are everywhere, some bring tears to your eyes while some bring a smile to your lips. Take some time to talk to the people who lived through it. Sharing is part of the healing process.

The clean up after a storm of this magnitude is no mean feat and progress at times has seemed agonizingly slow. The BVI Recovery and Development Authority (RDA) have indicated that all derelict vessels will be cleared by November 2019 as they implement their staged recovery plan that works in conjunction with the private sector to address needs at both community and tourism sectors.

The Islands are going strong once again, although complete recovery still has a way to go. Sailing in the Virgins is still as good as ever and as our readers know, revenue from Charter Boats feeds the economic arteries of the islands and we are proud that cruising sailors from around the world have been such a critical link in the chain of recovery. When planning your Virgin Island adventure, plan to enjoy the restaurants and beach bars whose owners and staff have worked tirelessly to be open for the season. They are there to support our enjoyment and in turn, we need to support them. The last few years has been difficult for all and your business is truly appreciated. Be generous and spend some money. They are ready. It's time to go sailing. Welcome to the Virgin Islands!

Simon Scott
Publisher

TABLE OF CONTENTS

TABLE OF CONTENTS

Chart From The United States To The Virgin Islands.

BAHAMAS

ATLANTIC OCEAN

CUBA

HISPANIOLA

JAMAICA

THE VIRGIN ISLANDS

PUERTO RICO

HORSE SHOE REEF

ANEGADA

14 N. MILES

NECKER I.

GT. TOBAGO

LITTLE TOBAGO

HANS LOLLIK

JOST VAN DYKE

GT CAMANOE I.

GUANA I.

DOG I.

SCRUB I.

BEEF I.

VIRGIN GORDA

TORTOLA

THATCH CAY

GREAT THATCH I.

SIR FRANCIS DRAKE CHANNEL

ROUND RK.

GINGER I.

ST. THOMAS

SALT I.

COOPER I.

ST. JOHN

PETER I.

CARIBBEAN SEA

DOG ROCK

NORMAN I.

BUCK ISLAND

35 N. MILES

0   5   10   15

SCALE IN NAUTICAL MILES.

VIRGIN ISLAND
CRUISING GROUNDS

N

NW   NE

W   E

SW   SE

S

BUCK ISLAND

ST. CROIX

Virgin Islands History

Nothing has influenced the history of the Virgin Islands more profoundly than their geography and physical makeup. Situated at the high point of the curving archipelago that swings from Trinidad to Florida, they survey strategically all of the Americas, and, with their steady trade winds and numerous sheltered harbors, it is not surprising that they rapidly became a center for sea routes to every point of the compass, providing a welcome pause in the lengthy trade lines between Europe and the riches of South and Central America. Having been described as "the place on the way to everywhere," they have long been desirable for both trading and military advantage, from the days when Spaniards sailed through carrying Mexican and Peruvian bullion to Spain until this century when the United States paid $25 million to buy the US Virgin Islands from Denmark in order to forestall any unfriendly foreign power from parking on their doorstep.

Sailors and sailing have therefore been at the core of Virgin Islands history from the moment the first Amerindians brought their kanawa (canoes) from the South American mainland and populated the Antilles.

The various migrations that occurred into the Caribbean from South America over the last thousand years have been identified with various archaeological complexes such as the Ciboney, Arawak and Caribs. However, the relationship amongst these different archaeological traditions remains obscure, although the old story of fierce and cannibalistic Caribs eating their way across the islands at the expense of the peaceable Arawaks is now seen as rather more the lurid colonial fantasy than a credible anthropological reconstruction of the early Caribbean.

Native words were adopted directly into European languages, as with canoe, tobacco, barbecue, potato, hurricane and, notoriously, cannibal.

increased so did Carib resistance which only provoked Emperor Charles V to order that the Indians "should be treated as enemies and given no quarter." Nevertheless, Carib military resistance to the Europeans lasted in one form or another until the start of the nineteenth century – and there was even a minor Carib War with the British in the 1930s.

Columbus discovered the Virgin Islands in 1493, on his second voyage to the New World. He anchored off Salt River Bay in St. Croix for fresh water and then was driven by unfavorable winds to Virgin Gorda. Seeing the numerous islands, he named them "the Virgins" in honor of St. Ursula and the 11,000 virgins who, threatened by the marauding Huns in 4th-century Cologne, sacrificed their lives rather than submit to a fate worse than death. Virgin Gorda may have got its name (fat virgin) because Columbus, viewing it from seaward, thought that it resembled a reclining woman with a protruding belly. As Spanish settlements

Piracy arose in general because various European nations who were unable to challenge Spanish dominance in the region directly, gave these pirates unofficial backing, in the form of letters of marque, to follow private enterprise or to indulge in smuggling, piracy and the harassment of Spanish settlements. Even a famous personage like Sir Walter Raleigh was therefore known to the Spanish as "El Pirata Ingles."

This combination of privateering and piracy (the distinction between the two wearing very thin at times) was to continue for several hundred years. A vast array of colorful and bizarre characters paused in the Virgin Islands, among them the well-known pirate Henry Morgan and the legendary Sir John Hawkins, who visited the area four times.

As the power of Spain waned, other countries began to colonize the West Indies more seriously, although piracy continued for a while, the struggling settlers being happy to trade their agricultural produce and materials for a share of the Spanish gold.

Eventually, however, the bullion treasures from America dried up and a process of colonization for commercial profit emerged. The Danes formally took possession of St. Thomas and, later, St. John; the English ousted the Dutch and gained a firm foothold in Tortola and Virgin Gorda; and the French settled in St. Croix but later sold it to the Danish West India Company.

The Spaniards continued to raid occasionally from their strongholds in Puerto Rico and Hispaniola through the late 1600s and piracy flared up intermittently in the early 1700s. Considerable cleaning up and law enforcement took place as the casual farming that had begun, merely in order to colonize the islands and break the Spanish monopoly, gave way to serious plantations which, unsubsidized by stolen Spanish gold, needed to trade at a steady profit.

Following the example of the original Spanish settlers, early plantation owners brought slaves from Africa. When the introduction of sugar cane production in the 1640s required a large, cheap and stable labor force, the number of slaves began to increase. For some time the colonies thrived. Sugar and cotton were valuable commodities and the plantations diversified into the production of indigo, spices, rum, maize, pineapples, yams and coconuts. In 1717 the first census taken in Virgin Gorda showed a population of 625, about half of whom were black. By the mid-1700s this population had grown to nearly 2,000 and the proportion of slaves throughout the Virgin Islands had increased dramatically.

Life on the plantations was extremely hard for the slaves and, as their majority on the islands increased, so did the restrictions on them and the severity of the punishments meted out to them for the breaking of these. Conflict over the slave trade was increasing; it had been outlawed in England in 1772 and the impetus for its abolition was growing.

The obstacles to plantation life increased, several hurricanes and droughts ravaged the islands, and the American Revolution and Napoleonic wars created a revival of enemy raids, piracy and fighting within the islands. The slaves suffered as a result and, as news of abolition elsewhere began to filter through to the West Indies, they began to make use of their by now considerable majority to rebel.

The slave rebellions coincided, more or less, with the introduction of the sugar beet in Europe, which dealt a fatal blow to the once great "trade-triangle" based on West Indian cane. By the mid-1800s the slaves were free and the white population had deserted the colonies.

For almost 100 years the Virgin Islands dozed peacefully, the freed slaves living quietly off the land and sea, though with some difficulty in years of drought and famine. Government was minimal. The islands struggled on with tottering economies. Virgin Gorda was visited briefly by Cornish miners who reopened the old Spanish mine in search of copper. An earthquake leveled all the churches in Tortola and the R.M.S. Rhone was wrecked off Salt Island. As late as 1869 the steamship Telegrafo was detained in Tortola and charged with piracy. Labor riots and rebellions occasionally protested the hardships. The United States began to show an interest in buying the Danish islands, afraid that they would be sold to a hostile nation such as Germany.

The islands moved into the 20th century without much change. An agricultural station was established in Tortola in 1900 in hopes of boosting the faltering economy, various homestead projects were begun throughout the island with little effect and the parent governments of each colony were forced to accept financial responsibility for the islands, which were fast becoming a liability.

The Callwood Distillery, Cane Garden Bay

The first world war was tightening the purse strings further, and by 1917 the Danes were happy to sell their Virgin Islands to the United States, which was eager to have a military outpost in the Caribbean. St. Thomas had long been a useful coaling station and harbor for steamships and was well positioned to defend the approaches to the Panama Canal.

Over the first half of the 20th century there was gradual social reform and progress towards local government. This process began to speed up as the tourist trade, boosted by the increasing ease of casual travel, began to grow. Situated conveniently close to the United States and blessed with a warm climate and a beautiful, unspoiled environment, the Virgin Islands rapidly became popular with tourists. This is an industry which needed only the natural resources of the islands to sustain their economies, and responsible tourism will also ensure that sustainability continues.

With the charter industry becoming the backbone of the islands, particularly in the BVI, sailors continue to make use of one of the finest sailing areas in the world. The quiet coves where Drake, Columbus and Blackbeard used to anchor are once more havens for fleets of sailing vessels and the modern adventurers who come to explore the Virgin Islands.

With thanks to Neil Whitehead, PhD

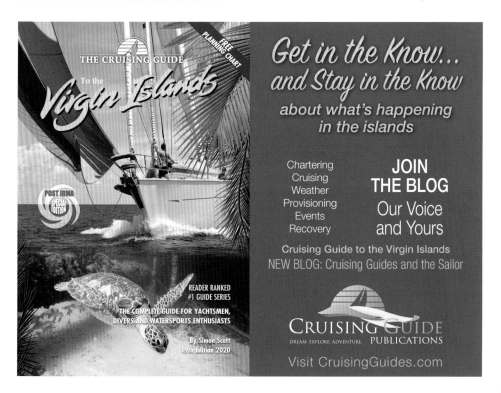

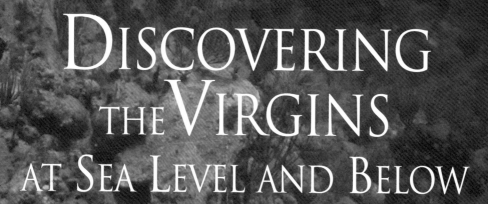

DISCOVERING
the VIRGINS
at Sea Level and Below

NATIONAL MARINE PARKS

BRITISH VIRGIN ISLANDS

Visitors come to the Virgin Islands to savor the magnificence of the area's natural resources –the steady, gentle tradewinds, glorious sunshine, crystalline waters, the splendor of the coral reefs and abundant sea life. This is a fragile area, however, which must be protected if it is to be enjoyed for many years to come.

The anchors of the charter boats have taken their toll in broken coral, destroying the incredible beauty below the sea that once housed many different forms of sea life. In an effort to defend the reefs against the carelessness of yachtsmen, the National Parks Trust has taken a firm stand and has installed mooring buoys developed by Dr. John Halas of the Key Largo National Marine Sanctuary. This mooring system is being used worldwide to protect reefs and prevent damage from anchors. It calls for a stainless steel pin cemented into the bedrock and a polypropylene line attached to a surface buoy. The system is very strong and extremely effective in eliminating damage when used properly.

MARINE PARK REGULATIONS

- Do not damage, alter or remove any marine plant, animal or historic artifact.
- All fishing – including spearfishing – is strictly prohibited. Lobstering and collecting live shells are also illegal.
- Use correct garbage disposal points; do not litter the area. Water balloons are prohibited.
- Water skiing and jet skiing are prohibited in all Park areas.
- No anchoring in the restricted area in and around the Wreck of the Rhone. When the mooring system is full, vessels should utilize the Salt Island Settlement anchorage and arrive by tender, using the dinghy mooring system provided.

MOORING USAGE REGULATIONS

- Vessels must legally have met BVI customs and immigration requirements, and have in their possession valid clearance forms and cruising permits.
- The buoys of the reef protection system are color-coded:
  Red: Non-diving, snorkeling and day use only (90 min. limit)
  Blue: Dinghies only
  Yellow: Commercial dive vessels only
- Vessels must attach to the buoy pennant, making sure to avoid chafing of the pennant against the vessel. If the configuration provided is not compatible with your vessel, an extension line must be attached to the pennant eye.
- All buoys are used at user's risk. While the moorings are the property of the BVI Government and are managed by the BVI National Parks Trust, neither bears the responsibility for any loss or injury resulting from the use of the system. Charterers may purchase permits through their charter companies, and visiting private yachts may purchase permits through customs. The fees are nominal and go directly to the Parks Trust for the installation and maintenance of the buoys.

NATIONAL PARKS TRUST
MOORING BUOYS IN THE BVI

For day use only with National Parks Permit

Norman Island
1. Angel Fish
2. The Caves
3. Ring Dove Rock
4. Black Forest
5. Santa Monica Rock
6. Water Point
7. Spyglass Wall
8. Brown Pants
9. Pelican Island
   & The Indians

Peter Island
10. Carrot Rock
11. Shark Point
12. Black Tip
13. Rhone Anchor
14. Fearless
15. Great Harbour

Dead Chest
16. Painted Walls
17. Coral Gardens
18. Blonde Rock

Salt Island
19. The Rhone
20. Rhone Reef

Cooper Island
21. Dry Rocks East & West
22. Haulover Bay
23. Mary L.
24. Incannes Bay
25. Cistern Point
26. Thumb Rock
27. Markoe Point

28. Devil's Kitchen
29. Carvel Rock

Ginger Island
30. Ginger Steps
31. Alice in Wonderland
32. Ginger Patch
33. Alice's Backside

Virgin Gorda
34. Fallen Jerusalem
35. The Baths
36. Fisher's Rocks

The Dogs
37. Great Dog South
38. George Dog
39. Bronco Billy
40. Cockroach Island
41. The Chimneys
42. Wall to Wall
43. Joes Cave
44. Flintstones
45. Dolphin Rocks
46. Seal Dogs
47. Mountain Point
48. Cow's Mouth
49. Paul's Grotto

Necker Island
50. The Invisibles

Scrub Island
51. Scrub Island
    Point
52. Scrub Island
    West

Great Camanoe
53. Diamond Reef

Guana Island
54. Monkey Point
55. The Chikuzen

Tortola
56. Brewers Bay
57. Green Cay
58. Great Tobago
59. Great Thatch

BVI MARINE PARK MOORINGS

The BVI National Parks Trust maintains moorings on the following islands:
Norman • Ginger • Pelican
Guana • The Indians
George Dog • Peter Island • Great Dog
Dead Chest • Cockroach • Salt Island • Tortola
Cooper • Virgin Gorda • Scrub Island
Great Camanoe • Sandy Cay • Green Cay
Tobago • West Dog • Seal Dog

RATE STRUCTURE

Private Vessel Fees –

BVI Registered Boats:
$75 per year

Foreign Registered Boats:
$150 per year

National Parks Trust
bvinationalparkstrust.org
Tel: 284-494-2069

Commercial Fees –

BVI Based Charter Boats:
$25 per boat/week (4 persons)
$35 per boat/week (6 persons)
$45 per boat/week (8 persons)
$55 per boat/week (10 persons)
Each added person pays $5/week

Foreign Based Charter Boats:
$50 per boat/week (4 persons)
$70 per boat/week (6 persons)
$90 per boat/week (8 persons)
$110 per boat/week (10 persons)
Each added person pays $5/week

Foreign Term Charter Yachts:
$750 annually (4 persons)
$1,050 annually (6 persons)
$1,350 annually (8 persons)
$1,650 annually (10 persons)

BVI Term Charter Yachts:
$375 annually (4 persons)
$525 annually (6 persons)
$675 annually (8 persons)
$825 annually (10 persons)

BVI & USVI Day Charter and
Dive Boats:
$3 per person/day (adult),
$2 (child)

10 Ways to Protect the Coral Reef

1. Realize that coral reefs are systems of slow growing animals that have taken many centuries to develop into what we see today. They are not rocks and standing on them or kicking them will cause substantial damage. Corals have very limited ability to recover from damages; breaking off a piece of coral is usually fatal, killing hundreds of years of growth.

2. Don't drop anchors or anchor chains on corals. Know what is below before you drop your anchor. If you aren't sure that you are over sand jump in the water with a mask to take a look. Dropping anchors and chains on coral crushes, pulverizes and dislodges the corals from the bottom. This destructive practice can be easily avoided by using a mooring to secure your boat or snorkeling to see what lies below your keel before you drop the hook.

3. Don't touch, kick or stand on coral. Don't drag dive equipment or cameras across it. Don't kick sand on it. Fins, cameras, dive gauges, and regulator second stages can crush coral polyps, or break off entire sections of coral. Sand kicked up by fins, feet or boat engines can smother corals, depriving them of sunlight and food they require for growth and life. And while small contacts may not be life-threatening, the additional stress may prove too much and become fatal. Abrasions also provide locations for infections in the coral, or places for invasion by marine micro-organisms.

4. Don't drive boats into reefs. While running aground is a nightmare for the cruiser, it is also fatal for the reef. Know where you are cruising. Pay attention to charts and navigation and limit distractions. Don't leave the helm while operating a boat and don't (or limit) cruising at night.

5. Don't pump-out holding tanks/bilges and don't add chemicals to these places. Pollutants in the form of sewage and oils are harmful to reefs. Nutrients in the sewage promote algae growth that out-compete coral for space on the reefs. (This is also why you should avoid urinating while snorkeling or diving. Use your boat's marine heads; that is why they are there.) Chemicals that are put into holding tanks and bilges are harmful to reefs.

6. Know where and how you can fish. Many cruisers love trolling and fishing, but before doing so, make certain you are in compliance with local regulations (either US or British).

7. Once you are aware and in compliance with fishing regulations, catch only what you will eat. Local reef fisheries are over-exploited, and fish play an important role in the ecology of the reef.

8. Take only pictures, leave only bubbles. Collecting shells and coral/live rock is illegal in the British and US Virgin Islands; even the "dead" rubble on shorelines. Shells, even ones that appear "empty" are illegal to collect. Photography or sketching is a non-destructive way to turn these finds into lasting memories.

9. Littering kills. Cruisers love Caribbean tradewinds, but care must be taken so articles don't blow off the boat into the water. Towels and wet clothes will blow off safety lines, sinking to entangle in the reef. Solid waste such as cups, napkins and plates that blow overboard are unsightly and destructive to marine life. Plastics smother reefs and harm turtles. Use proper trash facilities for solid waste, and don't let towels or trash blow off your boat into the water.

10. Avoid fuel spills. Use extreme care when fueling your boat and dinghy. If you do spill gas, don't use any dispersants such as detergents or soap. This causes oils to sink to the bottom and smother corals. Oil spills are an environmental and safety hazard, and legal violation.

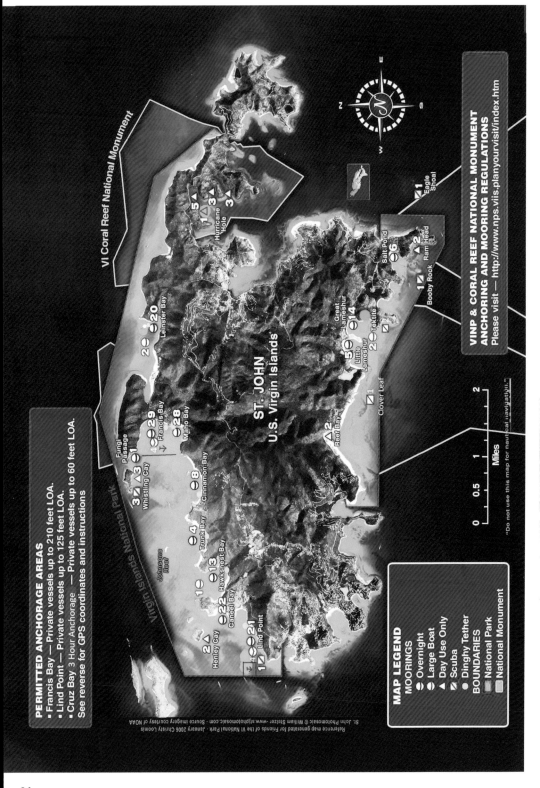

ST. JOHN
U.S. Virgin Islands

VI Coral Reef National Monument

Virgin Islands National Park

PERMITTED ANCHORAGE AREAS
- Francis Bay — Private vessels up to 210 feet LOA.
- Lind Point — Private vessels up to 125 feet LOA.
- Cruz Bay 3 Hour Anchorage — Private vessels up to 60 feet LOA.
  See reverse for GPS coordinates and instructions

**VINP & CORAL REEF NATIONAL MONUMENT
ANCHORING AND MOORING REGULATIONS**
Please visit — http://www.nps.viis.planyourvisit/index.htm

MAP LEGEND
MOORINGS
- Overnight
- Large Boat
▲ Day Use Only
▨ Scuba
● Dinghy Tether
BOUNDARIES
■ National Park
■ National Monument

Miles
0   0.5   1   2

"Do not use this map for nautical navigation."

Reference map generated for Friends of the VI National Park · January 2006 Christy Loomis
St. John Photomosaic © William Stelzer ·www.stjphotomosaic.com · Source imagery courtesy of NOAA

Hurricane Hole
Leinster Bay
Francis Bay
Fungi Passage
Maho Bay
Whistling Cay
Cinnamon Bay
Trunk Bay
Johnsons Reef
Hawksnest Bay
Cancel Bay
Henley Cay
Lind Point
Reef Bay
Clover Leaf
Little Lameshur
Great Lameshur
Tektite
Salt Pond
Ram Head
Booby Rock
Eagle Shoal

24

Virgin Islands National Park, St. John, US Virgin Islands

By Carol Bareuther

Coral reefs reflecting sapphire seas, pristine beaches rimmed with palm trees, and lush green hills unmarred by resorts or residences... The paradisiacal beauty of the Virgin Islands National Park is like a movie scene that makes you want to jump in and instantly become immersed. But slow down. To really appreciate the charms of this southernmost US park, you have to add some new lingo to your vocabulary. *Limin'*, meaning to "hang around idly," as defined by the late Virgin Islands historian and park ranger, Lito Valls, is a verb best carried out by forgetting time, setting aside the to-do list and enjoying your surroundings in a lazily, leisurely, limin' sort of way.

Marine Scene

Secluded coves, dazzling beaches and wondrous coral reefs have lured pleasure boaters to Park waters. In addition, the Virgin Islands rank as one of the Caribbean's premier diving and snorkeling locations. Several dive shops rent snorkel and scuba gear and run trips to offshore reefs. Park waters are open to sports fisherman with hand-held rods, and bone fishing along the flats by Leinster Bay is excellent.

Over the last two decades, however, the sheer number of visiting boats has accelerated damage to sea grass beds and coral reefs due to anchor damage. To protect these natural resources, the Park has installed 182 moorings – 154 on the North Shore and 28 on the South Shore, and established protected zones around several of the more sensitive sea grass and reef areas. Starting in 2002, the Park implemented a fee for the overnight use of these moorings. To pay the mooring fee several "iron rangers" (small kiosks) are located in several of the bays. Envelopes are provided for enclosing the fee, with a place to note your vessel's name and the date. Rangers patrol the bays regularly to insure compliance.

Using the National Park Mooring System

There is no reservation system for moorings, but one may be developed in the future. Moorings are in high demand from December to March, while September and October usage is low because of the threat of hurricanes. Boaters may only stay in Park waters for a maximum of 30

nights in a 12 month period and no longer than seven consecutive nights in one bay.

Park moorings are safe, easy to use and identified as white balls with blue stripes. Moorings are fixed to the sea bottom with either a sand screw or a stainless steel eyebolt, which is cemented directly into coral pavement. To pick up a mooring, grab the floating mooring line, or painter, and tie it to a short bowline on the vessel. Don't raft boats together or set anchors while on a mooring. All moorings are checked and maintained by Park Service personnel, however please do report any safety defects to a park ranger so they can be promptly repaired. The moorings are not designed for rough weather use. In high wind or heavy sea conditions, it is recommended that vessels anchor in a protected bay.

PARK ACTIVITIES

The Cruz Bay Visitor Center is a short walk from the public ferry dock, and is open daily from 8am to 4:40pm. The center contains exhibits, a park video, brochures, maps, and books. Park rangers can help you plan your visit, which may include island hikes, historical tours, snorkeling, cultural craft demonstrations, and evening campground programs.

From January through April, the non-profit Friends of the National Park offer seminars with topics ranging from outdoors photography to archeology, natural history and traditional West Indian cooking.

Hurricane season extends from June through November. The Park provides ongoing information for visitors including where to go in the event of a serious storm.

PARK REGULATIONS

ANCHORING AND MOORING

* There are only three permitted anchor zones within the Park and Coral Reef Monument: Cruz Bay Creek for vessels 60 feet and under. Max time limit is three hours. Lind Point for vessels up to 125 feet and Francis Bay for vessels up to 210'. Vessels must anchor to shoreward of a line from America Point to Mary Point (GPS coordinates available) and 300 feet from the mooring field.

* Vessels with an overall length greater than 210 feet, and commercial vessels over 125 feet, are prohibited from anchoring or mooring within Park waters.

* Large Vessel Moorings: In addition to the standard moorings for vessels up to 60 feet, there are larger moorings identified by a red stripe designed for vessels over 60 feet. These are located as follows: Lind Point 4; Hawksnest Bay 1; Maho / Francis Bay 4; Leinster Bay 2; Great Lamshur Bay 2

* Mooring balls are identified as follows:
Vessels to 60 feet -
White Ball with blue stripe
Vessels to 125' -
Large ball with red stripe
Orange ball with blue stripe -
Snorkel or dive

* Motorized vessels or vessels under sail shall not enter or anchor in areas identified as Boat Exclusion Areas.

* Anchoring is prohibited within beach access channels marked by red and green buoys.

* Setting of anchors is prohibited while on NPS moorings. Vessels using NPS moorings may not use additional ground tackle.

* Rafting of vessels is prohibited while on moorings provided by the NPS.

* Securing vessels to moorings using stern cleats is prohibited.

* NPS moorings shall be vacated if sustained winds exceed 40 mph.

* NPS moorings shall not be modified by any user.

* Vessels anchoring or mooring within Park waters may not exceed 30 nights in a calendar year and no more than seven consecutive nights in one bay.

* Boats are limited to 30 nights per calendar year in Park waters. Moorings are provided on a first-come, first-served basis.

PARK RULES & REGULATIONS

* Vessels less than 26 feet length overall may access NPS beaches where channels have been designated by a red and green buoy to drop-off or pick-up passengers.

* The use of drones is prohibited without a special permit from NPS

* Recreational kite surfing is prohibited in boat exclusion areas and moorings areas. Commercial kite surfing is prohibited within Park waters.

* Operating a vessel in excess of five mph or creating a wake in mooring fields or within 200 feet of a mooring field is prohibited.

* Trash being disposed of from vessels may not exceed two 10-gallon bags

and must fit inside NPS trash containers identified for vessel trash in Cruz Bay, Francis Bay, Leinster Bay, Salt Pond and Little Lameshur Bay.

* Each vessel is required to pay an overnight fee of $26.00 per night when mooring or anchoring in the Park between 5:00pm and 7:00am. Failure to pay the overnight fee is prohibited.

* Coral is very fragile and easily damaged by anchors, human touch, feet and flippers. Coral damaged by one person can take hundreds of years to re-grow. Remember, "If it's not sand, don't stand." Coral and other sea life can also cause injury to people when touched.

* It is illegal to dump litter in Park waters or on land. Dispose of litter in designated receptacles throughout the Park.

* No dumping of waste from vessels, use your storage tanks.

* Water skiing and jet skiing are not permitted in Park waters.

* Kayaks, dinghies, rafts or any other motored or rowed vessels must stay outside demarcated swim areas. Boats 26 feet or less may access the beach using channels marked by red and green buoys, but may not anchor in this channel. Boats may pick up NPS moorings.

* Fishing is allowed outside of swim areas, but not in Trunk/Jumbie Bay. Spear guns are prohibited anywhere in Park waters.

* Caribbean spiny lobster catch is limited to two per person per day and the season is October 1-March 30. Whelk must be larger than 2.5" and take is limited to one gallon per person per day, and 3/8" lip thickness.

* Collecting plants and animals – dead or alive – or inanimate objects, including cultural artifacts, coral, shells, and sand is prohibited. Metal detectors are not allowed anywhere in the Park.

* Camping is allowed only at Cinnamon Bay Campground.

* Fires are permitted only on grills at designated picnic areas.

* Feeding marine and terrestrial wildlife is prohibited and may be dangerous to you.

* Pets are not allowed on Park beaches, in the campground or in picnic areas, but may be walked – leashed – on trails.

* Glass bottles are not permitted on Park beaches.

PRIVATE VESSEL SIZE LIMITS

CONTACT INFORMATION

It is highly recommended that you look at these websites before boating in the Park to get any updates to the current information, and to familiarize yourselves with the Park rules and regulations.

Virgin Islands National Park
1300 Cruz Bay Creek, St. John, USVI 00830
Tel: 340-776-6201
Email: virg@us-national-parks.net
www.nps.gov/viis
www.virgin.islands.national-park.com

Friends of the VI National Park:
www.friendsvinp.org

Mooring & Anchoring Guide for the Virgin Islands National Park:
www.nps.gov/viis/planyourvisit/
boater-information.htm

ST. JOHN NATIONAL PARK		
Length on Deck	**North Shore**	**South Shore**
12 ft or less	May anchor only in sand and not within 200ft of a mooring field	May anchor only in sand and not within 200ft of a mooring field
13 to 60 ft	Must use moorings	Must use moorings
61 to 125 ft	Must use large boat moorings (see above) or specified anchor zones	Must use large boat moorings (see above) or specified anchor zones
126 to 210 ft	Prohibited from using moorings – must anchor in sand at Francis Bay 200 feet seaward of mooring field (at depths greater than 50 feet) and shoreward of a line drawn from Mary Point to America Point	Prohibited from mooring or anchoring
Greater than 210 ft	Prohibited from mooring or anchoring	Prohibited from mooring or anchoring

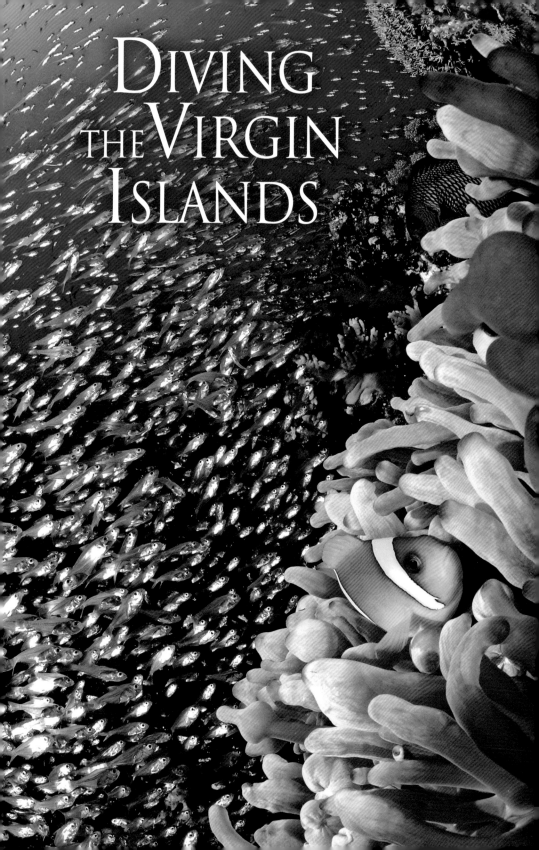

DIVING
THE VIRGIN
ISLANDS

DIVING THE VIRGIN ISLANDS

The Virgin Islands are one of the best sailing and cruising areas in the world. They are also recognized as one of the top dive destinations.

The wreck of the R.M.S. Rhone has become synonymous with the BVI in dive circles, regarded by many as the best wreck dive of the Western Hemisphere.

Superb reefs for both snorkeling and diving are found in and around most of the anchorages. The U.S. Virgin Islands have a series of underwater parks: Trunk Bay, St. John, Buck Island, St. Croix and Coki Beach, St. Thomas. In the British Virgin Islands, the island of Anegada has over 300 documented shipwrecks.

Servicing the needs of the visiting yachtsmen, many professional dive shops and dive tour operators have set up businesses, providing complete services from equipment rental and air tank refills, to tours and instruction.

For the non-diver, a resort course will enable you to explore the underwater world with the aid of an instructor. Full certification courses are available from the individual dive shop operators conveniently located throughout the islands.

The rules and regulations of the marine parks of both the U.S. and British Virgins are similar.

BVI DIVE SITES

Dive operators of the Virgin Islands, through a cooperative effort, have pooled information to give you these brief but picturesque descriptions of 20 of their favorite locations:

Painted Walls: Long canyons, a cave, a sponge-encrusted tunnel, barracudas, rock beauties, angelfish and a variety of pelagic fish make the Painted Walls an exciting and picturesque dive with 28 to 50-foot depths.

The Rhone: Just about everyone in diving has heard of the classical wreck, the RMS Rhone. Even those who have not visited the BVI have seen the Rhone in Columbia Pictures' treasure diving epic, *The Deep*. An ocean steamer, 310 feet in length, this magnificent vessel sank off Salt Island during an extremely violent hurricane in 1867. After over 140 years of silent slumber in 20-80 feet of water, this great ship remains remarkably intact with much of her decking, rigging, steam engine and propeller still visible. Gilded with colorful sponges and flourishing corals, the Rhone is perhaps the most impressive shipwreck in the entire Caribbean.

Rhone Reef: Two coral-encrusted caves are located in less than 25 feet of water at Rhone Reef, Salt Island. A variety of hard and soft corals, fish, turtles and the occasional shark can be found here. Due to its proximity to the Rhone, it is a protected area.

Great Harbour: Directly across the channel from Road Town Harbour lies a large, protected bay on the north side of Peter Island. At the center of this bay is a shallow coral reef less than 20 yards

offshore, beginning in 8 feet of water. Loaded with colorful sponges and a marvelous array of small marine life, the reef slopes gently to approximately 18 feet, then drops vertically to a depth of 40 feet.

Indians: The Indians are four large rock formations that rise from the ocean floor to a height of about 90 feet. Deepest depth is 50 feet on the westward side. The Indians have just about everything for the snorkeler as well as the scuba diver; brain, finger, star and elkhorn corals are abundant, as are gorgonians and sea fans.

Caves: The caves at Norman Island can provide many hours of fun for snorkelers. There is a large variety of subjects for the underwater photographer such as schools of dwarf herring or fry. These fish provide food for the many pelicans in the area. The reef in front of the shallow caves slopes downward to a depth of 40 feet.

Angelfish Reef: One of the best sightseeing dives is a sloping reef located off the western point of Norman Island. Depths here range from 10–90 feet. The high point of your dive will be a visit to the bottom of the channel where a large colony of angelfish resides. There is plenty of fish action at this particular site because of the swiftly flowing currents in the nearby channel and the close proximity to the open sea.

Cooper Island: The southeastern shore of Cooper Island, called Markoe Point, is a sheer rock wall that plunges some 70 feet to the ocean floor. Nurse sharks are frequently encountered lying on sandy floors at the base of small canyons formed by the rugged walls of the island.

Scrub Island: The south side of Scrub Island is a splendid reef with depths of up to 60 feet.

Little Camanoe: The northeastern tip of Little Camanoe offers a 30-foot reef dive. The coral overhangs in this area are exceptionally good. Caution: ground seas.

Seal Dog Rock: Plenty of pelagic fish. Depth of 80 feet. Caution: may have a current. This dive is recommended for experienced divers.

George Dog: The rocky point in the anchorage at George Dog is an easy 25-30 foot dive for beginning divers.

Invisibles: (East of Necker Island) Spectacular soaring peaks from 4-70 feet from surface. Flashing schools of every kind of fish, sleeping nurse sharks and all forms of sea life abound.

Visibles: (Southwest underwater pinnacle off Cockroach Island) Caves, canyons, resident 8-foot green moray & nurse shark. Depths to 70 feet. Spawning area for many species of jacks, snappers, and groupers.

Chimney: (West Bay of Great Dog) Winding canyon goes to a colorful underwater arch. Many coral heads with an unbelievable variety of small sea creatures.

Joe's Cave: (West Dog Island) Cathedral-effect cave with schooling glassy-eyed sweepers. Clouds of silversides overshadow a variety of eels, pelagic fish and other species, with an occasional school of bulky, splashing tarpon.

Van Ryan's Rock: (Off Collison Point, Virgin Gorda) Huge lobsters, turtles, and plenty of fish among brilliant corals and swaying sea fans.

Ginger Island: Mushroom coral heads 15-20 feet high, great visibility. Graduated shelves ending at 70-90 feet in a huge sand patch. You will see stingrays and huge Goliath grouper.

South side of Great Dog Island: Reef runs east and west, 100 yards of island coral, butterfly fish. Exciting dive locations, each more unusual than the next. Expect to see just about anything!

Anegada Reef: Graveyard of some 300 documented shipwrecks dating from the 1600s to the present. Spanish galleons and English privateers with uncountable treasure.

The Chikuzen: This 245-foot ship was sunk in 1981 and provides a fantastic home for all varieties of fish, including big rays and horse-eye jacks. The depth here is less than 80 feet. Located about 5 miles north of Camanoe Island.

BVI Dive Operators

Blue Water Divers
Nanny Cay Marine Center, Tortola
Tel: 284-494-2847
www.bluewaterdiversbvi.com
Full Service Dive Shop, PADI/SSI

Dive BVI (with 3 locations)
1. Leverick Bay Resort
North Sound, Virgin Gorda
Tel: 284-495-7328
2. Virgin Gorda Yacht Harbour
Tel: 284-495-5513
3. Scrub Island Resort
Tel: 284-340-0829
www.divebvi.com
PADI 5 star rating. Full service shops
with dive boats.

Jost Van Dyke Scuba & Eco-Tours
Great Harbour, Jost Van Dyke
BVI Tel: 284-443-2222
US Tel: 757-287-2731
www.jostvandykescuba.com
Full service dive shop with tours for divers,
snorkelers and ecological island tours.

Sunchaser Scuba
Bitter End Yacht Club
North Sound, Virgin Gorda
Tel: 284-344-2766
www.sunchaserscuba.com
PADI and NAUI pros offer full service,
underwater video, with dive boats.

Last Stop Sports
(with watersports location and bike shop)
Last Stop Bike Shop at Port Purcel,
Road Town, Tortola
Tel: 284-343-0214
www.laststopsports.com
Scuba rentals plus all kinds of watersports
from fishing to kayaking

BVI SNUBA
Tel: 248-341-0660
www.bvisnuba.com
Leverick Bay, Virgin Gorda
Underwater adventure without extra
equipment of certifications needed.

Sail Caribbean Divers (with 3 locations)
1. Hodges Creek Marina
2. Cooper Island
3. Mariner Inn, Tortola
Tel: 284-495-1675 or 284-541-3483
www.sailcaribbeandivers.com
Full service. PADI Gold Palm IDC Resort
instruction, rentals two dive boats

UBS Dive Center
Culture Ville, Tortola
Tel: 284-346-0024
Your own dive boat for the day, or tours
and instruction available

We Be Divin'
Village Cay Hotel & Marina
Tel: 284-494-4320
www.bviscubadive.com
Diver courses, rental, rendezvous service,
private charters

For USVI Dive Operators list, visit www.cruisingguides.com/ DiveOperatorsUSVI

DIVING IN THE U.S. VIRGIN ISLANDS

The diving between the various US Virgin Islands is considerably different, St. Croix 35 miles to the south is characterized by very deep diving and marine life that thrives on steep, deep walls. Most of the sites are on the north coast. St. Thomas and St. John are close enough to share many of the same sites and consequently there is a reasonable overlap of dive operators. The dive terrain is similar at both islands. A recompression chamber is located at the hospital on St. Thomas. Here is a sampling of the dives from all three islands:

Cartenser Sr.: (Off St. Thomas, near Buck Island) A spectacular dive on the intact, coral-encrusted hull of a World War I cargo ship in 50-foot depths. Tours easily arranged.

Cow and Calf: Two rocks between Christmas Cove and Jersey Bay, 5 feet below the surface. The lee side of the western rock provides intricate arches, ledges and caves. Many angelfish and beautiful coral.

Christmas Cove: Good beginner's dive on the northwest side of Fish Cay in 40 feet of water. Swim amongst the coral heads. Plenty of fish.

Dog Rock: For advanced divers on the northwestern side of Dog Island in 40-50 foot depths. Rock and coral ledges and caves. Caution: This one can be rough.

Coki Beach: A good place to snorkel off the beach. Coral ledges.

Little Saint James: A 40-foot dive on the lee side has some deep ledges to explore, sheltering various schools of fish.

Twin Barges: Located off Limetree Beach lie two wrecks sunk approximately in the 1940s. Although visibility is limited outside

USVI DIVE SITES

the wrecks, the clarity improves inside the ships' chambers.

Carvel Rock: Off of the northern side of this rock, near St. John, in depths to 90 feet, big schools of pelagic fish pass through colorful, sponge-encrusted caves.

Thatch Cay: Divers at the Tunnels here explore 8 different arches and tunnels.

Scotch Bank: Off St. Croix, this popular dive spot is a favorite for spotting stingrays and manta rays.

Long Reef: A 6-mile-long reef which provides dives at depths from 30-50 feet.

A forest of coral, including pillar and elkhorn colonies.

Salt River: This area has two distinct walls. The East Wall plunges from 50-100 feet, revealing many caves and caverns. The West Wall peaks at 30 feet and tumbles to 125 feet. The colors of the sponges grasping the crevices and pillars are awesome.

Buck Island: Off St. Croix, this national monument features abundant tropical fish and a jungle of huge staghorn and elkhorn coral. An absolute must for anyone visiting St. Croix.

Frederiksted Pier: (St. Croix) 30-foot-deep pilings offer splendid diving day or night. The pilings provide a home for bright sponges and algae, as well as sea horses, crabs and octopus.

Cane Bay, Davis Bay and Salt River: All have walls of coral from 20 feet to over 1000 feet. Several anchors have been discovered along the wall. One of the most-photographed anchors is nestled in sand at 60 feet on the Northstar Wall.

MEDICAL EMERGENCIES

In the event of diving related emergencies, contact the U.S. Coast Guard Search and Rescue on VHF 16 or telephone 340-776-3497 for immediate assistance. There is a recompression chamber in St. Thomas at the Hospital Chamber telephone 340-776-2686 or 340-776-8311, Divers Alert Network (919) 684-9111, 24 hours or call 800-446-2671.

Your charter company also can be of great assistance, and should be contacted if you run into a problem.

37

PLANNING THE CRUISE

CRUISE PLANNING LOGISTICS

Each year thousands of sailors from both sides of the Atlantic converge on the Caribbean to explore the thousands of coves and anchorages and discover the many wonderful cultures and colors that it offers. Many will arrive by air from the U.S. or Europe, to charter a boat, while others will make the passage aboard their own vessels.

When contemplating a cruise around the Virgin Islands there are a myriad of questions and issues to be asked and answered. We have tried to address some of the more germane issues here and a visit to our website will offer an enhanced reference guide for those looking to cruise the waters of the Virgin Islands.

The considerations for information are somewhat different depending upon which of the above options is chosen. The cruiser will require a deeper understanding of the Caribbean weather patterns on a seasonal basis, while the charterer will require a completely different set of data points. We have tried to strike a reasonable balance in this regard.

Cruising Your Own Boat

Cruisers en route to the Virgin Islands from North America have several options when contemplating a winter in the Caribbean;

To the Caribbean via the Bahamas:

Cruisers can migrate their way down the east coast, or intra-coastal waterway, to Florida, and then embark on the "Thorny Path" to the Virgin Islands. The Thorny Path is a long, sometimes difficult path that routes them across the Bahamas where they will encounter the effects of the easterly tradewinds as they enter the tropics en route to the Virgin Islands. Bruce Van Sant, in his book A Gentleman's Guide to Passages South describes this route in detail and offers excellent advice on how to avoid many of the difficulties. It should be noted that while the passage from the Bahamas to the Virgin Islands islands is a popular choice for cruisers due to the ability to island hop and therefore avoid long offshore passages, it is also a very challenging during the winter months when the tradewinds deliver a steady 20-25 knots from the east and the days are short.

The northern limit of the Northeast tradewind belt is approximately 30 degrees north, which places it north of Miami and south of Jacksonville. This is where the so called Horse Latitudes meet the tradewind belt and therefore lighter conditions prevail. With this in mind a reasonable alternative for those sailors willing to make the offshore passage would be to head due east from Miami across the Gulf Stream and south of Abaco via the Northwest Providence Channel above 25 degrees then continue due east or even a little north of east until reaching the 70th meridian and then turning SE. The more easting that you can make, the better. An ideal passage would take you east to 65W (also known as I-65) before turning due south for a lively tradewind reach to the Virgins.

The US East Coast to the Caribbean:

For those contemplating making the offshore passage of some 1500 miles, from the US they will typically depart from ports like Newport, RI or Norfolk, Virginia at the

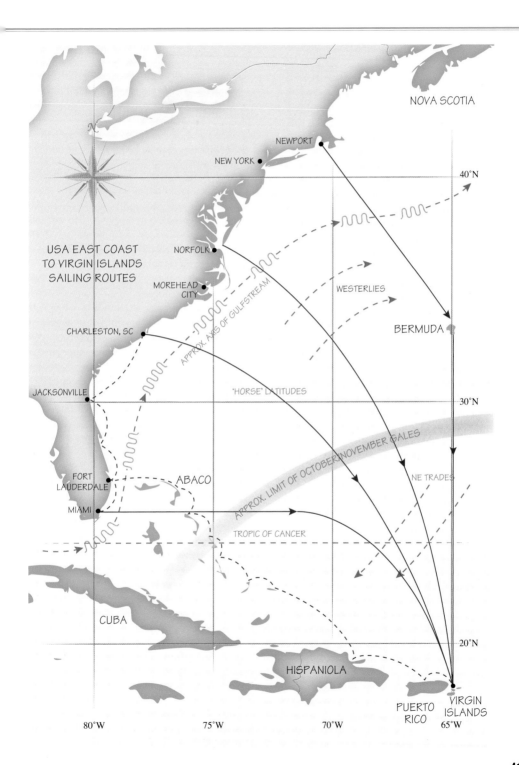

NOVA SCOTIA

NEWPORT

NEW YORK

40°N

USA EAST COAST
TO VIRGIN ISLANDS
SAILING ROUTES

NORFOLK

MOREHEAD
CITY

WESTERLIES

CHARLESTON, SC

APPROX. AXIS OF GULFSTREAM

BERMUDA

JACKSONVILLE

'HORSE' LATITUDES

30°N

APPROX. LIMIT OF OCTOBER/NOVEMBER GALES

FORT
LAUDERDALE

ABACO

NE TRADES

MIAMI

TROPIC OF CANCER

CUBA

20°N

HISPANIOLA

PUERTO
RICO

VIRGIN
ISLANDS
65°W

80°W   75°W   70°W

41

CRUISE PLANNING LOGISTICS

mouth of the Chesapeake Bay during October or early November in order to catch the short weather window between the end of the hurricane season and the start of the winter gales in December. This is a real blue water offshore experience; the passage time is approximately 10-12 days during which you will encounter some challenging weather conditions including a Gulf Stream crossing. Cruisers departing Newport will probably schedule a stop in Bermuda before heading due south to the Virgin Islands.

Mid-Atlantic Coast to the Virgins:

This route allows for a later departure, but because of the lower latitude precludes a stop in Bermuda unless forced to change plans due to gear failure or weather. Since the Gulf Stream, at this departure point, runs closest to the US coastline it will be encountered one day into the cruise. This also allows a strategy that gets you across the Gulf Stream just ahead of a front which will see the wind clocking and bringing a northerly component which makes for treacherous crossing conditions in the Gulf Stream. Once again the strategy should be to get as far east as possible and below latitude 30 degrees before heading south. The use of a weather routing service is highly recommended at this time of the year in order to position yourself properly to deal safely with approaching weather fronts and the Gulf Stream.

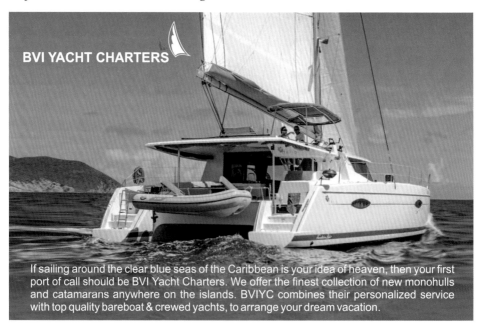

BVI YACHT CHARTERS

If sailing around the clear blue seas of the Caribbean is your idea of heaven, then your first port of call should be BVI Yacht Charters. We offer the finest collection of new monohulls and catamarans anywhere on the islands. BVIYC combines their personalized service with top quality bareboat & crewed yachts, to arrange your dream vacation.

+1 284-494-4289

charters@bviyc.com
www.bviyachtcharters.com

There are two cruising rallies that depart Virginia Beach around the first week of November. The Salty Dawg Rally (www.saltydawgrally.org) is designed for cruisers with blue-water experience and is a no-cost participation model. The Caribbean 1500 (www.worldcruising.com) is open to all for a fee and attracts around 70 participants annually. Both rallies provide an excellent way to make the passage in the company of other cruisers and with the added confidence of knowing there is a support system close at hand. Both rally organizers conduct excellent safety seminars on offshore passage making and boat safety during the weeks prior to departure.

Yacht Transport: There is also the option of having your vessel shipped to the Virgin Islands, thereby saving the wear and tear on your yacht. Dockwise Yacht Transport (www.yacht-transport.com) departs from Fort Lauderdale to St. Thomas in late November at a cost of about $25,000 for a typical 45' sailboat. Seven Seas Yacht Transport also have service from Newport, RI. to St. Thomas departing October and November. Peters & May Global Yacht Transport (www.petersandmay.com) also offer schedules at this time for both Europe and the USA departure points.

Europe to the Caribbean: Caribbean bound sailors departing Europe and the Mediterranean before the onset of winter will be able to take full advantage of the northeast tradewinds on their pas- sage across the Atlantic. The ARC rally departs annually from the Canary Islands in late October, with a fleet of 100+ vessels ending on the island of St. Lucia in the Windward Islands. After cruising the Windwards the boats generally work their way north through the Leeward Islands and then onto the Virgin Islands. Some consideration needs to be given as to where the vessel will be at the start of the next year's hurricane season. From the Caribbean most boats depart in mid spring when routes north are ideal. Vessels heading back to Europe will make a stop in Bermuda and for those heading for the east coast of the USA a stop at Turks and Caicos makes an enjoyable sail, reaching with the Antilles current behind you, or a leisurely cruise through the out islands of the Bahama chain on your way home.

The Virgin Island landfall: Approaching the Virgins from the north the skipper will have to make a small navigation course adjustment in order to compensate for the Antilles current which flows to the west at approximately ½ knot. Some caution should be taken not to allow yourself to get any further than 64 ° 30' west in order to be clear of the infamous reefs of Anegada. If the plan is to make an official entry into the BVI then consider leaving the island of Jost Van Dyke to starboard then sailing up the coast to Great Harbour to make your clearance. If you are heading for the USVI you can continue on to St. John or consider leaving Jost Van Dyke and Tobago to port before proceeding to Cruz Bay, St. John which is the preferred port of entry over St. Thomas.

Customs Considerations: The British Virgin Islands: Yachts visiting the BVI for the first time will be required to pay an

CRUISE PLANNING LOGISTICS

Annual Tonnage Fee, which is based on your yacht's net tonnage up to a limit of $55. If the vessel is to remain in the BVI for more than one month, there is a fee of $200 to temporarily import the yacht for up to one year. When arriving in the British Virgin Islands you must immediately proceed to a port of entry and clear Customs and Immigration. The skipper may present him/herself on behalf of the entire crew with passports, ships documentation and proof of clearance from the last port of call. If you are arriving after-hours, raise the yellow Q flag and if possible notify customs by phone. In some instances it is possible to arrange for after hours clearance. Overtime fees will be applied. Guns of any kind are not allowed in the BVI. You must declare them and the police will take them and give you a receipt so that you can pick them up on your way out of the BVI.

In addition to the fees above, see the section Customs, Immigration & Formalities for details on Cruising Permit & National Parks fee structure.
BVI Customs: 1-284-494-3475
BVI Immigration: 1-284-494-3471

The US Virgin Islands: Vessels arriving in the USVI, regardless of flag or crew nationality, are required upon entry into US waters, to contact (via telephone) the nearest designated location and provide:
• Name, DOB and citizenship including passport number
• Name of vessel/documentation number
• CBP user fee number if applicable
• Homeport and current location
• Return contact number

Then (unless instructed to the contrary) proceed to the nearest port of entry, where the captain and crew are required to present themselves in person with documentation.

Yachts over 300 gross tons must send Advance Notice of Arrival to the U.S. Coast Guard 24 hours prior to arrival or they will not be admitted into the USVI. (Check nvmc.uscg.gov/nvmc for details of Advance Notice of Arrival "NOA.") Non-USA crew or guests must have the requisite visas. For yachtsmen already in the Caribbean, U.S. visas can be obtained from the U.S. Embassy in Barbados after first obtaining an appointment. For non US yachts wishing to visit the US Virgin Islands under the 90 day visa waiver program (ESTA) the process is explained in the Cruising Information section under Customs & Immigration.

Cruising permits are not required in the USVI, however, vessels remaining six months or more are required to register with the Department of Planning & Natural Resources Environmental Enforcement Office (340-774-3320).

Vessels traveling between the BVI and USVI must clear out of BVI waters at one of the ports of entry (Road Town, West End, Tortola, Great Harbour, Jost Van Dyke, Spanish Town, Virgin Gorda, Gun Creek, Gorda Sound VG) and clear into U.S. waters at either Cruz Bay, St. John, Charlotte Amalie, St. Thomas or Gallows Bay, St.Croix.

When arriving into the U.S. Virgin Islands from the B.V.I. you must go to Customs

44

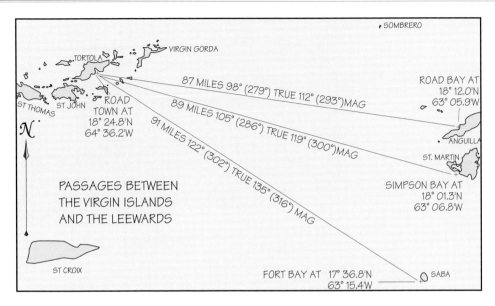

PASSAGES BETWEEN
THE VIRGIN ISLANDS
AND THE LEEWARDS

87 MILES 98° (279°) TRUE 112° (293°)MAG

89 MILES 105° (286°) TRUE 119° (300°)MAG

91 MILES 122° (302°) TRUE 135° (316°) MAG

SOMBRERO

VIRGIN GORDA

TORTOLA

ST THOMAS   ST JOHN   ROAD
TOWN AT
18° 24.8'N
64° 36.2'W

ROAD BAY AT
18° 12.0'N
63° 05.9'W

ANGUILLA

ST. MARTIN

SIMPSON BAY AT
18° 01.3'N
63° 06.8'W

ST CROIX

FORT BAY AT   17° 36.8'N
63° 15.4'W

SABA

and Immigration first. If you arrive at night you should hoist the yellow quarantine flag and wait until Customs and Immigration are open in the morning and not leave the boat before clearing in with the officials. U.S.V.I. Customs and Immigration offices: Cruz Bay, St. John - Charlotte Amalie, St. Thomas - Redhook, St. Thomas- Gallows Bay, St. Croix.

USVI Customs & Border Control:
1-877-305-8774

South to the Leeward Islands

The northern most islands of the Leeward Islands, Anguilla, St. Martin and Saba, lie around 80-90 miles east of the Virgin Islands and getting there entails crossing the Anegada Passage. A current from half a knot to a knot and a half usually flows in a westerly to northwesterly direction. The tradewinds blow from the easterly quadrant. All of this makes it really easy to sail from the Leewards to the Virgin

Islands; it is downwind and downcurrent. Conversely, the trip from the Virgins is tough, with both wind and current on the nose. Unless the wind is way in the northeast, you are unlikely to be able to lay even Saba on one tack, so unless you like heavy weather beating in short seas, avoid the strong Christmas winds. Approaching cold fronts can be preceded by calm days, which could provide a weather window if a 90 mile motor sail works for you. If schedule dictates that you must sail south during periods of strong north-easterlies, an alternative course would take you southeast from the Virgin Islands to Saba (passing west of the Saba Bank) and onto St. Kitts before heading east.

When conditions are favorable, it is best to depart the Virgin Islands from the most northerly point in order to deal with the wind and current. The BVI departure points would be via the Round Rock Passage, south of Virgin Gorda, or the Necker

Island Passage, north of Gorda Sound. A late afternoon departure should get you into St. Martin by midday the following day.

The Leeward Islands are covered in the *Cruising Guide to the Northern Leeward Islands* and the *Cruising Guide to the Southern Leeward Islands,* by Chris Doyle, available from the bookstore at www.CruisingGuides.com.

West to the Spanish Virgins

Sailing west to the Spanish Virgins is usually a broad reach or a run, depending upon departure point, wind direction and intended destination. The Antilles north equatorial current flows in a westerly or northwesterly direction at 0.5-1.5 knots. Departing from St. Thomas, you will have to plan on clearing customs in Culebra since St. Thomas is a free port. Your route should take you either to the north of Isla Culebrita (WP 18°20.0N, 65°14.0W)

where you will make your entrance to Culebra via the channel west of Culebrita and northeast of Culebra, or to the south around Grampus Banks to the red buoy Fl. R 4 sec. '2' (WP 18°40.30N, 65°12.50W). The distance is 10-15 nautical miles depending whether you are departing from WP UV608 by Salt Cay or WP UV606 east of Saba Island. It should also be noted that when it is blowing hard, the sea can pile up on the Grampus Banks making it quite choppy.

Depart St. Thomas early enough to get you there while the sun is still overhead, since the navigation around the reefs will require good light. Plan on spending your first night at Dakity Harbor, behind the reef entrance to Ensenada Honda. The following morning you can proceed to the head of Ensenada Honda to clear in at Dewey.

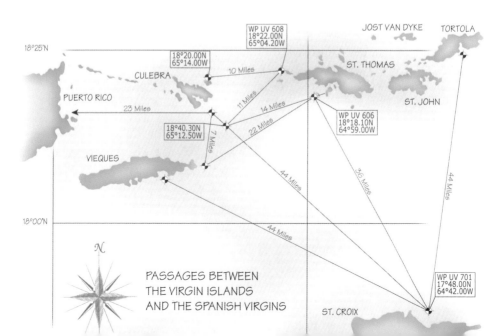

PASSAGES BETWEEN THE VIRGIN ISLANDS AND THE SPANISH VIRGINS

CHARTERING A YACHT

A successful charter could be called the art of managing everyone's expectations. We all expect the weather to be ideal with sunny tradewinds, perfect snorkeling, a comfortable boat; but gauging the temperament of the crew and managing the dynamics is key. Evaluating the crew's expectations and selecting the right location, boat, charter company, and itinerary can make all the difference.

TIME OF YEAR

As the first blasts of cold arctic air make their way across Canada and the northeast of the USA, many sailors start contemplating a Caribbean sailing holiday during the months of January through March. Because of the popularity of these (high season) months, the rates are appreciably higher and availability limited so early planning is essential. The tradewinds are also highest during this period and therefore one can expect generally settled weather with gusty wind and sea conditions (18-25 knots). The shoulder seasons are reflected with lower rates, but keep in mind that school holidays are often busy and demand drives cost. Thanksgiving and Easter holidays fill quickly, so make your plans as early as possible.

During the spring and summer months, the rates are generally lower and the anchorages less crowded as sailors launch and sail their vessels in home waters. We have always enjoyed May, when the weather is settled, the charter rates reasonable, and the anchorages are not crowded. Hurricane season officially starts in June, however early hurricane activity is very rare.

CHARTERING A YACHT

Chartering continues through August with an appreciable drop-off during September and early October when school holidays end. Charter rates at this time are at their lowest. Temperatures throughout the Virgins remain stable year round with the coolest temperatures during the winter months between a low of 74°F and a high of 84°F during the day. During the months of June, July and August the temperature will increase to a low of 79°F at night with daytime temperatures around 89°F.

SELECTING A CHARTER COMPANY

Choosing a bareboat, captained, or fully crewed sailing charter can seem a bewildering experience, especially if it's your first time. You will have to choose among different sailing locations, models and sizes of boats, provisioning plans and equipment options, not to mention the additional services of a sailing instructor, land accommodation, etc.

Before you are able to select the right charter company for your sailing vacation, you will have to answer a few questions and establish criteria for decision-making: Catamaran or monohull? Traditionalists ourselves, we enjoy shorthanded cruising on a monohull, but when we have a group of friends or family sailing together and partying in the Virgins, a catamaran offers additional accommodation and specifically outside living area making it our favorite choice.

Determine the crew size, level of expertise, general appetite for activity, and available budget. A charter holiday is comprised of airfare, provisioning, personal expenses and charter fee. Before you sign on the dotted line make sure that you have all the details and know what your overall costs are.

Look on the websites of the various charter operators listed in the back of the major sailing publications and familiarize yourself with the individual offerings. Another route is to call an independent charter broker. Charter brokers can help charterers find the perfect yacht and crew for their trip. Selecting a crewed charter can be difficult and a broker can help match your needs to a specific crew or type of vessel as well as provide quotes from several different companies. They are paid by the ship's owners or operating companies, so their services are available at no cost to the traveler. The two most common charter broker trade organizations are the American Yacht Charter Association (AYCA) and Charter Yacht Broker's Association (CYBA).

Your available budget will often determine both the size and age of the vessel and associated equipment, therefore it is imperative that your budget and expectations are aligned. Leading brand companies such as The Moorings, Sunsail, Marine Max Vacations or Horizon who offer charter fleets all over the world, will typically keep a vessel in service four to five years. These vessels are pre-specified with the builder, and have identical equipment in order to keep the logistics of maintenance under control.

Other fleet operators like TMM, BVI Yacht Charters or CYOA manage and charter yachts for individual owners. They are likely to have different types of vessels available with owner-customized equipment. Footloose Charters as well as Conch Charters specialize in taking yachts out of the tier one fleets at the end of their initial term and offering them at substantial

CHARTERING A YACHT

discounts. The important thing to consider is more the level of maintenance than the actual age of the vessel.

Whichever way you decide to go, make sure that you compare offerings and understand the total costs and trade-offs involved. Ask about sailing restrictions, chase boat coverage, service guarantees and before and after charter procedures and briefings. Do not be reluctant to ask the questions. There are also online postings, such as www.CharterAdvisors.com that can offer feedback from recent charterers.

WHAT TO EXPECT

When you book your charter vessel, the charter company will send you a packet of material, or in some cases, have you download it from their website. This will include a charter contract, sailing resume, provisioning and beverage preference list, inventory list, passenger list and projected arrival information. This information will be sent back to your charter company or broker so that appropriate arrangements for provisioning and transportation can be put in place prior to your arrival on the island.

Upon arrival at the airport or ferry, there will be a taxi or bus from the company waiting to take you to the marina.

Upon arrival at the marina, depending upon boarding time, you will be taken to the yacht and a staff member will set up a time for both an area chart briefing and a boat check out. The sooner you can get your gear put away, provisions stowed, beer chilled and briefings complete, the sooner you can cast off and get into the rhythm of the islands. Check all gear and

inventory thoroughly and ask as many questions as you need to at the briefing.

Charter companies will give you copies of Cruising Permits and Parks Permits where applicable, along with contact numbers for communication. Unless otherwise specified, your vessel will be provided with a navigation chart and basic navigation tools. In many cases, there will be an electronic chart plotter aboard also. Don't forget to take your copy of the *Cruising Guide to the Virgin Islands* and *Planning Chart!*

We highly recommend that you make the first overnight anchorage a relatively short sail from the base. A one to two hour sail gets you to a nearby anchorage where everyone can finish unpacking, get the boat organized, take a dive over the side and share a drink in the cockpit before firing up the grill for dinner.

TYPICAL SAILING ITINERARIES

When planning your Virgin Island sailing trip it is important to determine the right balance between sailing, snorkeling, exploring etc. How experienced is the crew? What is the general appetite for enthusiastic tradewind sailing? Are there divers aboard? Do you and the crew want to eat ashore every night? All of these factors will impact the way you plan your sailing adventure.

One thing is clear, you should plan an itinerary with a blend of activities to suit everybody aboard and not try to fit everything into a seven-day cruise. The real pleasure of a vacation is having the freedom to change plans, stay in a beautiful anchorage for an extra day, or keep sailing when the conditions are perfect.

Typical Sailing Itineraries

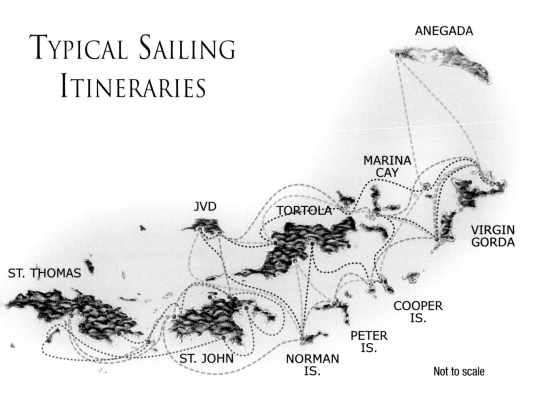

ANEGADA

MARINA CAY

JVD

TORTOLA

VIRGIN GORDA

ST. THOMAS

COOPER IS.

PETER IS.

ST. JOHN

NORMAN IS.

Not to scale

BVI, Nanny Cay - 10 Days

Day	Anchorage
1	Treasure Pt. / Norman Island
2	Pelican Is. / Jost Van Dyke
3	Sandy Cay / Little Jost Van Dyke
4	Bubbly Pool / Cane Garden Bay
5	Monkey Point / Marina Cay
6	The Baths / Gorda Sound
7	Anegada
8	Anegada / Gorda Sound
9	The Dogs / Cooper Island
10	Salt Is. / Peter Island

USVI, Charlotte Amalie / BVI - 10 Days

Day	Anchorage
1	Christmas Cove, Gt. St. James
2	Caneel / Leinster Bay, St. John
3	Annaburg Ruins / Jost Van Dyke
4	Marina Cay / Trellis Bay
5	Gorda Sound, Virgin Gorda
6	The Baths / V.G Yacht Harbour
7	Salt Is. / Peter Island
8	The Indians / Norman Is.
9	Hawksnest Bay, St. John
10	Charlotte Amalie, St.Thomas

BVI, Road Town - 7 days

Day	Anchorage
1	Cooper Is.
2	Marina Cay / Trellis Bay
3	The Baths / Gorda Sound, VG
4	The Dogs / Cane Garden Bay
5	Sandy Cay / Jost Van Dyke
6	White Bay/ Norman Is.
7	The Indians / Peter Is.

USVI / Benner Bay - 7 Days

Day	Anchorage
1	Hawksnest Bay, St. John
2	Leinster Bay, St. John
3	Coral Bay, St. John
4	Lameshur Bay, St. John
5	Water Is. St. Thomas
6	Christmas Cove, Gt. St. James
7	Benner Bay

TRAVEL PLANNING

The first day is critical and should be planned so that you get the crew to an anchorage; into the water and relaxed as soon as possible. Allow them to get accustomed to the environment and de-stress. Don't overdo it with a long sail to weather.

Anegada and the U.S. Virgins:
For planning purposes; to add Anegada to your itinerary when sailing from the British Virgins, you will need 10 days. Likewise to add St. John and St. Thomas we suggest a 14-day charter. This of course changes if you are taking a power cat or motor craft.

The possibilities are endless and we offer the suggested itineraries as a starting point only. The actual route and timing should be adjusted daily based upon the prevailing weather conditions and crew comfort. When planning your sailing holiday, make sure you allow at least a day on both ends for travel. Depending upon your originating point and time of arrival, you may want to consider a first-night hotel stay or, when available, a sleep-aboard. Your charter agent can help you decide.

For my own part, it takes me three days to de-stress and stop worrying about the office. After that I need seven days minimum to sail and explore the islands. More time is better of course but try not to pack so much into your time in the islands that the crew feels that they are on a European tour bus vacation. Determine a loose itinerary and allow it to evolve on a daily basis with input from your crew.

WHAT TO BRING ON YOUR TRIP

At the top of the list is to bring any prescription medications you are taking along with some medication for sea sickness. Although, there are good pharmacies in the Virgins, it might be difficult to replace if you forget to bring them. It is also good to bring along your own toiletries and bug spray. Speaking about prescriptions of a different kind, bring what you anticipate needing for your stay. Be certain they are in the correct and properly labeled pharmacy containers.

However, in the case that you experience an unexpected medical issue, the new Peebles Hospital in Road Town meets all of the national or international standards that any hospital in the UK or US would meet." They oversee nine community clinics on different islands in the chain.

Some charter companies supply fins, masks and snorkels, however, I always bring my own snorkel and mask.

The sailing days on the water in the tradewinds and sun are very comfortable and it is easy to forget just how strong the tropical sun can be. Bring a good sunscreen with you and keep applying it throughout the day. Hats and water wicking shirts with long sleeves are a sensible idea as they help evaporate perspiration while protecting you from the sun's rays.

Polarized sunglasses are a must for keeping the glare from water and sun under control, they also enable you to see water color and reefs clearly. Make sure to bring your camera along with extra camera batteries, SD cards or data storage. There will certainly be images that you will always want to see again and remind you of a great adventure.

CURRENCY AND CREDIT CARDS

The U.S. dollar is the local currency in both the U.S. and British Virgin Islands. Since you will be spending a lot of time on small islands, it is a good idea to keep several hundred dollars in cash, preferably in smaller denominations in order to pay for mooring fees etc. Most of the mooring balls you may pick up in the BVI anchorages cost around $30-$35 a night.

Major credit cards are honored at most establishments throughout the US and BVI. American Express cards are seldom accepted throughout the BVI and small beach bars have no way of handling card transactions, so cash is king! There are a few ATMs in more populated areas.

Before leaving home, call your bank and the credit card companies you plan to use and notify them you will be traveling to the U.S. and British Virgin Islands. This way they will be less likely to hold up any transactions of the cards you use, thinking that your card may have been stolen.

WHAT NOT TO BRING

(A) Scuba gear – Bring your own regulator, face mask, etc., but don't bring weight belts and tanks. They are available for rent throughout the islands.

(B) Food items – Unless you have special dietary needs, food is readily available.

(C) Surfboards and windsurfers – These items present a problem for the major airlines and a nightmare for the smaller commuter airlines. They are available for rent. Make prior arrangements with the appropriate charter company or agent.

Remember that you will probably purchase a few items while in the islands and some allowance should be made for such purchases when packing.

The ideal amount of luggage to bring on a sailing holiday should fit in a duffel bag above your airline seat. This will save your worrying about checking bags and waiting with baited breath to see if they show up on the other end.

FIREARMS

Some cruisers feel more secure with guns aboard for protection. If you are bringing firearms on your vessel into the U.S. Virgin Islands, the firearms must be licensed. When clearing Customs, all firearms and ammunition must be declared to Customs. Before arriving in the U.S. Virgin Islands call Customs first to ensure the regulations have not changed.

Firearms in the British Virgin Islands are prohibited and must be declared to Customs when you enter the British Virgin Islands. Customs will confiscate the firearms, leave them at Police Headquarters, and give the owner a receipt. When leaving the BVI the guns may be claimed from Police Headquarters with the receipt. Please check with BVI Customs before arriving with guns in the event that regulations have changed.

TRANSPORTATION

AIR SERVICE

Traveling to and from the Virgins is very straight forward. Most of the larger bareboat companies have travel agents who work closely with them and are in touch with special air fares and hotel accommodations.

From the United States: San Juan, Puerto Rico is the main hub into the Caribbean for visitors arriving from the US. It should be noted that where possible, it is far more convenient to fly with a company who offers a through-fare to the BVI via interline agreements and strategic partnerships with local operators such as Seaborne Airways and Cape Air. Otherwise, you'll have to get your bags in San Juan and check in again. San Juan (SJU) is serviced by Delta, Spirit, Jet Blue, Southwest, and American Airlines. Connecting flights to the Tortola (EIS) via Cape Air, Seaborne, Inter-Caribbean, Air Sunshine and Interlink. Cape Air has service from PR direct to Virgin Gorda.

Via St. Thomas (STT): Another option is to fly directly into St. Thomas and take the ferry to West End or Road Town, Tortola. There is also a direct ferry to Virgin Gorda on a limited schedule. Many of the flights from the US to St. Thomas arrive late afternoon, leaving a very narrow window to get to the ferry terminal and onto the last departing ferry. Check the schedule. There are plenty of good hotels throughout the islands, however if you are traveling at the height of the season, recognize that The Virgins are an extremely popular tourists destination for all sorts of tourists and water sports enthusiasts. Consequently, air travel and hotel accommodations should be organized and booked well in advance. If your flight does arrive too late to catch the ferry, there are some water taxi options that often work out less expensive than hotels: Foxy's Water Taxi (284-441-1905), Dohm's Water Taxi (340-775-6501), Dolphin Water Taxi (3470-774-2628). The

ISLAND AIR TRAVEL

The following airlines service the BVI:	Caribbean Wings (charter) 919-523-7094	The following airlines service the USVI:	Jet Blue 800-538-2583
Go BVI / BVI Airways bviairways.com	Fly BVI (charter) 284-340-5661	Air Sunshine 800-327-8900 954-434-8900	LIAT 866-549-5428 888-844-5428
Air Sunshine 800-327-8900 954-434-8900	Island Birds (charter) 284-495-2002	American Airlines 800-433-7300	Seaborne Airlines 866-359-8784 787-946-7800
Cape Air 800-227-3247 508-771-6944	LIAT 866-549-5428 888-844-5428	Bohlke International Airways (charter) 340-778-9177 800-653-9177	Spirit Airlines 801-401-2222
	Seaborne Airlines 866-359-8784 787-946-7800	Cape Air 800-227-3247 508-771-6944	Sun Country 800-359-6786 800-924-6184
			United Airlines 800-864-8331

Many of the airlines that fly in to the British Virgin Islands also fly to the U.S. Virgin Islands. Also check with your tourist agency and online for the latest information.

rate from Red Hook, USVI to West End, Tortola, based on a party of 4 is $100 per head plus $45 processing fees per person.

From Europe: Major carriers will route you through Antigua (ANU) or St.Maartn (SXM) with island connections to the BVI with Liat or Air Sunshine. Direct routing in Puerto Rico may also be possible.

Private Air Charters: Depending upon the size of your party and arrival times, it may prove practical to use a private charter company (see listing below). Caribbean Buzz Helicopters can also provide charters between Puerto Rico, St. Thomas, Tortola, Virgin Gorda or Anegada.

FERRY SERVICE

When traveling from one island to another or between the British and U.S Virgin Islands, local ferries are a quick and convenient option when not using your yacht.

In the USVI ferries run between St. Thomas and St. John on an hourly basis. Direct service is available to the BVI from both Charlotte Amalie and East End (Red Hook).

In the BVI, service to Jost Van Dyke leaves from West End and Virgin Gorda has regular service from Road Town and Trellis Bay. Service to Anegada is available from both Roadtown and Trellis Bay.

Since local ferry companies tend to rearrange schedules with some frequency, it is always prudent to call and check departure times in advance.

Contact www.visitusvi.com / www. bviwelcome.com / www.bvitourism.com.

FERRIES

Road Town Fast Ferry 284-494-2323, 340-777-2800; Road Town/Virgin Gorda/Anegada/St. Thomas USVI, www.tortolafastferry.com

TRANSPORTATION

New Horizon Ferry 284-495-9278; Tortola/Jost Van Dyke/ Tortola www.newhorizonferry.com

North Sound Express 284-495-2138; Tortola (Beef Island)/Virgin Gorda (the Valley) and Leverick Bay

Bitter End Ferry 284-494-2746; Gun Creek/ Bitter End Yacht Club Check status, not operational at press time

Speedy's 284-495-5235; Government jetty (next to Virgin Gorda Yacht Harbour); Road Town/Charlotte Amalie/Trellis Bay, www.bviferries.com

Native Son 284-494-5674, 340-774-8685; Tortola/Charlotte Amalie, St. Thomas/ Red Hook, www.nativesonferry.com

Inter Island Boat Services 284-495-4166, 340-776-6597; West End Tortola/Cruz Bay/Red Hook, www.interislandboat-services.com

Smiths Tortola Fast Ferry 284-495-4495, 340-775-7292; Road Town, West End, Charlotte Amalie, St. Thomas, www.bviferryservices.com

Saba Rock 284-495-7711; Any dock in North Sound

Scrub Island 284-395-3440; Trellis Bay/ Scrub Island

Peter Island Ferry 284-495-2000; Baughers Bay, Road Town/Peter Island

Marina Cay 284-494-2174; Trellis Bay/ Marina Cay

Norman Island Ferry Service 284-494-0093 Hannah Bay, Tortola/Pirates Bight, Norman Island

CAR RENTAL

Both the BVI and USVI have developed adequate car rental agencies to cope with the needs of the growing tourist industry.

Prices are slightly higher than on the U.S. mainland, but considering the high cost of freight and the limited life expectancy of vehicles in the islands, the differential is not excessive. Most major rental companies have local branches throughout the Virgins and advance reservations can be made.

Also, many locally owned and operated companies are also represented. If you are chartering during the peak months (December-April), try to reserve well in advance to avoid delays. In both the U.S. and British Virgins, remember to drive on the left.

TAXI SERVICE

All points of debarkation are more than adequately serviced by taxis. The airports and ferry docks are often lined with taxis.

It is common in the islands to see open safari buses, which can carry up to 20 passengers in natural "air-conditioned" comfort. Taxi fares tend to be expensive throughout the islands and taxis are not metered! However, there are official taxi rates in both the BVI and USVI, and the prudent traveler should inquire of the rate beforehand so that there are no misunderstandings.

The major charter-boat companies will arrange transportation to pick you up upon arrival at the airport, but, such service should be arranged at the time of booking the charter.

THE PRICE OF PARADISE

TAXIS

The following fares give you an idea of how much taxi fares can be. Prices are subject to change. Always ask how much a fare will be before getting in the taxi.

SAMPLE TAXI FARES IN THE BVI
From Beef Island Airport to Road Town:
1 person $27; 2 people $14 each; 3+ people $12 each

SAMPLE TAXI FARES IN THE USVI
From Charlotte Amalie to Compass Point:
1 person $12; $9 extra for 2 people

DINING OUT

Food for thought... Traveling around the islands, you'll note menu prices in restaurants are often higher than those in your home town. All food is shipped or flown in and then re-transported to other islands. Electricity and fuel are also expensive, so at the end of the day, profit margins are pretty skinny, all of which can be further exacerbated by the seasonality of the destination. Throughout the islands you can expect a 15% service charge to be added to the check.

SAFETY, HEALTH & EMERGENCIES

SUN PROTECTION

Although it may seem difficult to comprehend as you dig your car out of the snow to get to the airport, the tropical sun is hot, especially on pale bodies that have been kept undercover throughout a northern winter.

The constant trade breezes keep the temperature pretty much ideal, but be careful not to spend too long out in the sun, as the combined effect of overhead tropical sun and reflection from both sails and water can cause severe sunburns.

Most charter yachts are equipped with bimini tops, however it is imperative to bring along some lightweight, long sleeve tops (preferably with SPF protection) and a pair of lightweight cotton trousers that can be used to cover up your legs in case of sunburn. A sailing cap or wide brimmed Tilly hat will keep your nose out of trouble.

If you are fair, then perhaps you should think about a wide-brimmed hat.

Suntan lotions are available throughout the islands. Heed the warnings of dermatologists regarding excessive sun exposure and do not go out into the sun without using an appropriate sun block or coverup. Start with at least

SPF 30. If you are careful, you will gradually develop a rich, golden tan without suffering a painful and potentially dangerous sunburn. *It is very important to make sure your sunscreen bottle is labeled "reef safe" as many contain chemicals that kill coral.*

SAFETY IN THE ISLANDS

As with any destination in the world, there is always a chanc e of having something of value targeted by a thief. If you take precautions in advance, then you can enjoy your holiday with less worry. If you are chartering a bareboat, direct any specific questions to your charter company.

The following are some suggestions to help keep your possessions safe from petty crime:

Valuables: Expensive jewelry can be left at home. It is too easy to lose rings, earrings etc. when swimming, beaching and sailing. The islands are very informal for the most part, beach bars are casual and it's unlikely you would want to wear anything fancy.

Passports: You can keep your passport with you or put it in a very safe place when leaving the vessel. We suggest using waterproof pouches that can be worn around the neck under a shirt that will fit a passport, some cash and credit cards. Leave your passport number with someone at home so that if you do lose it, it will be easier for Immigration to help you.

Cash: Of course you'll need some cash, but there are more and more ATMs located throughout the islands. Credit cards can be replaced if lost or stolen. Just make sure you have left your credit card number with someone at home and bring the telephone number listed on the card to call and report a lost or stolen card.

Leaving your vessel: Most boats can be locked at the companionway hatch after dogging the portholes.

Dinghies: Most charter boats are equipped with metal cables and locks. When going ashore, lock your dinghy to the dock to avoid having it "borrowed." Also, at night or when leaving the dinghy with the boat, make sure you lock it to the boat. Vessels with dinghy davits should raise the dinghy out of the water at night or when leaving the dinghy and the boat.

Nights aboard at dockside: If you are unsure of the level of security while sleeping dockside, you might want to lock the companionway while leaving the hatches open for ventilation unless of course you have air conditioning aboard.

For your personal safety, the usual rules apply. Don't go anywhere where you feel uncomfortable, especially alone. Use caution as you would anywhere else. After several rounds of rum punch, anyone can become more vulnerable to crime, and it is not safe to be operating motor vessels after having a few too many.

The Virgin Islanders are very warm, friendly and helpful. The environment is mostly benign. But, as you would anywhere in the world, take a few simple precautions, relax, and enjoy your stay.

WATER SAFETY

The waters of the Virgin Islands are essentially a benign area. When people think of tropical waters, man-eating sharks, barracuda and giant moray eels come to mind. The truth of the matter is that more injuries are sustained by cuts from coral or by stepping on sea urchin spines than by encounters with underwater predators.

It is against BVI law to import jet skis. If you have a jet ski aboard you must declare it at customs when entering the BVI. Jet skis can be rented from local rental shops in certain locations.

Jet Skis are forbidden in the National Park Service waters in St. John and St. Croix.

Sharks: There are many large sharks around the waters of the Virgins, but they remain largely in deep water. It is highly unlikely that you will ever see a shark during your cruise.

Moray Eels: These creatures are shy by nature and make their homes in rocks and crevices in the reef. They will protect themselves from perceived danger, so do not reach into caves or crevices unless you can see inside.

SAFETY, HEALTH & EMERGENCIES

Barracuda: You will, without doubt, see numerous barracuda of various sizes while snorkeling the reefs. They are curious fish and are likely to stay almost motionless in the water watching your movements. They will not bother you, and it is best to show them the same courtesy.

Coral: Exercise extreme caution around all coral as cuts and scratches can become infected quickly. Familiarize yourself with the various types of coral and

remember to stay well clear of the fire coral. To preserve the reefs, do not touch the coral, with your fins, your hands or anything. *Take only pictures, leave only bubbles.*

Manchineel Trees: Familiarize yourself with this dangerous tree that grows along the shoreline, the manchineel tree has small green fruit that look like apples. Both the fruit and the sap are extremely toxic and can cause severe burns and rashes.

BVI BEACH SAFETY FLAGS

Red & Yellow Flags - mark areas of water that are patrolled by lifeguards. These are the safest places to swim.

Black & White Chequered Flags - mean an area of water that has been marked out for use by craft, for example wind surfing, surf boards or dinghies. For your safety do not swim in this zoned area.

Red Flags - these indicate danger. *Never swim when the Red Flag is flying.* At the Baths, Devils Bay & Spring Bay the Red Flag also indicates that the yachts are prohibited from using the mooring field.

Yellow Flags - these indicate that you should take caution: weak swimmers are discouraged from entering the water. At the Baths, Devils Bay & Spring Bay the Red Flag also indicates that the yachts should take caution when using the mooring field.

Purple Flags - indicate a marine life warning, for example Jelly Fish. The Purple Flag may also be flown with Yellow or Red Flags.

For More Information Visit: www.bvidef.org

Sea Urchins: These black, spiny creatures are found in abundance throughout the islands. They can be seen on sandy bottoms and on reefs and rocks. If you stand on one or inadvertently place your hand on one, it is likely that one or more of the spines will pierce your skin and break off. Do not try to dig the spines out of your skin. Call a doctor for assistance.

Jelly Fish: During the summer months these unwelcome visitors arrive. Check the water before entering, wear a chafe guard if possible. If stung try not to touch the wound but use vinegar or rubbing alcohol to neutralize the toxins.

Lionfish: This invasive species is growing in numbers and destroys coral and local fish populations. They are extremely attractive and venomous! Do not touch them. If stung apply the hottest water possible to the affected area and contact VISAR.

Don'ts: Observe the following rules, you will add to your enjoyment of the cruise:

1. Don't swim alone, at night, or in heavy surf.
2. Don't wear jewelry when swimming.
3. Don't reach into crevices or caves.
4. Don't spear a fish and leave it bleeding in the water or in a bag at your waist.
5. Take no marine life without a permit!
6. Don't touch or anchor in coral under any circumstances.

SEASICKNESS

For a small number of us, one of the downsides of a sailing holiday can be, of course, seasickness. This can be one of the few times you can feel so badly that you are afraid that you won't die! Although the Virgin Islands have relatively little wave action there are those who just look at a boat and turn green. It can happen at the most unpredictable times, and seasickness is always every bit as embarrassing as it is miserable for the victim.

Over the years we have seen and heard all kinds of remedies, and have tried most of them. Here is a list of products to help you prepare for your trip and act like an old salt:

1. One favorite is Sea-Bands. These elastic wrist bands have a small, plastic button that when placed in the right acupressure point on the inside of your wrist, helps to relieve symptoms. The bands come with easy instructions. They have no side effects, and are comfortable to wear. You may purchase them at drug stores. There are also other similar brands available. We have tried these numerous times with people who suffer from motion sickness at the slightest movement and have found them very successful.

2. An old, natural remedy that again, has no side effects and is safe to use is ginger capsules. Ginger has a settling effect on the stomach. These capsules are available in most health food stores.

3. Dramamine, Marezine, and Bonine are the old stand-by, over the counter antihistamines. Dramamine in particular can make you very, very drowsy. You can miss some good times if you are sleeping the days away, however, it is better than being sick.

Never overload dinghies

4. For a prescription drug, ask your physician for Transderm Scop. This is only sold as a prescription, and can have some side effects. It does have some restrictions and is not safe for everyone. Transderm Scop comes in the form of a medicated patch that is worn behind the ear for three days at a stretch.

Avoid reading and going below when you are underway. The fresh breeze can help, and also remember to look at the horizon instead of the waves passing next to the boat. Good luck, and let us hear from you if there are any other miracle cures around.

MOSQUITOES

When in the Virgin Islands, make sure to bring some good bug spray. There are three diseases that are transmitted by mosquitoes. One is called Dengue Fever and the other one is called Chikungunya and the most recent is the Zika Virus. The symptoms of Chikungunya are a rash, arthritis, headaches, high fever, back pain, nausea and vomiting. Zika can have no symptoms but people may experience: pain in the back of the eyes, joints, or muscles, fatigue, fever, chills, loss of appetite, or sweating. Also common is eye redness, headache, skin rash, or vomiting. Zika can be sexually transmitted and can cause serious birth defects in unborn children. Women and their partners wishing to become pregnant should check the CDC for important information before going to Zika affected areas. www.cdc.gov/zika

If you are ashore or on the boat and you detect mosquitoes spray yourself with bug spray and consider putting on a long sleeve shirt, long pants, and maybe even a scarf.

While these diseases are not rampant, you should be aware of them and if you manifest any of the above symptoms you should seek medical assistance.

TROPICAL FISH POISONING

Ciguatera, also known as tropical fish poisoning, is a disease which can affect people who have eaten certain varieties of tropical fish.

The results of such poisoning can be very serious and, although seldom resulting in death, can cause severe discomfort. Victims of ciguatera poisoning are often ill for weeks and some symptoms may persist for months.

One problem with fish poisoning is that it is impossible to differentiate between toxic and nontoxic fish. The fish itself is not affected by the toxins and therefore appears quite normal and edible. The toxins cannot be tasted and washing, cooking or freezing will not render them harmless.

Symptoms of Ciguatera
In most cases, the symptoms will appear within three to ten hours after eating the toxic fish. The first signs are nausea, vomiting, diarrhea and stomach cramps.

Later, the patient may also start to suffer from a wide variety of neurological ailments, including pains in the joints and muscles, weakness in the arms and legs, and/or a tingling sensation in the feet and hands. A tingling sensation around the lips, nose and tongue is also common.

At the onset of any of the above symptoms, the patient should ask, "Have I eaten any fish today?" If the answer is "yes," seek medical attention.

Types of Fish Carrying Ciguatera
The fish most likely to carry the toxins are the larger predatory fish associated with coral reefs. These include barracudas, grouper, snapper, jacks and parrotfish. It should be noted that only certain species in each family are associated with the toxins. Therefore, it is a good idea to check with a local fisherman before eating your catch.

The fish that are considered safe are offshore fish such as tuna, wahoo, swordfish, marlin, and dolphin. Others include sailfish, Spanish mackerel, small king mackerel and yellowtail snapper.

MEDICAL RESOURCES

Hospitals and Health Clinics
TORTOLA

Peebles Hospital
Road Town
284-852-7500

B&F Medical Complex
Open daily from 7:00am
Mill Mall Bldg., Wickham's Cay I
284-494-2196

Bougainvillea Clinic
Cutless Bldg.
284-494-2181

Eureka Medical Clinic
Omar Hodge Bldg., Wickham's Cay I
284-494-2346

Penn Medical Center
284-499-2261
Pharmacy: 284-340-4211
www.pennmedci.com

VIRGIN GORDA

Apex Medical Complex
284-495-6557

JOST VAN DYKE

Jost Van Dyke Clinic
284-852-7798

ST. JOHN

Cruz Bay Family Practice
340-776-6789
Emergency and Family Practice, 24/7

Myrah Keating Smith Community Clinic
340-776-8900

ST. THOMAS

Schneider Regional Medical Center
Sugar Estate, St. Thomas
340-776-8311

Red Hook Family Practice
340-775-2303

Yacht Haven Family Practice
340-776-1511

ST. CROIX

Governor Juan F. Luis Hospital
340-778-6311

Emergencies
BVI

For Police, Fire or Ambulance:
Dial 999 or 911

Virgin Island Search and Rescue (VISAR) Dial 767 (SOS) from any telephone, or 284-499-0911

USVI

Emergency 24 Hour, Police, Fire, Ambulance 911

U.S. Coast Guard
VHF 16. 340-776-3497, 340-344-3537

In the case that you experience an unexpected medical issue, the new Peebles Hospital in Road Town meets all of the national or international standards that any hospital in the UK or US would meet." They oversee nine community clinics on different islands in the chain. CEO Darlene Carty-Baptiste is quoted saying, "Regardless of one's inability to pay, no one is turned away. This applies to visitors as well as us."

SCUBA Emergencies
There is a re-compression chamber in St. Thomas at the hospital
340-776-8311, 340-693-6215

Divers Alert Network:
International hotline: 919-684-9111

PROVISIONING

As the fleets of charter vessels throughout the islands continue to expand, so do the provisioning services that support them. Access to fresh fruits and vegetables, meat, poultry including gourmet items is a mainstream industry and one that has expanded beyond Road Town, in the BVI, to the smaller islands and anchorages and to online ordering. All supermarkets stock both wines and spirits and a number of companies specialize in yacht provisioning.

A sailing holiday usually includes eating ashore at various establishments around the islands and to this end it should be a major consideration when ordering provisions. Don't over order! Determine how many nights you are likely to be ashore and order accordingly. Food is expensive in the islands and eating ashore is a major part of the experience.

Most charter companies in and around the Virgin Islands offer the charter party a choice of provisioning programs or put them in touch with local companies that specialize in the provisioning of yachts. Here are a few of your choices:

A) Allow the charter company to provision for you from a pre-selected plan to save on sailing time. The main plans are full provisioning, which includes 3 meals a day, or the popular split program, which eliminates some evening meals so you can eat ashore. If you are considering this, ask the charter company for a sample menu.

B) Provision yourself from one of the local markets or delicatessens. This is a good idea if you have specific dietary needs, but it is time-consuming, and when analyzing costs, taxi fares and sailing time should be considered. However, many of the local markets have a surprisingly sophisticated array of products.

C) Have an independent provisioning company prepare your provisions in advance and have them delivered to the boat or swing by and pick them up.

Boatside delivery from Good Moon Farm, Trellis Bay

PROVISIONING

Provisioning lists can be faxed or emailed in advance, allowing you the luxury of choosing your provisioning from home.

Some excellent options for online ordering are:

Riteway Food Markets: 284-340-2263 (www.rtwbvi.com) have a well-thought-out format and will deliver to your boat or villa on Tortola free of charge. They offer an excellent selection of wines and spirits.

Good Moon Farm: 284-542-0586 (www.goodmoonfarm.com) Good Moon Farm specialize in locally grown fresh produce for the yachting community. Now fully established as the sole local organic provisioning option in the BVI's inclusive of meats, seafood and poultry, Good Moon Farm is central to a network of local food producers including weekly supplies of produce from farmers in Dominica. Their online wish list allows you to place your order before leaving home and it will be picked, packed and delivered the day you arrive to your charter company or villa anywhere in the BVI. They also have an excellent Good Moon Farm Box option, priced to your needs. Good Moon Farm also delivers fresh greens and fruits every day to Aragorn's Studio in Trellis Bay, where they are sold from beautiful baskets in front of the studio or brought out to the anchorage in Aragorn's boat shop. If an order is placed on line it can also be delivered to Aragorn's studio in Trellis Bay for convenient pick-up.

TICO Wines & Spirits: 284-494-2211 (www.ticobvi.com) are both retailers and wholesalers of an extensive line of wines and spirits. Delivery (over $150) is free on Tortola or for orders under $150, a $10 delivery fee is charged.

RESTOCKING ALONG THE WAY

However you provision your vessel you will probably wish to augment your supply at some point along the cruise. Major items are available in Road Town, Manuel Reef, Nanny Cay, Soper's Hole, Cane Garden Bay, Trellis Bay, Maya Cove and East End in Tortola. Provisioning is available in Virgin Gorda Yacht Harbour, the Bitter End, and Leverick Bay in Virgin Gorda. In the U.S. Virgins you will be able to provision in Cruz Bay, Redhook, Charlotte Amalie, and in Christiansted, St. Croix.

TORTOLA/ROAD TOWN

ROAD REEF
RiteWay Food Market
Tel: 284-347-1162 or
284-494-2263
www.rtwbvi.com

**ROAD TOWN/
WICKHAMS CAY I & II**
Dockmaster's Deli
Tel: 284-494-2771

Bobby's Marketplace
Tel: 284-494-2189
bobbyssupermarket.com

French Deli
Tel: 284-494-2195
frenchdelibvi.com

RiteWay Food Market
Tel: 284-347-1188
www.rtwbvi.com

One Mart Foods
Tel: 284-494-6999/4649
onemartfoods.com

TICO Wine & Spirits
Tel: 284-340-6730/6777
www.ticobvi.com

EASTERN TORTOLA

FAT HOG'S BAY/EAST END
RiteWay (East End)
Tel: 284-347-1257
www.rtwbvi.com

TRELLIS BAY
Good Moon Farm
284-542-0586
goodmoonfarm.com

Trellis Bay Mkt Bar/Grill
Tel: 284-495-1421
trellisbaymarket.com

SCRUB ISLAND
Gourmet Market/Café
Tel: 284 394-3440

WESTERN TORTOLA

CANE GARDEN BAY
Bobby's Market
Tel: 284-494-2189
bobbyssupermarket.com

**Cane Garden Bay
Provisioning**
Tel: 284-495-9660

WEST END
Harbour Market
Due to open Nov. 2019
www.rtwbvi.com

**WEST END
(POCKWOOD POND)**
Seafood Kingdom
Tel: 284 495 1100
www.rtwbvi.com

**MANUEL REEF /
SEA COWS BAY**
Manuel Reef
Supermarket
Tel: 284-494-0931

VIRGIN GORDA

**VIRGIN GORDA YACHT
HARBOUR**
Buck's Markets
Tel: 284-495-5423
bucksmarkets.com

Cash & Carry
Tel: 284-340-2263
www.rtwbvi.com

Rosy's Enterprises
Tel: 284-495-5245
www.rosysvg.com

Supa Valu Ltd
Tel: 284-495-6500

NORTH SOUND
Bitter End
*Provisioning Store to
open November 2109*
Tel: 800-827-2392

OIL NUT BAY
Oil Nut Bay Marina Mkt
Tel: 284 393 1000

LEVERICK BAY
Chef's Pantry
Tel: 284-344-1621

GUN CREEK
Buck's Supermarket
284-495-7368

ANEGADA

Pam's Kitchen
Tel: 284-345-5436

Lil'Bit
Tel: 284-495-9932

JOST VAN DYKE

Camila's Superette
Tel: 284-495-9930

JVD Grocery
Tel: 284-343-6443
www.jvdgrocery.com

Rudy's Marketplace
Opening Sept/Oct 2019
Tel: 284-340-9282 or
284-340-5771

ST. JOHN

CRUZ BAY
Starfish Market
Tel: 340-779-4949
starfishmarket.com

Dolphin Market
Tel: 340-776-5328
dolphinmarkets.com

CORAL BAY
Love City Market
Tel: 340-643-0010

Dolphin Market
Tel: 340.776.5005

ST.THOMAS

CROWN BAY
Pueblo Super Market
Tel: 340-774-4200
www.wfmpueblo.com

**YACHT HAVEN GRANDE/
HAVENSIGHT**
Pueblo Super Market
Tel: 340-774-2695
www.wfmpueblo.com

Natural Food Grocery
Tel: 340-775-3737
FB: NaturalFoodGroceryVI

The Fruit Bowl
Tel: 340-774-8565
thefruitbowlvi.com

EAST END / RED HOOK
Moe's Fresh Market
Tel: 340-693-0254
www.moesvi.com

Sami's Fresh Mart
Tel: 340-714-6278

Cost-U-Less
*Reopening fall 2019,
check for current info.*

ST. CROIX

CHRISTIANSTED
Bi-Rite Supermarket
Tel: 340-718-6045

J&W Grocery
Tel: 340-713-8100

Cost-U-Less
Tel: 340-719-4442

**Food Town
Supermarket**
Tel: 340-718-9990

Food Plaza Extra East
Tel: 340-778-6240

Pueblo Supermarket
Tel: 340-718-0118

Expressway Market
Tel: 340-713-8080

FREDERIKSTED
Stop & Shop
Supermarket
Tel: 340-692-2771

**Supersave
Supermarket**
Tel: 340-772-3030

TEAGUE BAY
Ziggy's Island Market
Tel: 304-773-8382

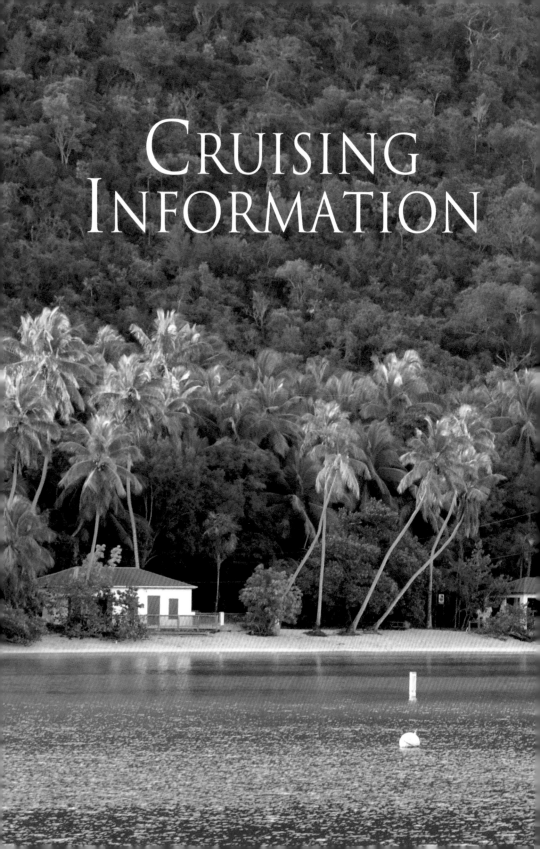

CRUISING
INFORMATION

HOW TO USE THIS GUIDE

The Cruising Guide to the Virgin Islands has been designed to incorporate both detailed information regarding a given anchorage and a quick visual guide to the cruising sailor, both with aerial photography and detailed anchorage charts.

The anchorage section of the guide is broken down by individual islands or groups of islands and color coded accordingly (see opposite page).

At the front of each section the reader will find a brief history or overview of the area, including a chart that is further broken down by individual anchorages shown by dotted red lines. A list of the relevant charts covering the area and the appropriate waypoints are also shown.

Turning to the individual anchorages; at the beginning of the text they are all identified with a *waypoint* location where applicable. *Navigation* gives the reader a quick fix on relevant distance to the anchorage and *Services* offers a one line overview on what is available.

The accompanying text is broken down by overview, followed by *Navigation and Piloting*, then *Anchoring* and finally detailed information on what to find *Ashore*.

At the back of each section, we have included a section entitled *Island Connections*. These pages are all sand colored and provide the reader with contact information for all the bars, restaurants and marine businesses around the islands.

The charts are accurate interpretations of the specific anchorages. They have been designed for vessels drawing about 6-6.5 feet and all water less than six feet is shown in yellow; once again allowing the skipper a quick reference for safety.

The *Guide* starts at Road Town, Tortola and continues counter clockwise around all of the anchorages in close proximity. This section is then followed by the Channel Islands east to Virgin Gorda and Anegada to then back west to Jost Van Dyke.

We have taken the liberty of starting the U.S. Virgin Islands at St. John, since that is a logical route for a vessel in transit to and from the BVI.

The information in this Guide has been collected over numerous years of living and cruising in the islands in addition to a formal annual area audit. The authors have made every attempt to keep the guide updated but acknowledge that sea conditions change and buoys may be misplaced, lost or off station. Use caution, be vigilant and keep us informed of any changes that should be posted on our website for fellow sailors.

CHART INFORMATION

Our charts are interpretive and designed for yachts drawing about 6.5 feet. Deeper yachts should refer to the depths on their charts.

 LAND   HILLS   ROADS PATHS

LAND HEIGHTS ARE IN FEET AND APPROXIMATE

 WATER TOO SHALLOW FOR NAVIGATION OR DANGEROUS IN SOME CONDITIONS

 SURFACE REEF   ROCKS DEEPER REEF

 NAVIGABLE WATER   DEPTHS ARE IN FEET AND APPROXIMATE

 CURRENT ✝ CHURCH   AERIAL

 MANGROVES ⚓ ANCHORAGE   PICK UP MOORING ONLY

 WRECKS DAY STOP ANCHORAGE NATL. PARK MOORING

GREEN BEACON
GREEN BUOYS (PORT)

RED BEACON
RED BUOYS (STARBOARD)

 ISOLATED SHOAL BEACONS & BUOYS

 N   E S

W

IALA B MARKS SHOWING DIRECTION OF DANGER (BUOYS & BEACONS)

 YELLOW BUOYS

 RED & GREEN DIVIDED CHANNEL BUOYS

 MOORING OR OTHER BUOY

 SECTOR

LIGHTS

FL = FLASHING, F = FIXED, L = LONG, Q = QUICK, M = MILES

LIGHT EXPLANATION:

FL (2) 4S, 6M

LIGHT GROUP FLASHING 2 EVERY FOUR SECONDS, VISIBLE 6 MILES

 WHITE (W)

GREEN (G)

YELLOW (Y)

RED (R)

Navigation

Paper Charts

It is possible to navigate through the U.S. and British Virgin Islands with a single paper chart, such as NIMA 25609 and our cruising guide. Many of the charter companies have duplicated this chart in one form or another as a handout for each charter group. If you're chartering, be sure to ask your charter company in advance which charts they'll provide you, when you'll receive them and whether the charts are yours to keep. In addition, ask if there is a plotter aboard and which software is included. Then take a careful look at the areas you intend to cruise and determine any additional chart coverage you may want. In many instances the company will provide a waterproof version of the area chart aboard the vessel as part of its permanent inventory.

Your own charts will allow you to plan your trip in advance and will also serve as a nice memento of your trip. Complete paper chart coverage of the Virgin Islands will range from about $50.00 to several hundred dollars, especially if you include electronic charts which are now very popular. The following paper charts or chart kits cover the Virgin Islands and surrounding areas and they are available from our website or larger chart agents in the U.S., Canada and Europe.

British Admiralty

2016	Puerto Rico to Leeward Islands
2006	Anegada to St. Thomas
2019	North Sound to Road Harbour

British Admiralty Leisure Folio:

5640	The U.S. & British Virgin Islands
	Kit contains 11 individual charts
	5640-(1-11)

National Image & Mapping Agency (NIMA):

25609	St. Thomas to Anegada
25610	Virgin Gorda Sound
25611	Road Harbour
25640	St. Thomas to Tortola
25641	Virgin Gorda to St. Thomas & St. Croix

IMRAY-Iolaire:

A23	The Virgin Islands
A232	St. Thomas to Virgin Gorda
A232	Tortola to Anegada
A234	Northeast Coast of St. Croix

NV Charts:

The Virgin Islands (St. Thomas to Anegada)
Chart Pack – The Virgin Islands
Pack contains 13 individual charts

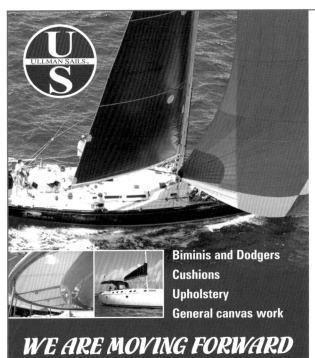

ELECTRONIC CHARTS & GPS

Most of the charter fleets throughout the Caribbean are now equipped with chart plotters pre-loaded with software. Before purchasing any electronic charts, ask your charter company or agent what equipment and supporting software is aboard.

Since electronic charts are derivatives of paper charts which in turn may have been produced from surveys conducted years earlier, caution should be exercised not to rely upon these charts as a sole source of information. Do not use zoomed in charts to establish waypoints around the islands, use only known waypoints so as not to corrupt data. Anegada is a prime example where the approach channel is shown in different locations depending upon the software being used.

In this age of information where smartphones and tablets are ubiquitous, companies like Navionics have developed apps that transform such devices into mini-chart plotters. Such devices should be used with caution, since you'll no doubt be roaming on a network outside of your plan and subject to high roaming rates.

These electronic charts cover the Virgins (and beyond) and are available from selected chart agents and marine electronic dealers in the U.S., Canada and Europe.

Maptech:	Companion CD charts
Admiralty Leisure:	Electronic versions of the Leisure Folio
NV Charts:	Companion CD charts
C-Map:	NAC501 Cuba to Trinidad
Garmin:	US030 Southeast Caribbean
Navionics:	3XG: Central and South America
Navionics:	Mobile App: Caribbean and South America

NAVIGATION

GPS (GLOBAL POSITIONING SYSTEM) & WAYPOINT GUIDE

Navigation throughout the Virgin Islands is mostly line of sight. It is of course mandatory to have updated charts aboard, both paper and electronic, but it is essential that you not rely on any one piece of information for the overall safety of your vessel. Your authors are not proponents of listing waypoint information that might be relied upon to take you through a narrow entrance in a reef. We have established waypoints outside of the anchorage and listed a suggested course. When necessary, post a lookout on the bow and never be complacent. Take visual sightings, depth readings and proceed with caution.

GPS has been known to fail, software has been known to give false readings. There have been reports of navigators finding themselves a couple of miles away from where they expected in places where the GPS showed good correspondence. Occasional errors are a possibility.

The Cruising Guide to the Virgin Islands has adopted the following system of waypoint identification:

The British Virgin Islands carry a designator of BV (British Virgins) while in the U.S. Virgins they will be designated as UV (U.S. Virgins).

They are further broken down by island or island group:

Tortola, BVI	100
Jost Van Dyke	200
The Channel Islands (Norman, Peter, Salt & Cooper)	300
Virgin Gorda and Anegada	400
St. John, USVI	500
St. Thomas	600
St. Croix	700

The waypoints pertaining to a particular section of the guide are listed on the leading pages and the entire waypoint list is also copied onto the free planning chart included with this guide. Virgin Island Waypoints can also be downloaded from our website at: www.cruisingguides.com/planning#IslandNavigation.

WAYPOINTS

WAYPOINT	DESCRIPTION	LATITUDE	LONGITUDE
Tortola		**North**	**West**
101	Road Town	18°24.80'	64°36.20'
102	Road Town/Kingston	18°24.50'	64°35.00'
103	Buck Island	18°25.10'	64°33.20'
104	Fat Hog	18°25.95'	64°33.20'
105	Beef Island	18°25.30'	64°30.90'
106	Marina Cay/Trellis	18°27.30'	64°31.50'
107	Cam Bay	18°28.55'	64°31.50'
108	Camanoe North	18°30.00'	64°32.40'
109	Guana Sound	18°27.70'	64°33.20'
110	Monkey Point	18°27.70'	64°35.00'
111	Guana North	18°30.00'	64°35.00'
112	Anderson/Rough Point	18°27.20'	64°39.80'
113	Cane Garden Bay	18°25.65'	64°40.20'
114	Soper's Hole N	18°23.70'	64°43.30'
115	West Point (Great Thatch)	18°22.80'	64°45.50'
116	Frenchman's Cay (S)	18°22.70'	64°41.90'
117	Nanny Cay	18°23.00'	64°38.50'
Jost Van Dyke			
201	Little Jost Van Dyke	18°26.60'	64°42.75'
202	Little Harbour	18°25.90'	64°43.05'
203	Great Harbour	18°26.10'	64°45.00'
204	White Bay	18°26.30'	64°45.80'
205	Tobago South	18°26.00'	64°49.50'
206	Tobago North	18°26.75'	64°50.00'
The Channel Islands			
301	Flannigan's Passage	18°20.60'	64°38.50'
302	Peter Island West Point	18°21.40'	64°37.00'
303	Dead Chest	18°22.00'	64°34.60'
304	Cooper Island	18°23.50'	64°31.00'
305	Round Rock Passage N	18°24.10'	64°28.20'
306	Round Rock Passage S	18°23.30'	64°27.10'
307	Carrot Rock, Peter Island	18°18.92'	64°34.25'
308	Peter/Norman Channel	18°20.00'	64°35.70'
309	Benures Bay	18°19.63'	64°36.40'
310	Pelican/Norman	18°19.70'	64°37.40'
311	The Bight, Norman Island	18°19.30'	64°37.50'
Virgin Gorda/Anegada		**North**	**West**
401	Baths	18°26.00'	64°27.00'
402	St. Thomas Bay	18°27.20'	64°26.90'
403	Great Dog	18°28.42'	64°26.80'
404	Dogs North	18°30.00'	64°29.20'
405	Cows Mouth	18°30.40'	64°25.20'
406	Mosquito Rock	18°31.30'	64°23.10'
407	Eustatia Passage	18°30.50'	64°18.70'
408	Necker Island Passage	18°32.20'	64°15.00'
410	Anegada Approach	18°42.40'	64°24.50'
411	Setting Point Channel	18°42.80'	64°23.65'

WAYPOINTS

WAYPOINT	DESCRIPTION	LATITUDE	LONGITUDE
St. John			
501	Johnson's Reef	18°22.15'	64°46.70'
502	Windward Passage	18°21.50'	64°47.80'
503	Cruz Bay	18°20.30'	64°48.78'
504	Chocolate Hole	18°18.50'	64°47.70'
505	Dog Rocks	18°17.30'	64°48.75'
506	Lameshur Bay	18°18.30'	64°43.80'
507	Rams Head	18°17.60'	64°41.70'
508	Coral Bay Entrance	18°19.40'	64°40.30'
509	Hurricane Hole	18°20.30'	64°41.90'
St. Thomas		**North**	**West**
601	Redhook	18°20.00'	64°50.00'
602	Cabrita Point	18°19.30'	64°49.60'
603	Cow & Calf	18°18.20'	64°51.30'
603a	Jersey Bay	18°18.50'	64°51.50'
603b	The Lagoon	18°18.86'	64°52.06'
604	Packet Rock	18°17.60'	64°53.40'
605	St. Thomas Harbor	18°18.60'	64°55.60'
606	Saba Is.	18°18.10'	64°59.00'
607	Sail Rock	18°16.80'	65°06.30'
608	Salt Cay Passage	18°22.00'	65°04.20'
609	Lizard Rock	18°23.40'	64°59.65'
610	Omen Rock	18°23.40'	64°57.50'
611	Little Hans Lollik	18°24.75'	64°55.00'
612	Hans Lollik	18°23.40'	64°53.70'
613	Middle Passage	18°21.50'	64°50.70'
St. Croix			
701	Central Navigation Point	17°48.00'	64°42.00'
702	Christiansted Hbr	17°46.00'	64°41.90''
703	Scotch Bank/Green Cay	17°46.60'	64°40.10'
704	Buck Island N	17°48.50'	64°38.00'
705	Coakley Cut	17°46.50'	64°38.50'
706	Salt River	17°47.80'	64°45.00'
707	West Point	17°45.00'	64°55.00'
708	East Point	17°45.00'	64°32.00'

NAVIGATION

THE BUOYAGE SYSTEM OF THE VIRGIN ISLANDS

The IALA Maritime Buoyage System has combined all the international requirements into a global standard. This single set of rules allows lighthouse authorities the choice of using red to port or red to starboard on a regional basis, the two regions being known as region A and region B. In the waters of the Caribbean where system B is used, the color red is used to mark the starboard side of the channel when approaching from seaward (red, right, returning). In this respect, it should be noted that the respective buoyage systems for both the U.S. and British Virgins are the same.

NAVIGATION

Pilotage through unknown waters is one of the major concerns of the cruising yachtsman. However, in the Virgins, where there is very little tidal rise and fall and only minimal current to worry about, pilotage is extremely simple. Since the weather is so warm, we don't experience any fog and you can almost always, the notable exception being Anegada, see the island for which you are heading (unless you are in a rare heavy rain fall).

The islands themselves are mostly high and volcanic, rising steeply from the crystal clear water. Reefs and shoals are not a major problem as they are usually well marked, and providing time is taken to study the pertinent guides and charts on a daily basis, your cruise around the island will be relatively stress free.

Since the islands in the chain are close together, you will have no difficulty in distinguishing them. By utilizing your chart or plotter and depth sounder you will always be able to locate your position without extensive navigation.

EQUIPMENT

Every cruising yacht should be equipped with the basic tools of navigation – compass, parallel rules, triangles, dividers, plotters, etc. However, it should be noted that in order to navigate throughout the islands, the only equipment needed besides a detailed chart is a compass, pencil and fathometer. Those wishing to brush up on navigational skills will find ample opportunity, although celestial observations are often difficult because of the proximity of the islands.

Reading the Water

There is no dark secret attached to the ability to read the depth of the water. It is merely the ability to distinguish water color. Experience is, of course, the best teacher; however, with a few practical hints and a pair of polarized sunglasses, even the novice will be able to feel his or her way into a coral fringed anchorage within a few days. When sailing over sandy bottoms, when the sun is bright you will be aware of large dark patches on the seabed, these are cloud shadows which will obviously be on the move. This phenomenon can be confusing since the shadow presents much the same as a grassy bottom.

It is important to have the sun overhead in order to distinguish reef areas. Do not attempt to negotiate a reef-fringed entrance with the sun in your eyes, and always have someone on the bow keeping an eye on the water in front of the boat.

Deep water of 50 feet and over will be "inky" blue. This can be lighter if the bottom is white sand.

A light green or turquoise would indicate a depth of 15-25 feet. If the bottom has rocks or coral, these will change the color to a brownish shade.

Water of 10 feet and under will show as a very pale shade of green if there is a sandy bottom, or a light brown if rocks and coral are present.

The Right of Way and Sailing at Night

A general rule of thumb is to stay out of everyone's way. There are times, however, when this is impossible and, in such instances, power boats should give way to boats under sail and all pleasure vessels should give way to commercial shipping. This being the case, it is important in close quarters to hold your course so that the other skipper can take appropriate action.

If you are crossing ferry traffic, it is prudent to keep a weather eye on approaching vessels and make every effort to stay well clear. Use your VHF channel 16 if you are in doubt and if you do alter course, make sure that the other skipper is aware that you have done so.

CRUISING ETIQUETTE

Freighters trading between the islands are often underway at night and at times are known not to use their running lights. Don't sail at night!

NAVY VESSELS & CRUISE SHIPS

When approaching a US Navy vessel or cruise ship, Coast Guard regulations state that you must slow your vessel to 5 knots within 500 yards and maintain a 200 yard distance at all times. Needless to say this is difficult in a harbor like Charlotte Amalie or Road Town where one has to pass large vessels at close quarters!

LOCAL CUSTOMS & DRESS CODE

Virgin Islanders are often rather conservative at heart and quite particular about dress. It is frowned upon to wear beachwear or bikinis into town or supermarkets. Topless sunbathing should be confined to the boat.

Great importance is set on greetings throughout the Virgins such as "good morning" or "good afternoon." It is considered rude to approach people with a question or to transact business without beginning with the appropriate greeting.

OVERBOARD DISCHARGE

In order to keep the waters of the Virgin Islands pristine, we as sailors need to do our part by making sure that we monitor and control the three major sources of pollution: sewage, garbage and oily waste. The National Marine Park System in both the BVI and USVI have a strict no discharge policy and are closely monitored for compliance.

Sewage - Untreated sewage should not be discharged in any harbor or within 1000 yards of the shoreline. In the USVI, Federal law prohibits discharge of untreated sewage within 3 miles of territorial waters.

All vessels should be equipped with holding tanks and the Y valve should be closed and controlled only by the skipper while the vessel is anchored or in a harbor. In the BVI there are limited pump out stations and these are prohibitively expensive so the skipper should plan to flush the tanks while in open water well away from the shoreline.

Garbage - Throwing or discharging garbage into the waters of the Virgin Islands is strictly prohibited by International MARPOL regulations. Please be sensitive and always carry refuse back to the boat. Don't leave it on the beach and don't throw anything into the water.**Oil and hazardous material** - It is absolutely prohibited to allow oily waste to enter the navigable waters of the Virgin Islands. Local marinas usually have controlled collection areas.

MOORING USAGE

Throughout the BVI in various anchorages you will find moorings available for you to use for a nightly fee. Most moorings will have the name of the restaurant or establishment where you should pay your fee, or in some anchorages someone will come in a small boat in the late afternoon – to collect the fee. This fee usually must be paid in cash. You should confirm that the mooring you are using is either a Moor-Seacure mooring or is professionally maintained. Boatyball, in conjunction with Moor Seacure, have developed an online reservation system that allows booking to be made starting at 7am each morning. You will be assigned a number depending upon your desired anchorage. The balls are all orange and clearly marked. Do not use these balls if you have no reservation.

In the BVI, National Parks Trust moorings are available for daytime use only, with a NPT permit that may be purchased at the same time as your cruising permit or at Customs & Immigration. The buoys within the park limits are designated by different colors. Yellow buoys are for commercial (dive) vessels, red buoys are daytime only and no diving is allowed while white buoys are limited to 90 minutes.

In the USVI National Park area, use of the mooring system is limited to vessels 60 feet and under. Please see details in the Diving, Snorkeling and Marine Parks section.

PICKING UP A MOORING BALL

1: Communications are critical. Make sure that you and your crew work out hand signals so that the crew member who is trying to pick up the mooring can direct the skipper back at the helm. Remember that the sound of your voice will be lost behind the noise of an engine and when you are facing forward looking at the approaching mooring, the skipper will not be able to hear you since you will be facing out to sea. Hand signals are imperative.

2: Before approaching the mooring ball, attach a dock line to a cleat and lead it through the fairlead and back over the lifeline. Remember that in tradewind conditions, the bow will blow off station rapidly once the vessel loses way, so it is important to get the line secured quickly. On a catamaran you will need to rig a second line to form a bridle. All moorings will be equipped with a pennant that terminates in a thimble through which to pass your line. *Do not attach the mooring pennant directly to the vessel.*

3: Approach the mooring buoy slowly and into the wind. The crew on the bow can use the boathook to indicate the location of the mooring in order to assist the skipper who will lose sight of it when in close quarters. Make sure your dinghy is pulled in short and secured. Use just enough power to reach the mooring and move it in reverse briefly once over the mooring to halt any forward motion.

4: The crew should be able to retrieve the pennant with the boat hook and lift it high enough to thread the dock line through the thimble and back through the same fairlead. Do not use the line as a bridle as the water motion and wind will "saw" through the line. Once the line is secure, let the skipper know with a "thumbs-up" and thread the second line.

5: If for any reason you miss the ball or lose control, do not try to hang onto it with the boat hook or your hands. Let it go and circle around for another try. Don't feel embarrassed, every sailor out there has been in a similar situation.

6: When leaving the mooring, simply have the crew member slip the ends of the two lines and allow the vessel to drift away from the mooring. Do not run over the pennant.

VIRGIN WEATHER

GENERAL CLIMATE

Located in the northeast tradewind belt, the Virgin Islands are blessed with excellent sailing conditions almost year round. During the winter months when the wind conditions are at their highest, the geographical makeup of the islands tends to shelter the sailing area, making for much easier sea conditions than one might logically expect in the vicinity of both the Leeward and Windward islands further to the south. That being said, it is important to understand the seasons of the Caribbean weather patterns which can be viewed as follows:

Winter (December–March) This period can be characterized by heavy sailing conditions with winds and seas reflecting the strong blustery tradewinds prevailing at this time. The winds at this time are also referred to as Christmas winds largely referring to the entire season versus late December and early January. The winds during this period can blow from 18-30 knots, more often than not in 3-4 day cycles created by passing high pressure systems.

Spring (April–June) This is perhaps the most settled time of the year and certainly my personal favorite sailing time. The winter tradewinds have diminished to a steady 10-15 knots from the northeast to south of east when not modified by tropical waves. Rainfall during this period is light.

Summer (July–October) Although hurricane season officially starts on June 1 and continues through November 30, statistically, early (June) tropical cyclone activity tends to occur in the western Caribbean. By mid-season, (July to early August) it is more likely to occur within a few hundred miles of the island chain. At the peak of the season (late August to September) it occurs mainly in the south of the north Atlantic, thousands of miles from the Virgins before reverting back in October to the eastern and then western Caribbean.

Fall (November–mid December)

A transitional season from the typical summer weather patterns with passing tropical wave activity, to the clearer, heavier tradewind conditions associated with non-tropical weather.

Note: An excellent reference source for cruisers wishing to understand Caribbean weather patterns is *Coastal and Offshore Weather: The Essential Handbook* by Chris Parker and available at his website www.caribwx.com.

WEATHER FORECASTS

Unlike that of most other parts of the world, the weather in the Virgin Islands is extremely stable. Forecasts are broadcast daily on most of the local stations:

The BVI, Tortola: ZBVI Radio 780 AM. Marine Forecast 08:05am (09:45am Sunday) Weather updates broadcast hourly on the half hour 07:30 to 21:30

St. Thomas: WIVI 96.1 FM (Forecasts at 07:30, 08:30, 15:30, 16:30 with hourly updates); WWWI 1000 (Forecasts hourly); WSTA 1340 AM; Radio Antilles 830 AM

St. Croix: WSTX 970 AM hourly

Puerto Rico: WOJO 1030 AM (English speaking all day at 6 minutes past the hour)

NOAA Weather is broadcast throughout the day on WX 3 or 4 or 6 on your VHF radio.

Internet Resources:
www.passageweather.com
www.caribwx.com
www.wunderground.com/tropical
www.windguru.com
http://hurricanes.noaa.gov (National Hurricane Center)

SSB (Single Side Band) Weather Net:
0630-0730	AST 8137kHz	USB
0730-0830	AST 8137kHz	USB
0830-0900	AST 8104kHz	USB
0900-0930	AST 12359kHz	USB
0930-1000	AST 1653kHz	USB

GROUND SWELLS

During the winter months of November through April, any significant weather in the North Atlantic will produce heavy swells along the entire north coast of the Virgins several days later. These ground swells have little effect on vessels under sail, but can turn a normally tranquil anchorage into pounding surf. Most anchorages exposed to the north are prone to this phenomenon – choose your anchorage accordingly.

WIND CONDITIONS

During the winter months of December through March the typical prevailing wind is from the northeast at 18-25 knots. The occasional stronger cold fronts, associated with low pressure systems, make their way southeast to reach the Virgin Islands. The initial effect will be lighter winds for several hundred miles ahead of the front. As a strong front approaches, the wind will

The Beaufort Scale (in knots)

FORCE	WIND	WMO CLASSIFICATION	ON THE WATER
0	Less than 1	Calm	Sea surface smooth and mirror-like
1	1-3	Light Air	Scaly ripples, no foam crests
2	4-6	Light Breeze	Small wavelets, crests glassy, no breaking
3	7-10	Gentle Breeze	Large wavelets, crests begin to break, scattered whitecaps
4	11-16	Moderate Breeze	Small waves 1-4 ft. becoming longer, numerous whitecaps
5	17-21	Fresh Breeze	Moderate waves 4-8 ft taking longer form, many whitecaps, some spray
6	22-27	Strong Breeze	Larger waves 8-13 ft, whitecaps common, more spray
7	28-33	Near Gale	Sea heaps up, waves 13-20 ft, white foam streaks off breakers
8	34-40	Gale	Moderately high (13-20 ft) waves of greater length, edges of crests begin to break into spindrift, foam blown in streaks
9	41-47	Strong Gale	High waves (20 ft), sea begins to roll, dense streaks of foam, spray may reduce visibility
10	48-55	Storm	Very high waves (20-30 ft) with overhanging crests, sea white with densely blown foam, heavy rolling, lowered visibility
11	56-63	Violent Storm	Exceptionally high (30-45 ft) waves, foam patches cover sea, visibility more reduced
12	64+	Hurricane	Air filled with foam, waves over 45 ft, sea completely white with driving spray, visibility greatly reduced

Virgin Weather

start to move south and then southeast immediately ahead of the cold front.

As the front passes the wind will shift to the northeast and increase to 20-30 knots with blustery conditions. By March, the winds start to move around to the east, and by June, they are blowing out of the southeast at 10-15 knots. During September to October, the tradewinds are weakest, and the weather can be less settled due to developing low pressure systems. By November, the high-pressure system around Bermuda starts to stabilize and 15-20 knot breezes become the norm.

Rain

While June through October is often characterized as the rainy season, heavy rain squalls can come at any time of year. The prudent skipper should be aware of an approaching squall by watching the sky and clouds to windward.

If a dark squall is approaching, it probably has considerable wind velocity on the squall line, and immediate action should be taken to shorten sail beforehand.

Storms and Hurricanes

Notwithstanding the devastating impact of two major hurricanes in 2017, The Virgin Islands generally have fewer storms than Long Island Sound in New York. When the islands do experience a tropical storm or depression, it is usually in the early development of the storm center, and the storms usually do not reach full intensity until they are north of the area. Should a storm approach the islands, remember that they travel very slowly;

consequently, with the communication systems used today, sailors can be assured of at least 48 hours warning.

In the event of a severe tropical storm or hurricane, approaching the Virgin Islands, you will be kept well notified by both the local radio stations, VHF marine advisory channels, SSB and, in the case of charter vessels, your local charter company. All major charter companies have well prepared hurricane plans and they will advise you how to proceed. All vessels in the Caribbean during the hurricane season should carefully monitor the progress of each tropical system and act accordingly. There are a number of hurricane holes throughout the Virgin Islands and should it be necessary to react to a storm warning, we recommend early action since the designated hurricane anchorages fill quickly:

Tortola: Paraquita Bay, Nanny Cay, Manuel Reef, Trellis Bay
Virgin Gorda: Biras Creek (under certain conditions)
St. John: Coral Bay, Hurricane Hole
St. Thomas: The Lagoon, Benner Bay

Tides and Currents

The tidal range throughout the Virgin Islands is about 12 inches, depending upon the time of year. You will probably be unaware of any fluctuation. However, you cannot rely upon the rising tide to float you off the odd sandbar. Currents in certain areas can reach 1-2 knots, namely through Pillsbury Sound between St. Thomas and St. John, the Durloe Cays in St. John, and in the narrows between St. John and Tortola.

Discover the world

While some people are happy with cookie-cutter vacations, we know you crave something more - like the exhilarating feeling of following your own compass and letting your inner seafarer roam free. For those wind-hungry freedom chasers that want more than the status quo, we're here for you and the world is waiting for you to pay it a visit. So get out there and grab life by the helm...

Bareboat | Skippered | Sail By The Cabin | Flotillas | Sailing Schools

Call 800.437.7880 or visit sunsail.com

COMMUNICATIONS

AREA CODES

British Virgin Islands	284
US Virgin Islands	340
Puerto Rico	787

Connectivity has become such a major factor in our lives that staying in touch with friends and family while traveling is now more a necessity than a luxury. For cruisers, being in touch is essential, whether it be for safety, weather information or just communicating with other cruisers.

CELLULAR TELEPHONES

For Virgin Island yachtsmen who need to keep in touch, cellular telephone service is generally available throughout the Virgin Islands. Cellular phones can be used for everything from checking in with the office, the family, or for local applications like ordering more provisions and making dinner reservations.

A word of caution: When you arrive in the islands turn your cellular data off so that you are not paying for unwanted "push" notifications. For both European and US phones it is advisable to check with your service provider regarding roaming charges while overseas. Another alternative would be to purchase or rent a local phone or SIM card for your personal unlocked smart phone. We purchased a phone with a local number for $50 and simply top off the minutes as required on a pay as you go basis.

Dialing toll free 800 numbers from the BVI will be charged at the normal rates for overseas calls.

To obtain a local BVI cell phone visit:
Cable & Wireless (Flow) – www.flow.com
Digicel – www.digicelbvi.com
CCT Global Communications – www.cctwireless.com
Renport at Wickhams Cay II rents cell phones.

Calling the US from a local BVI phone number is expensive (check the plans) but by giving friends and family the local BVI number and having them call you makes it an inexpensive call for all parties.

VHF

Almost every boat sailing the Virgins will be equipped with a VHF radio. Apart from single side band for offshore communications, VHF is used for all local traffic.

The channels vary from boat to boat, but the most commonly used frequencies are listed below.

Channel 16: Initial calling, standby and inter-national distress frequency. Switch to a working channel after contact is established

Channel 12: Portside operations (Charter company to yacht)

Channel 6: Ship-to-ship, safety

Channel 24, 85, and 87:
W.A.H. Virgin Islands Radio

Channel 67:
VISAR working frequency

Channel 68, 69, 71, 78, 79, 80: Non-commercial working channels

Channel 22A: Coast Guard ("A" is US mode), make initial contact on channel 16

Channel Wx-1 (162.55, Wx-2(162.4), Wx-3(162.475): NOAA Weather broadcasts

Do not allow children or crew members to use the VHF without adequate instruction.

MAKING DINNER RESERVATIONS

Where telephone service is non-existent, many restaurants stand by the radio on VHF Channel 16 and will then have you switch to another working channel to complete your request. It is frowned upon by the local licensing authority to use the VHF Channel 12 for reservations.

RADIO PROCEDURE

Before attempting to make a VHF radio call, think it through. Understand the procedure and the limitations of the equipment you are using.

The call should begin with two repetitions of the station or vessel being called, followed by the name of your yacht, followed by the word "over". It is important to terminate with the "over" as the other party will then key his/her mike and reply.

Example: "…Moorings, Moorings: this is the vessel Bodacious; over…"

If you get no response, repeat the call. If there is still no response, try again in five minutes. When contact is to be terminated, the party will sign off: "…This is Bodacious, clear with Moorings…"

EMERGENCY
US COAST GUARD: 787-729-6770
VISAR: 999 or 911 or 767 (SOS)

COMMUNICATIONS

DISTRESS CALLS

In case of a real, life threatening emergency, you use VHF Channel 16, key your mike and repeat the following: "…Mayday, Mayday, Mayday. This is the vessel Bodacious; over…"

Repeat three times until contact is made. Then give your location and the nature of your problem. It is important to state only the pertinent information and not to cloud the situation with emotion.

When stating your location it is critical to give, in addition to lat/long, both the name of the harbor, if applicable, and the island to avoid confusion. There is a Great Harbour in both Peter Island and Jost Van Dyke, and a Little Harbour in both Peter Island and Jost Van Dyke!

- Stay calm; don't panic.
- Don't allow anyone to use the radio unless they are familiar with the procedure and the problem.

The US Coast Guard monitors VHF 16 radio 24/7/365.

VISAR: From the BVI, call 767 (SOS) or 284-499-0911.

INTERNET AND EMAIL

If you need reliable email and web access during your trip, it is recommended that you contact www.flow.com, www.digicel.com or www.cctwireless.com (all local BVI) to purchase a prepaid data plan that can be used with your personal smart-phone as a WiFi hotspot or alternatively rent or buy a portable USB modem. A local

BVI data plan is usually for a 30 day period and costs in the range of $30 for 2 GB.

For more casual users, cruisers should experience little difficulty in locating a WiFi hotspot or cyber café on most of the larger islands throughout both the USVI and BVI. Available bandwidth varies as more often than not, the WiFi system is a router sitting on the manager's desk. Most restaurants offering WiFi require a security code (the expectation is that you purchase something).

VOIP (Voice Over Internet Protocol): When reasonable bandwidth is available, phone calls can be made utilizing a VOIP service such as SKYPE, which enables you to use your tablet, phone or computer to place a call to another device, assuming they are online. You will want to turn off the video in order to preserve bandwidth. SKYPE also has a more interesting feature which is called SKYPE out. This allows you to call a telephone number from your device. You will need to establish an account but the charges are minimal. The software can be downloaded to your computer for free or you can utilize the SKYPE app on your smartphone providing it has a WiFi function.

SSB (SINGLE SIDE BAND):

The primary Caribbean hailing frequency is 8104.0 USB. Once contact is established you will need to switch to a working frequency. This frequency is also used at 8:15am each morning to broadcast the Safety & Security Net.

CUSTOMS, IMMIGRATION & FORMALITIES

PORTS OF ENTRY

Since the Virgin Islands are divided between the US and Britain, you may be crossing international boundaries during your cruise. Therefore it is necessary to clear customs when entering and leaving each respective territory. Failure to observe this formality could result in substantial fines or even the loss of your vessel.

US Virgin Islands: US Customs and Immigration at the waterfront in Charlotte Amalie (tel: 877-305-8774) are open from 8am-noon and 1pm-5pm Monday through Saturday. Sunday they are open from 1pm to 5pm.

Cruz Bay, St. John: Customs and Immigration (tel: 877-305-8774) are open from 7am to 5:30pm seven days a week. In Christiansted, St. Croix at Gallows Bay, (tel: 340-773-1490), Customs and Immigration are open from 8am to 4:30pm Monday through Friday. Vessels arriving on Saturdays and Sundays must contact the customs at the airport 340-778-0216. All crew members are to present themselves for clearance in the USVI.

ESTA Visa (Electronic System for Travel Authorization): For foreign (non US) nationals arriving by boat wishing to use the ESTA 90 day visa program, you will have to apply online well in advance of your travel date and you must be in possession of the ESTA upon arrival. Since this program only allows you to arrive in the USA by commercial carrier you will need to take a ferry from the BVI to St. John or St. Thomas, where you will be finger printed and have your passport(s)

stamped for a 90 day period. At that point you can get back on the ferry to the BVI, clear your vessel out of BVI waters and proceed to Cruz Bay, St. John where you will notify them of your arrival and clear the vessel in. This is not a loophole but a legitimate use of the current system. There are no extensions available under this program so if you have extended cruising plans you will need to apply for a full visa prior to departure from home waters.

British Virgin Islands: To clear in to the BVI, proceed to the nearest BVI port of entry for inbound clearance. Often, if your stay is short and of a known duration, you will be permitted to clear in and out at the same time.

Vessels are allowed to anchor in the harbor prior to making their official entry but may not proceed directly to a marina unless using a ships agent. If arriving after hours, raise the yellow "Q" flag and do not go ashore.

When clearing in it is necessary to have in your possession the Ship's Papers, passports for all crew members and clearance papers from last port. In the BVI only the skipper needs to present him/herself at customs and immigration. The remaining party must stay on the vessel until formalities are complete.

CUSTOMS, IMMIGRATION & FORMALITIES

It is recommended that you wear proper attire when making your clearance.

All crew and passengers must have a valid passport and some nationals may need a BVI visa. If you have questions regarding the need for visas contact your nearest British Embassy or call BVI Immigration at 284-494-3471.

All visitors will be admitted for up to 30 days, should additional time be required application should be made to the immigration department in Road Town or Virgin Gorda as it cannot be extended at the port of entry. Our recommendation in this regard is to use the Virgin Gorda office since the work load is lighter and therefore waiting time is reduced to a minimum. Extensions will only be issued 4-5 days prior to expiration.

Hours of Operation: Road Town at the ferry terminal & West End at the ferry terminal: 7:45am -6pm Mon-Sat, 7:45am-7pm Sundays and public holidays. Jost Van Dyke and Spanish Town, VG: 8:30am-4:30 daily.
Gun Creek, VG: 8:30am-4:30pm Monday to Friday, 9am-2pm Sat- Sun.

Overtime Hours: Additional fees will be charged as follows: Immigration, Mon-Sat 4:30pm - 8:30pm and Sundays and public holidays. Customs, Mon-Fri after 3:30pm and Saturday and Sunday after 12:30pm.
After-hours clearing may be arranged in advance. Additional fees will apply. Call Customs at 284-494-3475 and Immigration at 284-494-3701 ext. 4700 to make after-hours arrangements.

Fees:
• Yachts visiting the BVI for the first time in a year will be required to pay an Annual Tonnage fee, this is based on the vessel's net tonnage.

• If the vessel is to remain in the territory over 30 days there will be a $200 temporary importation fee for up to one year (BVI registered boats are exempt).

• Cruising Permits for charter vessels (see page 73)

National Park fees:
• Private vessels: BVI vessels $75 annually Foreign vessels $150 annually

• BVI based charter vessels: $25 weekly up to 4 persons plus $5 per person

• Foreign based charter vessels: $50 weekly for 4 persons plus $10 per person

• BVI Charter companies will issue permits for customers, private yachts should call 284-494-3904 or visit the office at 57 Main Street, Road Town

PORT CLEARANCE

For vessels in the United States Virgin Islands over 300 tons gross weight, and any vessel carrying paying passengers or paid crew in and out of U.S. waters are now required to submit an advance Notice of Arrival/Departure (NOA/D) to the U.S. Coast Guard before calling at or departing from U.S. ports.

This notice must be filed electronically to the (NVMC) National Vessel Movement Center website at www.nvmc.uscg.gov, who can answer questions and provide downloadable forms.

CRUISING PERMITS

For more information call:

US Coast Guard regulation and related questions: 202-372-1244.

Marinas catering to megayachts often offer clearance services to assist in the clearance procedures. Check with the marina offices in advance.

LOCATIONS OF CUSTOMS

St. Thomas: Wharfside at the ferry dock, Charlotte Amalie, Yacht Haven Grande

St. John: Waterfront at Cruz Bay

St. Croix: Gallows Bay at Christiansted

Tortola: Road Town at the Government Dock West End ferry dock

Virgin Gorda: Government Dock, Spanish Town, Gun Creek, Yacht Club Costa Smeralda

Jost Van Dyke: Government Dock, Great Harbour

BVI CRUISING PERMITS

For yachts chartering within the waters of the BVI there is a daily tax payable at the time of clearance or at the commencement of charter. Private yachts with non-paying guests and family aboard are not required to carry a cruising permit. Dive boats, day charter and sport fishing boats should contact customs at 284-494-3701 for the complete fee schedule.

December 1st - April 30th
A: Foreign vessels $4/person per day
B: BVI (recorded) vessels $2/person per day

May 1st - November 30th
A: Foreign vessels $4/person per day
B: BVI (recorded) vessels $0.75/person per day

Cruising Permits are issued at Customs at time of clearance and are valid for a specific timeframe. BVI based charter companies will issue the appropriate permit based upon booking dates.

Failure to comply with the law can result in a $5,000 fine.

BVI NATIONAL PARKS TRUST PERMIT

In order to use the moorings provided in the BVI marine parks, it is necessary to purchase a National Parks Trust permit. BVI charterers may purchase these permits through their charter company and visiting yachts may purchase them at customs when clearing in. For private cruising (non-charter) vessels the fee is $75 annually for BVI registered vessels and $150 annually for foreign vessels. Charter fees are listed above.

The fees are nominal and go directly to the Parks Trust for installation and maintenance of the buoys. See page 398 for further details.

FISHING PERMITS IN THE BVI

It is illegal for a non-resident to remove any marine organism from the waters of the British Virgin Islands without first obtaining a recreational fishing permit. Call the Fisheries Department at 284-468-2700.

THE ANCHORAGES OF THE
BRITISH
VIRGIN ISLANDS

ROAD TOWN TORTOLA, BVI

Road Town, the capital of the British Virgin Islands, is the center of commerce, shipping and social activity. Centrally located on Tortola's south coast, Road Town is situated on the west side of Road Harbour, the longest natural harbor on the island.

Road Town has a rich history. On August 1st, 1834 the Emancipation Proclamation was read at the Sunday Morning Well. This gave slaves their freedom, even though slavery had been officially abolished in 1807. In 1853 a town-wide fire destroyed nearly every building in Road Town. The fire spread because of angry rioters protesting an increase on the cattle tax. Rioters eventually set fire to most of the plantations across the island.

The past two decades have been witness to tremendous growth and development throughout the BVI and Road Town has emerged as a haven for yacht chartering and a center for tourism. The town is a unique blend of past and present. The more recent developments have become a hub for the commercial and administrative buildings of the BVI, while the quiet charms of years gone by remain, like treasures, to be discovered by visitors arriving by air or sea. The oldest building in Road Town, Her Majesty's Prison on Main Street, dates from the 1840s and is undergoing transformation into a museum.

The latest addition to this vibrant town is Pier Park, recently completed to accommodate arriving cruise ship passengers, offering the visitor access to some duty free shopping and a couple of excellent places to eat and drink including Myett's Chill Zone and Aromas, a martini and cigar bar looking out across the harbor.

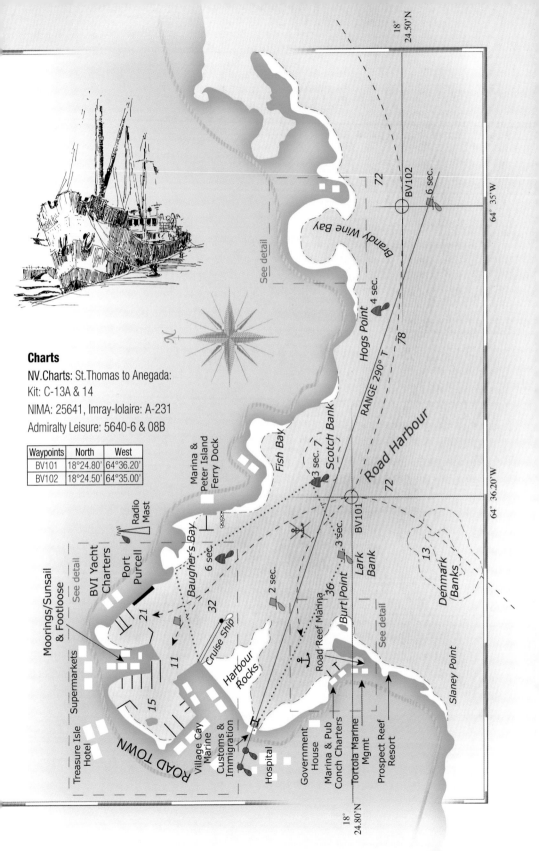

Charts

NV.Charts: St.Thomas to Anegada:
Kit: C-13A & 14
NIMA: 25641, Imray-Iolaire: A-231
Admiralty Leisure: 5640-6 & 08B

Waypoints	North	West
BV101	18°24.80'	64°36.20'
BV102	18°24.50'	64°35.00'

18°
24.50'N

18°
24.50'N

64° 35'W

64° 36.20'W

Brandy Wine Bay

Hogs Point

6 sec.

BV102

72

4 sec.

RANGE 290° T

78

Road Harbour

Scotch Bank

3 sec.

72

BV101

3 sec.

Lark
Bank

13

Denmark
Banks

Slaney Point

Fish Bay

Marina &
Peter Island
Ferry Dock

Radio
Mast

BVI Yacht
Charters

See detail

Port
Purcell

Baugher's Bay

6 sec.

2 sec.

36

Burt Point

Road Reef Marina

See detail

Moorings/Sunsail
& Footloose

Supermarkets

Treasure Isle
Hotel

21

32

11

15

Cruise Ship

Village Cay
Marine

Harbour
Rocks

ROAD TOWN

Customs &
Immigration

Hospital

Government
House

Marina & Pub
Conch Charters

Tortola Marine
Mgmt

Prospect Reef
Resort

18°
24.80'N

Road Harbour

Waypoint: BV101- 18°24.80'N 64°36.20'W
Navigation: 6nm east of Soper's Hole at the west end of Tortola
Services: Port of Entry to the BVI

There are ten marinas within Road Harbour and they can be broken down by area. To the west upon entering the harbor is Fort Burt Marina, HR Penn Marina and the Road Reef Marina. Tucked in behind the cruise ship dock at the head of the harbor are the two large marina developments known as Wickham's Cay I and II. Once inside the breakwater on the starboard side is the extensive facilities of the Moorings and on the other side of the entrance is Village Cay Marina and Inner Harbour Marina. To the north beyond the Port Purcell area and behind the seawall to starboard of the Moorings is the Joma Marina, home to BVI Yacht Charters and to port, the service facilities of Tortola Yacht Services. Further to the southeast and to starboard upon entering Road Harbour is Baugher's Bay.

Navigation & Piloting

Road Harbour is approached from the south or west via the Sir Francis Drake Channel and the entrance is largely free of obstruction for the cruising sailor. There is no reason to use the buoyed channel on the eastern side of the bay as it is intended for deep draft commercial or cruise ship traffic. There is however, a range between the outer green buoy (flashing 6 sec) near waypoint BV102 (Brandy Wine Bay) on the eastern side of the bay and the government/ferry dock in the center of town. This course is 290° true.

Make your approach at the center of the bay (waypoint BV101). This will place you between the red buoy (flashing 8 sec) marking Scotch Bank (7.8 feet/2.37m of water) and the green (flashing 3 sec) marking Lark Bank (14.4 feet/4.38m of water). Although there is plenty of water inside the Lark Bank marker, do not get too close to shore as a reef extends east from Burt Point.

The inner green marker (flashing 2 sec) marks the extremity of Harbour Rock that extends to the southeast from the new government administration building. Vessels heading into Fort Burt Marina, HR Penn Marina and Road Reef Marina should leave it to starboard. No anchoring is allowed north of a line between the government ferry dock and the Lark Bank green marker in order to keep the ferry route clear. For vessels clearing into the BVI from the USVI or other foreign ports, do not tie up alongside the government dock, as the surge can be excessive and the ferry traffic makes this difficult. Anchor off the Fort Burt Marina and take the dinghy ashore.

Road Harbour at night

Scotch Bank

Fl.R.8s

BV101

18°24.80N
64°36.20W

Fl.R.6s

Fl.G.3s
Lark Bank

Fl.G.2s

Burt
Point

FORT BURT & ROAD REEF MARINAS

Waypoint: BV101- 18°24.80'N 64°36.20'W
Services: Ice, Fuel, Marina, Taxi, Restaurant, Chandlery, Garbage disposal, Provisioning

Tortola

Navigation & Piloting

Once inside the buoys at the mouth of Road Harbour, head for the government dock (approximately 292°m) until the Fort Burt and HR Penn Marina are abeam.

Make sure that you leave the inner green buoy (marking the SE end of Harbour Rocks) to starboard. This approach will bring you clear of the reef that extends to the north from the mangroves at Burt Point. Approach the docks and anchorage from the northeast in order to avoid the sandbar that extends to the north from Road Reef. There is a buoyed channel (7ft/2.2m) northeast from the HR Penn Marina which takes you to the docks. If you are going to anchor you will have to pick a spot to the northeast clear of the various moorings situated either side of the channel.

18° 24.88'N

18

6

6

5

6

6   13

3

7

3

H.R. Penn Marina

Fort Burt Marina   Fuel

Conch Charters

Fort Burt Hotel

8

Marine Police

Burt Point

Tortola Marine Mgmt
VISAR
Doyle Sails

N

7.5

Road Reef

64° 36.77'W

FI.G.2s

Proceeding to Road Reef Marina, unless you have prior clearance from the marina (VHF 12) or are returning a vessel to the TMM charter base, we do not recommend committing to the channel owing to limited maneuvering room once inside. Make your turn to port when you are close to the HR Penn Marina docks, leaving Fort Burt Marina, Conch Charters and Smiths Ferry dock to starboard. There are a couple of shallow spots close to the roadside beneath Fort Burt Hotel, so favor the port side of the channel as you enter the pool of Road Reef Marina.

Ashore
FORT BURT MARINA
Both HR Penn & Fort Burt Marinas accept transient boats, call them on VHF 16 or pull alongside and check for slip availability with the dockmaster. Fort Burt Marina has gas and diesel and is the home of Conch Charters, established in the BVI over twenty years ago. Steeped in history, Drake's Point Restaurant at Fort Burt (up the hill from the marina) has an amazing view of the harbor, Drake's Channel and the islands to the south.

ROAD REEF MARINA
Road Reef Marina is managed by Tortola Marine Management (TMM), a charter boat company in business for thirty years! Electricity, ice and water are available as well as WiFi from the TMM office. The marina can accommodate vessels 60 feet in length, with a maximum draft of 7.5 feet. The beam size is unrestricted. The marina is open daily from 8am-5pm and they monitor VHF channel 12.

In the same complex that houses the marina office is the marine division of the British Virgin Island Police, the Royal BVI Yacht Club, VISAR Base Station, and Doyle Sailmakers. Road Reef Plaza next door to the marina has a variety of shops including a RiteWay Market that sells provisioning to the yachting community. Crandall's, a West Indian bakery, is across the road from Road Reef Marina.

The Government Dock

As the main port of entry to the British Virgin Islands, all vessels arriving from the U.S. Virgin Islands or other foreign ports must clear with customs and immigration before proceeding to a marina.

To clear Customs and Immigration in Road Town anchor off the Fort Burt Marina and the skipper can dinghy in to clear customs. You may only bring your dinghy to the dock since it is for the use of the ferries only. You must clear in before you or your crew can go ashore or to a marina. The captain can bring the necessary papers without his crew. Please see the section on Customs and Immigration in the Planning the Cruise section. If you arrive after Customs is closed, put your yellow quarantine flag up and remain on the vessel, anchored out until customs opens. You can call Customs and Immigration to announce your arrival and to tell them you will be in when they open: telephone 284-494-3475.

Discover the
TMM
Difference

THE TMM DIFFERENCE

Luxury bareboat charter in the **British Virgin Islands**

Our team provide a personal service and truly care about your charter experience.
Since 1979 friendly and memorable staff have welcomed our clients, delivering first-hand
local knowledge of the British Virgin Islands. Year after year we strive to deliver this
experience whilst maintaining a diverse fleet of modern yachts at competitive prices.

All the information you need to book a charter can be found on our website, www.sailtmm.com

charter@sailtmm.com
1-800-633-0155

For yacht sales enquiries please contact Don at
1-284-340-6393 or don@sailtmm.com

Representing these fine yacht manufacturers:

ROAD TOWN INNER HARBOUR
WICKHAM'S CAY I & II

Tortola

THE MOORINGS MARINA
VILLAGE CAY MARINA
INNER HARBOUR MARINA

Navigation: 1nm from harbor entrance
Services: Full service marina, Fuel, Ice, Water, Provisioning, Laundry, Garbage disposal, ATM, WiFi, Restaurants, Marine support services. No moorings available inside breakwater, moorings and anchorage outside of breakwater.

Navigation & Piloting

From waypoint BV101 between the red and green buoys at the entrance to Road Harbour, head NW at approximately 311°m. This will take you clear of the green buoy (fl 2 sec) marking the extremity of Harbour Rock (leave to port) and inside the cruise ship dock (note a quick flashing 3 sec light marking the dolphin at the end of the dock) and position you at the green marker outside of the breakwater and entrance to the Inner Harbour Complex. You can take this marker either side as there is 25 feet of available water. Although often an uncomfortable anchorage due to the exposure to the southeast, there are 10 moorings in place just south of the breakwater that allow for a lunch stop or a quick run ashore for provisions. Dinghies can be landed at Village Cay or the Moorings. These moorings are controlled by the Ports Authority who will collect for overnight stays.

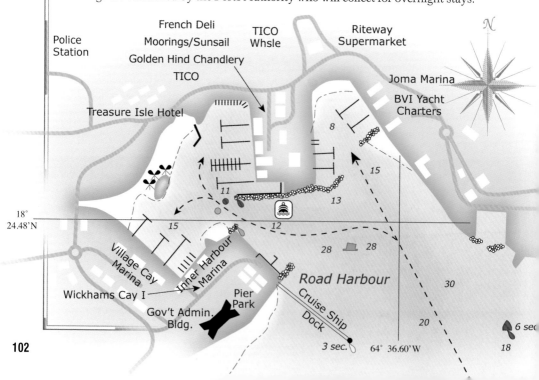

Proceed through the double breakwater (80 feet wide) and on through a final set of port, starboard markers just inside of the breakwater where you will have 15 feet of water depth since the entrance was changed and dredged. To starboard is the Moorings / Sunsail marina complex where fuel, water and transient slips are available (VHF 12). To port is Village Cay Marina and Inner Harbour Marina with a controlling depth of 11 feet. Call the dockmaster for instructions, both marinas monitor VHF 16. There are no mooring buoys within the basin.

VILLAGE CAY MARINA

Services: Full service marina, Fuel, Water, Ice, Laundry, Restaurants, Provisioning, WiFi, ATM, Hotel, Pool, Gift shop, Spa, Dive shop, Car rental
Call VHF 16 or 284-494-2771

Village Cay Marina, conveniently situated in the center of Road Town, is a great place to spend a couple of days while you re-provision, explore Tortola or prepare yourself for the next round of sailing guests.

The marina has 106 fixed slips that can accommodate vessels up to 109' in length with draft to 11'. Amenities include fuel, water, 110v and 220v shore power, cable TV, a swimming pool, showers, garbage disposal and free WiFi. There is a 24 hour

security and surveillance system in place. Navigare Yachting now operate their charter fleet from A dock. For slips, water or fuel call the dockmaster on VHF 16 or telephone: 284-494-2771 or book a slip online. Daily dockage rates are approximately $1.50 per foot year round.

The marina complex also offers 22 nice (small) hotel rooms for overnight guests with views of the marina and The Village Cay Restaurant offers waterside dining in a casual environment, a great spot to eat and drink while watching the harbor traffic. Visit the dive shop, boutique and the Oasis Salon and Spa.

For provisioning and deli food on the run, the Dockmaster's Deli is right in the marina complex or RiteWay Supermarket and TICO (for beer, wines and spirits) are a short taxi ride away. From Village Cay, you are a short walk away from the center of Road Town with access to banks, restaurants, taxis, ferries and the administrative offices of the BVI government. A few minutes from the marina is a little hole in the wall bar and restaurant, the Wolf Trap, that is a casual, outside place to get WiFi and to enjoy a light meal or a glass of wine or beer. Walking towards the ferry terminal you will pass the local crafts and gift center, a village of brightly painted Caribbean structures where local merchants display crafts, clothing and gifts. Across the street is Pusser's Bar and Restaurant, a good place to stop for a cold one when your low alcohol level light starts to blink or for a real espresso coffee and snack stop into Omar's.

For something different take a walk over to Pier Park, the new support facility for the cruise ship dock. The entire development has been nicely orchestrated and there is duty free shopping available and several interesting spots to stop and enjoy a drink or something to eat. Myett's Chill Zone is a good place to enjoy a drink looking out across the harbor or Aromas upstairs bar is a good place to enjoy a drink and a cigar.

INNER HARBOUR MARINA

Services: Dockage, Water, Ice, 110 / 220v, Restaurants, Provisioning, Marine chandlery

VHF 16 or 284-494-3010 or cell: 284-499-1144 (Betito Frett)

Inner Harbour Marina is located to port as you enter the basin and is adjacent to Village Cay Marina. This small marina services mainly long term clients but transient dockage is sometimes available. At the time of our last survey, the docks were being used as a repair center for hurricane damaged vessels with ongoing work all around.

There are 22 slips with 11-12' draft. Water and ice are available but no fuel at the time of our last survey. Adjacent to the marina in the Mill is the Marine Depot, a well-stocked marine chandlery. For your provisioning needs, the Ample Hamper is situated

nearby although, at the time of our last survey it was closed for hurricane repair and conducting all business on-line. We are told that the owner intends to have the retail store open in time for the season 2019/20.

From the marina numerous banking facilities are close at hand including Scotia Bank, First Caribbean and Banco Popular (most have ATM services).

The large multi-story building to the south houses the administrative offices of the BVI government, which is adjacent to the cruise ship terminal and the local village shopping market.

A short walk puts you on Main Street with access to all of the Road Town shops and restaurants.

Dockmaster: Call VHF 16 or 284-494-3010 or call 284-499-1144.

THE MOORINGS SUNSAIL MARINA COMPLEX (WICKHAM'S CAY II)

One of the Caribbean's most comprehensive marina facilities, The Moorings marina on Wickham's Cay II is the base for several charter companies operating within the Moorings marine group. The marina is home to the Moorings, Moorings Power, Moorings Luxury Crewed Yachts and Sunsail Charters. Dockage is also available for visiting yachts when there are available slips but reservations should be made in advance as dock space is scarce.

The Mariner Inn Yacht Club has been completely refurbished after the hurricane with a complete update to the restaurant facilities. The restaurant and bar is open seven days a week serving breakfast, lunch and dinner. Guests staying in the marina are welcome to use the restaurant and to use the swimming pool.

The hotel has 32 recently renovated rooms overlooking the activity in the marina in addition, there are also seven, five star luxury rooms with a view of Road Harbour and the Sir Francis Drake Channel.

At the southern end of the complex you will find the The Moorings Village, the main reception area for charter services and home to Charlie's Restaurant and Bar (named for Charlie Cary, a co-founder of the Moorings). It is perched over the water at the base of "B" dock. Charlie's is open for lunch and dinner (until late) with an in-house pizza oven and an upscale menu. It is casual, with no reservations required. Also at the village you will find a provision center, boutique, a sales office for the Moorings yachts, concierge services and a spa. If you need to cool down, try the café for an ice cream or a thirst quenching beverage from the coffee bar.

Charter services for Moorings, Moorings Power and Moorings Crewed Yachts are located on docks A and B at the inner harbor. For transient overnight dockage and

Moorings Marina

docking instructions, check with the marina for availability (VHF 12) before heading to "C" dock. Dockage is on finger piers and can accommodate vessels with a draft of 9 feet. Vessels up to 120 feet may tie up at the "T" dock when it is available. Amenities include water, ice, and electricity. Fuel (gasoline and diesel) and ice are sold at the bulkhead between docks "B" and "C".

Sunsail is located on the "D" dock. The Sunsail office is at the base of the dock. Behind the office are showers and an ATM. Last Stop Sports rents water toys and dive equipment. Hiho's shop sells casual fun surf clothing. There is also a gift shop with t-shirts, books, and gifts to bring home with you. Renport rents mobile phones and WiFi modems for use aboard in addition to items such as 12 volt blenders and iPods. You can also rent DVDs for the trip in case you get a rainy day. If you are interested in purchasing a Sunsail boat, the brokerage office is nearby.

Other related services on Wickhams Cay II:

Across the road from the Moorings marina is the Moorings boatyard facility originally known as Tortola Yacht Services. Purchased by The Moorings in order to service the needs of their ever growing fleet, to the best of our knowledge they are not extending hauling services to private vessels.

The Golden Hind Chandlery. Relocated from their earlier location next to the boat yard in late 2018, they are now housed in a purpose built facility close by on Wickhams Cay II. They have an excellent inventory that has been greatly expanded and also carry their own line of RIB's and Tohatsu outboards. Matt Hood and his team are always willing to go the extra mile to accommodate special needs. At this point there is no website. Telephone 284-494-2756.

Nautool Machine, next to the boatyard, are stainless steel fabricators and capable of custom design at a reasonable price.

Provisioning:

Located within walking distance of the marina is RiteWay, a major supermarket chain with branches throughout the islands. The selection is excellent and you can call a taxi for the return trip. TICO is also located close to the marina where you can shop for beer, wine, liquor and other beverages. Across the street from TICO on the corner of the highway is The French Deli and Bakery. They carry a brilliant selection of cheeses and pâté along with authentic baguettes and pastries. If you have the time, make this a lunch stop as the sandwiches are excellent.

PORT PURCELL/JOMA MARINA
Navigation & Piloting

From the green buoy just outside of the breakwater to the Inner Harbour complex, proceed to the north and enter the small basin leaving the stone breakwater that connects with the Moorings to the west, to port. A second shorter breakwater to starboard extends from the northeast adjacent to Port Purcell.

Once inside the breakwater, there is a new marina facility immediately on your port hand (this marina will not be available until a breakwater is built to protect from swells), further north is the dock associated with The Moorings boatyard service area. On the starboard side is the

Joma Marina complex and home to BVI Yacht Charters. The water depth is 8-10 feet and 15 feet on the "T" dock.

BVI YACHT CHARTERS

BVI Yacht Charters operate the marina along with their charter fleet which utilizes most of the available dock space. As the season gets busy, freeing up some slips, they are able to accommodate some transient visitors by prior arrangement. Situated within walking distance of Riteway supermarket across the road, TICO on Wickham's Cay II as well as Parts & Power, this is a very convenient location. The marina monitors VHF 16 and is open from 8am to 5pm daily. Telephone 284-494-4289

Government House

Baugher's Bay

Waypoint: BV101 - 18°24.80'N 64°36.20'W
Navigation: 0.5nm NE from the buoyed harbor entrance
Services: Restaurant, Ferry, Commercial marina

Navigation & Piloting

From waypoint BV101 at the entrance to Road Harbour, Baugher's Bay is a little over a half mile ahead to the northeast on your starboard side. The anchorage is straight forward with no obstructions. As you approach the marina, there is a large mooring buoy due west of the breakwater. This is for the fuel tanker, so keep clear. If you are anchoring, the preferred location would be to the south of the small breakwater, in order to keep out of the way of the Peter Island ferry that uses this location.

Ashore

For those going to Peter Island Resort, this is where the Peter Island ferry picks up and drops off passengers. The pickup spot is to the left of the old CSY marina looking from the sea.

The old marina is a commercial marina used by the Road Town Fast Ferry and not available for transient boats.

111

Ashore in Road Town

When going ashore in Road Town, it is important to observe the local dress code, which prohibits swimwear, brief attire, and shirtless males. In order to avoid embarrassment, please cover up!

Road Town is a unique blend of architectural character, blending old West Indian houses, complete with red tin roofs and Victorian dado work around the porches with newer concrete structures that accommodate the administration and finance sectors. Since a good part of Road Town, as we know it today, is built on reclaimed land, the main arterial access through town is actually not Main Street but Waterfront Drive. Main Street runs parallel and can be accessed via any side street. A walk down Main Street toward the east from Peebles Hospital to the

cemetery at the bottom of Joe's Hill, will reveal all sorts of delights tucked away behind newer buildings or squeezed shoulder to shoulder along Main Street.

Fort Burt located at the western end of town opposite the Pub and Conch Charters base is a small fort that once guarded the approaches to Road Harbour. Built by the Dutch and later rebuilt by the English, the fort now houses a hotel and restaurant affording the visitor spectacular views of the harbor.

Government House situated at the south end of Main Street, is a classic example of British colonial architecture and home to the appointed governor. Except on special occasions, it is not open to the public.

The Philatelic Bureau of the post office, across the street from the Sir Olva Georges Square, is a must stop for anyone who would like to take home a collection of the exotic and colorful stamps of this tropical territory.

The Virgin Island Folk Museum is housed in a small traditional West Indian house on Main Street and contains artifacts from various periods including pre-Columbian and plantation. There are also marine artifacts from the RMS Rhone along with a small gift shop.

Her Majesty's Prison dates back to the 18th century and is the oldest building in Road Town. There are ongoing plans to convert it into a museum. During our first visit to Road Town in the early 70's we were strolling along Main Street taking pictures when a young man approached us explaining that he was actually a prisoner in the jail, serving time for marijuana possession. According to his story, since he was a fruitarian they would let him out of the jail every day to purchase some fresh fruit. He told us that he wanted books to read, so we returned to the boat and found him, among other titles, a copy of Siddhartha by Herman Hesse that deals with a spiritual journey of self-discovery, a subject matter we felt befitting given the circumstance.

St. George's Anglican Church right next door to the prison was originally constructed during the 18th century but was partially destroyed by a hurricane and later rebuilt. The Proclamation of Emancipation was read from the pulpit of St. George's and a copy is kept inside.

Sunny Caribbee Spice Company and Art Gallery is located in a delightful old West Indian house. The shop carries specially packaged herbs and spices from the islands that make wonderful gifts for friends or yourself. The air-conditioned art gallery is next door with art treasures displayed for sale. They have a large selection of paintings and prints from all over the Caribbean.

On the waterfront opposite the ferry terminal and taxi stand, you will find Pusser's Company Store and Pub. This is a delightful, air-conditioned pub where you can cool down with a beer or lemonade and a deli sandwich or pizza. If you haven't tried a Pusser's Painkiller, this may be just the right time! Friday nights the Pub is jamming at happy hour. The Pusser's Company Store, with tropical and nautical clothing for ladies and men, watches, luggage and nautical accessories attached to the pub, leads to Main Street. Further along Waterfront Drive is Capriccio di Mare offering breakfast, lunch and dinner from 8am. They also serve a great cappuccino while you wait for the ferry arrival across the street and gaze at the boating activity in the harbor.

Across the street is the brightly colored Crafts Alive Market, right on the waterfront featuring local souvenirs of all kinds, including t-shirts hats, baskets, shell work and more.

Pier Park located adjacent to the cruise ship pier was opened early in 2016. The cultural and entertainment complex is a state of the art marketplace with 60 plus businesses that support restaurants, bars, retail shopping and showcases the BVI's cultural heritage.

The shopping is duty free and there are often dancers, musicians and local entertainment. Walk down to Myett's Chill Zone and relax with a cool drink looking out over the harbor or stop by Aromas martini and cigar bar. A dinghy dock is in the short term plan that will give cruisers the ability to visit the park from the anchorage.

Sage Mountain National Park

Continuing along Main Street, Joe's Hill Road on the left leads up to Sage Mountain National Park or over to Cane Garden Bay. The panoramic view is breath-taking at the top of the hill and the temperature is usually cool and breezy.

If you are up for an adventure and don't mind a light hike, a visit to the Sage Mountain National Park is highly recommended. Although not officially a rain-forest due to lack of precipitation, this 92-acre reserve includes the 1,780 foot Mt. Sage and a forest with 15 to 20 foot tall fern trees, Bulletwood trees, West Indian and Broadleaf Mahogany and White Cedars (the BVI national tree). Hikers on the park's trails will pass the scattered remains of old houses and a variety of orchids, and might spot several species of birds, including the Antillean crested humming-bird and the pearly-eyed thrasher.

Back in Road Town, if you are still feeling energetic, continue on Main Street past Sunday Morning Well, past the courthouse and high school to the botanical gardens across the street from the police station.

The J.R. O'Neal Botanic Gardens is a four acre park, recently reopened after the hurricane and maintained by the National Parks Trust and the BVI Botanical Society. The gardens, which include a lush array of indigenous and tropical plants also encompass the ruins of the century old agricultural station.

Established in 1979, the gardens were named after the BVI's first conservationist, Joseph Reynold O'Neal who was also a leading figure in the formation of the National Parks Trust and the establishment of the BVI's first national park at Mount Sage National Park.

As you enter the gardens you will walk through the avenue of royal palms leading to the fountain, which makes a captivating entrance for visitors.

Paths disappear into corners of the garden lined with colorful blossoms draped over shady pergolas.

The botanic collections represent the different habitats of the BVI such as the rainforest, coastal environments and dry forests, in addition to displays of exotic species and an extensive collection of palms. A gazebo of orchids both native and exotic can be discovered by the pond, where lilies float and turtles swim. The nursery at the garden is an important repository for endangered species of flora found within the BVI, ensuring their survival from habitat loss.

The gardens are a refreshing place to stop away from the hustle and bustle of Road Town. There is a small entrance fee and donations are always welcome.

Many other shops and services, too numerous to mention, are waiting for you to discover in Road Town. Pick up a copy of The Welcome Magazine, available for free throughout the island, which lists all restaurants, shops and activities.

ISLAND CONNECTIONS

EMERGENCIES
999 or 911
VISAR (Virgin Island Search and Rescue)
Tel: 767 (SOS), or
+1 284 499 0911
www.visar.org

ROAD REEF

MARINAS
Road Reef Marina / Tortola Marine Mgmt.
Tel: 284-394-2751
www.sailtmm.com
operations@sailtmm.com
FB: sailTMM
VHF 12
Water, electricity, ice, showers, WiFi, (call ahead for slip availability), 8am-5pm 7 days/week

Village Cay Resort & Marina
Tel: 1 284 494 2771
www.villagecaybvi.com/marina
marina@villagecaybvi.com
VHF: 71
Call to reserve slip
Dock slips, fuel, electrical, water, trash & oil disposal, ice, showers, laundry, WiFi, deli
7.30am-6pm

CHARTER COMPANIES
Conch Charters
Tel: 284-494-4868
www.conchcharters.com
FB: conchchartersbvi
VHF channel 16
Pub, showers, WiFi, water, electricity
8:30am-5pm 7 days/week

Tortola Marine Management (TMM)
Tel: 284-394-2751
www.sailtmm.com
operations@sailtmm.com
FB: sailTMM
VHF 12
Water, electricity, ice, showers, WiFi, (call ahead for slip availability), 8am-5pm 7 days/week

PROVISIONING
Riteway Food Market
Tel: 1 284-347-1162,
284-494-2263
www.rtwbvi.com
FB: RiteWayFoodMarkets
Online ordering, free delivery
7am-9:30pm 7 days/week

SAILMAKERS
Doyle Sailmakers
Tel: 284-494-2569
www.doylesails.com

RESTAURANTS
Crandall's Pastry Plus
Tel: 284-494-5156
FB: CrandallsPastry
Across from Road Reef Marina, BBQ, roti, bakery items
M-F 5:30am-4pm,
Saturdays: 5:30am-2pm

The Rooftop by Brandywine
Tel: 1 284-440-2301, 1 284-494-2200
FB: therooftopbybrandywine
Lunch, dinner, specialty

cocktails, music, rooftop view
Tue-Fri 12pm-11pm, Sat 5-11pm, Sun-Mon closed

Capriccio di Mare
Tel: 284-494-5369
FB: CapriccioBVI
Breakfast, lunch, dinner, Italian, pizzas, pasta, espresso
8am-10pm, reservations recommended

Omar's Fusion
Tel: 1 284 345-4771
www.omarfusion.com
FB: omarsfusion.bvi
Asian fusion cuisine
Lunch 11am-4pm, happy hour 4-6:30pm, dinner 6-9:30pm

Pusser's Road Town Pub
Tel: 284-494-3897
www.Pussers.com
FB: pussers.BVI
Pizza, take-out, roti, jerk, outdoor & indoor seating, WiFi, sports games
11am-9:30pm,
bar 9am-11pm

Maria's By The Sea Hotel & Restaurant
Tel: 284-494-2595
www.mariasbythesea.com
FB: mariasbythesea
breakfast 7-10am, lunch 11am-3pm, dinner 4-9pm, specialty cocktails

WICKHAM'S CAY I

MARINAS
Village Cay Resort & Marina
Tel: 1 284 494 2771
www.villagecaybvi.com/marina
marina@villagecaybvi.com
VHF: 71
Call ahead to reserve slip
Dock slips, gas & diesel, electrical, water, trash & oil disposal, ice, showers, laundry, security, WiFi, deli
7:30am-6pm

RESTAURANTS
Water's Edge Restaurant (at Village Cay Marina)
Tel: 1-284-494-2271
www.villagecaybvi.com/restaurant
International cuisine, pizza, cocktails, waterfront view, DJs, BBQ night, Sunday brunch, reservations recommended
7:30am-9pm

PROVISIONING
Dockmaster's Deli (Village Cay Marina)
Tel: 284-494-2771
Gourmet salads, sandwiches
Mon-Fri 6:30am-4pm

Bobby's Marketplace
Tel: 284-494-2189
Bobbyssupermarket.com
Free delivery and pickup, groceries, beer, wine, fresh produce
7 am-12am 7 days/week

Sunny Caribbee Spice Co. & Art Gallery
Tel: 284-494-2178
www.sunnycaribbee.com
Caribbean seasonings, preserves, coffee, arts & crafts

DIVING/ WATERSPORTS
We Be Divin'
Tel: 284-494-4320
www.webedivinbvi.com
webedivin@bviscuba.com
FB: webedivinbvi
Dives up to 6 people, 3,5,8 hour tours, multi tank dives, RMS Rhone, Indians, other spots Snorkel & beach shop
8am-5pm 7 days/week

CHANDLERY
Marine Depot BVI
Tel: 284-494-0098
FB: marinedepotbvi
Chandlery, marine supplies, pumps, refrigeration, batteries, fasteners, electronics, nautical gifts, engine supplies, clothing, fishing gear
M-F 8am-5pm,
Sat 8:30am-1:30pm,
closed Sun

MARINE/ BOATYARD SERVICES
Richardson's Rigging Services
Tel: 284-494-2739 or 284-499-4774
rrsbvi@gmail.com
FB: Richardsons-Rigging-Services-Ltd

WICKHAM'S CAY II

MARINAS
The Moorings Marina
Tel: 284-393-2331
www.moorings.com/base-guide/tortola
FB: TheMooringsBVI
VHF 16
Fuel, marine slips, bar, coffee shop, restaurant, security, WiFi, laundry services, showers
7am-11pm, 7 days/week,
July-Sept:8am-10pm

CHARTER COMPANIES
The Moorings
Tel: 284-393-2331
www.moorings.com/base-guide/tortola
FB: TheMooringsBVI

BVI Yacht Charters
Tel: 284-494-4289
www.bviyachtcharters.com
FB: bviyc
Skype: bviYachtCharters

Footloose Charters
Tel: 1 800-814-7245
www.footloosecharters.com
FB: FootlooseCharters

Sunsail
Tel: 284-494-2226
www.sunsail.com
FB: sunsailusa

ISLAND CONNECTIONS

CHANDLERY
Golden Hind Chandlery
Tel: 284-494-7749 or
284-494 2756
ghc@surfbvi.com
Marine guide books, charts,
gear, gifts
M-F, 7am-5pm, Sat:
8am-12pm, closed Sun

MARINE/ BOATYARD SERVICES
Nautool Machine
Tel: 284 346 3187
www.nautool.com
john.robinson@nautool.com
Specialize in biminis & rails

WATERSPORTS/ ECO-TOURS
Ground Sea Adventures BVI
Tel: 284-343-0002 or
284-499-1620
www.groundseabvi.com
FB: groundseaadventures
Surfing, eco tour, SUPs,
island hikes, mangrove
kayaking, kite surfing
8am-6pm

RESTAURANTS
Charlie's Restaurant & Bar
Tel: 1-284- 393-3602
www.marinerinnbvi.com/
dining
Call for reservations,
dockside, Italian/Caribbean
cuisine, 7am-10pm

Ginny's Coffee Shop
Tel: 1-284- 393-3603
www.marinerinnbvi.com/
dining
Pastries and sandwiches,
variety of coffee, quick bites

The Mariner Inn Restaurant
Tel: 1-284-393-3619
www.marinerinnbvi.com/
dining
Local & international cuisine

French Deli & Gourmet Shop
Tel: 1-284-494-2195
www.frenchdelibvi.com
European products, fresh
baked products, breakfast,
brunch, lunch, deli, bakery,
bistro, wine, orders/
provisions. M-F: 8am-6pm,
Sat 8am-3pm, closed Sun

Verandah Restaurant (Treasure Isle)
Tel: 284-444-2501
treasureislehotelbvi.com/
dining.php
Breakfast, lunch, dinner
daily with excellent views,
European-Caribbean cuisine,
happy hour, Sunday brunch

SpyGlass Lounge (Treasure Isle)
Tel: 1(284) 444-2501
treasureislehotelbvi.com/
dining.php
Cocktails & tapas
Wed -Fri

The Poolside Deck (Treasure Isle)
Tel: 284-444-2501
treasureislehotelbvi.com/
dining.php
Appetizers, cocktails, tapas
daily

PROVISIONING
Rite Way Food Market
Tel: 1 284-347-1188
www.rtwbvi.com
Produce, fresh & frozen
meat, fish, beer, wine,
household, etc.
7am-10pm 7 days/week

One Mart Foods
Tel: 284-494-6999 or
284-494-4649
www.onemartfoods.com
FB: OneMartSupermarket
In-store and online
ordering, delivery, seafood,
produce, meat, alcohol,
snacks, drinks, frozen food,
health & beauty
Mon-Thur 6am-10pm,
Fri-Sun 6am-11pm

TICO Wine & Spirit Merchants
Tel: 1 284-340-6730 or
284-340-6777
www.ticobvi.com
FB: TICOBVI
Beer, wine, spirits, mixes,
online ordering, pickup or
delivery (order ahead)
M-F 10am-5pm, Sat
9am-3:30pm, Pasea Estate
Store: M-F 9am-6pm, Sat
9am-3:30pm,
Closed Sunday & holidays

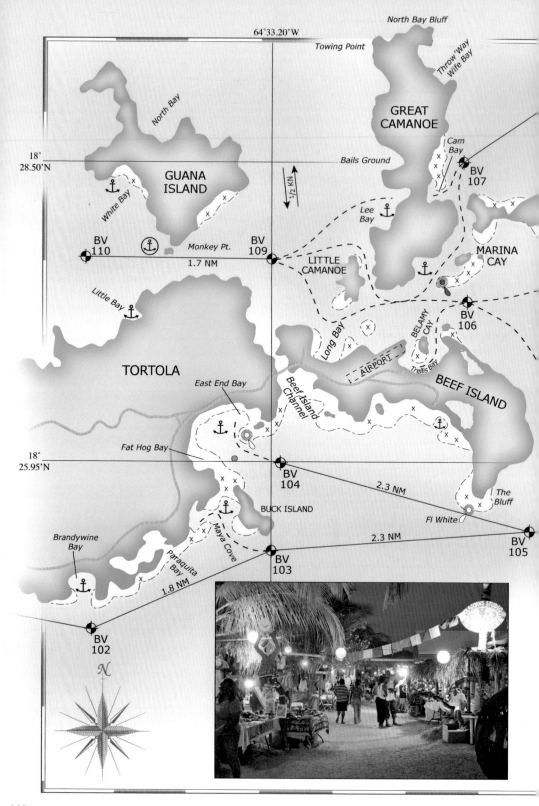

North Bay Bluff

Towing Point

64"33.20'W

Throw'Way
Wife Bay

GREAT
CAMANOE

North Bay

Cam
Bay

18°
28.50'N

Bails Ground

BV
107

1/2 KN

GUANA
ISLAND

Lee
Bay

MARINA
CAY

White Bay

BV
110

Monkey Pt.

BV
109

LITTLE
CAMANOE

1.7 NM

BV
106

BELAMY
CAY

Little Bay

Long Bay

AIRPORT

Trellis Bay

TORTOLA

East End Bay

BEEF ISLAND

Beef Island
Channel

Fat Hog Bay

18°
25.95'N

BV
104

2.3 NM

The
Bluff

BUCK ISLAND

Fl White

2.3 NM

BV
105

Brandywine
Bay

Maya Cove

Paraquita
Bay

BV
103

1.8 NM

BV
102

N

118

EASTERN TORTOLA

SCRUB
ISLAND

Waypoints	North	West
BV101	18°24.80'	64°36.20'
BV102	18°24.50'	64°35.00'
BV103	18°25.10'	64°33.20'
BV104	18°25.95'	64°33.20'
BV105	18°25.30'	64°30.90'
BV106	18°27.30'	64°31.50'
BV107	18°28.55'	64°31.50'
BV108	18°30.00'	64°32.40'
BV109	18°27.70'	64°33.20'
BV110	18°27.70'	64°35.00'
BV111	18°30.00'	64°35.00'

Charts

NV.Charts: St.Thomas to Anegada: Kit : C-13 & 14

NIMA: 25641, Imray-Iolaire: A-231

Admiralty Leisure: 5640-6,7,3B

BRANDYWINE BAY

Waypoint: BV102-18°24.50'N 64°35.00W
Navigation: 1nm NE of Road Harbour; 4nm W of Beef Island Bluff
Services: Restaurant, Garbage (at head of beach)

Tortola

This lovely curve of a bay with a stunning white sand beach is just east of Road Town on the southern side of the island. It provides a comfortable overnight anchorage in the usual east/southeast tradewinds, but can develop an uncomfortable surge if the wind moves to the south. Close to Road Town and East End, Brandywine is a great last night dinner ashore anchorage.

Navigation & Piloting

Brandywine Bay is tucked in behind a reef that extends out from both sides of the headlands. The opening between the two sections of the reef is wide and safe for entry in the center with a depth of 10 feet. The entrance is straightforward and easy to see in reasonable light. It should be noted that the bay shoals off on all sides.

Anchoring & Mooring

Although the Brandywine Estate Restaurant, situated on the headland to the east of the bay and overlooking the Sir Francis Drake Channel, has in the past maintained several moorings in the center of the bay exclusively for dinner guests, the current owners indicate that although there are a couple of private moorings in place, they do not maintain them and therefore recommend that guests use their own ground tackle. There are also several moorings in front of the white condominiums to the east, they are private and in shallow water.

If you are anchoring, position yourself in the center of the bay as it shoals to both the east and west. If there is any indication of a southerly surge entering the bay you may want to consider a stern anchor in order to keep the bow of your vessel facing the entrance to the bay.

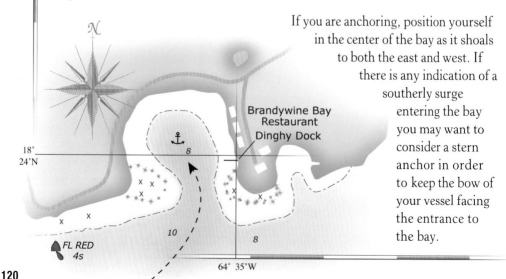

Brandywine Estate
Restaurant

Ashore

As you face the row of condominiums on the water's edge on the eastern side of the bay, you will see the Brandywine Estate dinghy dock located about 50 yards to their right. Construction on additional condominium units and docks was underway at the time of our survey so this may affect the location of the access path. Once ashore, follow the pathway to the left of the dock to where it meets the concrete road on the Brandywine Estate, and then it is just a short walk up the hill to the restaurant.

Although severely damaged during the storm, owners Regis and Claudine have done an amazing job rebuilding and revitalizing this restaurant. Brandywine Estate monitors VHF channel 16 after 2pm and is available by telephone (284-495-2301) all day for reservations and instructions for mooring (if they should install some in the future).

Brandywine Estate, with views of the boats in Sir Francis Drake, serves delicious French and Caribbean cuisine and the food is as spectacular as the view from the terrace. They are open for lunch and dinner daily, except Tuesdays. There is an outside lounge that is breezy with a front row view of the channel.

The white sand beach at the head of the bay is a good spot for a walk, a swim, or just lazing the day away. Garbage can be deposited in the green dumpster by the roadside. A park project is underway at the NW end of the beach however progress is slow and completion has been further delayed by the storm.

Maya Cove

Hodges Creek

Waypoint: BV103 18°25.10'N 64°33.20'W

Navigation: 2.5nm NE of Road Harbour

Services: Restaurants, Dockage, Moorings, Water, Fuel, Ice, Garbage disposal, Scuba shop

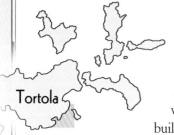

Tortola

Maya Cove or Hodges Creek as it is shown on the charts is approximately a half mile west of Buck Island on the southeastern shore of Tortola. Sheltered by the reef, it is always cool and relatively free of bugs. At the time of our last visit (May 2019) the marina was closed. The docks were clear of all wrecks but work was just starting on the building infrastructure. According to the owner, Mr.Penn, the marina and associated services will be open for business by November 2019. This includes, transient dockage, moorings, restaurant etc.

The small marina on the eastern side of the bay by the entrance and the marina at the head of the bay to the north are both private marinas and do not take transient yachts. The large three story building with the red roof is the Hodges Creek Marina, a full service facility. Moorings may be available via the marina on VHF 16. There is limited room to anchor due to the mooring field but a good alternative is to anchor in

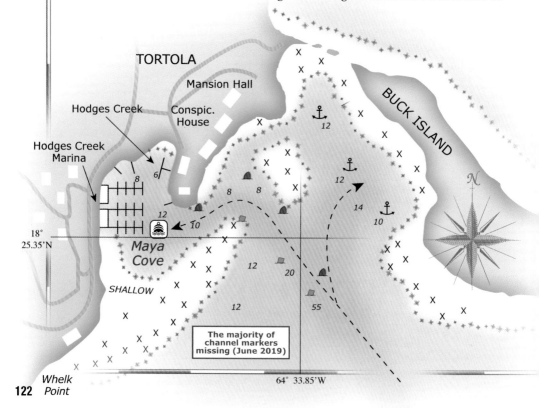

TORTOLA

Mansion Hall

Hodges Creek

Conspic. House

Hodges Creek Marina

BUCK ISLAND

Maya Cove

SHALLOW

12

12

8

8

8

6

12

10

12

20

12

55

12

14

10

12

10

N

18° 25.35'N

The majority of channel markers missing (June 2019)

64° 33.85'W

Whelk Point

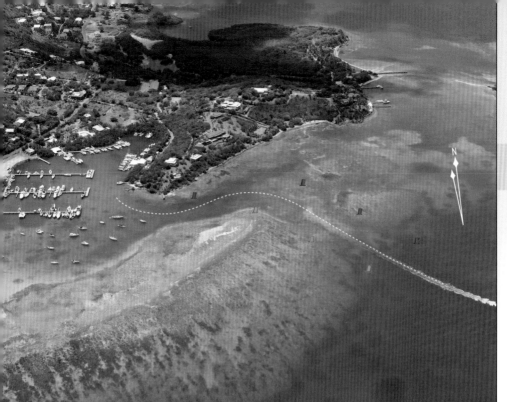

the lee of Buck Island in 7-10 feet of water (see below). Hodges Creek is home to The Catamaran Company and Sail Caribbean Divers.

Navigation & Piloting

When approaching Maya Cove from the west, it is well to remember that the reef extends from Whelk Point all the way to the buoyed entrance at the northeastern end of the reef. Entry should be made under power.

From the Buck Island waypoint (BV103) the channel markers are easy to see and are located under a promontory of land approximately 75-100 feet high. At the time of our last survey, there were only two key buoys in place with the starboard hand red marker indicating the edge of the reef and the green strategically placed at the tip of the reef to port around which the channel takes a 90 degree turn to port. Proceed into the anchorage, but do not head too far into the southwest corner of the cove as it shoals off rapidly.

BUCK ISLAND

From the waypoint (BV103) work your way up into the northeastern corner where you can anchor in 7-10 feet of water on a sand bottom off the western shore. Very few yachts anchor here which makes it even more attractive. In certain sea conditions the anchorage can be rolly, but generally it provides a safe anchorage. Do not go too far up toward the northwest tip of the island since it shoals off rapidly. There is no passage between Buck Island and Tortola and no landing is permitted on the island itself.

Ashore

Hodges Creek Marina is a full service marina which provides water, ice, and showers; and they monitor VHF-16.

At last edit, two service companies were operating: The Catamaran Company with its fleet of charter catamarans and Sail Caribbean Divers.

The marina restaurant was under renovation when we last visited and the marina management indicate that they will have a new facility, management and probably name identified in the next few months. As in the past it is assumed that the new restaurant will serve breakfast, lunch and dinner where you can look out across the channel while dining.

Sail Caribbean Divers maintain their headquarters at the Hodges Creek Marina and offer dive tours and instruction.

Provisioning: For your provisioning needs, RiteWay Supermarket at East End is a short taxi ride away. Their hours are 7am to 9pm Monday through Saturday and 7am to 6pm on Sunday. If you have online access via WiFi, RiteWay has an excellent online ordering system where you can check off the items required which are then accumulated in a shopping cart for secure check out and payment. The order can then be delivered to the marina free of charge if it is over $150. Visit RiteWay online at www.rtwbvi.com or call the provisioning group at 284-347-1188.

Hodges Creek Marina

Fat Hog's Bay & East End Bay

Waypoint: BV104 - 18°25.95'N, 64°33.20W
Navigation: 4.2nm NE of Road Harbour;
Services: Marinas, Restaurants, Fuel, Ice, Water, Provisions, Dive shop, Showers, Garbage disposal, ATM, Yacht charter, Chandlery, Laundry

Fat Hog's Bay and East End Bay are located just north of Buck Island and west of the Bluff on the point of Beef Island. These well-protected bays are conveniently located in the middle of the BVI cruising grounds and very close to the airport. Surrounded by the area known locally as East End, the bays are well populated by local fishermen and cruisers. It should be noted that both Harbourview and Chalwell Marinas suffered severe damage during the hurricane and at the time of our last survey there were no docks in place.

Navigation & Piloting

Both anchorages are easily accessible from Sir Francis Drake Channel by leaving Buck Island to port and transiting between the green can and Red Rock, a 20-foot high rock formation marking the southwestern end of Red Rock Reef. Inside of the entrance be aware that Fat Hog's Bay shoals off to the west so head due north to

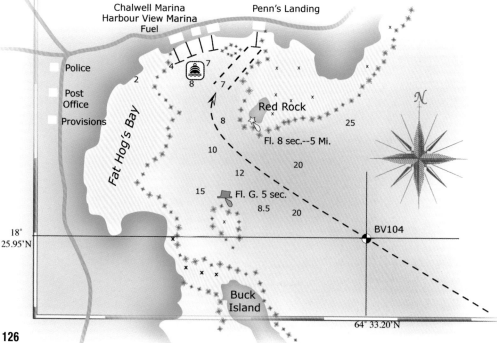

the Harbourview and Chalwell Marinas or turn to the east toward the moorings field or the buoyed channel into Penn's Landing Marina. Do not attempt to cross directly from Harbourview Marina to Penn's as there is a shallow area to the west of the marked channel.

Anchoring & Mooring

The average depth from Red Rock into East End Bay is about 9 feet (2.7m) with good holding ground and excellent protection behind the reef. There are 10 mooring balls in front of the Chalwell Marina, or further to the east there are 22 moorings managed by Penn's Landing. The depths of these moorings vary from less than 5' to 8' and all the balls are numbered so call Penn's Landing on VHF 16. Please do not anchor within the mooring field or obstruct the channel by anchoring inside of it.

Ashore

Three marinas operate within Fat Hog's Bay: Harbourview Marina, Chalwell Marina and Penn's Landing. These marinas are conveniently very close (2 miles) to the airport.

The Harbourview Marina lost the entire dock in the storm and it is doubtful that equipment can be mobilized in order to support a rebuilding effort that would be in time for the 2019/20 season. The marina office is open from 8am to 5pm daily and monitor VHF channel 16. Amenities include ice, water, laundry facilities (make sure to bring some quarters), showers and a few rooms for those wishing to get a break from the boat for a night or two. An outside bar is available pool-side for marina guests and others to gather for an afternoon drink.

Harbourview Marina includes the following businesses: Harbourview Marine Supply Chandlery; The Honey &

Spice Pastry Shop and HUM poolside restaurant and bar, open for both lunch and dinner. Across the street is Emile's Cantina serving Mexican fare (dinner only, closed Tuesdays).

Further to the east is the Chalwell Marina where once again the dock structure was damaged, so no dock services are available. There is the modern, well equipped East End Laundromat where you can leave laundry or stay and do it yourself, in a clean well managed environment.

For provisions, Quickmart has a provisioning store at the Chalwell Marina and RiteWay East End Food Market has a store right next door to the Harbourview Marina offering a deli counter, fresh meats and great produce. Parham General Store is also just a walk away between Penn's Landing and Harbourview Marina where you'll find household items and many fix-it tools and parts – they are

closed on Sundays. There is an ATM at Thelma's just east one block from the Harbourview Marina dock.

Penn's Landing offers water, ice, showers and overnight dockage in addition to yacht management services. Call Scott or Carris on VHF16. The moorings, maintained by Moor-Seacure, can be paid at the office. The Red Rock Restaurant & Bar at Penn's is open for dinner and offers great casual seaside dining. Open M-F 5:30-9:30pm or later, Saturday: lunch 11:30am-3pm, Sunday: brunch 10am-3pm, dinner: 5:30pm-close. Bar opens daily at 4pm. Call 284-442-1646.

Fuel (diesel and petrol) is available at Alphonso's Gas Station which is located just east of Penn's Landing. You can bring the vessel alongside the bulkhead where you can purchase dinghy fuel, liquid propane gas and ice.

Looking Northwest across Beef Island toward Guana Sound

BLUFF BAY
(BEEF ISLAND)

Waypoint: BV104 - (Fat Hog's Bay) 18°25.95N, 64°33.20W
Navigation: 2nm west of East End Bay
Services: Good snorkeling, Escorted kayak exploration
Caution: Reef Entrance / No Navigation Markers

For those who would like to get away from the crowd, Bluff Bay is situated on the south coast of Beef Island about 0.75 nm from Beef Island Bluff and provides a comfortable, sheltered anchorage behind a reef entrance. The suggested approach is from the southwest in good light with a lookout on the bow. Identify Whale Rocks to starboard and the reef protecting Hans Creek to port. The channel axis runs approximately northeast. Favoring the starboard side of the channel, pass

through the entrance in 10 feet of water and turn to port where you can drop your anchor in 8-9 feet on a sand bottom.

For a fascinating SUP or Kayak eco tour of the protected mangrove area of Hans Creek, contact Alex at 284-499-1620 or visit them at www.groundseabvi.com. They run their tours from this location and Alex, a local BVI born guide will show you newly born lemon sharks and explain the fragile ecosystem of the bay.

HANS CREEK

7   8

10

12

WHALE ROCKS

BLUFF BAY, BEEF ISLAND

Trellis Bay (Beef Island)

Waypoint: BV106 - 18°27.30'N 64°31.50W
Navigation: 5nm due west of Virgin Gorda Yacht Harbour; .75nm due south of Marina Cay
Services: Moorings, Provisions, Restaurants, WiFi, Ice, Water sports rentals, Ferry service, Art studio, Gift shops, Garbage, Car rental, ATM, Laundromat

Tortola

Located on the north shore of Beef Island, Trellis Bay was, at one time, a major anchorage with a large marine railway and jetty built by the Polish navigator and explorer Wladek Wagner, who adopted Trellis Bay as home for his family in the 1950s. Wagner also built the stone building on Bellamy Cay as well as the smaller stone buildings lining the bay.

The anchorage is well protected even in adverse weather conditions and its proximity to the airport makes it convenient for embarking and disembarking passengers, as it is a short 5 minute walk from the terminal to the beach bars and establishments lining the inner bay. At the creative heart of Trellis Bay is Aragorn's Studio, a center for local arts and crafts and home to the renowned fire ball sculptures and host of the Full Moon Party.

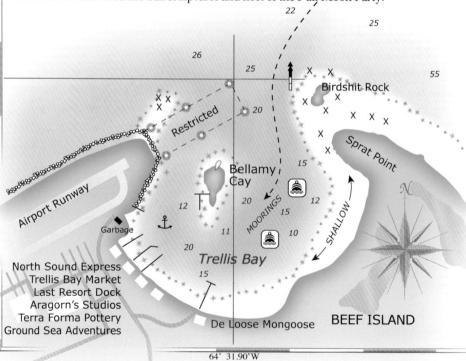

North Sound Express
Trellis Bay Market
Last Resort Dock
Aragorn's Studios
Terra Forma Pottery
Ground Sea Adventures

Post hurricane; Trellis Bay has been somewhat rearranged by Irma. Suffering some major storm damage and leaving many vessels on the beach in various levels of maritime distress. The fragile dock infrastructure, supporting the east end ferry services, was also badly damaged and many of the familiar shops and beach bars were still rebuilding (June 2019). Bellamy Cay (Last Resort) will be closed for the season 2019/20.

That being said, the RDA (Recovery & Development Agency) informs us that tenders are already in for the removal of derelict vessels and replacement of navigation aids which all should be accomplished prior to November 2019. In addition we note that there is new energy developing in the bay and some exciting new projects underway. The famed Fire Ball Full Moon Party continues as in the past, De Loose Mongoose is being completely rebuilt under new ownership, the Trellis Bay Market & Roti Bar have extended their patio and a new dock is in place, Marché Bar & Grill have also extended both menu and service area.

Navigation & Piloting

When approaching from the east and rounding the bluffs of Beef Island, you will be on a lee shore and if sailing, watch for wind shifts caused by the landmass. There is also tendency for the sea to become confused in this area, notably in the winter months when sea conditions are more boisterous. Follow the shore line northwest until you can identify the rocks awash at the tip of Sprat Point (locally known as "Bird Shit Rock"), marked by a yellow/black cardinal "north" marker. Leave the marker to port and enter the bay via the unmarked channel between Bellamy Cay and Sprat Point in 20 feet of water.

The yellow buoys to starboard (six in place June 2019) were strategically placed to mark the extremities of the airport runway proposed "restricted" zone and all vessels entering the bay should leave them to starboard. The airports/Port Authority confirms the intent to replace the missing buoys, however no immediate action is contemplated. The area within the yellow buoys should be considered a no-anchor zone.

Anchoring & Mooring

Due to the numerous cruising yachts resident in the bay, the anchorage often appears crowded upon entering, however there is usually sufficient room to find a spot to anchor or pick up a mooring ball, except on a busy full moon party night when an early arrival is key. Moorings are available on a first come basis with the orange balls are serviced by Moor-Seacure and Kevin & G will come by in the evening and collect the fee. The remaining balls to the west of Bellamy Cay are private and to the best of our knowledge are not serviced.

Anchoring is tight, because of the strategic placement of the mooring balls there is usually some room at the southeastern end of the bay for catamarans or to the west behind Bellamy Cay for deeper draft monohulls. The bottom is hard packed sand so make sure your anchor is well set. Ferry traffic use the west side of the anchorage as an unofficial channel and there is always ongoing activity so allow room for them to maneuver in the southwest corner of the bay adjacent to the docks. Do not anchor within the actual mooring field which is administered by the NPT and who have the authority to issue fines as appropriate.

When entering the bay and transiting from the southeast side of Bellamy Cay to the southwest do not turn too quickly as a sand bar/reef extends from Bellamy Cay south into the bay, the end of which is occasionally marked with a small buoy or ships fender. The area to the south of Sprat Point is shallow so avoid it. There are usually some shallow draft cruising vessels tucked in there, giving the impression that the anchorage extends further than it does. On the eve of a full moon party, it is recommended that you make plans to arrive early afternoon in order to secure a mooring or anchorage.

Full Moon party at Trellis Bay

Ashore

Trellis Bay offers an interesting and fun combination of restaurants, ferry connections, water sports, entertainment, local artists, local crafts and local organic provisions. Visiting Trellis gives you a wonderful insight into a low key local beach community. It is a short trip from Marina Cay or Scrub Island and worth the time to visit this artist community, have a breakfast in one of the beach bars or chill in the world's largest hammock while your crew visits Aragorn's studio.

Dinghies: Due to the storm, many docks were damaged and therefore the situation will evolve as repairs are made. Today you can land the dinghy at the Trellis Bay Market dock at the west end of the beach or the Bellamy Cay dock in the center. By November 2019 we were informed that the new owners of D'Loose Mongoose will have their new dock(s) in place. Make sure dinghies are well secured and during the winter months, when the wind is blowing hard, be sure to tie them on the leeward side to prevent them from getting caught under the dock.

Provisions: At the west end of the bay is the brightly colored Trellis Bay Market which provides an excellent selection when you are running low on provisions. Ice, beer, wine, fresh and frozen meats and vegetables are all available in this small store. The market it accessible from the water via its private dock. The adjacent laundry was demolished in the storm and it is hoped that it will be back in place for the 2019 season.

For local grown provisions, Good Moon Farm delivers fresh greens and fruits every day to Aragorn's Studio where they are sold from beautiful baskets in front of the studio or brought out to the anchorage in Aragorn's boat shop. It is also possible to order online at the Good Moon Farm website and pick up the fresh produce at the Trellis Bay studio the following day.

Garbage: Bags should be taken to the dumpster located at the western end of the beach. Please do not leave trash in any other container as it tends to overflow and attract animal life. Ice and garbage disposal is also available boat-side each morning courtesy of Kevin and G (note the matching t-shirts), a delightful couple who service Trellis Bay, Marina Cay, Cooper Island and Great Harbour, Peter Island daily. Call them on VHF 16.

Car Rental & ATM: For cruisers wishing to rent a car or to access an ATM, you will need to walk across to the airport terminal where there are three major rental companies. The ATM is inside the lobby opposite the rental car service desks.

Full Moon Party: The Trellis Bay Full Moon Party has become a must-see happening for BVI visitors. Check the dates in the ad above and plan your vacation around the moon. Arriving early in the day is recommended as the anchorage gets very crowded. The fire ball full moon party retains the carnival air of excitement it always has. Each month, as the moon waxes full, Aragorn's huge iron orbs with cut out designs are set ablaze along the water front. This signals party time everywhere along the bay, which, we might add, usually fills up early in anticipation of the celebration.

If you've been to The Full Moon Party, you won't forget it. If you haven't, you won't want to miss it. Some love to climb

in to the giant purple hammock to look at the stars while others want to take a break from dancing while they enjoy the famous West Indian buffet. Then, there are those who crowd the hammock for a great photo to send home. Over the years, the moon has inspired many stories of fact and fantasy about this ever morphing natural satellite. There have been tales circulating forever about the full moons mystical, magical powers and the effect of its heightening of emotions. Scientists debunk this theory except in a very small percentage of people. Those who have attended a Full Moon Party will probably disagree. Their emotions are definitely heightened by the music, dance, drink, food and the aura that surrounds it all. It's a time when even the shiniest of heads, figuratively, let their hair down and give way to this very contagious party spirit in a fun, family friendly environment.

Restaurants: At the east end of the bay, De Loose Mongoose (de Goose) is now under new ownership who are well underway with construction with a "soft" opening planned for November 2019. Neil Kline, Operations Manager & local chef, tells us that there will be two docks, one for commercial traffic (ferries) and one for dinghies. There will be three bars, a coffee bar, cocktail bar, and rum bar. The environment will be family friendly with a Sunday Caribbean buffet brunch with live music. Neil's background in the food business is apparent when he talks enthusiastically about the menu being a reflection of the Caribbean melting pot of cuisine. Fresh seafood, fish and fungi, and other adaptations of local cuisine

GOOD MOON FARM
TURNBULL ESTATE, TORTOLA

We deliver...

EAT LOCAL GROWN
ORGANIC FOOD

Visit our website or call 1 284 5420586

WWW.GOODMOONFARM.COM

along with pizza and other bar favortites. WiFi will be available to patrons.

Further to the west is Marché Bar & Grill who have recently expanded their menu to include a Sushi bar. The bar was crafted in the BVI from reconditioned cypress that was salvaged from an Irma damaged roof. The tables are from the same cypress but with a Sapele Mahogany inlay. They feature a variety of food, coffee drinks, ice cream and smoothies in addition to beer, wine and mixed drinks. The restaurant is open every day except Monday from 11 am to 10 pm. Call them at: 284-545-0259.

At the west end of the bay next door to the Trellis Bay Market is one of my favorite stops, the Trellis Bay Market Bar and Grill, a lively place to eat and mix with the locals in a fun, casual environment. The "roti-wrap" is the commercialization of roti and curry as a fast food item in the Caribbean. Various wrapped "rotis" are served including chicken, fish, shrimp and vegetable. Take some back to the boat for lunch or dinner (don't forget the mango chutney). The grill is lit every Friday and Saturday producing the best BBQ and jerk on the island. During the monthly full moon party BBQ and jerk are served

along with their specialty Goat Water. Open 6am to 10pm daily and 8am to 6pm on Sunday (call (284-495-1421).

Aragorn's Studio: The Trellis Bay Village is a haven for artists and local craftsmen; an access point for BVI local culture. At the heart of the creative energy is Aragorn Dick-Read, master craftsman and fire sculpture artist. Aragorn is also famous for his copper sculptures and one of a kind wood-cut and etching print t-shirts. The gallery walls offer a stunning display of sculptural talent. Aragorn has exhibited his art all over the world from China to New York and London to Kazakhstan; he is also available to undertake private or public art commissions. Visitors are encouraged to visit the back of the studio where "the magic" is being made.

135

Pottery Studio: Next door in the pottery studio is Debbie who has worked with Aragorn for over 13 years and who now operates independently as TerraForma. Debbie is an incredibly talented artist and has earned a reputation as one of the top potters in the Caribbean. A kiln demonstration area is located adjacent to the studio and live demonstrations in Raku pottery firing are always a part of the full moon experience. Debbie also holds pottery classes. Hours 9-5pm Tuesday - Saturday Call: (284) 345-8983.

When at anchor at Marina Cay or Trellis Bay, keep an eye out for Aragorn's boat shop laden with t-shirts, crafts, fresh bread and organic fruits as he or his employees go boat to boat around the anchorage. The boat only carries one percent of what you will see on shore, so make the trip to the studio for the other 99%.

Exploration: For an interesting, new and unusual side trip, consider linking up with GroundSea Adventures. Alex Dick-Read, Aragorn's brother, operates SUP or kayak tours through the last pristine mangrove eco-system in the BVI. Hans Creek, a BVI Fisheries protected area, gives you a beautiful close to nature experience for all ages. Alex and his guides offer deep local knowledge that will take you through the importance of this impressive, peaceful and inspiring sanctuary. You will see baby lemon and black tip sharks, just born, large stingrays and a plethora of juvenile reef fish that grow up in the protected waters before venturing out to the reefs. The smart way to book this popular tour is online before you leave home and schedule the three hour trip into your itinerary whilst sailing up the channel. Alternatively, you can sail straight into the shelter of Bluff Bay to meet your guide at the entrance to the lagoon, or if you are in Marina Cay or Trellis Bay, link up with the Ground Sea crew at Aragorn's Studio for the short ride over to the south side of Beef Island. Should some of the party wish to hike while others paddle the mangroves, there is a mountain trail to the top of Beef Island that provides awesome views across the channel.

Alex also operates an extensive range of custom hiking tours all through the islands. Contact them at (www.groundseabvi.com) or call 284-499-1620.

Kayak

Hike

Surf

SUP

Driftwood fish at Aragorn's Studio

Aragorn at work

Tortola sloop Esperanza

MARINA CAY
SCRUB ISLAND & CAM BAY

Waypoint: BV106 18°27.30'N, 64°31.50'W
Navigation: 8nm NE Road Harbour, 4.5nm west of Virgin Gorda Yacht Harbour
Services: Restaurant, Hotel, Fuel, Ice, Water, Garbage disposal, WiFi, Pusser's Store, Ferry to Trellis Bay, Snorkeling

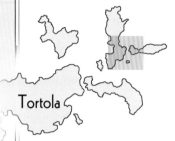

Tortola

Marina Cay, nestled behind a reef and lying between the islands of Camanoe and Scrub, is easy to enter and provides visiting yachtsmen with good holding in an all-weather anchorage. There are numerous mooring balls available, therefore limiting anchoring to the northeast between Marina Cay and Scrub Island or southwest behind the mooring field where you will be a little more exposed.

Navigation & Piloting

Approaching Marina Cay from the east, you have three choices. The recommended route is to go around the north end of the island. There is good water up to the large, conspicuous rock that marks the northeast end of the reef. Leave it to port and pass

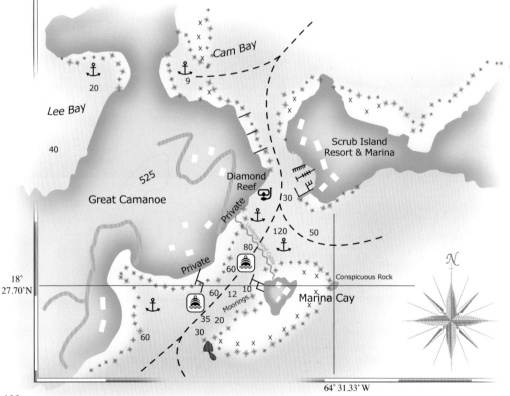

SCRUB IS.

MARINA CAY

Rocks Awash

GREAT CAMANOE

N

between Marina Cay and Scrub Island into the anchorage.

Alternatively, approaching from the south or west, you should favor the southern tip of Great Camanoe. A red buoy marks the southwest extremity of the reef. Leave it to starboard as you enter the anchorage.

If the light is good, and you are approaching from the north or northeast, it is possible to approach Marina Cay between Scrub Island and Great Camanoe. This transit should be made under power and only in good light. From waypoint BV107, proceed through the channel which, although narrow, carries 25 feet. On your port hand will be the Scrub Island Resort and Marina, and ahead will be Marina Cay.

Anchoring & Mooring

Numerous fully maintained moorings are available on a first-come basis. Moorings are maintained by Moor-Seacure and payment ($30) can be made at the marina. There are some additional balls that have been laid in the small bay to the west of Marina Cay by the management of Great Camanoe. We understand that someone will come by and collect the fee ($30). If you are anchoring, keep clear of the mooring field by anchoring further to the northeast between Marina Cay and Scrub Island, or to the southwest. Also be aware of the underwater cable between Great Camanoe and Marina Cay, just to the north of the dock. There are signs indicating the location, but they are not always evident.

Camanoe Island is private and off limits to visiting yachtsmen. Please be considerate with respect to the proximity of the private homes on Camanoe, keeping noise levels down and respecting the residents' privacy.

Ashore

Marina Cay, like many establishments, was severely impacted by the passing of Hurricane Irma. The old Pusser's restaurant on the beach was completely destroyed, the docks severely damaged along with the Pusser's Company Store. At the time of our last survey (May 2019) the restaurant had been relocated to the head of the dock under a large canvas canopy with the small bar in close proximity. The restaurant offers casual dining at the grill often with live entertainment.

The marina/fuel dock still operates offering fuel, ice, water, garbage disposal, laundry facilities and showers for yachtsmen. They monitor VHF channel 16. Marina Cay provides free ferry service from the main dock in Trellis Bay – check with them for departure times. The Scrub Island ferry also stops here en route to and from Trellis Bay. This is a free service leaving Scrub Island on the half hour.

Marina Cay is an amazing islet almost surrounded by a reef. It is an idyllic spot, the quintessential tropical island. Regrettably the lasting impact of the 2017 hurricane is still in evidence and the island lacks the polish and energy that was in evidence before the storm. On the horizon (2020) there is a major revitalization planned that will transform the character into a Caribbean farm to table environment that sounds exciting!

Shopping: The old Robb White House on the highest point of Marina Cay has now been converted to the Pusser's Company Store stocked with their quality tropical and nautical clothing, unique accessories, gifts and sundries.

When at anchor at Marina Cay or Trellis Bay, keep an eye out for Aragorn's boat shop laden with t-shirts, crafts, fresh bread, and organic fruits as he or his employees go boat-to-boat around the anchorage. Aragorn's boat only carries one percent of what you will see at his store on shore, so make the trip to the studio to see the other 99%. There's something for everyone!

Snorkeling: There is excellent snorkeling on the reef around the island and located just off the shoreline of Camanoe between Marina Cay and Scrub Island is a NPS designated snorkel area, Diamond Reef, where you can tie your dinghy and enjoy some pristine snorkeling. Dive BVI offers dive trips and instruction daily. An air station is in operation and Ocean Kayaks and Hobie Cat rentals are available.

SCRUB ISLAND MARINA

Navigation: Approach from the north via Waypoint BV107 18°28.55N, 64°31.50W
(Cam Bay) between Scrub and Camanoe or follow directions to Marina Cay

Services: Full service marina, Ice, Water, Showers, Restaurants, Hotel, Provisions, Ferry to Trellis Bay, WiFi, Sailing School, Dream Yacht Charters

Just to the north of Marina Cay is the BVI's luxury development: Scrub Island Resort, Spa & Marina. The marina is tucked into the western end of Scrub Island and protected by a natural reef and breakwater. This 55-slip, full-service marina was opened in mid-2010 and is equipped to accommodate vessels up to 160 feet. In addition to the marina, the resort offers two restaurants, a gourmet market and café and world-class hotel rooms overlooking the marina. The restaurants are open to visiting yachtsmen and a dinghy dock is located at the foot of the middle dock.

The marina has a maximum depth of 15 feet, but vessels over 7 feet should contact the marina prior to arrival. The approach depth is 25 feet. The marina monitors VHF channel 16/74 or call 284-394-3440. The dock master, Savio, has been there for 9 years and along with his assistant Paul, they will take very good care of you. There is no fuel available at the marina for environmental concerns.

Ashore

The Scrub Island Marina offers 55 deep water slips available for lease or transient docking, and is equipped to accommodate vessels up to 160 feet. It should be noted that Dream Yacht Charters are operating from this location, and their transient docking is more flexible between Sunday and Thursday when the Dream YC fleet is out on charter. Available at the marina is ice, water, electricity (110v/ 220v with 30/50/100 amp), garbage disposal ($5 per bag), and wireless internet. Water is $0.20 per gallon and dockage is $1.50 -$2.50 per foot (seasonal). You can also purchase provisions at the gourmet market near the marina or enjoy fresh deli sandwiches or pizza sitting out on the patio. It is (open from 10am).

Facilities include restrooms, showers and changing facilities. Laundry valet is also available. Scrub Island is an amazing resort close enough to Tortola for easy access with ferries and water taxis.

Donovan's Reef is the name of the casual bar and restaurant overlooking the pool and down the channel. At night the lights from Beef Island and Trellis Bay sparkle. It is casual, open air dining, serving lunch and dinner. The menu features American and Caribbean cuisine. No reservation needed.

For more elegant dining you will want to try the Cardamon & Company restaurant, nicely situated to take advantage of the sweeping views of Camanoe Pass and surrounding waters. The Restaurant serves dinner; reservations are requested.

You can get to Scrub Island from Tortola by water taxi if you aren't on a boat. The water taxi leaves from Trellis Bay at the North Sound water taxi dock (in Trellis Bay). It is a short trip over to Scrub Island. The water taxi is free for resort and marina guests and runs hourly from 6:30am to 10:30pm. departing Trellis Bay at 45 minutes past the hour.

Cam Bay looking southeast

CHART YOUR COURSE.
AND FEEL FREE TO WANDER.

Dive into the true spirit of the British Virgin Islands
while sailing the best-kept secret in the Caribbean.
Hop off your boat and immerse yourself in the unique
culture, endless adventures and discoveries waiting
to be made on and offshore. Nearly 600 nautical
miles and 60 islands await you.

BVITOURISM.COM | 1-800-835-8530

Tortola | Virgin Gorda | Jost Van Dyke | Anegada | Cooper Island | Guana Island
Little Thatch | Necker Island | Norman Island | Peter Island | Saba Rock | Scrub Island

THE
BRITISH
VIRGIN ISLANDS
NATURE'S LITTLE SECRETS

Entrance to Cam Bay

CAM BAY

Waypoint: BV107 18°28.55'N 64°31.50'W
Navigation: 0.6nm N of Marina Cay; 6.4nm from Mountain Point VG
Services: None. National Marine Park.

Cam Bay is a small delightful anchorage located on the eastern shore of Great Camanoe. Many of the charter companies have placed it off limits but the crewed charter captains have used it extensively when the charter party needed a little solitude. Cam Bay is not hard to enter but there is limited room once inside so if you see more than four to five boats at anchor you may want to regroup and anchor at Marina Cay or tie up at Scrub Island Marina for the evening.

Tucked in behind the reef you get the cooling effect of the trade winds but retain the calm and protection of the reef.

Navigation & Piloting

Approaching from the north from waypoint BV107 proceed south toward the Scrub Island Cut, Cam Bay will be to starboard.

The entrance to the bay is protected by a reef that starts at the northern end and continues south for some distance. The entrance is about 200 feet wide and carries 10 feet of depth. The reef from the southern end of the bay extends approximately 200 feet to the north before the opening. Enter under power with good light and someone on the bow. Head for the beach before turning to starboard for a short distance and then rounding up within 150 feet of the reef. Drop the anchor in about 10 feet of water, take a quick dive to check the anchor is well set and enjoy the solitude. Do not proceed too far to the north since the water shoals off quickly.

Approaching from the south, via Scrub Island Cut, Cam Bay will open up to port. Make sure you have identified the location of the reef before making your entrance. Do not anchor in the entrance since you will not benefit from the protection of the reef and will probably have to endure a rolly uncomfortable evening.

CAMANOE PASSAGE
GUANA SOUND

Waypoint: BV109 - 18°27.70'N 64°33.20'W
BV110 - 18°27.70'N 64°35.00'W

Tortola

Traveling west to Guana Sound from Marina Cay or Trellis Bay, two routes are available and both need to be fully understood prior to starting the transit. The first is the narrow passage between Great and Little Camanoe and the second is between Little Camanoe and Beef Island (Tortola).

CAMANOE PASSAGE

Many of the charter operators insist that only the narrow passage between Great Camanoe and Little Camanoe be used. The channel, although narrow, carries nearly 20 feet of depth and it is recommended that it be negotiated under power, since the wind will become erratic due to the land formation. Stay to the center of the channel and identify the rocks on the northeast corner of Little Camanoe before turning to port and into the Guana Channel. When a ground swell is present during the winter months the water can break heavily on this small reef.

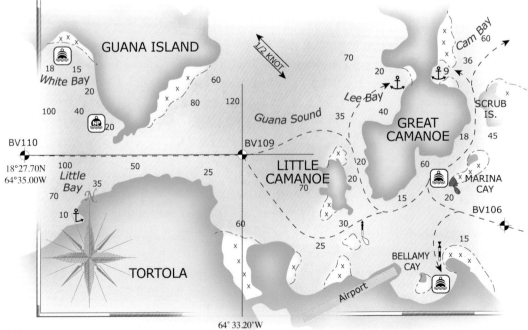

The Camanoe Passage

The image labels: BEEF ISLAND, TRELLIS BAY, BELLAMY CAY, AIRPORT, ROCKS, GREAT CAMANOE, SHOALS, LITTLE CAMANOE, REEF, LITTLE CAMANOE PASSAGE

CAMANOE PASSAGE

BEEF ISLAND PASSAGE

There are two notable obstructions to navigation to be aware of when using this passage to pass into Guana Sound, the reef that extends from the southwest end of Little Camanoe and the shoal that lies to the south of the yellow cardinal marker due south of the Camanoe passage. Due to airport restrictions (see Trellis Bay) it is suggested that your approach from the east is toward the southern tip of Little Camanoe until you identify the yellow cardinal marker which must be left to port. Once past the marker do not turn west, but head southwest until you are clear of the reef. The reef to starboard extends southwest from Little Camanoe, after which you are in deep water and the approach to Guana Sound is clear of obstruction.

THE GUANA CHANNEL

Heading due west from the north end of Little Camanoe, toward Monkey Point, you will enter Guana Sound and the Guana Channel that divide Tortola and Guana Island. Although the channel looks narrow from a distance, there is a minimum of 1/4 mile at the narrowest point and 25 feet of water under your keel. Sailing to the west with the wind on your quarter you should be able to sail through. Keep to the center of the channel leaving Guana and Monkey Point to starboard. As you pass the point you will see yachts at anchor across the sandy area that joins Monkey Point to the rest of Guana Island.

LEE BAY (GREAT CAMANOE)

Waypoint: BV109 (Guana Sound) 18°27.70'N 64°33.20'W

Navigation: 2.1nm due east from Monkey Point; 2.7nm NW of Trellis Bay

Services: None

Although often ignored in favor of the more popular anchorages in this region, Lee Bay on the west coast of Great Camanoe provides a quiet respite for those wishing more seclusion. Lee Bay is well protected in most weather conditions and cooled by the breeze that flows over the saddle of land that provides a backdrop for Cam Bay on the other side of the hill. The approach to Lee Bay from the east is via the passage between Great and Little Camanoe. The passage can carry 20 feet and although narrow, is straightforward. There is a rock on the northeast end of Little Camanoe, be sure to identify it and stay clear toward the center of the channel. Lee Bay will open up to starboard. Approaching from the west from Guana and Monkey Point, head to the northern end of Little Camanoe until you can identify the Bay. The entrance is straightforward with no obstruction.

Anchoring & Mooring

The best spot to anchor is in the northeast corner of the bay in front of the saddle of the hill in 15 feet of water. The holding ground is good, and besides the occasional low coral growth, the bottom is clear. Please take care not to anchor in coral.

When a northerly sea condition is present during the winter months and surf is breaking on the northern tip of Camanoe, the resulting ground swell can work its way into this anchorage. Depending upon the condition, a second anchor should be deployed or an alternative anchorage identified until sea conditions return to normal.

White Bay, Guana Island

Monkey Point, Guana Island, with White Bay in background

MONKEY POINT/GUANA ISLAND

Waypoint: BV110 - 18°27.70'N 64°35.00'W
Navigation: 1.7nm due west from Little Camanoe; 4.5nm E of Rough Point (BV112)
Services: National Park Moorings

At the southern tip of Guana Island is a delightful anchorage known as Monkey Point. An excellent day anchorage, Monkey Point is situated on the western side of the rocky outcrop that marks the southern extremity of the island. There are 10 National Park moorings in place for those with a permit. (Yellow balls are for commercial use only.)

The small beach area and excellent snorkeling make this a great lunch stop. When there is a northerly swell running, the anchorage can be rolly.

Monkey Point, Guana Island

WHITE BAY/GUANA ISLAND

Waypoint: BV110 - 18°27.70N 64°35.00W
Navigation: 4.5nm W of Rough Point (Waypoint BV112) / 0.8nm north of Monkey Point
Services: None (this is a private island) / Moorings

Easily identified by the long stretch of beautiful white beach, White Bay is located on the southwest side of Guana Island, less than a mile from Monkey Point. Open to both the south and west, during the winter months, when a northerly ground sea is running, this anchorage is not recommended. The anchorage, located at the northern end of the bay, has a coral shelf that extends to the south and in an ongoing effort to protect the coral from further damage caused by indiscriminate anchoring, numerous private moorings have been laid by the hotel who make them available for yachtsmen at $30 per night. Since the placement of the moorings restricts available anchoring room, boats wishing to anchor at White Bay should do so to the south or west of the mooring field in 15-20 feet of water. Do not anchor on or near corals, which will appear as darker patches on the sea bottom, and do not allow your anchor chain to run over or drag across these sensitive and fragile ecosystems. Guana is a private island and access to the beach facilities is for hotel guests only. There are no public facilities.

To the north of the anchorage, separating White Bay from Muskmelon Bay to the north you will notice a rock formation that looks like a large iguana's head and known locally as Guana Head Rock for which the island is named. Muskmelon Bay to the north is a designated marine protected area and should be considered a no-anchor zone. The moorings have been laid down by the hotel to preserve the corals and are for daytime use only.

LITTLE BAY/TORTOLA

Navigation: .75nm SW of Monkey Point
Services: None

Sailing west from Monkey Point or east from Jost Van Dyke, there are numerous white sandy beaches apparent to the south. They are all exposed, but when the weather is calm, we recommend Little Bay as a lunch stop only. If there is any surf activity apparent on the beach, do not anchor here. Use the anchorage at Monkey Point or continue further east through the cut. The bottom is sandy and holding is good in 10-15 feet of water.

ISLAND CONNECTIONS

EMERGENCIES
999 or 911
VISAR (Virgin Island Search and Rescue)
Tel: 767 (SOS), or
+1 284 499 0911
www.visar.org

BRANDYWINE BAY

RESTAURANTS
Brandywine Estate Restaurant
Tel:1 284-495-2301
FB: Brandywine-Estate-Restaurant
Ocean view, chef curated menu, European cuisine, cocktails, brunch, wine
Tue-Th 5-11pm;
Fri-Sun 12pm -11pm

MAYA COVE/ HODGES CREEK

MARINAS
Hodges Creek Marina:
Will be for the winter season 2019/2020, no further details available at time of printing

CHARTER COMPANIES
The Catamaran Company BVI
Tel: 284-344-3722
www.catamarans.com
FB: catamaranco
9am-5pm 7 days/week

DIVING/ WATERSPORTS
Sail Caribbean Divers
Tel: 1-284-541-3483
www.sailcaribbeandivers.com
FB: sailcaribbeandivers
Dive courses & scuba expeditions, private dive and snorkel trips, SUP and kayaking, weekly gear rental (diving and watersports)
8am-5pm 7 days/week

FAT HOG'S BAY

MARINAS
JY Harbour View Marina
Tel: 284-495-0165
284-496-0165
www.bviharbourview.com
11am-9pm

Penn's Landing Marina
Tel: 284 441-1134
www.pennslandingbvi.com
FB: PennsLandingMarinaBVI
VHF 16
12 slips, water, electricity, showers, WiFi, 20 moorings, restaurant
8am-5pm 7day/week

Chalwell Marina
VHF 16

CHANDLERY
Harbourview Marine Supply
Tel: 284-495-2586

PROVISIONING
RiteWay (East End)
Tel: 284-347-1257
www.rtwbvi.com
Fresh produce, seafood, meat, wine, spirits, gluten free, vegan, provisioning
7am–9pm 7 days/week

RESTAURANTS
JY Harbour View Marina Bar & Restaurant
Tel: 284-495-0165 or
284-496-0165
www.bviharbourview.com
FB: JYHVM
Burgers, fish, lobster, wings, cocktails, apps, music
11am-3pm, 5pm-9pm or later

Red Rock Restaurant & Bar
Tel: 284 442-1646
www.bviredrock.com/restaurant
FB: redrockrestaurant-andbar
Waterfront dining, bar menu, cocktails, fresh, seasonal, organic, international, pizza, happy hour, call for reservations
M-F 5:30pm-9:30pm,
Sat lunch 11:30am-3pm,
Sunday: brunch 10am-3pm,
dinner: 5:30pm, drinks at 4

TRELLIS BAY

DIVING/WATERSPORTS
Ground Sea Adventures
Tel: 284-499-1620
www.groundseabvi.com

PROVISIONING
Kevin & G
Ice delivery and garbage, pick-up by boat, (makes the rounds in anchorages)

Good Moon Farm
284-542-0586
FB: goodmoonfarmbvi
www.goodmoonfarm.com
Fresh, organic local produce and more. Online ordering, in store grocery

Trellis Bay Market Bar & Grill
Tel: 284-495-1421
www.trellisbaymarket.com
FB: trellis.bay
7am-6pm 7 days/week

RESTAURANTS
De Loose Mongoose
(Due to open October 2019)

Trellis Bay Market Bar & Grill
Tel: 284-495-1421
www.trellisbaymarket.com
FB: trellis.bay
Breakfast, lunch, dinner:
Roti, BBQ, jerk, ribs, burgers, wings, pizza.
Full moon parties, reservation requested
M-Th 6am-8pm,
F-Sat 6am-10pm,
Sun lunch and dinner
11am-9pm,
Daily happy hour 4-6pm

Marché Bar & Grill
Tel: 1 284-494-3626
FB @Marche-Bar-and-Restaurant
Sushi, Asian & local cuisine, bar, full moon party, reservations encouraged
Closed Mon,
Tue-Sun 8am-11:30pm,
full moon 9am-2am

SHOPS
Aragorn's Studio
Tel: 284-495-1849
www.aragornsstudio.com
FB: aragornsstudio
Art, pottery, t-shirts, gifts

TerraForma BVI
FB: TerraFormaBVI
Tel: 1 284-345-8983
Mon-Sat 9-5, closed Sundays, pottery & gifts

FERRY SERVICES
Speedy's
Tel: 284-495-5240 or
284-495-5235
info@speedysbvi.com
www.bviferries.com
FB: virgingorda.transport.speedys
Virgin Gorda-Road Town & back, Virgin Gorda-Beef Island & back, Virgin Gorda, Charlotte Amalia St. Thomas, check site for schedule and rates

Sensation Ferries
www.sensationferries.com
Tel: 1-284-340-2723
FB: VirginIslandsFerries
Virgin Gorda-Tortola
Check website for schedules and fares

Inter Island Boat Services
Tel: 1 340-776-6597
interislandboatservices.com
FB: InterIslandboatservices
St. Thomas & St. John-BVI,
Tortola, Anegada, Jost Van
Dyke
Check website for schedule

Scrub Island Ferry
(Complimentary to guests)
Tel: 1 284-394-3440
www.scrubisland.com
FB: ScrubIsland

MARINA CAY

Marina Cay Pusser's
Tel: 284-494-2467
marinacay@pussers.com
Pussers.com
FB: Pussers.Marina.Cay

SCRUB ISLAND

MARINAS
Scrub Island Marina
Tel: 284 394-3440
www.scrubisland.com
FB: ScrubIsland
VHF 74
Electricity, water, ice, trash

RESTAURANTS
Cardamon & Co.
Tel: 284-4394-3440
www.scrubisland.com
Fine dining, amazing views
Dinner, daily, reservations
requested

Donovan's Reef
Tel: 284 394-3440
www.scrubisland.com
Open air, poolside, chill vibe
Breakfast, lunch, dinner,
reservations encouraged

**One Shoe Beach Bar &
Grill**
Tel: 284 394-3440
www.scrubisland.com

PROVISIONING
Gourmet Market & Cafe
Tel: 284 394-3440
www.scrubisland.com
Deli, fruit, sandwiches,
provisions, coffee, baked
goods, cheeses, snacks,
wine, liquor
Open daily

CHARTER COMPANIES
Dream Yacht Charter
Tel: 1 284-345-2185
dreamyachtcharter.com
FB: DreamYachtCharter
infona@dreamyachtcharter.
com

DIVING / WATERSPORTS
Dive BVI
Tel: 284-340-0829
info@divebvi.com
www.divebvi.com/
FB @DiveBVI
SSI, PADI and NAUI
Checkout dives, rendezvous
pickup service, day trips,
open water dive course,
multi-tank trips, contact
to book

Offshore Sailing School
Tel:284-4394-3440
www.scrubisland.com

WESTERN TORTOLA

Charts
NV.Charts: St.Thomas to Anegada: Kit: C-13 &14
NIMA: 25641, Imray-Iolaire: A-231
Admiralty Leisure: 5640-5&6

Mercurius
Rock

BV
206

Cable
Rock

GREAT TOBAGO

4.2 NM

LITTLE
TOBAGO

King
Rock

BV
205

4.3 NM

5 NM

N

THATCH CAY

UV
613

Middle Passage

GRASS CAY

MINGO CAY

CONGO CAY

Hawk

UV
502

Leeward Passage

SAINT THOMAS

64° 50'W

Waypoints	North	West
BV112	18°27.20'	64°39.80'
BV113	18°25.65'	64°40.20'
BV114	18°23.70'	64°43.30'
BV115	18°22.80'	64°45.50'
BV116	18°22.70'	64°41.90'
BV117	18°23.00'	64°38.50'

18°
28'N

LITTLE JOST VAN DYKE

GREEN CAY

JOST VAN DYKE

White Bay

Great Harbour

Little Harbour

BV 201

SANDY CAY

BV 112

Brewers Bay

BV 204

BV 203

BV 202

BV 113

Cane Garden Bay

18°
25'N

Carrot Bay

3 NM

3.6 NM

Cappoons Bay

1740
Mt. Sage

BV 114

Thatch Island Cut

Long Bay

Smugglers Bay

TORTOLA

Sea C
Bay

Nanny Cay

GREAT THATCH

WEST END

Windward Passage

LITTLE THATCH

Sopers Hole

Fort Recovery

BV 117

BV 115

The Narrows

3.3 NM

FRENCHMANS CAY

BV 116

WHISTLING CAY

Francis Bay

Leinster Bay

United Kingdom
United States

Cinnamon Bay

SAINT JOHN

64° 40'W

BREWER'S BAY

Waypoint: BV112 – 18°27.20'N 64°39.80'W
Navigation: 2nm North of Cane Garden Bay;
5nm West of Guana Is.
Services: Beach bar, Ruins, Snorkeling

Without question, Brewer's Bay, on the northern coast of Tortola, is one of the most beautiful unspoiled bays in the Virgin Islands. During the winter months it is vulnerable to northerly ground swells owing to the northerly exposure and has been posted as an "off-limits" anchorage by many charter companies due to the extensive coral and charted underwater cables. In the 35 years we have been writing this cruising guide we are unaware of anyone fouling the cable, however it is our job to point out the stated obstructions.

When the weather is settled we highly recommend this anchorage where you will find yourselves in limited company.

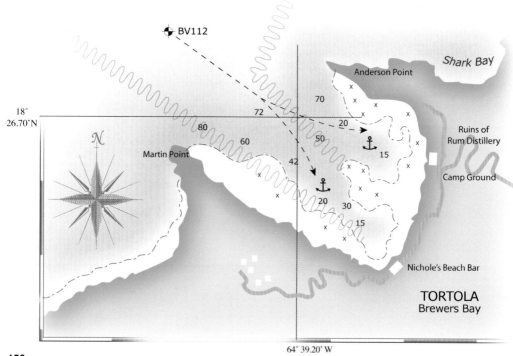

Navigation & Piloting

Brewer's Bay is divided by a reef that extends from the shore out toward the northwest. There are two anchorages; the northern one which is more protected from the swell that works its way round the point, and the southern anchorage which is easier to negotiate, but a little more exposed. Both anchorages require good light overhead and someone posted on the bow to spot for coral heads. Do not enter this anchorage in times of northerly ground swells!

From the waypoint (BV112) west of Anderson Point head into Brewer's Bay on a course of 120°m. This will take you toward the lower (right) anchorage. It is suggested that you visually locate the center or middle reef before working your way into the anchorage where you can drop the hook in 15-20 feet of water. Do not anchor in coral and do not pick up any moorings. The northern anchorage remains the most popular and there is a large patch of sand that is apparent to the north of the center coral formation that provides an ideal place to drop the anchor.

Ashore

While the snorkeling is excellent, time should also be taken to explore ashore. For those interested in a shore side hike, it would be worthwhile walking up the hill to the east toward Mount Healthy to see the ruins of Tortola's only remaining windmill. Only the base of the original mill has survived the passing years, along with the crumbling remains of the old distillery building at the northern end of the beach. There is also a very casual beach bar called Nicole's at the southern end of the bay. The Brewer's Bay Campground is located on the beach toward the northern end.

Mount Healthy Windmill

CANE GARDEN BAY

Tortola

Waypoint: BV113 – 18°25.65'N; 64°40.20'W
Navigation: 4nm NE Soper's Hole;
5nm East of Great Harbour, JVD
Services: Moorings, Ice, Water, Fuel, ATM,
Restaurants, Entertainment, Provisioning, Garbage
disposal, Taxi, WiFi

Regarded by some as one of the more beautiful anchorages in the BVI, Cane Garden Bay is picture postcard material, with a white, palm-fringed beach stretching the entire length of the bay and a backdrop of green hills climbing 1500 feet to Sage Mountain and the rain forest.

Cane Garden Bay suffered severe flooding and storm damage during Irma and a $1.7 million dollar grant was established to repair and upgrade the beach and general environment. Excellent progress was evident during our most recent survey, but evidence of the storms impact is noticeable.

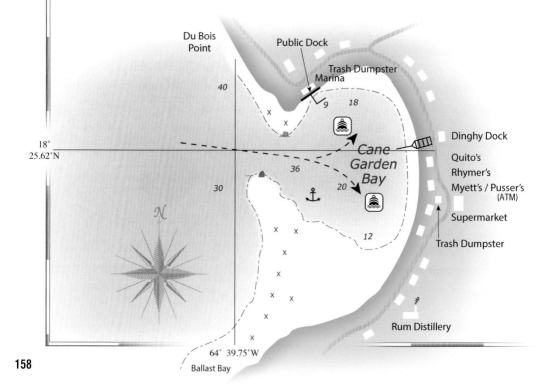

Cane Garden is now a day-trip destination for cruise ship passengers bused over from Road Town, the logical consequence being the appearance of an array of ubiquitous beach chairs and sun umbrellas along the length of the beach.

When the weather is settled Cane Garden is a delightful anchorage with good holding, however, during the winter months, when the northerly ground swells build and the surf is breaking on the reef, it is advisable to seek another anchorage.

Navigation & Piloting

Approaching from the west, you will sail past Smuggler's Cove, Belmont, Long Bay and Carrot Bay before reaching Cane Garden Bay. If you have any doubt, or your GPS is not working, line up the south side of Jost Van Dyke directly under the peak of Tobago and this range will bring you to the entrance.

The entrance to Cane Garden is toward the northern end of the bay; the reef extends both north and south and is marked with two sets of red and green buoys. During our last visit (May 2019) both sets of buoys were missing. Should this be the case then use your chart plotter when entering. Enter between the buoys and once well inside the reef you will have plenty of room to anchor on a sand bottom or pick up one of the numerous mooring balls. The various establishments usually send an emissary out in a dinghy to collect mooring fees just about the time you are settling into the first gin and tonic.

Anchoring & Mooring

When anchoring, keep clear of the marker buoys (missing May 2019) designating the swimming area. The bottom affords excellent holding in 15-20 feet of water. The moorings usually identify the establishment responsible for collecting the fees.

PUSSER'S *at Myett's*

On the beach . . . Cane Garden Bay, Tortola . . . Beautiful Night & Day

LUNCH & DINNER, A delightful blend of West Indian & American cuisine.

- AND -

Pusser's Company Store, fully stocked with the Pusser's Collection of the Caribbean's most extensive line of Tropical, Nautical, Casualwear.

ECLECTIC, TRADITIONAL, FUNCTIONAL, COMFORTABLE, *Certainly Not Fashion!*

For Reservations call: 495-9381 • 495-4554

SHOP THE PUSSER'S CO. STORE ONLINE AT WWW.PUSSERS.COM

Owing to the mountainous backdrop to the bay, the wind tends to change direction, so check your swinging room in relation to other vessels, particularly if you are on an anchor and close to the mooring field. Please exercise caution maneuvering through the bay as there are often swimmers making their way across the bay by way of the great circle route. During the winter months, If there is a northerly ground swell developing, the prudent skipper will seek another anchorage.

Ashore

To experience a sunset at Cane Garden Bay is nothing less than a special magic that creates an unforgettable memory. It is a quintessential Caribbean beach with the sounds of reggae in the background, the palm leaves rustling in the trade winds and the long white beach framing the clear turquoise waters of the bay.

The dinghy dock in Cane Garden Bay is located in the middle of the bay by the rocks. It was severely damaged by the storm and had only received some repairs when we last visited. Extreme caution should be used when using this dock and the adjacent stairway to the road. On the northwest side of the bay is the Cane Garden Bay public dock where you can tie up to fill your water and fuel tanks and buy ice at Hodges Gas Station. However, there are no overnight facilities at this dock. The dock head has approximately 9 feet of water, be sure to check the depth at the dock before moving your boat there. Do not attempt to tie up at the dock with a ground sea running. There is a garbage dumpster adjacent to the marina.

Cane Garden Bay is lined by several terrific beach bars for the choosing. There is almost always live entertainment nightly at one establishment or another, or at several! Check ashore to find where the music will be on any given night.

Next to the dinghy dock is Quito's, newly refurbished and serving lunch and dinner. Quito performs alone and with his band, The Edge, several nights a week. Quito's is a favorite amongst both visitors and locals. The place is jamming when the band is playing! Quito's new hotel is now finished and should be considered the first "high rise" on the CGB beach.

Just west of Quito's on the beach is Paradise Club open from 7am serving delicious breakfasts, lunch, dinner and drinks at the bar inside, or on the deck outside. Paradise Club sustained considerable damage but a resilient crew kept the place open.

Rhymer's Beach Bar and Restaurant further west along the beach is the pink building. Rhymer's serves breakfast, lunch and dinner daily with live entertainment on special occasions. Ice, telephones, showers, and a small market stocking most necessities, are available on the premises.

Further down the beach and well worth the walk is Pusser's at Myett's Garden Grill Restaurant, nestled in the palm trees. The restaurant, which is now a joint venture with Pusser's is open for breakfast, lunch and dinner daily with reservations. Stop in for happy hour. There is usually live music playing most nights featuring calypso, funk or reggae. Check out the Pusser's Company store and Olivia's Corner Store. An ATM is available if you need to replenish cash. Try the new spa for some massage therapy, facials, manicures and hair waxing. The communications center is complete with telephones, fax and computers with high-speed internet. WiFi is also available to guests. Myett's also rents watersports equipment including kayaks, SUPs, snorkel gear and other fun non-motorized water toys.

For a different experience in a local setting, try Banana's Bar and Grill across from the taxi stand and park. The atmosphere is comfortably elegant, clean and sophisticated. The menu runs from $15-$25 for an entree and there is a comfortable bar to lean on. Reservations recommended.

The Elm Restaurant and Bar is open daily until 7pm, 5pm on Sundays. They have live music and barbecues on Friday and Sunday afternoons. Elm also has guest cottages available.

Supplies can be purchased from a well-stocked branch of Bobby's Market on the road behind the beach, or at Callwood's Grocery Store, Rhymer's Beach Bar, and Pleasure Boats and Provisioning. There is a police station located near Bobby's Market. There is also a garbage dumpster across from Bobby's.

Mr. Callwood's Rum Distillery at the south end of the bay affords visitors a glimpse back into history. White and gold rum are still produced from the cane grown on the hillsides and the product bears the label Arundel from the name of the estate purchased by the Callwood family in the late 1800s. It is recommended that you ask permission prior to wandering around the distillery and the purchase of a bottle or two is expected.

Callwood Distillery

Pusser's at Myett's

Cane Garden Bay

Soper's Hole/West End

Tortola

Waypoints: BV115(N) 18°22.80'N, 64°45.50'W;
BV116(S) 18°22.70'N, 64°41.90'W
Navigation: 7nm SW Road Harbour;
4.5nm SE of Jost Van Dyke
Services: Note: At press time, Soper's Hole was
still under construction and therefore the implied
services to follow assume that construction
continues as planned, on time and that all parties
can come to terms on contractual matters.
BVI Port of Entry, Provisions, Dockage, Moorings, Ice,
Water, Fuel, WiFi, Laundry, Slipway, Restaurants,
Taxi, Car rental, Garbage disposal

West End is shown on the charts as Soper's Hole, a very deep well-protected harbor,
about a mile long, lying between Frenchman's Cay to the south and Tortola. It is a port of
entry for vessels arriving and departing British waters, and a ferry stop between the
British Virgin Islands and the US Virgin Islands. Ferries also depart from this bay to
Jost Van Dyke.

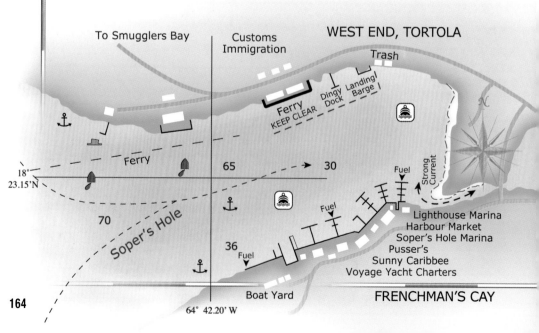

Navigation & Piloting

Approaching from the north the favored passage would be to enter Soper's Hole between Steele Point at the west end of Tortola and Great Thatch. There is plenty of water but be prepared for some pretty fickle wind changes and occasional heavy gusts off the surrounding hills. If you are entering from Drake's Channel, slip in between Little Thatch and Frenchman's Cay. Once again there is deep water fairly close to shore but be prepared for a strong current.

As you enter the anchorage, there is a buoyed channel on the northern side of the bay. This is largely for commercial craft and leads to the customs and immigration services located at the government ferry dock; private vessels should proceed east down the center of the anchorage. Vessels wishing to clear in and out of the BVI are permitted to anchor, or to pick up a mooring. The dinghy dock servicing the ferry terminal was destroyed by the storm along with the terminal. The BVI Government have indicated that a new temporary facility will be in place by October 2019 that will allow the reinstatement of ferry traffic between the USVI and BVI. It is hoped that a new dinghy dock will be included in the plan.

Anchoring & Mooring

The harbor is so deep in places that yachts will find themselves in 60-70 feet of water. There are numerous mooring balls available at the normal rate for overnight, (no charge for a short lunchtime stop) but should you decide to anchor and assuming the vessel is under 50 feet the best place is up in the northeast corner where the water depth is 20-35 feet or to the west of the mooring field in deeper water.

There are moorings available from Soper's Hole Wharf & Marina, which are maintained by Moor-Seacure and can be paid for at the marina. Further to the west there are mooring balls available from Soper's Hole Yacht Services. Be sure not to obstruct the slipway. Most of the marinas monitor VHF 16.

Customs & Immigration

The following information assumes that the BVI Government are able to build a temporary terminal to facilitate international clearance of commercial vessels in time for the 2019/20 season. If this does not happen then commercial vessels will continue to clear in Roadtown.

The original terminal, shut down since 2017, remains in the planning stage. The BVI Government indicated that an extension to the existing temporary facility that would enable international arrivals from neighboring islands, would be in place and operational by season 2018. That date came and went! The current plan calls for the facility to be up and running for the season 2019/20. This temporary solution would include a trailer, restrooms and enough area to house, Customs and Immigration in addition to ticket counters for the various ferry services. They are open Monday through Saturday from 7:45am to 6pm and 7:45am to 7pm on Sundays and public holidays. Vessels arriving in the BVI after hours are required to fly a yellow "Q" flag, and the crew must remain aboard until the vessel is properly cleared. Credit cards are accepted over $25.

Ashore

Post Irma: It should be noted that the West End/Soper's Hole anchorage sustained heavy damage from the storm and rebuilding efforts have been ongoing. During our last visit (May 2019) we were delighted to note that Frenchman's Cay was in the midst of being rebuilt as close as possible to what it was pre storm. For those of you who have visited in the past, you'll remember the quaint iconic village of shops and restaurants painted in bright tropical and pastel colours, with gingerbread trim and craftsmen detail.

At that time, the entire dock and bulkhead system was undergoing repair and rebuilding with cranes and heavy

equipment working on turning a page back in history, at least visually. Logically all the service companies, with the notable exception of Voyage Yacht Charters, Soper's Hole Marina, Omar's Restaurant and the slipway were closed.

The following information is predicated upon the docks and infrastructure being finished by October/November 2019 but there are never any guarantees as weather and availability of construction equipment and materials can be capricious. Although the anchor businesses, like Pusser's and Harbour Market, have indicated that they will be up and operational by season, their time to market is contingent upon the dock work and infrastructure completion. As this edition of the *Cruising Guide* heads to the printer, hulls and abandoned and dismasted boats still lay on the sand spit at the head of the harbor, hopefully gone by season.

For provisioning, the two story Harbour Market (Riteway) will be opening again and is located at the base of the marina east of Pusser's. Normal opening hours are 7:45am to 6:30pm. Harbour Market offers a large variety of provisions, gourmet foods, liquor, beer and wine. Credit cards are accepted.

Soper's Hole Marina is open 8am to 5pm along with Voyage Yacht Charters. The marina can accommodate vessels up to 180' with a 20' draft. Slips and moorings are available, as well as well as fuel, water and ice. VHF16. Shower facilities are available for marina guests.

Dockage, water and ice are also available at the Lighthouse Marina. They are open from 8 am to 5 pm. Slips are available for yachts up to 160' with a draft of 25-35'. Call ahead. Duty-free bulk fuel can be arranged by prior appointment. Admiral Marine Management has been owned and operated by Olly Alsop since 2007. They offer long and short term yacht management and full project management. Richard Stein is operations manager and will add a lot of assistance and bit of humour to your day. Located within the marina is the newly rebuilt Admiral Pub, offering a full service bar as well as some good food. The menu is simple just a different dish every night. Expect lawn games for participators as well as spectators.

The two story Pusser's Landing will be back featuring waterfront dining with two restaurants and bars, an outdoor terrace and the Pusser's Company Store. Downstairs, the restaurant offers a more casual ambiance, with an open air bar, on the deck dining and the Company Store which carries Pusser's special line of nautical and tropical clothing, watches, and nautical accessories. Upstairs the Crow's Nest Restaurant offers a more elegant dining experience although the menus are the same. Friday, Saturday, and Sunday nights you can dance to the sounds of live music! Pusser's is open seven days a week and monitors VHF channel 16. WiFi is available.

For a completely different dining and bar experience try Omar's Fusion restaurant, located down toward the boatyard. Owner operated, they serve a fusion of Indian inspired dishes at a reasonable price. There is also a bar with some outside seating. For a morning coffee or breakfast Omar's Café next to the Harbour Market nicely situated in a small courtyard they feature, in addition to a great breakfast menu, a variety of coffee drinks, ice cream, smoothies, pastries, beer, wine, sandwiches and snacks. WiFi is available.

It is our understanding that the Arawak boutique will be back with their excellent selection of merchandise including clothing and accessories, along with Sunny Caribee for a unique selection of Caribbean spices and island gifts. Regrettably the building that houses Blue Water Divers will not be finished until early 2020 but they can be contacted at their Nanny Cay base.

Further to the west, Soper's Hole Yacht Services (boatyard) has, in addition to a standard travel lift, a KMI SeaLift that can haul almost any kind of vessel up to a 14 foot draft including monohulls and catamarans. The yard offers fuel, water, showers, provisioning and WiFi. Security is provided around the clock. They are open Monday through Friday from 8am to 4pm. Discounted bulk diesel fuel is also available by arrangement.

Rental cars by the day or week can be obtained from Shaun Smith at Soper's Hole Car Rentals on Frenchman's Cay behind the Soper's Hole Marina office (284-547-9652). If Shaun doesn't have a car available, try Denzel Kline, located on the road toward town, they will deliver a rental vehicle to a west end location.

Laundry services are available on Frenchman's Cay just to the west of Omar's Fusion restaurant. Alternatively on the north side of the harbour, just a short walk towards town, there is another laundry service (Surbash) where you can DIY or leave it and pick it up later in the day.

Pre-storm there was a small but well stocked marine chandlery store (Sink or Swim Marine Supply) to the east of Harbour Market in a lime green building at the end of the boardwalk. We assume that they will open again once the dock infrastructure is completed. The building also houses a sister company L'Amore where you can indulge in a gelato sitting under an umbrella outside. They also serve coffee drinks, sandwiches and smoothies.

All photos taken pre-hurricane

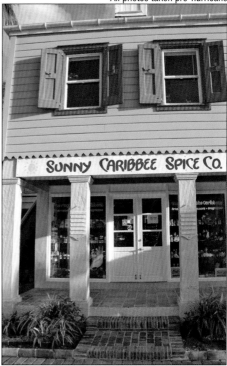

169

Nanny Cay
(Hannah Bay)

Tortola

Waypoint: BV117 (18°23.00N, 64°38.50W)
Navigation: 2.2nm SW of Road Harbour / 4.2nm East of Soper's Hole
Services: Full service 200 berth marina, Chandlery, Hotel, Ice, Garbage disposal, Provisions, Restaurants and bars, WiFi, Pump out, Fuel, Water, Nanny Cay is not a port of entry

Approaching Hannah Bay or Nanny Cay from Road Town to the east, or Soper's Hole to the west, the first landmark will be the masts of the boats hauled out in the boatyard and at the dock. Nanny Cay forms a peninsula, jutting out from the south coast of Tortola and was originally developed by dredging an entrance through the reef at the south end of the bay. Fully protected from the northeast trade winds, Nanny Cay Marina and Hannah Bay Marina offer a full service marine environment. There is no room for anchoring once inside the breakwater and no moorings are available.

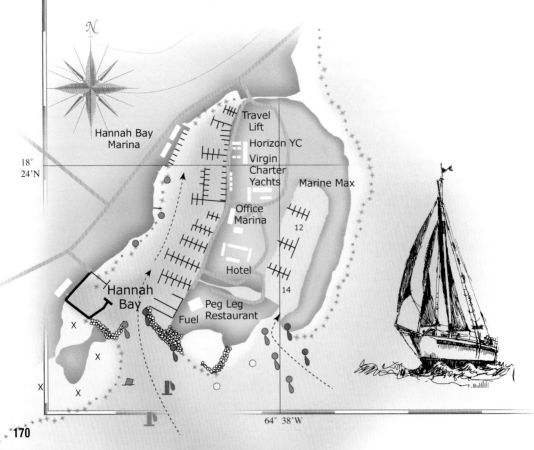

N

Hannah Bay Marina

Travel Lift

Horizon YC

Virgin Charter Yachts

Marine Max

Office Marina

12

Hotel

14

18° 24'N

Hannah Bay

Peg Leg Restaurant

Fuel

64° 38'W

Navigation & Piloting

Whether making your approach from the east or west it is advisable to stay a quarter mile off the shoreline in order to avoid the coral and shoal water extending from the south shoreline of Tortola and to the east and north into Sea Cow Bay.

Recent expansion of the marina complex has included a second entrance channel to the east of the main entrance. Both channels are well marked with two sets of markers, but it advisable to check with the dock master (VHF16/68) before entering. There are two yellow buoys between channels defining the shoreline. Yachts with a draft over ten feet (but with a maximum of 11.5 feet) should call the marina first for instructions on VHF channel 16 as access is dependent on the state of the tide.

Head for the southernmost point of Nanny Cay until the lighted red and green channel markers are visible. The main channel will be to port. Stay in the center of the channel and follow the red and green markers NNW between the breakwaters and into the bay. The inner markers are on the breakwater. The first set of markers inside the breakwater are stakes and the channel will carry 10 feet. There are invariably several yachts anchored to the west just inside the entrance, this is shallow and designated as a no anchoring zone. The 20 slip marina on your port hand (Hannah Bay) is operated by Nanny Cay. Hannah Bay Marina is to your port and the Nanny Cay Resort & Marina extend off to the right.

Since the Nanny Cay Marina runs at high occupancy, it is advisable to contact the marina on VHF 16 or 68 prior to arrival should a berth be required. The fuel dock and pump out station is on your starboard hand just beyond the breakwater. Hours of operation are 8am to 6:30pm. Remember that this is a floating dock so adjust your fenders accordingly.

Ashore

Post Irma, almost all of the docks have been replaced and starting at the fuel dock are renumbered A-K. The 200 slip marina can accommodate yachts up to 140 feet long, 10-foot draft, and 33 feet wide. Amenities available within the marina include two high- speed fuel docks; 120/220V electricity; luxury shower facilities and restrooms; water and ice from Nanny Cay's own R/O plant; pump out station; laundry; garbage disposal; and 100% site-wide backup power. Storage lockers may be rented through the marina. There is also a First Bank ATM on-site at the Nanny Cay taxi stand by the marina office.

The new outer marina expansion project is now operational and the new docks (L-R) are now in use. There is a fuel dock as you enter the new marina basin and the docks start at L. Marine Max in their new home, operate from the innermost docks, adjacent to their new operations center. Expansion will continue providing an additional 120 slips suitable for yachts 30-75' with T-heads and bulkheads capable of berthing mega yachts to 160' in length. The first half of the new marina has a controlling depth of 14', the second half 12'. The 6.5 acre outer marina peninsula will have eight new condo blocks each with four, three bedroom condo units.

Provisioning: Riteway Supermarket provides both retail and provisioning services. The market is well stocked and organized. CYM Management stocks a good selection of South African wines, soft drinks and food products.

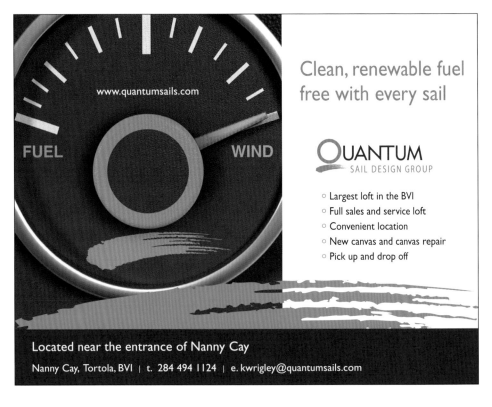

Chandlery: The Nanny Cay Chandlery is now independent and housed in a new two-level building with over 4,000 square feet of retail and office space on the ground floor and a further 2,000 square feet of warehouse space upstairs enabling the provision of a large inventory on-island with a high level of convenience and stock availability. Open 7 days a week. Mon-Fri 8am-5pm, Sat 8am-4pm, Sun 8am-3pm.

Marine Services: There is a wide variety of services based at Nanny Cay and a complete listing can be obtained from their website (nannycay.com). Cay Electronics have been operating since 1982 and moved to Nanny Cay from Road Town several years ago. Yacht Management Services are provided by Johnny's Maritime, who have been operating for 25 years (284-494-3661), or CYM Yachts (official Oyster repair center).

Mechanical and refrigeration services are well represented by Aquadoc, Tradewinds Yachting Services, Marine Maintenance Services, BVI Marine Management and Marine Cooling Systems (284-441-6556). Tradewinds is

NANNY CAY

the BVI Yamaha dealer and service center. They also supply Caribe, Walker Bay and AB inflatables. Located behind the Galley Café, they have a fully stocked parts department, factory trained technicians and a new management team focused on the customer experience.

Quantum Sails: A full service loft, the team can build and repair your sails and provide expert custom canvas work (284-494-1124).

EXCEPTIONAL VACATIONS

DIFFERENT IN EVERY WAY

UNITED *by* WATER
MARINEMAX
VACATIONS

2015 Winner
Best BVI Yacht
Charter Company

CHARTER YACHT VACATIONS TO BE ENVIED

Indulge in an unforgettable adventure aboard a new custom built power catamaran where you will discover the British Virgin Islands in a whole new way. Where unprecedented upgrades are standard and custom designs are spacious for your luxury vacation. Exceeded only by our team's service commitment and expertise, discover why your experience will be different in every way.

Charter Yacht Ownership Program:
Benefits to owners include fixed monthly payments, zero operating expense and professional MarineMax management. *Financing available. Trade-ins considered.*

Yacht Charter Vacations
888-461-5497 • 813-644-8071

38   44   48
Power Catamarans

Yacht Ownership Program
866-934-7232 • 813-644-8070

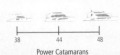

www.marinemaxvacations.com

174

For shipwright and rigging services, visit The Yacht Shop. Rigging Services: Richardson's Rigging (284-494-2739) and Wickhams Cay II Rigging, now located just to the west of the marina (284-494-3979).

Painting and gelcoat services are provided by BVI Painters and V.I. Marine Refinishing.

Yacht Charter Services: Horizon Yacht Charters (284-494-8787), a highly regarded charter company, makes Nanny Cay Marina their base of operations, along with MarineMax, who have recently moved their base of operations from Scrub Island to Nanny Cay, operate a fleet of custom charter designed power-cats from 38-48'. They are located at the outer marina in their new facility and can be reached by

VHF16 . Virgin Charter Yachts operated by Alexia and Gary Lucas operate a fleet of 16 power yachts that include two luxury fully crewed Sunseeker yachts in addition to bareboat, powerboats and monohulls. They operate from H-dock 284-495-2526 or VHF 16. Vacances Sous Voiles (VsV) are Hanse dealers and offer bareboat and crewed services.

Boatyard: Nanny Cay's full-service boatyard has storage for 260 yachts and two boat lifts. One is a conventional Acme Marine Hoist capable of lifting monohulls up to 68 feet long, 10 feet draft and weighing up to 50 tons. The other is a wide-body Marine Travelift, capable of lifting and moving catamarans up to 32 foot beam and 70 tons in weight making it the widest lift capacity in the BVI and the largest capacity lift of its type north of Trinidad.

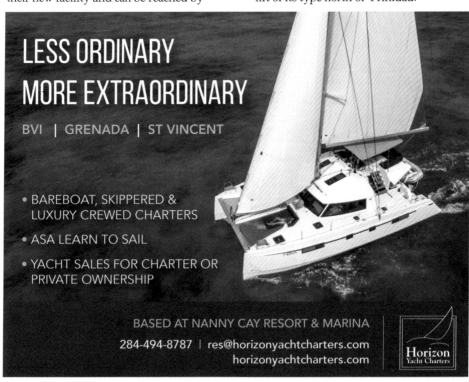

Nanny Cay also offers a highly secure cradle storage system that earned its status as an approved hurricane storage facility by Pantaenius, one of the world's leading insurers of luxury yachts.

Hotel: The hotel, nestled in a tropical garden, offers standard and deluxe hotel rooms as well as the recently completed waterfront two and three-bedroom townhouses. The townhouses can accommodate up to six guests and offer a view of the channel. They also have private decks with dock space for a small powerboat. Post Irma almost all of the hotel rooms have been refurbished.

Shopping & Gifts: For the shopper, Arawak Boutique sells clothing, souvenirs and interesting gifts.

Restaurants & Bars: Complementing the marina are two restaurants and a beach bar. The Galley Café is open for lunch and dinner in the heart of the marina. The Beach Bar, on the beach adjacent to the pool has become a full scale restaurant for casual dining since the destruction of Peg-Leg Landing in the storm. For dinner, chairs and tables are set out on the sand offering a casual

Caribbean experience. Both are open seven days a week. Captain Mulligan's, located at the entrance to the Nanny Cay complex is a casual sport's bar serving hot wings, ribs and burgers in an open air environment from 11am daily.

Dive, Powerboat Rentals & Sailing Schools: Blue Water Divers, a well-established dive company, has been based in Nanny Cay for over twenty years. They operate a dive shop, conduct dive tours and perform in-water bottom cleaning. Nanny Cay is their main base of operations. Island Time rents powerboats by the day, or longer.

There is property-wide free WiFi access for guests. There is currently no Customs and Immigration at Nanny Cay. You must clear in at one of the ports of entry.

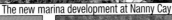
The new marina development at Nanny Cay

SEA COW BAY/MANUEL REEF MARINA

Waypoint: BV117 18°23.00'N; 64°38.50'W

Navigation: 5.5 nm NW West End,
2nm SW Road Harbour

Services: Dockage, Water, Ice, Garbage Disposal,
Showers, Electricity, Restaurant, Market,
Chandlery, Laundry

Tortola

Tucked up into the coastline north of Nanny Cay is Sea Cow Bay and Manuel Reef Marina. Totally protected from the prevailing trades, this 40 slip marina has matured substantially since our last visit and provides an excellent spot for owners to leave their vessels under management service while away from the island. The maximum water depth is 9 feet.

Navigation & Piloting

Approaching from the southwest (BV117) and the Sir Francis Drake Channel, continue past Nanny Cay until you are able to see all the way up into Sea Cow Bay and the end of the dock at the marina (about 329°m). The shoreline is dotted with reefs so make sure

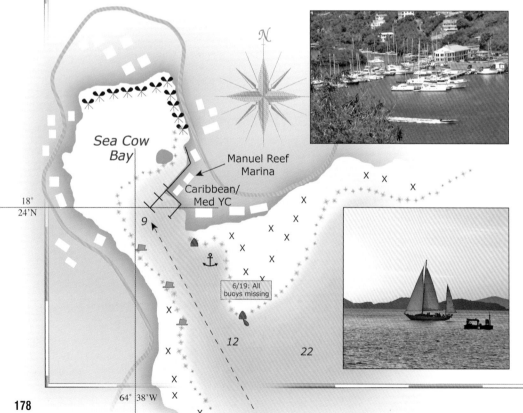

Sea Cow
Bay

Manuel Reef
Marina

Caribbean/
Med YC

6/19: All
buoys missing

9

18°
24'N

12

22

64° 38'W

you are in the center of the channel. Since the hurricane all navigation markers are missing (May 2019) so caution should be exercised in order to identify the edge of the outer reef on your starboard hand due south of the condominium buildings. At the time of the last survey, the center of the channel was marked with an outer PVC post and an inner red buoy (floating). It is recommended that you contact the harbormaster on VHF16 for updates to navigation aids. The first dock, north side is utilized by MedCaribbean Charters. The south side is very shallow.

Anchoring & Mooring

Owing to the very shallow nature of Sea Cow Bay, the only option other than docking at the marina would be to anchor in 10-12 feet of water just out of the channel on the starboard side

before the bulkhead. There are usually two or three yachts anchored here, so make sure that you do not swing into the channel.

There are two docks, both with T-heads. The second dock is for transients. Call the marina on VHF 16 for docking instruction. The Marina Manager is Dean Simmonds and Henry is the dock master. There are 10-15 transient slips at $1.30/foot for monohulls and $1.60 for cats. There is no fuel. Water is $0.15 per gallon.

Ashore

Manuel Reef Marina is conveniently situated between Nanny Cay and Road Town. The marina offers electricity, water, showers and a large laundry facility.

Provisioning is available from the Manuel Reef Supermarket, which is clean and well organized although not adequate for a full provisioning service. Right next door is the Captain's Choice Chandlery that is surprisingly well stocked. Owned and operated by Natalie Etwaru.

MedCaribbean Charters operate a fleet of 15 yachts (monohull and catamaran) and moved to Manuel Reef from East End after the storm. Owners William and Maria offer late model yachts at very reasonable prices in a European style charter service.

A full laundry service (BMS) is available daily 6am to 7pm or you can do it yourself (284-541-2405)

C&R's Car and Jeep Rentals can be reached at 284-494-0573.

Gene's Restaurant and Bar (284-495-3086) is closed Tuesdays, serving lunch and dinner. There is also Dr. Georges Medical Clinic if you need some help. They can be reached by telephone at 284-494-0971.

The Sensus Gym is on the top floor. 123 Hulls Yacht Sales also offers repairs and yacht management services. The marina is also the base for Sabbatical Yacht Charters and The Captain's Compass Yacht Charters. Storage units are available from the marina office.

ISLAND CONNECTIONS

999 or 911
VISAR (Virgin Island Search and Rescue)
Tel: 767 (SOS), or
+1 284 499 0911
www.visar.org

BREWER'S BAY

RESTAURANTS
Nicole's Beach Bar (Brewer's Bay)
FB: Nicoles-Brewers-Bay-Beach-Bar
Beach bar serving island drinks with a great view

CANE GARDEN BAY

EMERGENCIES
Police
Tel: 284-368-5371

RESTAURANTS
Quito's Gazebo & Inn
Tel: 1 284-495-4837
www.quitosltd.com
FB: QuitosGazebo
Breakfast 7-10am daily, mimosas, Bloody Marys and pancakes. Lunch 11am-4pm daily, burgers, wraps, pizzas. Live music and happy hour at 5pm. Dinner: burgers, jerk BBQ etc. Free WiFi and beach chairs for customers.

Banana's Bar & Grill
Tel: 1 (284) 440-3252
FB: Bananas-Bar-Grill
Daily lunch & dinner 11am-10pm, cocktails, frozen drinks, water view, pizza, conch fritters, burgers (Friday can takeout)

Elm Beach Bar
Tel: 284-494-2888
FB: Elm-Bar-Cane-Garden-Bay

Dinner: tuna, ribs and chicken specials, BBQ nights, live music

Rhymer's Beach Bar & Restaurant
Tel: (284) 495-4639
FB: Rhymers-Beach-Hotel
www.rhymersbvi.com
Breakfast 8-11am, lunch 11am-5pm, burgers, chicken, roti, conch fritters, dinner 6-9pm, happy hour 5-7pm: lobster, shrimps, fish, mahi, swordfish, tuna

Pusser's at Myett's
Tel: (284) 495-9381/ 4554
www.myetts.com/pussers-at-myetts
FB: MyettsBVI
Breakfast, brunch, lunch 8am-3pm; dinner, 6-10(ish) pm, happy hour 4-7pm

Paradise Club Lounge Bar & Restaurant
Tel: 284-345-2541 or 284-495-9910
FB: paradiseclubvi
Lounge, live music, DJs Sun-Th 10am-10pm, Fri-Sat, 10am-12am

PROVISIONING
Bobby's Market
Tel: 284-494-2189
bobbyssupermarket.com
Fresh meat, wines and liquors, fresh produce. Free pickup and delivery anywhere in the BVI 7am-12am 7 days/week

Cane Garden Bay Pleasure Boats & Provisioning
284-495-9660

WEST END / SOPER'S HOLE

CUSTOMS & IMMIGRATION
West End Customs
Tel: 284-495-4221

West End Immigration
Tel: 284-495-4443
www.bvi.gov.vg
Check for current business hours to clear in.

MARINAS
Soper's Hole Wharf & Marina / Voyage Charters
Tel: 284-346-5550 or 284-346-5501
FB: Sopers-Hole-Wharf-Marina-West-End-Tortola-British-Virgin-Islands
VHF 16
Dockage, mooring balls, water, diesel, gasoline, ice 8am-5:30pm

LightHouse Marina/ Admiral Marine Management
Tel: 284-340-1715 or 284-340-1716
www.admiralbvi.com

CHARTER COMPANIES
Voyage Charters
Tel: 284-346-5501
Tel and WhatsApp: 284-346-5550
bvi@voyagecharters.com
FB: VOYAGEcharters
VHF: 16/11
Dockage, mooring balls, water, diesel, gasoline, ice 8am-5:30pm

MARINE/BOATYARD SERVICES

B&G Marine Services
Tel: 1-284-345-2656
www.bgbvi.com
FB: bgbvi
info@bgbvi.com
Install/repair/maint. of mechanical, electrical, AC, refrigeration, solar, wind, hydroelectric, plumbing (fresh/gray water, septic, watermakers), varnish, interior/exterior detailing

Soper's Hole Yacht Services
Tel: 284-495-4589
VHF 16
sopersholeyachtservices.com

RESTAURANTS

Pusser's Landing
Restaurant & Bar
Tel: 284-495-4554 Pre-Storm#
www.pussers.com

Omar's Fusion
Tel: 284-495-8015
www.omarscafebvi.com

Omar's Cafe
Tel:284-495-8015
www.omarscafebvi.com

Admiral's Pub
Lighthouse Marina
Tel: 284-340-1715
www.admiralbvi.com

CAR RENTAL

Soper's Hole Car Rental
Tel: 284-346-9652 or
284-547-9652
sopersholecarrental.com
shcarrentals@outlook.com

PROVISIONING

Harbour Market
284-495-4423

Seafood Kingdom
(Just outside of Soper's Hole)
Tel: 284 495 1100
FB: seafoodkingdombvi
Best way to order: seafood.
kingdom22@gmail.com
Seafood, responsibly sourced, individually packaged, 24-hour orders. Free delivery to all major bases.

NANNY CAY

MARINAS

Nanny Cay Marina
Tel: (284) 394 2512
www.nannycay.com/marina
FB: nannycay
VHF 16, 8am-6:30pm daily
100+ slips, 8 for megayachts, 2 fuel docks, electricity, ice, pump-out, garbage, showers, bar, restaurant, chandlery, boatyard, haul-out, painting, rigging, electronics, surveyors, engineering, woodwork

RESTAURANTS

The Galley
Tel: 284-394-2512
nannycay.com/restaurants
FB: nannycay
Lunch & dinner: pizza, burgers, rotisserie chicken, sandwiches

BEACH BAR

Tel: 284-394-2512
nannycay.com/restaurants
FB: nannycay
Open 11am

Grill Shak
Tel: 1 284 394 2512
nannycay.com/restaurants
BBQ every night, specials

Captain Mulligan's Sports Bar
Tel: 284-494-0602

FB: Captain-Mulligans
Burgers, wings, pizza
11am-12am

PROVISIONING

Rite Way
Tel: 284-347-1188
www.rtwbvi.com

HOTELS

Nanny Cay Hotel
Tel: 284-394-2512
www.nannycay.com

MARINE SERVICES

Nanny Cay Boatyard
Tel: 284-345 2658
nannycay.com/boatyard
Haul/launch, 3 lifts, haul-out, marine engineering, woodwork, painting, rigging, electronics, surveyors, can accommodate over 50 tons, wide lifts, 32' beam

BVI Marine Management
Tel: 284-340-2938 or
284-541-7615
service@bvimm.com
Welding, fabrication, machining, engine repairs, refitting, repowering
8:30am-5pm

Cay Electronics
Tel: 284-494-2400
www.cayelectronics.com
rob@cayelectronics.vg
Marine systems engineers, navigation, marine electronics, installation, servicing, nav equipment, (Raymarine, Garmin, etc), sales, repairs, power or sail
M-F 8:30am-5pm

Johnny's Maritime Services
Tel: 284-494-3661
FB: Johnnys-Maritime-Services

ISLAND CONNECTIONS

Charters, repairs, can rendezvous outside of Nanny Cay

BVI Painters
Tel: 284-494-4365 or
284-499-2862
www.bvipainter.com
Brightwork, coppercoat, fibreglass, gelcoat scratch repairs, hand polishing, marine refinishing, osmosis repairs, painting, AwlGrip and varnish, antifouling, scratch and dent repair

BVI Yacht Sales
Tel: 284-544-6607 or
284-494-3260
www.bviyachtsales.com
info@bviyachtsales.com
M-F 9am-5pm

Caribbean Marine Surveyors
Tel: 284 346-1576 or 284 346 2091
www.caribsurveyors.com
info@caribsurveyors.com,
Survey types: insurance, purchase, phase-out, tonnage, cargo, and damage

Wickham's Cay II Rigging
Tel: 1 284-345-3979 or
284-494-3979
www.wickrigging.com
FB: WickhamsCayIIRigging
info.wickrigging@gmail.com
Rigging, chandlery with large inventory, rigging inspections, tunes, winch servicing, splicing, bridles, dinghy & tender towing/lifts, complete re-rigs, unstepping/stepping masts, hydraulics

Richardson's Rigging Services
Tel: 284-494-2739 or
284-499-4774
rrsbvi@gmail.com

VI Marine Refinishing
Tel: 284-494-0361 or
284-499-1636
vim@surfbvi.com
vimrefinishing@yahoo.com

SAIL LOFT
Quantum Sails
Tel: 284-494-1124
www.quantumsails.com

DIVING/ WATERSPORTS
Blue Water Divers
Tel: 284-494-2847
www.bluewaterdiversbvi.com
FB: Blue-Water-Divers-British-Virgin-Islands
WhatsApp: 284-340-4311
Skype: bluewaternanny
VHF 16
Multiple boats, dive tours and certification courses, certified PADI training facility, SSI dealer, quality equipment, multiple dive sites & dive options, contact to reserve

CHARTER COMPANIES
Virgin Motor Yacht Charters
Tel: 284-495-2526
www.virgincharteryachts.com
FB: virginmotoryachts
9am-5pm 7 days/week

Horizon Yacht Charters
Tel: 284-494-8787
www.horizonyachtcharters.com/bvi/nanny-cay-base
Skype: Hycbvi.reservations

MarineMax Vacations
Tel: 888-461-5497
marinemaxvacations.com

CAR & BOAT RENTALS
Island Time
Tel: 284-495-9993
www.islandtimeltd.com
FB: islandtimebvi
info@islandtimeltd.com
Rentals, variety of sizes and types of powerboats and RIBS, cars, adventure tours, boat and jeep tours, water taxi 8:30am-5pm, 7 days/week

MANUEL REEF MARINA

Manuel Reef Marina
Tel: 284-4 94-0445
manuelreefmarinabvi.com

RESTAURANTS
Gene's Bar & Grill (Manuel Reef Marina)
Phone: 284-545-7765
robin.sookraj3@gmail.com
Drop in or call for reservations

PROVISIONING
Manuel Reef Supermarket
Tel: 1 284-494-0931
FB:bvisupermarket
bviparkandsave@gmail.com
9am-8pm 7 days/week

CHARTER COMPANIES
MedCaribbean Charters
Manuel Reef Marina
Tel: 284 346 2242
info@medcaribbean.com
English & Spanish

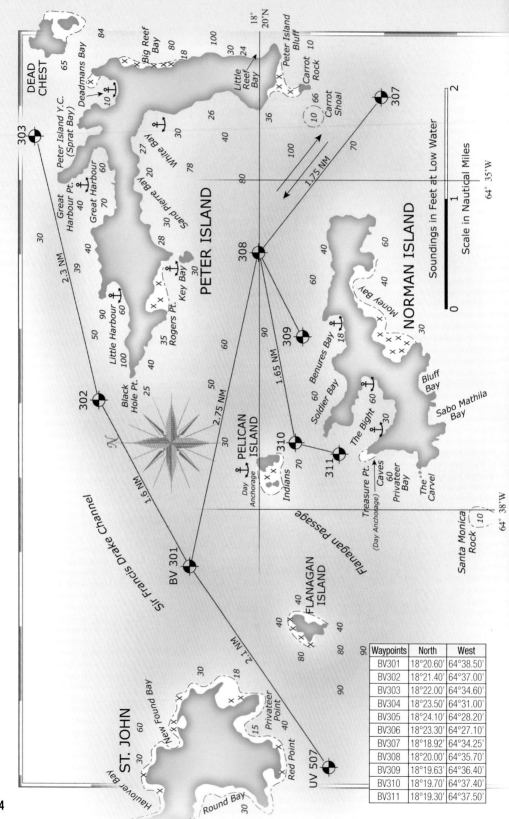

Waypoints	North	West
BV301	18°20.60'	64°38.50'
BV302	18°21.40'	64°37.00'
BV303	18°22.00'	64°34.60'
BV304	18°23.50'	64°31.00'
BV305	18°24.10'	64°28.20'
BV306	18°23.30'	64°27.10'
BV307	18°18.92'	64°34.25'
BV308	18°20.00'	64°35.70'
BV309	18°19.63'	64°36.40'
BV310	18°19.70'	64°37.40'
BV311	18°19.30'	64°37.50'

THE CHANNEL ISLANDS
NORMAN & PETER

The Sir Francis Drake Channel, named for the famed and successful circumnavigating privateer and Queen's rogue, has also been known as *Freebooter's Gangway* and played host

Charts
NV.Charts: St. Thomas to Anegada: Kit C-13 & 14
NIMA: 2561, Imray Iolaire; A-231
Admiralty Leisure: 5640-5, 6, 7

to the famous and infamous characters who underpin the golden age of piracy as England fought to sabotage Spain in an effort to gain wealth and territory. Today the channel provides an ideal sailing ground for the visiting yachtsman, offering many excellent anchorages and dive sites to explore within a short distance of one and other. Norman Island is replete with history of buried treasure and discovery. Visit the William

The Bight

Thornton (Willy T) in the Bight for an evening of fun, or eat ashore at Pirates Bight. Snorkel the caves at Treasure Point or dive the Indians. Further to the north is Peter Island with many beautiful bays in which to anchor, turquoise water to snorkel and shipwrecks on which to dive. Discover the wreck of *RMS Rhone* at Salt Island, Manchineel Bay at Cooper Island and The Dogs at the head of the channel, all with their own charm and attractions. It would be easy to spend an entire week discovering this incredible chain of islands.

THE BIGHT
NORMAN ISLAND

Waypoint: BV311 – 18°19.30'N; 64°37.50'W
Navigation: 5.7nm SSW Road Harbour
Services: Restaurants, Bars, Moorings, Trails, WiFi, Snorkeling, Dive shop

Norman is the first island of any size that, together with the islands of Peter, Salt, Cooper and Ginger, form the southern perimeter of the Sir Francis Drake Channel.

Often referred to by the locals as "Treasure Island", legends of Norman Island are rich with stories of buried pirate treasure. A letter of 1750 stated, "Recovery of the treasure from Nuestra Senora buried at Norman Island, comprise 450,000 dollars, plate, cochineal, indigo, tobacco, much dug up by Tortolians."

The main anchorage on Norman Island is the Bight, an exceptionally well-sheltered anchorage.

Navigation & Piloting

Approaching Norman Island from the south, Santa Monica Rock located 0.7nm SW of Carvel Rocks, covers a small area that is covered by 11-12 feet (3.6m) of water. While this is of no concern to the average yachtsman, during periods

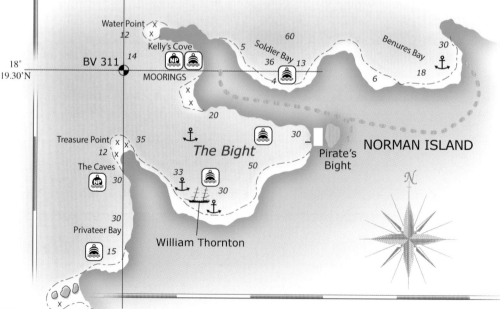

KELLYS COVE

THE BIGHT

TREASURE POINT

PRIVATEER BAY

Carvel
Rocks

of heavy swells it is well to take note. Approaching from the northeast, leaving Pelican Island to starboard, Ringdove Rock is located approximately 300 yards west of Water Point and has 14 feet (4.3m) of water over it.

If your approach brings you by Pelican Island, remember that you cannot pass between the Indians and Pelican Island.

The entrance to the Bight is straight forward and without hazard. Enter between the headlands, keeping in mind that there is shoal water just off both points. Kelly's Cove, a delightful small anchorage at the northern end of the bay, will be immediately identifiable upon rounding Water Point into the Bight.

Anchoring & Mooring

Considerations when deciding where to pick up a mooring or drop anchor in the Bight are whether to be near the partying or away from it. The William Thornton (Willy T), a converted steel schooner, anchored in the SW section of the Bight can be lively late into the night; the same applies to Pirates Bight Beach Bar & Grill ashore; if you are hanging on a mooring just offshore.

If you are planning to anchor there are a couple of options other than in deep water behind the mooring field in the center of the bay; in the southwest section of the bay to the east and west of The Willy T there is space for 5-6 vessels to swing clear of the moorings, at the head of the bay to the south of Pirates Bight, taking care not to obstruct the channel to the service dock and up in the northeast corner of the bay along the shoreline. The anchorage is deep, so you will need to get far enough in to anchor on the shelf in 15-30 feet of water. If you do anchor instead of picking up a mooring be sure that you are well clear of the moorings and have plenty of room to swing without fouling a mooring buoy.

There are numerous mooring buoys in place that you may pick up on a first come basis at the current rate (these moorings are not maintained by Moor Seacure).

Someone will come by dinghy to collect the mooring fee usually in the early evening. Be aware that the wind tends to funnel down through the hills, giving the impression that the weather is much heavier than it is once you are outside of the bay.

Ashore

Located in the Bight of Norman Island is the William Thornton, a floating restaurant named for the architect of the U.S. Capitol building. An earlier version of the Willy T, as it is affectionately named, was lost in Hurricane Irma and the hulk which lingered on the shoreline of the Bight for months, is destined to become a man made reef to be enjoyed for years to come by divers and snorkelers. After the storm, the owners were given notice that they had to move the replacement vessel from its original home in the Bight to Great Harbour, Peter Island; here it enjoyed the same popularity but with the underlying tension that it would be required to move yet again! In June of 2019 the new BVI government determined that they could move back to Norman Island. Gone to come back as they say in the islands.

The vessel is a converted 100 foot schooner. Lunch is served from noon to 3pm and the bar is open daily from noon. Nicknamed the "Willy T," stories abound about many wild nights of partying aboard. The ambiance is casual, noisy and often riotously fun with the usual suspects taking a leap of faith from the stern of the upper deck into the water below, with or without bathing attire. The "Willy T" monitors VHF 16.

Pirates Bight Beach Bar & Grill commands a view of the Bight from the head of the bay. This is a great place to watch the sunset and escape the boat for a while with a a couple of rum punches. Happy hour is from 4-6pm. Lunch is served from 11:30-4pm, and dinner in two seatings, one at 6pm.and the other at 7pm. Reservations are advised. They feature West Indian and international cuisine, prices range from $10-$20 for an appetizer and $18-$30 for dinner. When we visited last we met Regina, a restaurant staff member from Jamaica who was full of smiles and information.

The buildings and general infrastructure suffered a good deal of damage during the storm and both buildings have now been completely rebuilt and executed in good taste. The second building originally known as "The Club"is now used only for weddings and special occasions. WiFi is available throughout the facility and they have an extensive boutique.

The dinghy dock is to the south side of the dock, there is a buoyed swimming area to the north and south of the dock adjacent to the well groomed beach. Caribbean Divers operates a dive shop and boutique from here and can arrange tours. There are numerous trails around the island and if you are planning a hike the staff will give you some suggestions and organize a search party if you do not return before dark. Take a phone, water and sunscreen. There is good snorkeling on the reef at the eastern end of the bay just south of the beach.

Kelly's Cove

A fine alternate anchorage to the Bight is Kelly's Cove, a small, secluded anchorage set against a rugged hillside backdrop. Close enough in proximity to the main anchorage and Treasure Point to allow access by dinghy, Kelly's Cove is a delightful anchorage that provides excellent snorkeling from the boat.

As you approach the Bight, Kelly's Cove is situated under Water Point to the east. The entrance is straight forward, but anchoring needs careful consideration owing to the limited amount of swinging room. There are five overnight moorings in this area leaving limited room for anchoring unless a stern line is taken ashore. If you are dropping the hook, make sure that it is not in coral and the water is shallow enough (20'-25') to control the swinging room due to back winding.

Close by, under Water Point, the National Parks Trust has installed several daytime moorings for snorkeling and diving. There is no charge assuming one has purchased a permit.

Treasure Point

A dinghy trip to Treasure Point and the caves for snorkeling and exploring is a must. Tie up your dinghy to the line strung between the two small round floats. This avoids dropping an anchor and destroying coral. You may also take your boat and pick up a National Parks mooring during the day (with a permit). In order to protect the coral from further destruction, no anchoring is permitted. If all of the mooring balls are taken, move further to the south where you can anchor, or pick up a mooring in Privateer Bay and dinghy back.

Bring your snorkel gear and a flashlight for some cave exploration. Caution: do not use your outboard engine between the dinghy mooring line and the shore as there are usually swimmers in the water. One of the charms of this area is the abundance of small colorful fish. Please do not feed them as it tends to make them aggressive.

PRIVATEER BAY

Further to the south of Treasure Point is Privateer Bay often used as a day anchorage to access both the caves at Treasure Point and Carvel Rock, which provides excellent snorkeling in the appropriate weather conditions. Exposed to the north but usually protected by the headland, Privateer Bay can make a delightful overnight stop in the right conditions and still be close enough to action in the Bight by dinghy.

Although nine mooring balls are now available, anchoring can prove problematic in this area, since the bottom drops off rapidly and patches of dead coral and rock on the seabed should be identified prior to setting the anchor. Anchor in 15-20 feet.

The Caves at Treasure Point

NORMAN ISLAND

SOLDIER BAY

THE BIGHT

BENURES BAY

BENURES BAY (NORTH COAST)

Waypoint: BV309 – 18°19.63'N; 64°36.40'W
Navigation: 6nm SW of Frenchman's Cay; 1nm east of Water Point
Services: Moorings (Soldier Bay), Trails

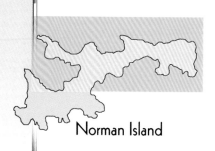

Norman Island

Under normal trade wind conditions, there are two delightful anchorages on the north coast that, while limited in available anchoring room, provide a tranquil setting a little out of the mainstream of cruising and charter traffic. Both of these anchorages should be avoided when the wind moves to the north for short periods during the winter months.

The larger and more protected of the two bays, Benures Bay lies to the east on the northern coast of Norman Island. The approach is straightforward as there is no shoal ground to be concerned about until you are in close proximity to the beach.

Anchor up in the northeast corner of the bay and as close to the pebble beach as possible. At the time of the last survey, no moorings were available. The bottom is sand, so the holding is excellent in 15-20 feet of water and the snorkeling is great. It should be noted, however, that wind and current often compete in this area and

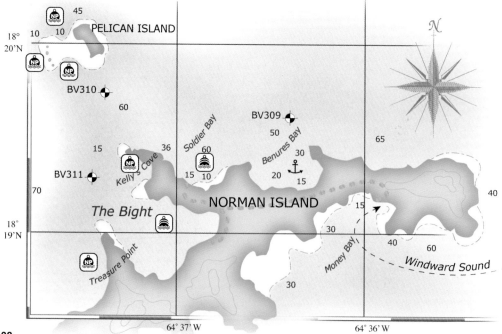

Benures Bay

you are likely to be back winded. To sit in the cockpit savoring a gin and tonic and watching the sun slowly set down the channel to the west is close to perfect. To access the trail, land your dinghy on the southeast end of the pebble beach and secure it to a tree. Walk back into the bush a few yards and you will pick up the trail that leads to the top at which point you can head southeast to Money Bay (bring swimsuits, sunscreen, a cell phone and water) or west to the Bight.

SOLDIER BAY

A little over half a mile east of Water Point is Soldier Bay, a small anchorage capable of accommodating a limited number of vessels and ideal during the summer months when the wind is light and the trade winds are blowing from the southeast. The entrance to Soldier Bay is free of any foul ground until the shoreline. If anchoring you will need to identify a sandy stretch to lay down the anchor in 25 feet of water or pick up one of the five mooring balls managed from Pirates Bight Beach Bar. Holding is good and the snorkeling is excellent.

SOUTH COAST / MONEY BAY

Location: 18°19.00'N ; 64°36.00'W
Waypoint: BV307 (Carrot Rock) 18°18.92'N; 64°34.25'W
Navigation: 3.2 nm east and south of Benures Bay
Services: Hiking trails

Tucked away on the south coast of Norman is an idyllic spot that can be used as a daytime stop or under ideal calm conditions overnight. Under certain conditions the swell can work itself into this little bay and therefore a stern anchor would prove prudent. A few years ago a breakwater was erected from both sides which effectively prevented anchoring by more than one vessel of any size.

Approaching from the east, you will pass the rocky headland forming the southeastern tip of Norman Island; stand well clear since you will be on a lee-shore and the sea conditions will reflect the fact that they have traveled unbroken for 100 miles or so.

Money Bay is located in the eastern end of the second bay to the west of the headland.

Care should be taken to make sure you know exactly where you are. There is plenty of water depth even though the seas are rough in this area.

Locate the entrance between the two rock breakwaters and proceed into the center of the bay, dropping the anchor in 10 feet of water on a sandy bottom. The ideal solution would be to run a stern anchor toward the shore which will keep your bow to the wind and head to the sea. There is a trail from the beach at Money Bay up to the ridge and back to the Bight or Benures Bay. Take water and sunscreen.

PELICAN ISLAND & THE INDIANS

Waypoint: BV310 – 18°19.80'N ; 64°37.40'W
Navigation: 5nm SE Frenchman's Cay, 5nm SSW Road Harbour
Services: National Parks Moorings, Excellent snorkeling / diving

Pelican Island and The Indians should be considered a day anchorage only. Located one mile NNW from Water Point and highly visible from the channel because of the unique formation of the four red rocks known as The Indians. Do not attempt to sail between Pelican Island and The Indians. Approach them from the north and pick up one of the ten Parks Trust mooring balls. A reef extends between the two and provides excellent snorkeling as does the area immediately around the Indians. As part of the National Parks Trust, this area is protected and no anchoring is permitted. If the moorings are taken you may consider anchoring in Kelly's Cove at the mouth of the Bight (0.5nm) and taking the dinghy over assuming you have a capable outboard and the sea conditions are light. There is a dinghy mooring line in place on the south side west of Pelican Island.

This anchorage is very exposed and can be uncomfortable. The snorkeling is excellent and well worth the trip. The Indians have just about everything for the snorkeler as well as the scuba diver; caves, tunnels, brain, finger and elk horn corals are abundant as are gorgonians and sea fans. In addition to the immediate area, there are two additional sites that are interesting, Pelican (30'-70') and Rainbow Canyon (15'-55'). Rainbow Canyon can be dived in almost any conditions, it is an easy beginners dive where you will find both hard and soft corals on big mounds of granite along with canyons, sea fans and colors that justify the title of Rainbow Canyon.

The Indians

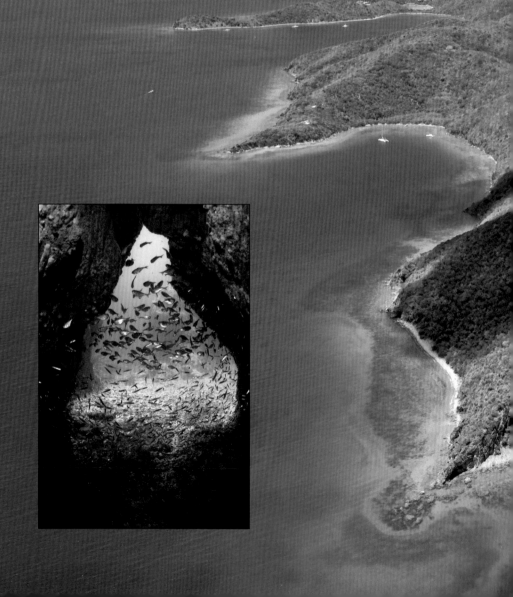

THE CHANNEL ISLANDS
PETER ISLAND

LITTLE HARBOUR

Peter Island

Waypoint: BV302 - 18°21.40'N; 64°37.00'W
Navigation: 3.2nm SE Nanny Cay
Services: Snorkeling

Sailing to the east the next island is Peter. Captain Thomas Southey wrote his impressions of the island in his chronological history of the West Indies over 100 years ago:

"In May (1806) the author with a party visited Peter's Island, one of those which form the bay Tortola, a kind of Robinson Crusoe spot, where a man ought to be farmer, carpenter, doctor, fisherman, planter; everything himself."

Navigation & Piloting

There are several good overnight anchorages on Peter Island, the westernmost of which is Little Harbour. Although it doesn't look it on the chart, Little Harbour is a well-protected overnight stop with good holding ground.

When approaching from the NW the first landmark is a dilapidated white house which is now difficult to see due to weeds and growth on the northwest point forming the eastern side of the harbor. There are no obstructions but do not cut the point too close as the reef extends 100 feet toward the west from the shore.

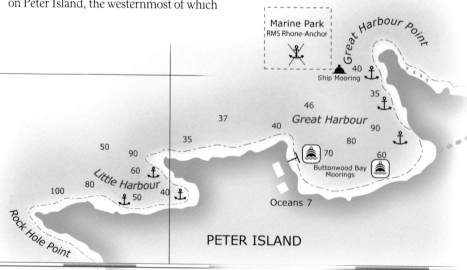

18°
21.63'N

Marine Park
RMS Rhone-Anchor

Great Harbour Point

40
Ship Mooring
35
46
37   40   Great Harbour   90
50   80
90   35
60   70   60
80   Buttonwood Bay   Moorings
100   Little Harbour
50   40
Oceans 7

Rock Hole Point

PETER ISLAND

64° 36' W

Little Harbour

Anchoring & Mooring

Little Harbour is deep (40-60 feet) in the center of the bay. There are no moorings and therefore the best spot to anchor is well up in the eastern reaches of the bay, in 15-25 feet over a sandy bottom. You will be back winded, so check your swinging room relative to other vessels and use two anchors if necessary. If the anchorage is crowded, anchor close to shore on the southern coast of the bay in order to stay in 25-35 feet of water. Be careful not to anchor in the coral reef on the southwestern side of the anchorage. It is 40-50 feet below the surface, and is not easy to see and therefore, easy to damage. Please help protect the coral reefs.

In recent years it is noted that more yachts are mooring stern to the shore on both the north and south sides of the bay. This tends to restrict the available room to anchor, due to the back-winding effect. A stern line tied to a tree or around a convenient rock will keep you from swinging, but make sure your anchor is well set.

Ashore

Peter Island is a private island. There are no facilities ashore at Little Harbour. It is a quiet, usually, well-protected harbor where you can watch the frigate birds dive for fish, watch the sunset and the stars and moon at night. It is often used by crewed yachts that anchor stern to the shore and tie off to a rock or tree.

The house you see on top of the point is now in ruins. Ashore in the bay are the remains of a dock. It is not recommended that you go ashore here.

GREAT HARBOUR

Waypoint: BV303 - 18°22.00'N; 64°34.60'W
Navigation: 4nm SSE Road Harbour
Services: Moorings, Restaurant, Bar, Trail

Great Harbour, situated on the north side of the island is approximately half a mile across and a well-protected anchorage that, until recent years, was largely neglected by the charter fleet because of the depth and lack of moorings. There is ample room to anchor along the eastern point although it can be tricky to locate an ideal location to get the anchor set.

Navigation & Piloting

Approaches to Great Harbour are clear and free of any obstruction. There is a large ship-mooring at the north end of the bay. Skippers should familiarize themselves with the location of the National Parks Trust protected area, the site of the lost anchor of the RMS Rhone that was sunk off of Salt Island in 1867, while attempting to gain sea room to the south in a hurricane.

Anchoring & Mooring

Entering Great Harbour, Buttonwood Bay and the Oceans Seven Beach Bar & Restaurant will be on the western side of the bay. There are numerous mooring balls available on a first come basis that extend from Buttonwood Bay across the southern end of the bay. Payment can be made ashore if you are staying overnight. To the east, in the inner corner of the bay is a protected fishing area, where local fishermen run their nets out into the bay. This area appears to have been adversely impacted by the hurricane and

much of the Sea-Grape foliage along the shoreline was destroyed. If anchoring, stay clear of this activity and locate a spot in about 20 feet of water to the west of the beach and east of the mooring field, or along the headland that extends to the northwest. Make sure your anchor is well set by reversing at 1500 rpm's and, if possible, take a snorkel and swim over it for peace of mind.

Ashore

Buttonwood Bay, on the western side of Great Harbour is home to the restaurant and bar called Oceans Seven. During our last survey (May 2019), Oceans Seven was closed and still under reconstruction due to hurricane damage. They indicated that they would be operational by season 2019/20.

You can pick up a mooring and jump in the dinghy, tie up to the dock and pay for your mooring at the restaurant. They request reservations for dinner – check to find out if they are having entertainment or special events. Oceans Seven is open daily from 10am- 9pm with happy hour at 4-6pm. They serve West Indian dishes as well as international. There are no garbage facilities ashore or any shops for provisioning. Landing your dinghy at the eastern end of the bay you can access a trail that will take you to Sprat Bay and from there you can hike to Deadman's Bay. Please note that the opening date for the Peter Island Resort has not been made official and therefore access across a construction zone will not be allowed.

FISHERIES PROTECTED AREA

SPRAT BAY PETER ISLAND RESORT

Peter Island

Waypoint: BV303 - 18°22.00'N; 64°34.60'W
Navigation: 4nm SSW of Road Harbour
Services: The Peter Island Resort is closed until further notice. (Moorings, Restaurant, Bar, Dockage, Fuel, Ice, Water, Dive shop, Trails)

Sprat Bay is easy to spot from the Sir Francis Drake Channel by the row of roofs comprising the hotel section of the Peter Island Resort. The entire bay, Deadman's Bay and several beaches on the south coast of Peter Island are part of the resort. It should be noted that as of June 2019 there has been no official notification of a projected opening date after the devastating hurricane of 2017 that inflicted major damage. Demolition and building crews were in evidence but no official date so it is unlikely that the resort will open for the 2019/20 season.

Navigation & Piloting

Making your entrance to Sprat Bay, it is important to familiarize yourself with the location of the reefs on either side of the channel. The main reef extends north and

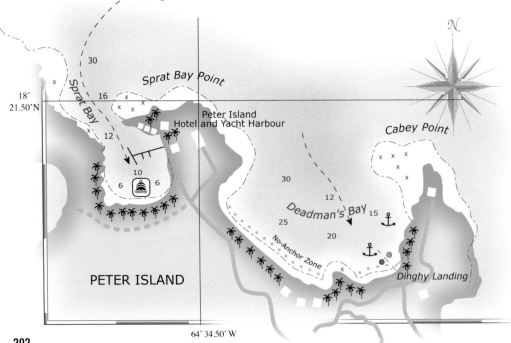

slightly west of the main bulkhead; so do not get too close to the western shore.

Entering on a heading of 141°magnetic, you can either tie up to the dock, which now sports new finger piers or pick up a mooring. Do not go too far into the southern end of the bay when maneuvering, as it is shallow. There are four moorings available (subject to change)for a fee of $65 per night (pay the dock master ashore). The moorings cannot be reserved in advance. The dinghy dock is located at the eastern part of the marina. You may call the dock master on VHF channel 16.

Ashore

Once again, the entire resort suffered considerable damage that entailed rebuilding large portions of the resort. As of press time we had received no notification of opening dates and therefore visitors should assume that no services are available unless independently verified from a local source.

Once open we expect the following to be the general structure: The Peter Island Resort dock has 15 mid-sized slips and can accommodate up to 3 additional vessels alongside and a 175-foot T-dock for larger vessels. The dockage rate for transient vessels is $125 per night up to 50 feet. Check with the dockmaster for the rates for larger vessels and to confirm current rates. For visiting day guests, the dock-age is $20 per hour (sometimes waived if you are having lunch in the restaurant); again confirm these rates by contacting the dockmaster. Pumping marine heads into the harbor is not permitted. Fuel is available as well as water. Garbage can be left for a fee of $5 and ice may be purchased at $4 per bag.

Originally built by Norwegians in the late 1960s, the resort has been completely renovated and now is undergoing a complete rebuild. The hotel and restaurants extend along the bulkhead. Yachtsmen docking at Peter Island are welcome to use the Tradewinds Restaurant, Drake's Channel Lounge, Deadman's Beach Bar and Grill, Little Deadman's Beach, the boutique, and the dive shop. Reservations are requested at the restaurants. Make sure to ask for the details of the dress code. There is no provisioning available at the resort.

Deadman's Bay

Waypoint: BV303 - 18°22.00'N; 64°34.60'W
Navigation: 0.5nm from Sprat Bay & 2.6nm west of Salt Island
Services: Snorkeling and trail; the Resort is closed

The easternmost anchorage on Peter Island, Deadman's Bay is a spectacular crescent of white sand with palm trees blowing in the trades. The anchorage itself is exposed to the north and therefore can be rolly due to the surge making its way around the northeastern point, making it a better day stop except in very settled southerly conditions. A reef extends 300 feet to the west from Cabey Point.

Anchoring & Mooring

Deadman's Bay is owned by The Peter Island Resort and visitors are asked to respect the rebuilding efforts to the hotel and beach pavilion infrastructure. This is a picture perfect beach to visit despite the sometimes rolly water action. The beach is divided by some rocks; the beach to the west is for the use of hotel guests only, and yachtsmen are requested to respect the line of buoys designating the swimming beach. However, when the resort is reopened, the Deadman's Bay Beach Bar is open to cruising and charter yachts as well as the hotel guests. In season the resort often holds beach barbecues here with steel drum bands playing on the beach.

There is a dinghy landing area, marked with red and green markers to the eastern end of the bay. The trail leads over to Little Deadman's Beach, an interesting beach to explore (the huts there are reserved for hotel guests) and connects to a 5-mile loop. Take water and sunscreen.

Deadman's Bay, looking across to Deadchest Island

The Real Dead Chest

Though there are few that haven't at least heard of the film *Pirates of the Caribbean*, most are unaware of the identity of the real Dead Chest Cay, Dead Man's Bay, and the actual hidden treasure chest full of "Pieces of Eight". The story unfolds in the British Virgin Islands, our very own veritable paradise.

On the south side of the Sir Francis Drake Channel and just to the east of Peter Island is the cay named Dead Chest. In the days of yore a "dead man's chest" was the name for a coffin, the outline of which you can make out when viewing the island from the northwest. Look even longer and the coffin appears to contain a shrouded body with a raised head. As long ago as the late 1700s the cay's moniker was Dead Chest, clearly marked on Jeffrey's 18th century chart of the Virgin Islands. Folklore has it that the infamous pirate Blackbeard marooned fifteen men on the cay with nothing but a bottle of rum. Some apparently tried to swim the half mile to Peter Island's eastern cove but didn't make it, giving this beautiful palm lined bay the ominous name, "Dead Man's Bay".

At a much later date author Robert Louis Stevenson researched events in the area, studying nautical charts (his passion), as well as historical events and Caribbean lore. The well documented piracy of a huge treasure, much of which had been buried on Norman Island, most likely provided him with valuable information the culmination of which resulted in the much loved Treasure Island. Thus, Dead Chest Cay came to be immortalized in the famous refrain:

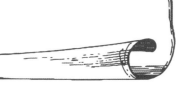

Fifteen Men on the Dead Man's Chest,
Yo-ho-ho and a bottle of rum!
Drink and the devil had done for the rest.
Yo-ho-ho and a bottle of rum!

Perhaps the most captivating aspect of the many similar themes of the film and the true story of the piracy in the Virgin Islands is that both involve treasure chests. In the BVI, a daring act of piracy led to the burying of a cache of treasure on Norman Island in the year 1750. Some 160 years after the event a treasure chest of "Pieces of Eight" was discovered in the southernmost cave on the leeward side of the peninsula that crests at Treasure Point. Mention of the discovery is made in no less than three publications!

"Yo–ho-ho and a bottle of rum!!"

Julian Putley is the author of "The Virgins' Treasure Isle," the story of the daring piracy and subsequent burying of it on Norman Island in the BVI.

KEY POINT, ROGER'S POINT & WHITE BAY
(THE SOUTH COAST OF PETER ISLAND)

Peter Island

Waypoint: BV308 - 18°20.00'N; 64°35.70'W
Navigation: 2nm NE Water Point (Norman Is)
Services: None

There are three anchorages on the south side of Peter Island that are worthy of mention, but some regard to sea and weather conditions should be noted when planning to anchor, since southerly conditions can make Key Point and Roger's Point uncomfortable.

Approaches and Anchoring

The ideal approach is from the SW and deep water. When approaching Key Point from the west, give Roger's Point a good offing since there is a small reef that extends to the southeast.

Key Cay is separated from the mainland (Key Point) by a narrow isthmus of land that allows the trade breeze to flow freely across the anchorage.

Tuck yourself up into the northeast corner and anchor on a sandy bottom in 15-18 feet of water. There are some coral heads in the area so make sure that you locate a good sandy spot before dropping the hook.

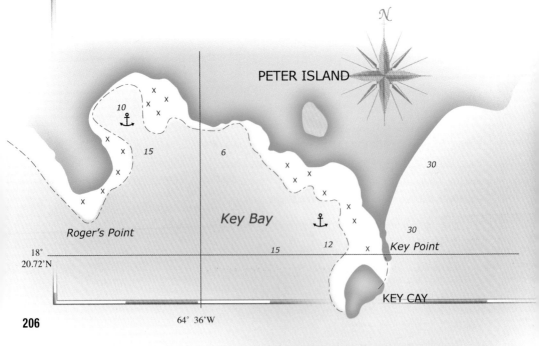

Key Point

White Bay

The snorkeling is excellent and the anchorage is open to the prevailing breeze, keeping it free from bugs. The island is private and no services are available.

Further to the west, northeast of Roger's Point, there is a small anchorage inside a coral lined channel that should only be attempted in calm conditions with good light and a lookout on the bow. The axis for entry is to the northwest and once inside you will be in 12-15 feet of water on a sand bottom. Snorkeling is good. This anchorage can also be accessed by dinghy from Key Point.

WHITE BAY

Waypoint: BV308 - 18°20.00'N; 64°35.70'W
Navigation: 3nm NE Water Point (Norman Is)
Services: None

Tucked up in the northeast corner of the island before the coast turns to the south, White Bay is a reasonable anchorage when the ground swells caused by the normal flow of current are not running. We would recommend it as a day anchorage only in normal conditions. An approach from the southwest is ideal and straightforward.

Making your approach from the south (waypoint BV307 Carrot Shoal), make sure that you give Carrot Rock on the southernmost tip of Peter Island plenty of sea room and are aware of the location of Carrot Shoal (covered by 9.5 ft/2.9m of water). There is a 1.5 to 1.75 knot current flowing through this area that can run to the northwest or to the southeast.

Anchor on a sandy bottom in 15 feet of water.

Since White Bay is for the use of guests of the Peter Island Resort, landing is not encouraged although access to beaches throughout the BVI is always available to the high tide mark.

WHITE BAY, PETER ISLAND

A Charter Cat anchored at Little Harbour

Little Harbour, Peter Island

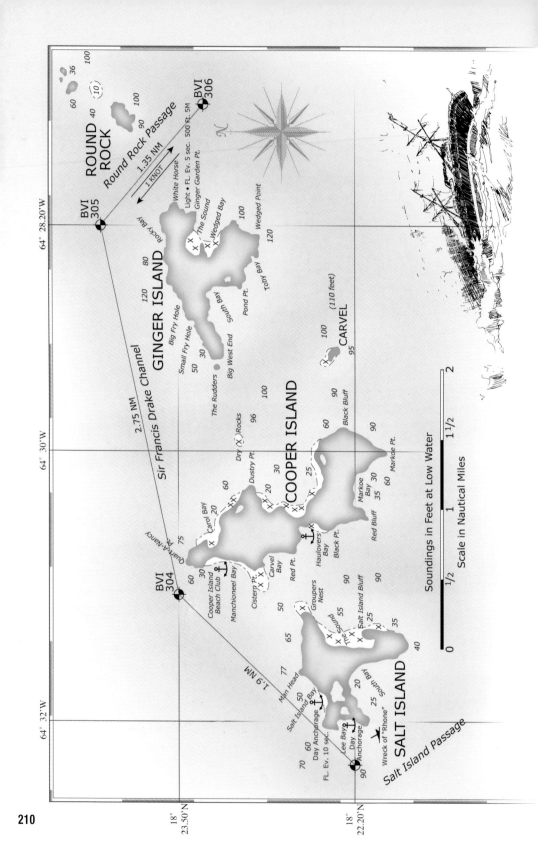

ROUND ROCK

100
36
60 40 (10) 100
90
100

BVI
305

BVI
306

Round Rock Passage

1.35 NM

1 KNOT

White Horse

Light • FL. Ev. 5 sec. 500 Ft. 5M

Ginger Garden Pt.

The Sound

Wedged Bay

Wedged Point

Rocky Bay

100
120

GINGER ISLAND

Sir Francis Drake Channel

2.75 NM

120 80

Big Fry Hole

Small Fry Hole

50 30

South Bay

Big West End

Pond Pt.

Toby Bay

CARVEL

(110 feet)

100

95

The Rudders

Dry (X) Rocks

96

Dustry Pt.

100

60

Black Bluff

90

90

Markoe Pt.

Markoe
Bay

30 35

60

Red Bluff

Quart-A-Nancy

75

Carol Bay

60 20

20 30

25

COOPER ISLAND

Cooper Island
Beach Club

Manchioneel Bay

60

30

Cistern Pt.

Carvel
Bay

50

Red Pt.

Haulovers
Bay

Black Pt.

BVI
304

Groupers
Nest

90

90

Salt Island Bluff

90

The Sound

55

25

35

65

Mpn Head

77

20

25

South Bay

40

SALT ISLAND

50

Salt Island Bay

Day Anchorage

Wreck of "Rhone"

Lee Bay
Day
Anchorage

FL. Ev. 10 sec.

60

70

90

Salt Island Passage

WN 6'T

Soundings in Feet at Low Water

Scale in Nautical Miles

0   1/2   1   1 1/2   2

64° 28.20'W
64° 30'W
64° 32'W

18°
23.50'N

18°
22.20'N

The Channel Islands
Salt, Cooper & Ginger Islands

The sailing and snorkeling paradise, formed by the chain of small islands designating the southern boundary of the Sir Francis Drake Channel (Freebooter's Gangway), Salt, Cooper and Ginger Islands, together with Fallen Jerusalem and The Dogs to the east are home to some of the most spectacular snorkeling and dive sites in the BVI, including the Wreck of the Rhone, Alice in Wonderland (Ginger Island) and Cistern Point off of the point of Cooper Island.

Ginger Island is uninhabited and has no tenable anchorages. Fallen Jerusalem was declared a national park and bird sanctuary in 1974 and has a small day anchorage, with excellent snorkeling, on the north side also accessible by dinghy from The Baths when the weather is light.

Waypoints	North	West
BV303	18°22.00'	64°34.60'
BV304	18°23.50'	64°31.00'
BV305	18°24.10'	64°28.20'
BV306	18°23.30'	64°27.10'

SALT ISLAND BAY

Waypoint: BV303 (Dead Chest) - 18°22.00'N;
64°34.60'W
Navigation: 5nm SE Road Harbour; 2nm east of
Peter Island
Services: National Park Moorings at Lee Bay

Salt Island, a little over two nautical miles east from Peter Island, is a relatively low island rising to less than 400 feet at the northern end. At the eastern extremity, a rock is awash and restricts the channel between Salt and Cooper Islands. Caution should be exercised in this regard. At the western end lies the famed wreck of the Rhone.

Named for the island's three evaporation ponds, Salt Island was once an important source of salt for the ships of Her Majesty's Royal Navy. The island and its salt ponds, although belonging to the Crown, were operated by the local populace. Each year at the start of the harvest, the Governor, as annual rent, accepted one bag of salt. In 1845, a barrel was quoted at one shilling and, although inflation has taken its toll, salt is still sold to visitors. The residents of the settlement just off Salt Bay have all moved off of Salt Island to the more populated islands with all the modern conveniences.

Anchoring & Mooring

Salt Island Bay, north of The Settlement is clear of hazards, but the prudent skipper is advised to ensure that the anchor is well set before going ashore. You may anchor in 10-25 feet of water on a sandy bottom from the Settlement east to Manhead.

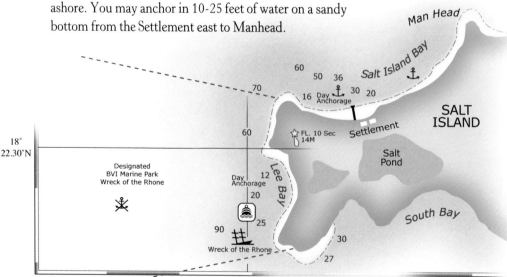

SALT ISLAND BAY

LEE BAY

MARINE PARK
RMS RHONE

N

Evaporation Pond, Salt Island

The small jetty was destroyed in the storm, but the remains are still in place and present a hazard. Landing the dinghy on the beach, make sure that you secure the dinghy on the beach, either by pulling it well up the beach or using the dinghy anchor to prevent the surge from liberating it.

During the high season, the anchorage to the west (Lee Bay) can get crowded with divers and snorkelers anxious to see the wreck of the RMS Rhone. Consider leaving the boat in Salt Island Bay and taking the dinghy around to Lee Bay where you can secure it to the dinghy tether by courtesy of the National Parks Trust.

LEE BAY

Although exposed and recommended as a day anchorage only, Lee Bay, located on the west end of the island, is an alternative to Salt Bay for those wishing to dive or snorkel on The Wreck of the Rhone. The National Parks Trust has installed moorings for the use of permit holders only. They are designed for boats under 50 feet to pick up in order to dinghy over to the Rhone. Anchoring over the Rhone or within the park is strictly prohibited as the National Parks Trust protects it. Constant anchoring by boats has destroyed some of the coral. Remember that the yellow mooring balls are for commercial vessels only. Watch out for divers!

Ashore

Salt Island has a few fishermen who fish off of the island, but it is no longer settled. There are no services or restaurants ashore.

The Royal Mail Steamer Rhone

"On the morning of October 29, 1867, the R.M.S. Rhone was at anchor outside of Great Harbour, Peter Island. The Rhone, under the command of Captain Robert F. Wooley, had left Southampton on October 2, 1867, and was taking on cargo and stores for the return crossing. The R.M.S. Conway, commanded by Captain Hammock, lay alongside.

The stillness of the tropical day was undisturbed as the sun blazed down from a clear sky upon calm seas. As the morning wore on, the barometer began to fall, hinting the weather might deteriorate. The seas, however, remained untroubled. Although the captains alerted themselves, work was allowed to continue. Captain Wooley hailed Captain Hammock that he did not like the look of the weather and, as the hurricane season was over, it must be a northerly brewing. Wooley felt they should shift to the northern anchorage of Road Harbour, Tortola.

About 11am, the barometer suddenly fell to 27.95 degrees. The sky darkened, and with a mighty roar a fearful hurricane blew from the north/northwest. The howling wind whistled through the shrouds and tore at the rigging. With engines going at full speed, the ships rode the storm.

At noon there came a lull in the storm. The Conway weighed anchor and headed toward the northern anchorage of Road Harbour. As she steamed across the Sir Francis Drake Channel, she was hit by the second blast of the hurricane. Her funnel and masts were blown away, and she was driven onto the island of Tortola.

The Rhone tried to weigh anchor during the lull, but the shackle of the cable caught in the hawse pipe and parted, dropping the 3,000-pound anchor and some 300 feet of chain. With engines running at full speed, she steamed seaward in order to seek sea room to weather the second onslaught. She had negotiated most of the rocky channel and was rounding the last point when the hurricane, blowing from the south-southeast, struck, forcing her onto the rocks at Salt Island where she heeled over, broke in two, and sank instantly, taking most of her company with her."

– Courtesy of R.M.S. Rhone
  by George and Luana Marler

The Wreck of the Rhone

COOPER ISLAND
MANCHINEEL BAY

Waypoint: BV304 - 18°23.50'N; 64°31.00'W
Navigation: 6nm SE Road Harbour
Services: Moorings, Ice, Restaurant, Hotel, Gift shop, Dive center, WiFi, Coffee bar, Microbrewery, Garbage disposal (boat service only)

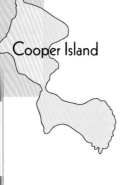

Cooper Island

Cooper Island, located northeast of Salt Island is less than two miles in length and about 500 feet high. On the east side of the island about 300 yards off of Dustry Point on the northeast side there is a patch of rocks aptly named Dry Rocks. Further to the south and less than a mile east-northeast of the southern extremity is the 110 foot high Carvel Rock.

BV304

18° 23.50'N

Quart-a-Nancy Pt.

60

x
x

55

30

Manchineel Bay

36

40

30

Cooper Island Beach Bar

50

Moorings

27

20

COOPER ISLAND

Dinghy Moorings

x

18° 22.80'N

Cistern Pt.

Grouper's Nest
x
x
x

36

Carvel Bay

55

6

Red Point

x

25

Hallovers Bay

25

SALT ISLAND

HAULOVER BAY

CISTERN PT.

Manchineel Bay

Navigation & Piloting

The principal anchorage on Cooper Island is Manchineel Bay located on the northwest shore. When approaching the bay from the north, around Quart-a-Nancy Point, you will be on your ear one minute and becalmed the next. The point shelters the wind entirely, and we would recommend lowering sail and powering up to the anchorage.

Traveling from Manchineel Bay south to Haulover Bay or approaching from Salt Island to the west, be aware of a rock barely awash just north of the eastern point (Grouper's Nest) of Salt Island. With Cistern Point on the Cooper Island side and the rocks off the end of Salt, the passage between the islands is restricted. We do not advise sailing through.

Anchoring & Mooring

There are thirty moorings in Manchineel Bay owned and operated by Moor Seacure. Twelve of these are

Boatyball moorings that can be reserved via their website on a nightly basis. All others are on a first-come basis. They can be identified by the pennant beneath the buoy and a pay-at-the-bar sticker. The fee is $30 per overnight stay. The other 10 most southerly moorings near Cistern Point are privately owned, and a dinghy will come to collect the fee. Anchoring is not permitted in the mooring field or in the seagrass. Manchineel Bay is one of the Department of Environment and Fisheries seven permanent seagrass monitoring sites that provide food and shelter for sea turtles and many species of fish. No anchoring is permitted.

Since this anchorage is popular, both as a first and last night stop, because of its proximity to Road Town, the mooring balls fill quickly and we have witnessed on many occasions two or three vessels racing through the anchorage toward the last mooring ball. With swimmers in the water, we urge restraint.

Ashore

There is a good sandy beach fringed with palm trees and offering views of many of the islands to the west including spectacular sunsets. Please exercise caution in your dinghy and look out for snorkelers and swimmers. The snorkeling is excellent at each end of the beach, and there is a dinghy line at Cistern Point if you wish to explore the deeper water. Dinghies may tie up at either of the two jetties to visit Cooper Island Beach Club, the Sea Grape Boutique, or Sail Caribbean Divers. WiFi is available at the Rum Shop and the most recent innovation has been the establishment of a microbrewery. Garbage service is available daily by boat pick up only. Keep your eye open for Kevin & G in their matching shirts, they usually are in the anchorage around 7.30am. Give them a wave or call them on VHF 16.

Under new ownership since 2009, Cooper Island Beach Club has undergone substantial renovations. The Harris family has also invested in many green initiatives behind the scenes, such as a state-of-the-art solar-powered system that provides over 75% of the resort's power. The restaurant serves a varied international menu and dinner reservations are essential in the busy season. Go ashore during the day, phone 284-495-9084 or call on VHF 16 before noon to avoid disappointment. Happy hour starts at 4pm and the bar deck features comfortable outdoor sofas and parasols for shade. Ice is usually available at the bar.

Cooper Island Beach Club has guest cottages available each with a private bathroom and beachfront balcony; perfect for before or post-charter, or just a night off of the boat.

Next to the Beach Club to the north the Sea Grape Boutique has resort clothing, island souvenirs, local art, books, and essential sundries you may need.

Although there is no regular schedule, the Beach Club boat goes to Tortola several days a week, to transfer guests or

to pick up supplies, so check at the office if you need transportation.

Sail Caribbean Divers, a PADI Five Star IDC facility offers a full range of scuba diving experiences catering to all levels. They will meet you at the Cooper Island jetty and within 15 minutes you can be diving on colorful coral reefs and some of the best wreck diving in the Caribbean, including the world-renowned wreck of the RMS Rhone. Their staff is on-site daily offering air-fills, PADI dive courses, and equipment rentals including kayaks and snorkel gear.

HAULOVER BAY

A little over half a mile south of Manchineel Bay is the small anchorage known as Haulover Bay (shown on UK Admiralty Charts as Hallover). Transiting between Salt and Cooper you will leave Cistern Point, the western extremity of Cooper, to port and do not venture too far west toward Salt Island. Directly north of the Grouper's Nest (eastern most point of Salt Island) is a rock awash.

Haulover is a reasonable overnight anchorage except during southerly conditions when it can be rolly. There is a reef at the south end of the bay so anchor in 20 feet of water.

THE DOGS (WEST DOG, GREAT DOG, GEORGE DOG & SEAL DOG)

Virgin Gorda

Waypoint: BV403 (Gt.Dog) - 18°28.42'N; 64°26.80'W

Navigation: 6.2nm NW Cooper Island, 2.5nm NW St.Thomas Bay, Virgin Gorda

Services: National Parks Trust Moorings, Snorkeling, Dive sites

Great, George, West and Seal Dogs lay a couple of miles to the west of Virgin Gorda, and generally speaking, have good water all around them. They are all in a protected area of the National Parks Trust. They make a delightful lunch stop on the way up from the islands to the south but when the northerly ground swells are running in the winter months they can be uncomfortable even as day anchorages.

It is not possible to sail or power between West and East Seal Dogs. If there is not a sea running there are three good daytime anchorages in the lee of Great Dog and George Dog.

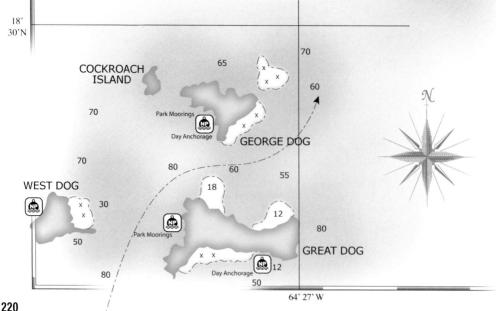

George Dog

On George Dog, the best anchorage is in the bay to the west of Kitchen Point. Pick up a National Parks Trust mooring just off of the beach and stay for lunch and a snorkel trip. The rocky point is also an excellent 25-30 foot dive for beginner divers.

Great Dog

Off of Great Dog there are two possible anchorages depending on the weather. The most common one is on the south side of the island. There are several National Parks Trust moorings you may use with your permit. The depth is between 20-30 feet and the bottom is rocky. The second spot is off the beach on the west coast and it also has National Parks moorings available. The snorkeling is excellent in both locations and for the scuba divers there are a number of excellent sites.

South side anchorage: The reef runs east and west. Over 100 yards of island coral, butterfly fish and scores of other species.

The Chimney (West Bay): A winding canyon leads to a colorful underwater arch. Many coral heads and an unbelievable variety of sea creatures.

GEORGE DOG

GREAT DOG

EMERGENCIES
999 or 911
**VISAR (Virgin Island
Search and Rescue)**
Tel: 767 (SOS), or
+1 284 499 0911
www.visar.org

SERVICES
Kevin & G
Ice delivery and garbage
pick up by boat

COOPER ISLAND

RESTAURANTS
Cooper Island Beach Club
Tel: 284-547-2002
www.cooperisland-
beachclub.com
FB: cooperislandbeach-
clubbvi
Closed Aug. 12 to Oct. 24
Lunch 12pm,
dinner 5:30-8:30pm
(reservations required),
happy hour 4-6pm
Coffee Box open 8:30am-
5:30pm. Espresso, gelato,
smoothies, fresh pastries
and freshly made salads.
Rum Bar open 2-10:30pm,
largest selection of rum in
the Virgin Islands, featuring
a range of house-infusions,
rare aged rums and classic
cocktails

SHOPS
Seagrape Boutique
Swimwear, fashion, jewelry,
artwork, gifts and art
FB: seagrapeboutiquecibc
8:30am-6.30pm

DIVING/ WATERSPORTS
Sail Caribbean Divers
Tel: 1-284-541-3483
sailcaribbeandivers.com
FB: sailcaribbeandivers
8:30am-4:30pm daily
Closed Aug. 11- Oct. 25
Dive courses all levels,
discover scuba program
at cooper, pickup /
rendezvous, private dive
& snorkel trips, SUP &
kayaking, daily gear rental

NORMAN ISLAND

RESTAURANTS
Pirates Bight
Tel: 284-443-1305
www.piratesbight.com
FB: NormanIsland
VHF 16/69
Lunch, dinner, 4-6pm
happy hour, cocktails, good
wine list, 11am-9pm, daily
(closed July 31-October 1)
Gift Shop

**William Thornton
(Willy T)**
Tel: 1 284-340-8603
www.willy-t.com
FB: WillyTBVI
VHF 16/74
Bar, lunch, dinner & fun
12pm-1am daily

PETER ISLAND

MARINA
**Peter Island Marina &
Resort**
Not currently functional.
Check www.peterisland.
com for updates

FERRY SERVICES
Peter Island Ferry
Check schedules & rates at
www.BVIWelcome.com

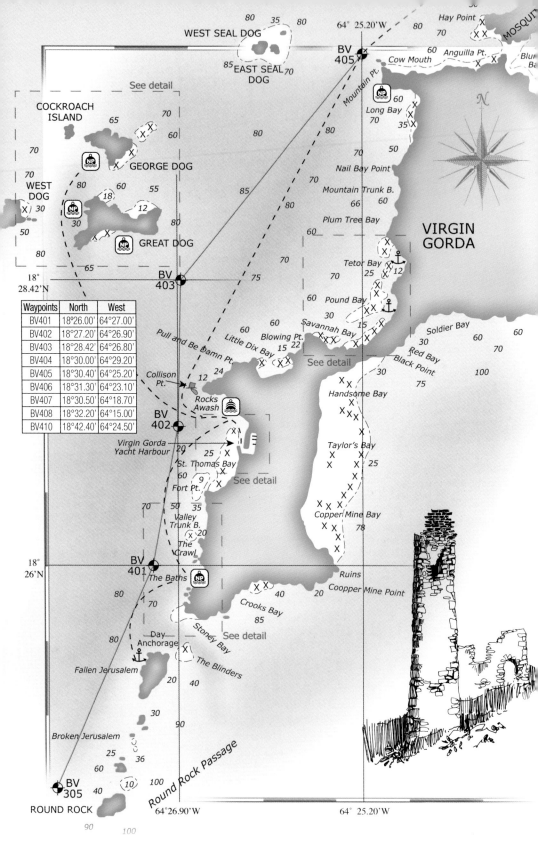

WEST SEAL DOG

80 35 80 64° 25.20'W 80 Hay Point X MOSQUIT
70 X X
BV 60 Anguilla Pt.
405 Cow Mouth X Blu
Ba

85 EAST SEAL 70
DOG

COCKROACH
ISLAND 65 70 NP 60
Mountain Pt. Long Bay
70 X X 80 70 35 X

WEST 80 60 GEORGE DOG 70 50
DOG 18 55 Nail Bay Point

70 NP 12 70 Mountain Trunk B.
30 66 60

50 GREAT DOG Plum Tree Bay
80 80 80 60 VIRGIN
GORDA

65 BV 75 70 Tetor Bay X
403 25 X 12
70 X

60 Pull and Be Damn Pt. 60 Pound Bay
60 30 X 15

Little Dix Bay Savannah Bay Soldier Bay 60 60
Blowing Pt. X 30 70
15 22 Red Bay
See detail Black Point 100
30 75

X X Handsome Bay
X X X

Collison 12 24 X X X
Pt. X
Rocks Taylor's Bay
Awash X 25
BV X
402 X

Virgin Gorda 20 25 X
Yacht Harbour X Copper Mine Bay
St. Thomas Bay 35 X X
60 9 X 78
Fort Pt. X See detail X X X

70 50 Ruins
Valley Coopper Mine Point
Trunk B. 20 20
The X
Crawl

BV NP
401 The Baths 40
80 70 20
Crooks Bay
85

80 See detail
Stoney Bay
Day X The Blinders
Anchorage
Fallen Jerusalem 20 40

30

Broken Jerusalem 90
25 36
60
BV 10 100
305 40
ROUND ROCK 64°26.90'W 64° 25.20'W
90 100

Waypoints	North	West
BV401	18°26.00'	64°27.00'
BV402	18°27.20'	64°26.90'
BV403	18°28.42'	64°26.80'
BV404	18°30.00'	64°29.20'
BV405	18°30.40'	64°25.20'
BV406	18°31.30'	64°23.10'
BV407	18°30.50'	64°18.70'
BV408	18°32.20'	64°15.00'
BV410	18°42.40'	64°24.50'

18°
28.42'N

18°
26'N

Round Rock Passage

VIRGIN GORDA

The island of Virgin Gorda is approximately 10 miles long with high peaks at the north and central areas. The Gorda Peak National Park at 1,370 feet contains trails you can follow to hike to the summit, but throughout the island there are numerous trails to follow within the National Park system, including those along and through the Baths. The Baths are a natural collection of slowly eroded boulders that line the south end of Virgin Gorda. Their beauty is iconic. The waters around Virgin Gorda offer the sailor a myriad of delights from the granite caves at the Baths to the deep anchorages of North Sound, a small archipelago of islands. Virgin Gorda has over 500 acres of designated national park including Fallen Jerusalem to the west.

Charts
NV.Charts: St.Thomas to Anegada: Kit C-12,12A,13
NIMA:2561, Imray Iolaire A-231
Admiralty Leisure 5640-2, 3, 7, 8A, 9

HISTORY

The first residents in Virgin Gorda history to populate the area were the Ciboney, Arawak, and Carib Indians. They lived by farming the land and fishing its abundant natural resources. Columbus came upon the entire string of Virgin Islands on his second voyage to the New World, in 1493, even though he never landed here. Seeing so many isles and cays, it is believed he named them after the 11,000 virgin followers of Saint Ursula, who were martyred in the fourth century (as the story goes). Virgin Gorda, the "Fat Virgin," as Columbus irreverently named the island for its resemblance from seaward to a generously sized woman lying on her back, was once the capital of the British Virgins with a population of 8,000 people.

After Columbus officially claimed the island for the Spanish crown, the island languished for nearly 200 years with minimal administration. During this period privateers and pirates such as the notorious Bluebeard and the likes of Captain Kidd used Virgin Gorda as a base of operations from which to harass and plunder Spanish galleons that passed through the reef-laced waters carrying home to Europe gold from

the New World. By 1870 the British had ousted the Dutch settlers from both Virgin Gorda and Anegada and built an agricultural base that brought prosperity to the region but which gradually eroded with the abolition of slavery in 1838.

Copper Mine Point

Tourism to Virgin Gorda was accelerated by the development of the Little Dix Bay Resort and the Virgin Gorda Yacht Harbour in the mid 1960s thanks to the efforts of the American philanthropist Laurance Rockefeller who was also instrumental in helping establish the foundations of the National Parks with the donation of Gorda Peak in 1974.

North Sound Looking West

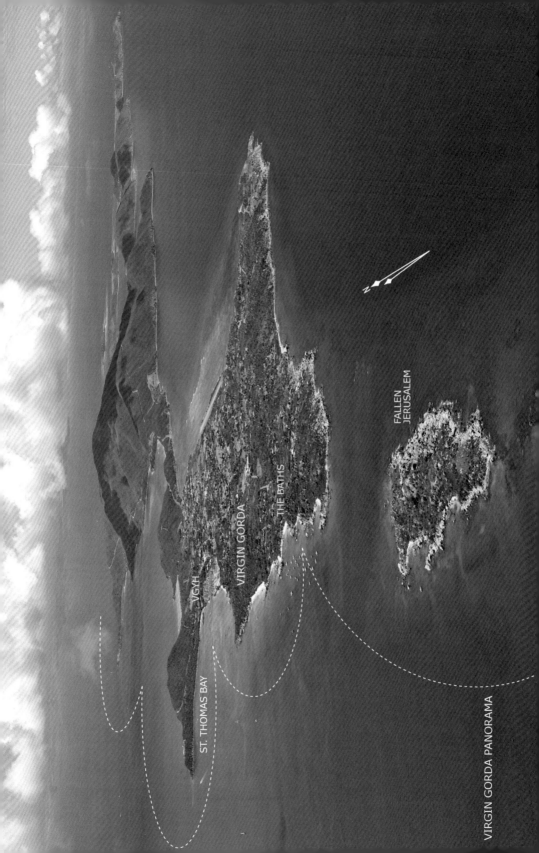

VGYH

VIRGIN GORDA

THE BATHS

ST. THOMAS BAY

FALLEN
JERUSALEM

VIRGIN GORDA PANORAMA

N

THE BATHS

Waypoint: BV401 – 18°26.00'N; 64°27.00'W
Navigation: 4.7nm NE Cooper Island;
1.4nm south of VGYH
Services: NPT Moorings, Restaurant, Beach bar, Trail

Virgin Gorda

When planning a trip around the island, it is essential to include The Baths. A National Park protected area, The Baths are located on the southwest tip of Virgin Gorda and characterized as an unusual formation of large granite boulders. Where the sea washes in between the huge rocks, large pools have been created where shafts of light play upon the water, creating a dramatic effect. The beach adjacent to The Baths is white and sandy and the snorkeling excellent. A trail has been established behind the beach, through the boulders, to Devil's Bay to the south.

Valley Trunk Bay

Little Trunk Bay

Rock

The Crawl

BV 401

18° 26'N

Spring Bay

VIRGIN GORDA

NP SWIM AREA

The Baths

National Park Boundary

TRAIL

TO CAVE DEVILS BAY

NP Devils Bay

SWIM AREA

Stoney Bay

64° 27'W

THE BATHS | SPRING BAY

During the winter season when ground swells are present, the anchorage is very exposed and at such times it is recommended that you anchor in St. Thomas Bay or take a slip at the Yacht Harbour and take a taxi ride to The Baths. The National Parks Trust has initiated a flag system to warn of dangerous seas in the area of The Baths. There is a flag pole at the beach, one at the top of The Baths, and one on Devil's Bay beach. There are plans to install more along the beach area to ensure that they are clearly visible to boaters.

This information will be provided in the National Parks Trust permit which is required in order to use National Parks Trust moorings. The permit can also be shown to gain access to The Baths (without additional payment) from the land should conditions require.

Navigation & Piloting:

Approaching from the south (waypoint BV305 Round Rock Passage North) keep Round Rock, Broken Jerusalem and Fallen Jerusalem well to starboard. The area has numerous uncharted rocks and a 2 knot current that can run northwest or southeast. When approaching from the Sir Francis Drake Channel, the first landmark will be the large rock formations. There are fine, white sandy beaches of varying sizes and The Baths are located at the second beach from the westernmost tip of Virgin Gorda. If there is a ground sea running, it is advisable to keep sailing into the Yacht Harbour and take a taxi to The Baths.

If you are powering or sailing further north towards the Yacht Harbour, be mindful of Burrows Rock, which extends 200 feet out from the small headland at the south end of Valley Trunk Bay.

Anchoring & Mooring

National Park Trust moorings are the only mode of securing the vessel in order to protect the coral as this is in part of the BVI National Park Trust. There is no anchoring at The Baths or Devil's Bay. Anchoring is permitted outside the boundary of the park which ends at the southern end of Valley Trunk Bay. National Park Trust moorings permit a three hour limit.

Since no vessels are permitted to land within the park, it should be noted that there are two dinghy mooring tether systems in place, one at Devils Bay at the southern end and one at the Baths. From this point everyone will need to swim ashore using the buoyed rope barrier as necessary. Weak swimmers should make use of a life jacket or a pool "noodle" when making their way from the dinghy tie-up area to the shore. They should also be cautioned to wear gloves if they intend to use the buoyed rope barrier line as support as submerged line will accumulate barnacles which can inflict nasty cuts.

Ashore

Take ashore only those articles that you don't mind getting wet and wrap cameras and valuables in a waterproof pouch or plastic bags.

Once ashore, the actual entrance to The Baths is unmarked but is at the southern end of the beach under the palm trees. Make your way in between the natural slot in the rocks (you will have to crouch) and follow the trail that leads inconspicuously between the huge granite boulders all the way to Devils Bay. Over the years this trail has been upgraded by the National Park Trust in order to accommodate the burgeoning

number of visitors arriving by cruise ship. There are handholds and wooden ladders to assist the less agile, but care should be taken and it is advisable to wear reef shoes or some kind of footwear.

Colorful stalls on the beach sell souvenirs, crafts and t-shirts. It is also possible to get a cold drink and sandwiches at the Poor Man's Bar right on the beach so bring some cash in a sealed plastic bag. Lockers, shower facilities and toilets are in close proximity. At the Top of The Baths you can enjoy breakfast, lunch, sushi and late lunch appetizers while enjoying the view of The Baths and the islands to the west or cool off in their fresh water pool. Meal service starts at 8am and they close at 6pm.

Dinner reservations are recommended by booking online at www.topofthebaths. com or calling 284-495-5497.

Caution; it is wise to check on the daily cruise ship arrivals in Road Harbour as eager tourists are transported to Virgin Gorda and The Baths, both by boat and taxi, which can create a crowded situation on and around the narrow trail. If possible, schedule your visit early in the morning or later in the afternoon. If you do encounter a group making their way through the rocks, it is best to allow them to pass since two-way traffic can present some frustrations when crouching and trying to walk contemporaneously. Rock-rage has been evidenced believe it or not.

SPANISH TOWN (St. THOMAS BAY)
VIRGIN GORDA YACHT HARBOUR

Virgin Gorda

Waypoint: BV402 (St.Thomas Bay) – 18°27.20'N; 64°26.90'W

Navigation: 4.3nm east of Trellis Bay;
1.4nm north of The Baths

Services: Port of entry, Ferry service, Full service 120-slip marina, Restaurants, ATM, Yacht repair facility, Boatyard, WiFi, Pump-out, Propane, Moorings, Laundry

Once the capital of the BVI, Spanish Town is still the major settlement on the island. Although opinions vary, it is commonly thought that Spanish Town is so called for the number of Spanish settlers who came to mine the copper ore at Copper Mine Point early in the 16th century. The mines were still working until 1867, and it is estimated that some 10,000 tons of copper ore were exported.

The Virgin Gorda Yacht Harbour is located in the middle of Spanish Town (or the Valley as it is more commonly referred to) and is the hub of shopping and boating activity on the south end of the island. Although badly damaged by Hurricane Irma in 2017, it is projected that all marina operations and service facilities will be rebuilt by season 2019/20.

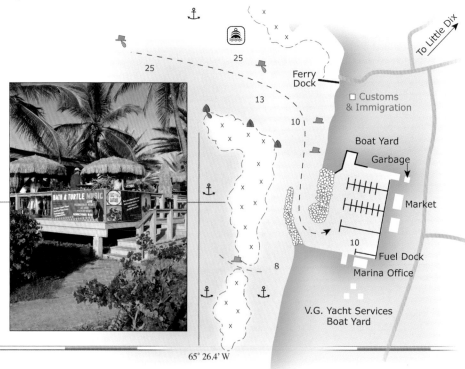

Virgin Gorda Yacht Harbour

Navigation & Piloting

Approaching St. Thomas Bay and the Virgin Gorda Yacht Harbour from the east, head for the northeast corner of the bay. Yachts traveling south from Gorda Sound should give a wide berth to Colison Point (4 sec fl. green buoy) as they have rocks awash at the end of the point.

For vessels wishing not to enter the yacht harbor, there is limited anchoring under the headland to the north in 15 feet of water on a sand bottom. There are also several moorings available for the usual $30 per night in addition to numerous private moorings in this area. During the summer months when the wind is well around to the east and the seas are calm, you can anchor to the west of the reef outside of the yacht harbor in about 6-9 feet of water. There is also a cut through the reef, south of the breakwater and marked with a single green can that is noted on the chart as a small boat passage, where several shallow draft catamarans spend the evening.

To enter the yacht harbor, you should familiarize yourself with the location of the St. Thomas reef that parallels the shoreline.

Approach the harbor on a line with the prominent ferry jetty in St. Thomas Bay. Leave the first two markers (green) to port. Immediately to starboard, you will see the first red buoy marking the north end of the reef. As you round the second red buoy, you will turn approximately 90 degrees to starboard and pass between another set of buoys before entering the harbor. Contact the harbormaster via VHF 16 to get your slip assignment before you enter the yacht harbor. There is no anchoring in the yacht harbor.

When leaving Virgin Gorda Yacht Harbour/St. Thomas Bay and heading north to Gorda Sound, be sure to give Colison Point a wide berth, as the rocks extend well out from the land into the water. There should be a green 4 sec fl. buoy marking this point. Make sure it is on station.

Ashore

Customs and Immigration are located at the town jetty, just a couple of minutes from the Virgin Gorda Yacht Harbour. They are open from 8:30am to 4:30pm daily. Sundays and holidays incur overtime charges. Upon entry from another country into the BVI proceed to Customs and Immigration. Only the skipper needs to go to present passports of the passengers and the ship's papers.

If you arrive after regular hours you must raise your yellow Q flag and call Customs at 284-495-5173 and Immigration at 284-495-5621. You must not leave your vessel until you have cleared in.

The marina has dockage for over 100 yachts and can accommodate 4-5 superyachts. The maximum length is 180 feet and the maximum width is approximately 35 feet. The controlling depth in the harbor is 10 feet.

Entering the marina, the fuel dock is directly ahead on the starboard side, in front of the marina office. Amenities include water, ice, fuel, oil, pump-out, WiFi, and power (110v, 220v and 110 amps). Showers and heads are included in the dockage fee. The marina office will answer all questions and help you with services and reservations. The dock crew will help you with electric and water.

At the time of the hurricane, plans were already underway to rebuild the marina service buildings and it could be said that the storm accelerated the demolition process. According to Keith Thomas, marina manager, the plans (June 2019) were to have the new service centers finished by November 2019 in time for the season. There will be a new market and provisioning center (where the old Buck's Market used to be) along with an expanded marine chandlery open 7:45am until 7pm (6pm on Sunday's) and new shower/restroom facilities. Across the parking lot, the retail center will also be rebuilt to accommodate Dive BVI, The BVI Tourist Board and other retail boutiques.

A new open restaurant and bar will be operating overlooking the marina serving casual cuisine in an informal casual setting. Garbage can be disposed of at the northern end of the marina building in the compactor. There is no fee if you are a marina guest.

Complementing the marina is a full service boatyard and dry storage facility adjacent to the harbor. The boatyard is serviced by a 70 ton Travel Lift that can haul vessels over 100 feet in length with a beam up to 22 feet. The recent 9 acre expansion of the boatyard at the north end of the marina is operational with a 350ton travel lift, with a beam of 40 feet and capable of hauling larger catamarans and megayachts. The boatyard offers complete services including shipwrights, marine mechanics, Awlgrip and osmosis

treatment. All yard services should be coordinated by the service manager, Jeremy Dougan (jdougan@vgyh.net) or call 284-499-5552

The greater marina complex offers numerous facilities including a bank (ATM), drugstore, provisioning, car rentals, taxis, dive shop and boutique, and other shops.

For divers, Dive BVI operates a full service dive shop offering daily tours as well as rendezvous dives from the Virgin Gorda Yacht Harbour. They also have an extensive boutique for water wear located in the retail center.

Beyond the marina complex there are several restaurants within easy reach. Just a few minutes walk down the road toward the ferry dock is the Bath & Turtle-Chez Bamboo, two sister restaurants under one roof, a cultural cornucopia of food, drinks and atmosphere. Enjoy a cool drink in the casual bistro surroundings at the inside bar or outside on the terrace bar in the balmy evening breeze and listen to the music of local bands and entertainers. For a more formal dining experience the inside restaurant, Chez Bamboo serves an interesting array of international cuisine and Rose, the owner, and her team will be there to welcome you. Hours of business: breakfast, lunch, dinner, 7am-9pm, bar until 10:30pm. (284-545-1861).

To the south of the marina, The Rock Café and CocoMaya, both highly recommended, are a ten minute walk from the marina. That being said, the road is narrow and the recommendation would be to take a taxi for $3-4 per head. CocoMaya is situated right next to the beach with a fire pit in the sand

and serving creative Caribbean cuisine with an Asian influence. Open from 3-10pm Tuesday-Saturday for drinks, late lunch and dinner, reservations advised.

The Rock Café is nestled amongst the fabulous Virgin Gorda boulders serving Italian and Caribbean cuisine. They serve dinner and happy hour starts at 4pm, and often have live music. Sam's Piano Bar is a favorite spot for a relaxing drink after dinner.

Fischer's Cove, next door to the marina, serves breakfast, lunch and dinner from 7:30am to 10pm daily in a casual, friendly atmosphere by the water.

Rosewood Little Dix Bay is scheduled to reopen for the 2019/20 season and is a taxi ride away and those wishing to look around the grounds are welcome for drinks and luncheon. Reservations are required for dinner. Although jackets are not required, shorts are not allowed in the dining room after 6pm.

Island Tour

If you have the time, take a taxi or rent a car and drive around the island. Traveling north you will drive past Little Dix Bay, Savannah Bay and the continuing vistas as you follow the west coast road toward Nail Bay and the ruins of an old sugar mill. A little further, as you turn to the east climbing toward Gorda Peak, you will find Hog Heaven Bar & Restaurant with amazing views across North Sound. Gorda Peak is 1,370 feet at its summit and a designated National Park with hiking trails. The return trip takes you past South Sound and back through Spanish Town then on to the copper mine ruins at the southeastern tip of the island. Access to The Baths is via a well-defined trail.

SAVANNAH BAY

Waypoint: BV403 (Gt.Dog) – 18°28.42'N;
64°26.80'W
Navigation: 2.3nm NE of VGYH
Services: Snorkeling
Caution: Reef entrance, no buoys

Virgin Gorda

During the summer months or when the ground swells are down and the weather is calm, there is a delightful anchorage behind the reef in Savannah Bay, however it can be very tricky to get in and navigate over coral heads to the anchorage. When the weather is calm, being anchored in Pond Bay is the quintessential Caribbean experience. If you are chartering this bay may be off limits.

Navigation & Piloting

The entrance to Savannah Bay behind the reef is at the southern end of the bay, just north of Blowing Point under Minton Hill. It is essential that you have good overhead light in order see the coral heads and a lookout posted on the bow.

Enter the anchorage about 325 yards off the point parallel to the headland. There is a small reef that extends from the headland on your starboard hand. Work your way into the bay until you are abeam of a white range marker painted

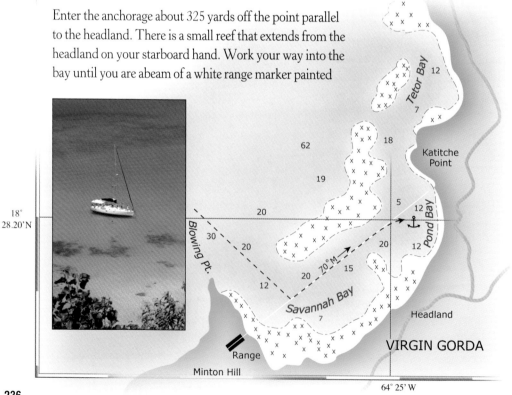

Savannah Bay

on the rocks under Minton Hill to starboard. When the range is abeam turn to port (about 70°M) and continue with caution toward the end of the beach under Katitche Point. You will pass over some coral heads but this will take you into Pond Bay where you can anchor in 12-15 feet of water on a sandy bottom. The snorkeling is excellent.

Tetor Bay further north is a complicated channel and should not be attempted except by dinghy. Watch for the small reef that extends from the headland on your starboard hand and work your way around the coral heads that comprise the center reef. Once inside, you can anchor in 7 feet of water.

MOUNTAIN POINT / LONG BAY

Services: NPS moorings, Diving and snorkeling

Situated just south of Mountain Point, before you enter Gorda Sound, Long Bay is a small delightful anchorage that is tenable only when there is no ground sea running and open to the south. The anchorage is easy to approach from the east. There are some National Park System Moorings in place for daytime use and a small beach at the head of the bay. Anchor on a sandy bottom in 15-29 feet of water. The snorkeling is excellent both on the reef that extends from the shore into the anchorage to the northeast and along the shoreline under Mountain Point.

Long Bay / Mountain Point, Virgin Gorda

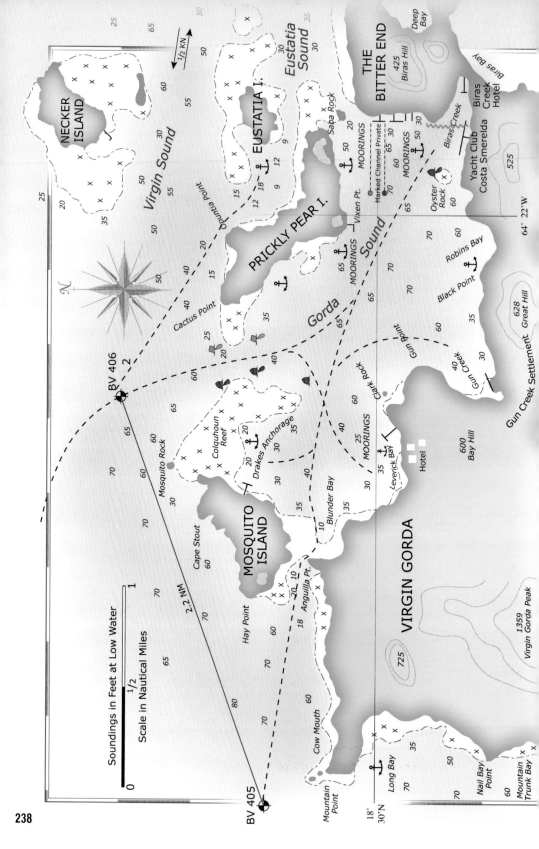

238

GORDA SOUND (NORTH SOUND)

Waypoint: BV406 (Mosquito Rock) – 18°31.30'N; 64°23.10'W

Navigation: 15nm NE Road Harbour; 3.6nm north of VGYH

Services: Moorings, Restaurants, Beach bars, Full service marinas, Hotels, Trails, Watersports

Located at the northern end of Virgin Gorda, Gorda Sound or North Sound, as it is sometimes called, is a large bay protected all around by islands and reefs.

It is an ideal place to spend several days exploring the reefs and relaxing. There are numerous restaurants and marina complexes here to suit almost everyone's taste and wallet. There are three entrances into the Sound but only one that is well marked. The western entrance via Anguilla Point is tricky and should only be used by those with local knowledge. Most bareboat companies place it off limits.

Oyster Rock

LEVERICK·BAY

DRAKE'S ANCHORAGE

GUN CREEK

MOSQUITO ROCK

COLQUHOUN REEF

BIRAS CREEK

YCCS

BITTER END

SABA ROCK

PRICKLY PEAR

N

GORDA SOUND

Northern Entrance
via Colquhoun Reef

Navigation & Piloting

Gorda Sound is best approached from the north. A prominent landmark is Mosquito Rock that extends 25 feet above sea level and marks both the northern extremity of Mosquito Island and the northern tip of Colquhoun Reef that arcs to the southeast into the Sound. The channel between Colquhoun Reef to the west and Cactus Reef to the east is marked with two sets of red and green buoys and the controlling depth is from 15 feet where the buoys are located to 35 feet in the center of the channel.

Leaving Mosquito Rock well to starboard, head for the first green buoy (flashing 6 seconds) that marks the port side of the channel when entering. This will keep you clear of both reefs. There is a red nun (fl.6 sec) to starboard marking the outer (eastern) limits of Colquhoun Reef. Proceed through the second set of markers (fl.5 sec) into clear water and Gorda Sound.

If you are proceeding to Leverick Bay or Drake's Anchorage, continue due south until you are south or east of the third red buoy marking the southern extent of the coral heads extending from Colquhoun Reef. It is imperative that you leave it to starboard in order to avoid going aground. Once past the buoy, you can proceed directly to either anchorage with clear water.

Traveling to the east, past Vixen Point, is a vast mooring field associated with both the Bitter End and Saba Rock. There is a privately marked channel to the docks of Bitter End, and another marking a channel past Saba Rock, into Eustatia Sound and the Oil Nut Bay Marina Village at Deep Bay.

There is one other navigational hazard in the Sound and that is Oyster Rock, which is to the west of the Biras Creek anchorage. The rock is marked with a red cone buoy.

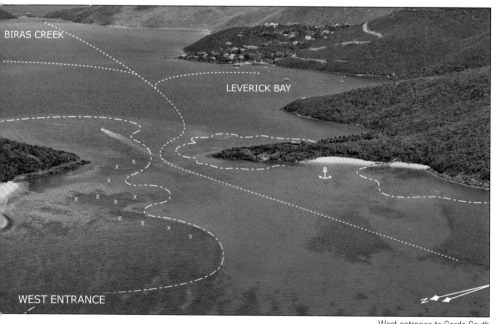

BIRAS CREEK

LEVERICK BAY

WEST ENTRANCE

West entrance to Gorda South

SABA ROCK

Navigation: 1.5nm NE of entrance channel
Services: Ferry, WiFi hotspot, Marina, Restaurant, Hotel

Originally developed by Bert Kilbride, Saba Rock is a tiny island sitting astride the channel to Eustatia Sound, between the Bitter End on Virgin Gorda and Prickly Pear Island. The island infrastructure suffered enormous damage as a result of Hurricane Irma resulting in the sale to a European resident of Virgin Gorda who has undertaken the rebuilding process.

Anchoring & Mooring

Approaching Saba Rock and the mooring field from the west it is difficult to know which moorings belong to Saba Rock and which ones to Bitter End. Generally the moorings to the north of the marked channel are those belonging to and maintained by Moor Seacure for Saba Rock.

If you plan to anchor, the best location to drop your hook is west of the mooring field, along the coast of Prickly Pear in 15-20 feet of water on a sandy bottom.

Ashore

At press time, there was no available information regarding the new buildings and plans for general infrastructure, although rebuilding was well underway. It should be assumed that the facility will be partially open for the season 2019/20 and updates will be posted on our website (www.cruisingguides.com).

Saba Rock under construction, June 2019

Vixen Point
(Prickly Pear Island / National Park)

Navigation: 0.9nm SE Colquhoun Reef Entrance;
Services: Moorings, Beach bar, Restaurant

Anchoring & Mooring

On the west side of Prickly Pear Island, to the north of Vixen Point and south of Cactus Reef, is a good spot to anchor in 7-12 feet of water. Caution should be taken to identify a shallow (5') finger that extends to the northwest just above Vixen Point. Another spot to anchor is just below this finger before reaching the mooring field closer to Vixen Point. A number of moorings are available off of the sandy beach and you may register and pay for them ashore at the restaurant. Additional anchoring space is available to the south of Prickly Pear behind the mooring field controlled by Saba Rock. You will have to anchor fairly close to the shoreline but holding is good in 15 feet of water.

Ashore

The Sand Box serves lunch from 11:00am to 5pm daily and dinner from 6:30 to 11pm in a casual beach bar atmosphere. They also serve a mean margarita! The beach is good for swimming and you have a clear view of the activity in the Sound while you relax. The Sand Box monitors VHF 16 or call 284-495-9122.

SABA ROCK

BITTER END
YACHT CLUB
EST. 1969. LAUNCHING AGAIN 2019-2020.

The Quarterdeck Marina
Bitter End Yacht Club 2.0

Bitter End Yacht Club's iconic nautical village returns to its roots
as the world's favorite yachting and watersports destination.

DOCKAGE · MOORINGS · YACHT MANAGEMENT · WATERSPORTS
RESTAURANT · BEACH BAR · BOUTIQUE · PROVISIONS

For dockage and dining reservations call 800.872.2392 or Hail us on VHF Channel 16   Visit us at WWW.BEYC.COM

BITTER END

Navigation: 1.3nm NE of North Sound Channel Entrance
Services: Moorings, Ferry, Full service marina, Restaurant, Watersports, Provisioning, Boutique, Trails, WiFi

Originally established in the late '60s by charter skipper, Basil Symonette, the original Bitter End consisted of a small dock, rustic bar, restaurant and a few sparse cottages. The Hokin family, sailors themselves, took over the stewardship in the early '70s and since that time transformed it into a world class resort and water sports center with global recognition.

Hurricane Irma made a direct pass over the island on September 6th. 2017 leveling what had taken 50 years to build. Nearly two years later Bitter End 2.0, as the family refers to it, is becoming a reality with an opening scheduled for the season 2019/20. Phase one is the marina village to be followed by new accommodations the following year.

Anchoring & Mooring

Located on John O'Point, the Bitter End is a resort hotel and marina that features water sports, recreational activities, restaurants, overnight dockage, guest rooms and moorings.

There are two sets of lighted buoys marking the approach for the North Sound Express ferryboat. Avoid anchoring near this channel to keep it clear for ferry traffic. The Bitter End channel and mooring field is a no wake zone.

The Bitter End maintains numerous moorings available for boats up to 60 feet at $35.00 per night that can be paid for at the new Quarterdeck Office with cash or credit cards (8am-5pm) or paid to the launch driver every evening from 3pm to 6:30pm (cash only).

The Quarterdeck Marina sells fuel and water at the fuel dock and is open from 8am to 3pm with a depth at the fuel dock of 10 feet. Vessels taking a berth will also

BITTER END

Bitter End Quarterdeck before Hurricane Irma

have electricity hookups. Depth in the marina is approximately 10-22 feet. Please make arrangements in advance. The Bitter End monitors VHF 16 or can be called by phone at 284-494-2745 or email: qdmanager@beyc.com

Ashore

The Bitter End is a unique nautical village catering to yachtsmen. The new development has been focused around visiting yachtsmen with a new open air two-story marina building with outdoor seating and a lounge offering views of the sound and associated marine activity where guests can gather for drinks, sunsets and celebrations.

We are told that there will be private bathing facilities and toilets for the use of marina guests, 24 hour security, enhanced wifi, a boutique offering the Bitter End line of watersport clothing in addition to other fashion items. The Clubhouse will return as a casual waterfront restaurant and beach bar. Provisions and gourmet offerings will be available from the general store.

Although not confirmed at the time of printing, garbage pickup is at your boat in the morning between 8 – 9am. Bags must be tied and there is a charge of $2 per bag. For those on moorings, you may call the launch on VHF 16, and request a free ride ashore on the Bitter End launch. The free service is daily from 6:30pm to 10:30pm each evening. For guests needing to visit the market at Gun Creek for more extensive provisioning options, it is possible to take the ferry from Bitter End to Gun Creek, shop for an hour and take the next ferry back for no charge. The ferry leaves Bitter End on the hour and Gun Creek on the 1/2 hour (no service 10am/1pm/8pm). This is subject to change so check with the marina manager.

Watersports: Venturing north from the marina along the newly enhanced beach area, watersport's enthusiasts will discover an all new club fleet of small craft available to visiting boaters. Hobie Waves, Lasers, Sunfish, 420's, kayaks, stand-up paddle boards plus other toys are available for rent.

Diving: SunChaser Scuba maintain their base at Bitter End and have operated almost continually through the rebuilding process. They offer daily dive trips, PADI courses, equipment rentals and air refills. VHF 16

Hiking: There are numerous trails throughout the Bitter End (map available from Activity Desk) and adjacent properties. They vary in intensity and take between 20 minutes (Guy's Trail) to 75 minutes (Alvin's Trail). Spectacular scenery can be viewed from the top so take your camera, sunscreen, water and wear a sturdy pair of shoes.

The Bitter End closes each year from mid-August to mid-October.

Saba Rock from Guy's Trail

From North Sound

The B.V.I. Government in conjunction with Oil Nut Bay have installed a buoyed (red and green) channel from the passage east of Saba Rock all the way past Deep Bay and the new marina development to Oil Nut Bay where a large upscale development continues. The channel is reported to carry 8 feet and joins a marked channel through the eastern end of the reef to seaward and into the Necker Island Channel. Skippers are encouraged to exercise extreme caution in this area. Anchoring in the southwest extremity of Deep Bay or Oil Nut Bay is discouraged.

Vessels wishing to transit through the Saba Rock channel and on to the anchorage behind Eustatia Island (Eustatia Sound) should note the location of the reef extending north from Saba Rock toward Eustatia Island. Post a knowledgeable lookout on the bow and proceed with caution. Make sure that you have good light overhead.

Grunt

Mangroves at Biras Creek

Bitter End Clubhouse (pre-Irma)

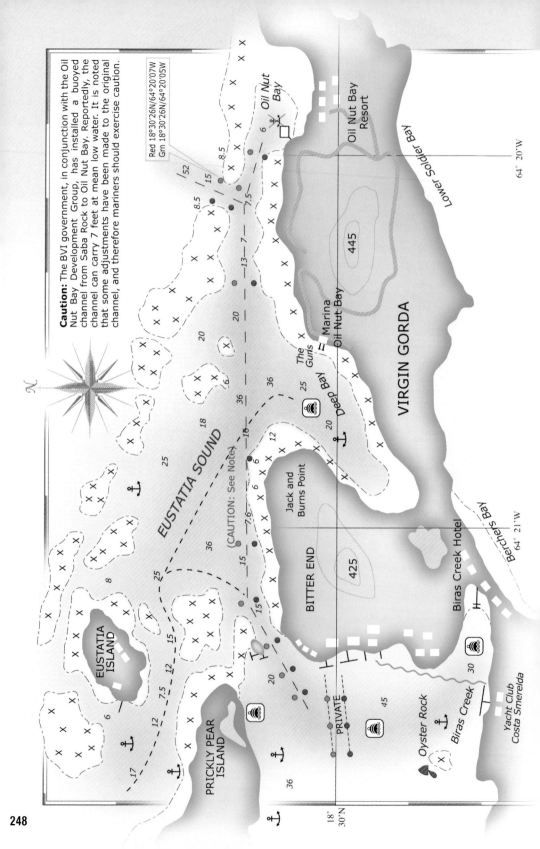

Caution: The BVI government, in conjunction with the Oil Nut Bay Development Group, has installed a buoyed channel from Saba Rock to Oil Nut Bay. Reportedly, the channel can carry 7 feet at mean low water. It is noted that some adjustments have been made to the original channel, and therefore mariners should exercise caution.

Red 18°30'26N/64°20'07W
Gm 18°30'26N/64°20'05W

Oil Nut Bay

Oil Nut Bay Resort

Lower Soldier Bay

64° 20'W

445

VIRGIN GORDA

Marina
Oil Nut Bay

The Guns

Deep Bay

EUSTATIA SOUND

(CAUTION: See Note)

Jack and Burns Point

BITTER END

425

Biras Creek Hotel

Betchers Bay

64° 21'W

EUSTATIA ISLAND

PRICKLY PEAR ISLAND

PRIVATE

Oyster Rock

Biras Creek

Yacht Club
Costa Smerelda

18°
30'N

248

EUSTATIA ISLAND AND EUSTATIA SOUND

Waypoint: BV406 (Mosquito Rock) 18°31.30'N; 64°23.10'W

Navigation: 1.7 nm SE of Mosquito Rock (Eustatia Island)

Services: None

Eustatia Sound is a magnificent area, located to the north and east of Bitter End and Saba Rock. The most sheltered overnight anchorage in the area is in behind Eustatia Island, which bounds the western end of the Sound. However, many skippers use the Sound as a day anchorage to enable diving and snorkeling along the stretch of reef that marks the northern extremity of the Sound and entrance to the Necker Island Channel.

This area is not well marked and caution should be exercised unless you are very familiar with navigating around and through coral. A good solution is to leave the boat on the mooring at Saba Rock or Bitter End and take the dinghy through the cut and out to the reef.

Navigation & Piloting

Approaching from the north or west (via waypoint BV406), leaving Mosquito Rock and the entrance to the Sound via Colquhoun Reef well to starboard, continue to the southeast leaving Prickly Pear Island to starboard. To the northeast you will see Necker Island and Eustatia Island will be visible ahead to the southeast. Once you are past Opuntia Point on the northeast tip of Prickly Pear, turn southeast and steer for the eastern tip of Prickly Pear until Eustatia Island is due east. Head for the southwest end of Eustatia where you will see a dock and drop the hook in 15 feet of water in the lee of the island. Do not make your entrance too far north as there is reef to the northwest of the island; favor the Prickly Pear side of the channel.

Eustatia Sound

DEEP BAY
OIL NUT MARINA VILLAGE

Navigation: 1.7nm NE of North Sound Channel Entrance

Services: Marina, Heliport, Fuel, Water. Ice. Moorings, Restaurant, Bar, Wifi, Garbage, Trails, Snorkeling

Located within Eustatia Sound to the east of Saba Rock, the Oil Nut Bay Village and Marina are accessed via a marked channel from North Sound. The channel carries 8 feet (2.4 meters) and joins a marked channel through the eastern end of the reef to seaward and into the waters of Necker Sound. Anchoring in Oil Nut Bay is discouraged.

Navigation & Piloting

From North Sound there is a marked channel between Saba Rock and John O'Point (Bitter End). Follow the channel to the east passing three sets of markers off the shoreline to the south before turning south into Deep Bay around Jack & Burns Point. The channel can carry 8 feet (2.4 meters), the shallowest areas are located adjacent to Saba Rock and at the eastern end of the channel where it turns north and flows out to Necker Sound. Skippers are cautioned to pay attention to the markers as there are patches of coral to the north and south of the transit line.

Anchoring & Mooring

The Oil Nut Bay Marina Village is open to all visiting yachtsmen. Eleven moorings are available for vessels to 60 feet at $30 per night. A larger mooring is available for vessels to 120 feet at $120 a night. The mooring fee includes a bag of ice if the mooring fee is made at the market. Vessels wishing to anchor will probably want to move further south into the bay in order to anchor in 20 feet of water on a sand bottom. Marina rates are $3 per foot in season and $2 per foot in the low season. Call the dock master on VHF 16 or 284-393-1000.

Ashore

The Marina Village is designed to accommodate vessels up to 100 feet with a draft of up to 8'. When complete the marina will offer up to 93 berths. For the season 2019/20 there are three piers that are designated from the east (1,2 and 4). Pier number 3 will be completed at a later date. A state of the art marina complex, Marina Village is anchored by the Nova Restaurant overlooking the secluded waters of Deep Bay. The restaurant offers a variety of cuisine including small shareable options. There is also a large covered lounge deck where sailors can relax and enjoy a drink including hand crafted cocktails.

The marina market offers a good selection of provisions including wine and all basic staples, plus grab-and-go deli items. There is also a bakery, coffee shop, boutique, and library. Access to the Beach Club facilities at Oil Nut Bay is available with a day pass for visiting yachtsmen at $120 per person.

Since the marina and Oil Nut Bay development is only accessed via private road or by sea, security is never an issue and for access to the hiking trails, check with the dock master, Nick Putman. There are two heliport landing areas available in close vicinity to the marina complex.

Deep Bay / Marina Village

BIRAS CREEK

Navigation: 1.8nm NE of Channel Entrance
Services: Hotel & Marina are closed until further notice (June 2019)

A very well-protected anchorage fringed by mangroves, Biras Creek Resort, at the head of the harbor, straddles a hill with stunning views of the beach on one side and the harbor on the other. The anchorage is accessible directly from North Sound. Oyster Rock, marked by a red nun will be on your starboard hand when entering. Regrettably the resort and marina closed in June of 2016 and later sustained considerable damage from Hurricane Irma. We understand that complete renovations and extensions to the property are underway (May 2019) but no clear date for opening has been communicated at press time. The marina still has a few long term tenants but should be considered closed for practical purposes.

There are a number of moorings in this anchorage and we confirm that they are being serviced and that someone will be around for the mooring fee. The anchorage itself, is lined with mangroves, many of which were damaged in the hurricane, but which remains very well protected and should be considered a hurricane hole in any passing disturbance. Depths range from 36 to 24 feet closer to the dock.

Caution should be taken to note the presence of an underwater cable that extends from the marina at Bitter End just off the coastline past Rat Point (sometimes referred to as "Wedding Point") and exits near the east end of the YCCS commercial dock.

The Biras Creek Anchorage

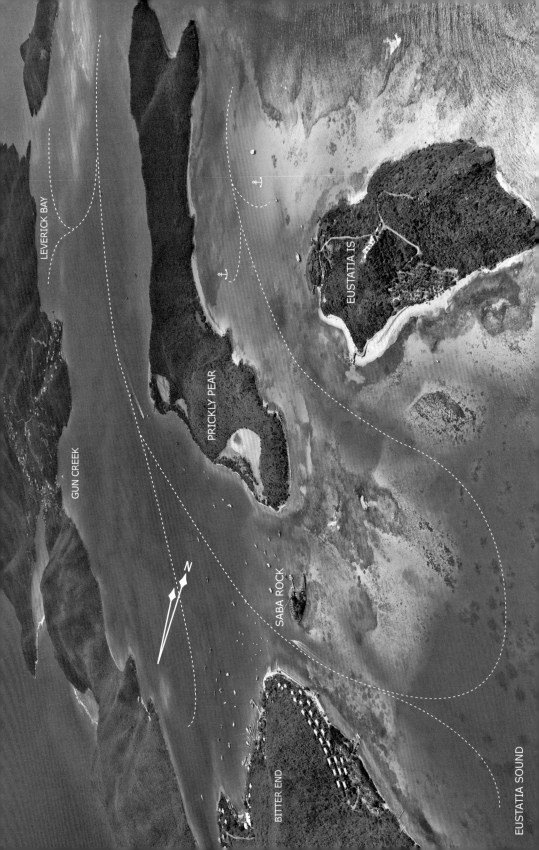

LEVERICK BAY

GUN CREEK

PRICKLY PEAR

N

SABA ROCK

BITTER END

EUSTATIA IS

EUSTATIA SOUND

Ashore

Although visitors are welcome to land their dinghies at the marina dinghy dock, they are not welcome to roam around the hotel while it is closed. They are welcome to use the trails that connect with those of The Bitter End, YCCS, the beach and the roadway to Oil Nut Bay. In this regard, visitors are requested not to litter and to leave minimal impact on the surrounding environment.

On your starboard side as you enter Biras Creek are the service buildings and associated docks for the resort. Like many other buildings in the vicinity, extensive damage was sustained as a result of the hurricane and at press time we have no definitive news about a reopening of the Fat Virgin Café. In the past, this has been a great spot for a casual lunch or dinner looking out across the water. When open the hours were from 10am for sandwiches, burgers, chicken and roti. Happy hour is 4:30-6:30pm with 1/2 price beers and wine. We look forward to seeing them back in business.

Yacht Club Costa Smeralda (YCCS)

Services: None: The facility is closed until further notice (June 2019)

The entire 2,500 foot dock system associated with the YCCS facility was destroyed when the eye of Hurricane Irma past almost overhead in September 2017. Since the facility cannot function without docks, the management have advised us that at the time we went to press, no decision had been made as to when the facility would reopen.

Gun Creek

Navigation: 1.2nm due south of Colquhoun Reef Entrance; 1.2nm SE of Leverick Bay
Services: Provisions, Ferry, Restaurant, Taxi, Garbage disposal, Note: June 2019, the Customs and Immigration station at Gun Creek was closed due to hurricane damage.

To the southeast of Leverick Bay, under Gnat Point, is the local settlement of Gun Creek, normally a Port of Entry into the BVI and small village.

Bakers Bay is exposed to the northeast and consequently during the winter months the anchorage can be choppy. If you are clearing Customs (see note on closure due to hurricane damage), you can anchor in 18-20 feet of water on a sandy bottom and tie your dinghy up to the dock adjacent to the Customs and Immigration building. This is also a ferry landing area so consideration should be given to local traffic. For vessels arriving from St. Martin or down island, Gun Creek makes a convenient port of entry and gives immediate access to the sheltered anchorages of Gorda Sound.

The Gun Creek mini market (Buck's) is located 5 mins up the hill on the right and is reasonably well stocked. For cruisers anchored at Bitter End, it is possible to take the free ferry from their dock to Gun Creek, take care of your shopping and return on the next ferry one hour later. Ferries depart Gun Creek on the half hour. Taxi and island tours can be arranged.

Although no official notification has been received regarding reopening this station, when open Customs and Immigration hours of operation have traditionally been from 8:30am to 4:30pm Monday through Friday and Saturday, Sunday and holidays they open 9:00am to 2:00pm. They do take a lunch break at 12:30pm to 1:30pm.

Classic Yacht at YCCS Dock (pre-Irma)

LEVERICK BAY

Navigation: 1nm SSW of the Colquhoun Reef entrance channel

Services: Moorings, Ferry, Full service marina, Restaurant, Dive shop, Hotel, Provisions, WiFi

Anchoring & Mooring

Leverick Bay Resort and Marina is one of those destinations that make North Sound a watersports haven. Heading for the marina from North Sound the water is fairly deep with a minimum of 16 feet at the marina. Leverick Bay monitors VHF 16 or you may call 284-495-7275. Pull in to the T dock for water (0.25c gal.), fuel and ice ($3.50 bag). There are approximately 36 moorings in the bay, the orange ones are by reservation only via the Boatyball website. All others are available to pick up on a first come basis, pay the $30 per night fee at the marina. On the southern side of the marina you will find the dinghy dock. The marina has 25 slips with electricity, fuel, ice, showers, trash disposal ($2.50 per bag) and laundry facilities. Slips are $1.50 per foot per night up to 69'. $2.50 per foot over 70'. Both moorings and dock customers are entitled to 100 gallons of fresh water, a free bag of ice and hot showers, along with use of the resort's swimming pool. The marina can also accommodate up to three mega-yachts for overnight stays. The deepest part of the marina is 24 feet and has room for a 300 foot mega-yacht.

For vessels wishing to anchor, there is room both behind the mooring field to the west in 25 feet water, or limited room inside of the mooring field in 12 feet of water. Make sure you are clear of the adjacent moorings.

Ashore

Leverick Bay is an entertaining watersports recreation center. You will find all the amenities you need including a pool, grocery market, 24 hour laundry, WiFi, and air conditioned rooms and villas. The Chef's Pantry and deli is located within the marina complex and offers a good range of product including meats and seafood, breads and pastry. Hours are 7am to 7pm daily.

The Restaurant at Leverick Bay has two very unique dining venues. The upstairs open air terrace overlooking the North Sound offers a seasonal menu of classic cuisine including such items as fresh Anegada lobster and beef tenderloin. (Price range for entrees $26-$45.) Reservations

How many reasons
do you need to visit paradise?

LEVERICK BAY RESORT & MARINA

Here, we offer them all!

Welcome to the marina and resort where **a true Caribbean vacation** is made to suit you. A treasure of **salty heart** and a **pirate soul** inspired by all those who want to live twice.

OUR AMENITIES INCLUDE: Virgin Gorda Villa Rentals, Jumbies Beach Bar & The Cove, The Restaurant, Pusser's Store, The Spa, Power Boat Rentals, BVI Snuba, Michael Beans Show, Moko Jumbies, Chef's Pantry Supermarket, Blue Rush Watersports, Arawak Store.

www.leverickbay.com
Tel.: 1 (284) 542 4014 • becky@leverickbay.com
MARINA • HOTEL • BEACH RESORT

recommended. The downstairs beach bar (Jumbies) offers a variety of pub items and Caribbean specialty drinks from 10:30am until 9pm daily. Friday nights feature a beach BBQ with a live band and a Moko Jumbies show (Caribbean stilt dancers). In season from Monday-Wednesday 5pm-7pm they feature Michael Bean, a musician would be pirate, sailor and showman who entertains visitors and turns "Happy Arrr" into a two hour beach party. Reservations recommended. Call 284-340-3005.

Watersports: Leverick Bay is a good base for exploring by land or by sea. Dive BVI is a full service dive shop servicing divers in Virgin Gorda since 1975. They provide a good opportunity for diving on some of the unique dive sites around North Sound. Leverick Bay Water Sports have power boats, dinghies, Hobie Cats, paddle-boards (SUP's) and kayak rentals for exploring the surrounding waters of North Sound.

For the shoppers, the Pusser's Company Store carries a unique line of nautical and tropical clothing for men and women along with watches and luggage presented as if you're in an antique nautical shop. Arawak, located at the foot of the dock, offer an excellent selection of tropical clothing and beach attire along with Batik wraps and gift items. Hours:9am-5pm daily.

Drake's Anchorage (South Bay) Mosquito (Moskito) Island

Tucked up to the east behind Colquhoun Reef and to the north of Blunder Bay, Drake's Anchorage as it is known is a delightful spot and a little off the beaten path. The breeze flows across the anchorage but the reef breaks up any chop. Here there are no moorings (yet) so it is an excellent spot to enjoy an anchorage that is not crowded.

Approaching the anchorage from the east, make sure that you are south of the red buoy marking the southern tip of the coral heads extending from Colquhoun Reef. Once past the buoy, continue west a short distance before turning northwest toward the docks. Anchor off the docks or under the reef in 15-20 feet of water on a sandy bottom.

Ashore

Originally developed in 1966 by renowned BVI treasure diver and adventurer Bert Kilbride, Drake's Anchorage was a favorite watering hole for cruisers. Bert sold the island in the early '70s and purchased Saba Rock where he lived and continued his dive business. Drake's Anchorage was finally closed in 2000 and later sold to renowned adventurer and entrepreneur Sir Richard Branson.

The island infrastructure was severely damaged due to Hurricane Irma and the rebuilding has morphed slowly with the earlier construction that was ongoing at the time of the storm. New docks have been installed and a lemur sanctuary further adds to the intrigue. The island is private and therefore no facilities are available to cruising yachts.

DRAKE'S ANCHORAGE

DRAKE'S ANCHORAGE
COLQUHOUN REEF
MOSQUITO IS
MOSQUITO ROCK

Looking across Colquhoun Reef to Drake's Anchorage

Josie feeding tarpon

Saba Rock

EMERGENCIES
999 or 911
VISAR (Virgin Island Search and Rescue)
Tel: 767 (SOS), or
+1 284 499 0911
www.visar.org

THE BATHS

RESTAURANTS
Top of the Baths
Tel: 1-284-495-5497
www.topofthebaths.com
FB: topofthebaths
Open daily 8am-6pm
Breakfast 8-11am,
lunch 11am-5pm,
sushi 11am-5:30pm

SHOPPING
Bamboula Boutique
Tel:284 542 9181
FB: BamboulaVG
Beach wear, beach cover-ups,
unique jewelry, purses, hats

Caribbean Flavor
Tel: 1 284-495-5914
FB: caribbean-flavor
Resort wear, fashion,
semiprecious jewelry, art
and souvenirs
9am-5pm

SPANISH TOWN

MARINAS
Virgin Gorda Yacht
Harbour
Tel: 284.495.5500
VHF 16/11
www.vgyh.vg
marina@vgyh.vg
8am-5pm daily

MARINE / BOATYARD SERVICES
Virgin Gorda Yacht
Harbour Boatyard
Tel: 284-495-5500
boatyard@vgyh.vg
7am-4pm weekdays

CHANDLERY
Virgin Gorda Yacht
Harbour Chandlery
Tel: 284-495-5706
chandlery@vgyh.vg
7am-4pm weekdays,
Saturday 8am-12pm

CAR RENTAL / TAXI
L&S Jeep Rental
Tel: 284-495-5297
www.landsjeeprentalstaxi-
andtours.com
FB: vgbestcarrentals

Speedy's
Tel: 284-495-5235
www.speedysrentals.com

PROVISIONING
Buck's Markets
Tel: 284-495-5423
www.bucksmarkets.com
Groceries, produce, wine,
liquor, fresh & frozen
meats, dairy and pharma-
ceuticals, provisioning,
online order, delivery.
Mon-Sat 7am-8pm
Sun: 7am-7pm

Cash & Carry Spanish
Town
Tel: 284-340-2263
www.rtwbvi.com
FB: RTWCashCarry
Grocery, frozen, produce,
spirits & more

Rosy's Enterprises
Tel: 284-495-5245
www.rosysvg.com
admin@rosysvg.com
Supermarket, provisions
orders, deliveries, produce,
meat, baked goods, liquor,
wine, beer
Mon-Fri: 8:30am-8pm,
Sat: 8:30am-8:30pm,
Sun: 8:30am-7pm

Supa Valu Ltd
Tel: 284-495-6500
Mon-Fri 8:30am-5:30pm

RESTAURANTS
Bath & Turtle-Chez Bamboo
Tel: 1 284-545-1861,
www.bathturtle.com
Breakfast, lunch & dinner specials, Asian fusion, sushi, burgers, pizza
7am-9pm, bar 'til 10:30pm

CocoMaya
Tel: 284-495-6344
cocomayarestaurant.com
FB @CocoMayavg
Call to reserve; Asian fusion, beach-front, lounge, waterfront, classic cocktails, wine list, menu on FB
Late lunch & dinner,
3-10pm, happy hour
3-6pm, closed Sun-Mon,

Fischer's Cove
Tel: 284-495-5252
www.fischerscove.com
Waterside serving breakfast, lunch and dinner, specializing in island cuisine
Reservations requested

Hog Heaven Bar & Restaurant
Tel: 1 284-343-0197
FB: Hog-Heaven-Bar-Virgin-Gorda
BBQ, bar, superb water view
10am-10pm

Rosewood Little Dix Bay
Due to open late 2019

The Rock Cafe
Due to open late 2019
www.therockcafe.vg

Wheelhouse Restaurant
Tel: 284-495-5230
Serving local West Indian fare; breakfast, lunch & dinner, rooms for rent

SABA ROCK

Saba Rock Marina & Restaurant
Under construction, coming back soon
Check for updates at:
info@sabarock.com
FB: sabarockresort

OIL NUT BAY
Private Resort Community

MARINAS
Oil Nut Bay Marina Village
Tel: 284-393-1000
www.oilnutbay.com
Mooring balls, berthing slips, garbage, electricity, water, ice, gas & diesel

PROVISIONING
Marina Market
Gourmet food, basic provisions, wine, spirits
8am-6pm daily

RESTAURANTS
Oil Nut Bay Coffee Shop
Espresso beverages, fresh baked pastries, cakes and breads
8am-6pm daily

Nova Restaurant
Bar: 11:00am-close
Restaurant: Sat-Wed
11:30am-9pm, closed
Th-Fr, Sunday brunch
10am-4pm, dinner 4-9pm

SHOPPING
Oil Nut Bay Boutique
Resort fashion, gifts, local crafts & art
8am-6pm daily

BITTER END

Bitter End Yacht Club
Tel: 800-827-2392
Due to open late 2019, including retail, restaurants, bar, provisions
Check for updates at
www.beyc.com
FB: BitterEndYachtClub

DIVING/WATERSPORTS
Sunchaser Scuba
Bitter End Yacht Club, North Sound Virgin Gorda
284-344-2766
PADI and NAUI pros offer full service, underwater video, with dive boats.
www.sunchaserscuba.com

LEVERICK BAY

MARINAS
Leverick Bay Resort & Marina
Tel: 284-542-4014, VHF 16
www.leverickbayvg.com/leverickbaymarina
FB @leverickbay
Mooring balls, boat slips, water, power, ice, fuel, pool, showers, electricity, laundry facilities, garbage disposal
8am-10pm daily

RESTAURANTS
The Restaurant at Leverick Bay
Tel: 284-541-8879
www.leverickbayvg.com/therestaurant
8am-10pm daily

Jumbies Beach Bar
Roti, burgers, conch fritters, sandwiches, salads, fish & chips, pizza, and cocktails. Friday beach BBQ buffet, Moko Jumbi dancers & live band at 7pm, 11am-9pm daily, happy hour 4-7pm

The Cove
Tel: 284-346-7241
Pub food, lunch or afternoon snack at the pool or beach
Food service 11am-9pm

SPA
The Spa at Leverick Bay
Tel: 284-346-1235
www.thebvispa.com
info@thebvispa.com
8am-8pm daily

DIVING / WATERSPORTS
Blue Rush Water Sports
Tel: 284-499-7515
bluerushwatersports.com
FB: bluerushbvi
Flyboarding, jet ski tours, clear-bottom kayaking, tubing; hobie cat, SUP & body-board rentals
9am-5pm daily

BVI SNUBA
Tel: 284-341-0660
Only place in BVI to SNUBA, due to open soon
FB: BVI-Snuba
8am-6pm, 7 days/week

CHARTERING COMPANIES
Bradley Powerboats BVI Ltd Charters & Rentals
Tel: 284-345-3941
virgingordapowerboat-rentals.com
Boat rentals from 13' dinghies to 30' powerboats
Call to book

PROVISIONING
Chef's Pantry Supermarket & Deli
Tel: 284-344-1621
chefspantry@leverick-bayrestaurant.com
Selection of gourmet items: seafood, special meats and cheeses, fresh baked breads and pastries, coffees, fine wines and spirits.
7am-7pm daily

SHOPPING
Pusser's Gift Shop
Tel: 284-495-7369
Clothing, accessories, souvenirs and gifts

ARAWAK
Gift shop, selection of tropical clothing, sarongs, accessories, UV beachwear, swimwear, batik art
9am-5pm daily

CAR RENTAL / TAXI
Speedy's Rentals & Taxi
Tel: 284-341-7145

ANEGADA THE DROWNED ISLAND

Anegada's translation from Spanish is the "Drowned Island." As Irma approached, the island was evacuated to escape any chance of this becoming a reality via the vengeance of the storm. To everyone's surprise, Anegada did just that, escaped the storm's worst winds. Although there was substantial damage, this small island community was quick to rebuild and celebrate their survival with a huge public party during December's famed Lobster Fest.

In contrast to the mountainous volcanic formation of the remainder of the Virgin Islands, Anegada is comprised of coral and limestone, at its highest point the island is 28 feet above sea level. Created by the movement between the Atlantic and Caribbean Plates, which meet to the northeast of the island, Anegada is 11 miles long and fringed with mile after mile of white sandy beaches.

Horseshoe Reef, which extends 10 miles to the southeast, has claimed over 300 known wrecks, which provide excitement and adventure for scuba diving enthusiasts who descend on them to discover their secrets. The reef also provides a home for some of the largest fish in the area, as well as lobster and conch. The numerous coral heads and tricky currents that surround the island, along with the difficulty in identifying landmarks and subsequent reef areas, have in the past made it off limits for many charter companies. Plan on spending at least two nights on Anegada. It is one of those special places.

64° 24.50'W

Charts*

NV.Charts: St.Thomas to Anegada:
Kit C-12,12A,13

NIMA:2561, Imray Iolaire A-231

Admiralty Leisure 5640-2,3,7,8A,9

Keel Point

Bone Bay

Windlass Bay

Soldier Point

Jack Bay

Loblolly Bay

Deep Bay

West End

Ruffling Point

Flamingo Pond

ANEGADA

ATLANTIC OCEAN

Settlement

Anegada Reefs Hotel

Pomato Pt.

Neptune's Treasure

10

40

13

25 BV 411

Numerous Coral Heads

Little Anegada

Salt Pond

White Bay

Pelican Point

Horse Shoe Reef

18° 42.40'N

BV 410

18° 42.40'N

36

24

30

12

East Point

35

20

15

30

Numerous Coral Heads

37

11.2 NM

40

60

30

Day Anchorage

20

Continuous Reef Breaks Heavily

50

60

36

40

30

55

65

39

60

50

40

60

55

50

55

N

66

55

Hawk's Bill Bank

The White Horse
(coral heads 3' high)

60

55

4

Robert Reef

10

6

70

10

70

66

50

30

48

70

60

80

BV 408

Waypoints	North	West
BV401	18°26.00'	64°27.00'
BV402	18°27.20'	64°26.90'
BV403	18°28.42'	64°26.80'
BV404	18°30.00'	64°29.20'
BV405	18°30.40'	64°25.20'
BV406	18°31.30'	64°23.10'
BV407	18°30.50'	64°18.70'
BV408	18°32.20'	64°15.00'
BV410	18°42.40'	64°24.50'
BV411	18°42.80'	64°23.65'

Necker Island

The Invisibles

BV 406

4.25 NM

Mosquito I.

Gorda Sound

BV 407

18° 30.50'N

Soundings in Feet at Low Water

0   1   2   3   4   5

Scale in Nautical Miles

VIRGIN GORDA

*Additional resources: For additional charts and updates, visit bvipirate.com

64° 18.70'W

SETTING POINT

Waypoint: BV410 (Setting Point Approach) 18°42.40'N; 64°24.50'W; BV411 (Channel) 18°42.80'N, 64°23.65'W

Navigation: 11.4 nm north of Virgin Gorda (North Sound Entrance)

Services: Moorings, Restaurants, Tours, Car rentals, Ice, Fuel, Dive tours, Gift shops, Hotels, WiFi, Provisions

Additional resources: For additional charts and updates, visit bvipirate.com

Anegada

Because of its low profile and surrounding coral heads, Anegada should be approached only in good weather conditions and with the sun overhead in order to see the bottom. Leave North Sound between 8:00 and 9:30am to arrive at the west end of Anegada with good light overhead in order to see the coral heads. When the wind moves to the southeast this anchorage can be a little choppy depending on wind strength.

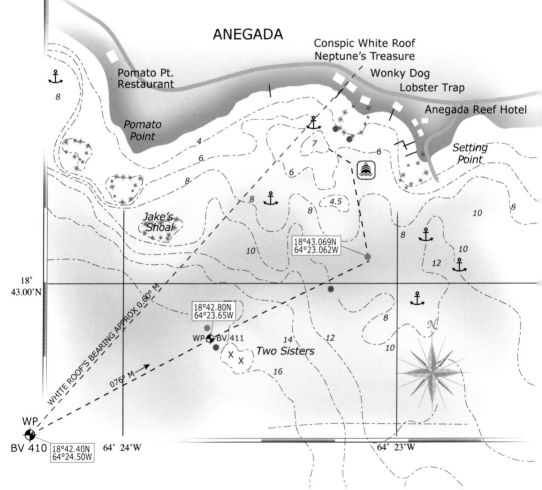

FLAMINGO POND
LOBSTER TRAP
ANEGADA REEF HOTEL
SETTING POINT
WONKY DOG

Navigation & Piloting

Departing from Gorda Sound (waypoint BV406) steer a course of 008°m, which will take you from Mosquito Rock to waypoint BV410 south of Pomato Point. The 1-2 knot current will set you down to the west and some compensation may be required as you approach the island. The 11.5 mile sail is usually a close reach. Do not lay a course directly to the outer channel marker at Setting Point as this will take you over shallow coral heads known locally as the Two Sisters situated to the southwest of the red channel marker. It will also take you very close to Prawny Shoal, located due south of Setting Point. If you are on course and not too far east, you will never have less than 20 feet of water under your keel until you reach the outer channel buoys. If you are north of 18°43N you have passed the channel entrance so turn around.

Owing to the low elevation of the island, the palms and pines will be sighted before the land. Do not turn off course until you have identified Pomato and Setting Points or verified your waypoint. From WP BV410 to Setting Point, the course is 076°m to the waypoint BV411 between the first set of buoys. The white roof of Neptune's Treasure should be bearing approximately 060°m. Depending upon weather conditions you should be able to visually identify the outer red buoy marking the channel into Setting Point. These buoys are small and sometimes difficult to see from a distance, especially when choppy.

It is important to note that many chartplotters will not accurately show the channel markers and their relative position to the land mass.

That is to say that much of the charting was taken from surveys developed years ago and therefore a prudent skipper will utilize known GPS coordinates to locate both the WP BV410 approach and WP BV411 between the two outer channel markers, since those positions are absolute regardless of charting inaccuracies. Do not establish waypoints from a zoomed in chart and do not be alarmed if your plotter does not show the buoy positions accurately.

At the time of the last survey (May 2019), the channel was defined by a set of red and green buoys at the entrance to the channel, a mid-channel red buoy, and a final inner green marker. At the inner green buoy, although unmarked, the channel turns NW into the anchorage and mooring field off of The Anegada Reef Hotel. Call Anegada Reef Hotel or Neptune's Treasure on VHF channel 16 for assistance. Prior to Hurricane Irma there was an inner set of red/green markers that identified the position of a sand bar NNW of the inner green buoy. Since that set is no longer in place, care should be taken to identify the exact location since there is less than 4'5" (1.35m) at low water.

POMATO POINT

When the weather is calm and the main anchorage is crowded, there is an anchorage in the small bay NW of Pomato Point, due north 1.2 nautical miles of waypoint BV410. Anchor in 12-15 feet on a sandy bottom. Sid's Pomato Point Restaurant is a tranquil spot for dinner although they do not have a dock to land the dinghy.

Anchoring & Mooring

Yachts drawing over 7 feet should anchor off the commercial dock, in line with the green buoy in 8-10 feet of water on a good sandy bottom. All others can make their way into the inner harbor where numerous moorings are available. Skippers should take note of the reef that extends east into the anchorage between the southernmost dock (Potter's) and the large concrete commercial dock at the end of the point. Caution should also be taken to identify the shallow area (less than 4'5" at low tide) NW of the inner green channel marker at N18°43.20' W64°23.25'. This small sandy area is shallow enough to cause concern for catamarans and monohulls. During our last visit, we saw a 4'5" draft catamaran aground. Monohull groundings are numerous and towing services are expensive. Proceed slowly and with caution. From the inner green marker, head north toward the dock base at Neptune's Treasure until you are abeam of Potter's dock, where you are well clear of the sandbar.

If you do decide to anchor, you will be in soft sandy mud and the holding is excellent. Since you will be in 8' water a 5 to 1 scope gets you 40' which limits your swinging room. Moor-Seacure/Anegada Reef Hotel has numerous mooring buoys available in the anchorage. In addition there are 10 orange Boatyball moorings (use Boatyball.com). There are also a number of additional

balls extending well back into the anchorage of uncertain heritage regarding the ground tackle. The one that we checked was secured to a concrete block that had not been buried in the sand and therefore allowed a hard concrete edge exposed in about 5.5' of water. We strongly suggest that if you are picking up one of these mooring balls, after securing the line you run the engine in reverse at top cruising RPM in order to be sure the ground tackle is secure. Peter, at The Wonkey Dog, tells us that he will also have an additional 20 moorings in place for the 2019 season and they will be on a no-charge basis for guests eating dinner at the restaurant.

Almost as soon as you arrive in the anchorage a dinghy or dinghies will be alongside the boat to collect the mooring fee, or to solicit a booking for dinner at one of the respective restaurants. We strongly suggest that you go ashore, walk the beach and then decide which establishment works for you and the crew before committing to a reservation. Barry will come by in a dinghy each morning to collect garbage for $3 per bag. He is most courteous and always happy to see you in the anchorage; he will

also collect fees for the (Moor-Seacure) moorings on behalf of Anegada Reef Hotel. The other ball fees will be collected by Jerry. For dinner reservations, take your time and decide at your own pace where you want to eat dinner. Just make sure your reservation is in as early as possible.

For vessels drawing less than 6 feet, the inner anchorage off of Neptune's Treasure is a good spot, limited in room but less choppy when it is blowing hard and with good holding. Regrettably the expansion of the mooring field has limited available anchoring room and therefore this area is more suitable for catamarans. From the main channel inner green marker, turn N toward Neptune's Treasure Dock keeping a sharp look out for the reef that extends to the SW from the point to the east of Neptune's Treasure. Historically there have been two PVC poles marking the outer extremity of the reef but they were not in place (May 2019). Leave the reef to starboard and anchor on a sandy bottom in 6 feet of water.

Ashore

One of the first things to do is to decide where you want to have dinner. Next,

make reservations. If you arrive in the afternoon, dining near the anchorage is best so that the only transportation you'll need is a dinghy. Most of the restaurants monitor VHF Chanel 16. If this doesn't work for you, a simple phone call will. Either way, we cannot stress this enough, Reservations by 4pm are mandatory! Only some establishments accept credit cards, so it is advisable to check ahead. Most businesses do accept traveler's checks in U.S. dollars and of course, U.S. currency. Euros are not accepted in the Virgin Islands. There is no ATM or bank in Anegada at present.

Dinghies can be landed at Anegada Reef Hotel, Potter's, Lobster Trap, Wonkey Dog and Neptune's Treasure. Garbage can be dropped off behind the buildings at Anegada Reef for $3 per bag and ice is available for $8 per bag. The team at Anegada Reef is also able to help you organize transportation to the north shore and assist with other logistics.

Restaurants: This island is a foodie's dream. If you are into lobsters, so fresh they are hauled from home traps during the day and on your plate by dinner, you've definitely come to the right place.

The Anegada way to cook a lobster is to grill it over an open flame and the result is a meal you won't forget. Most of the restaurants feature lobster on their menus but you will not get one without a reservation. This is serious business (especially if you're hungry!).

The Anegada Reef Hotel is the place to dine waterfront and under the stars. Dress casual or dress up either way, your feet will be in the sand while you sit at a lovely set table, complete with candles. Attentive servers will bring you the wine list and anything else you may need. Either way, the fish and the lobster are *Anegada good* (and that is good)! You'll also want to try the ribs. The old "Honour Bar'" still exists. It is often an afternoon gathering place for both locals and visitors. The Anegada Reef Hotel has 10 rooms; 4 deluxe and 6 standard. The Boutique closest to the dock is also part of the complex.

The Wonky Dog Café is just a short walk if you continue west on the beach or if arriving by dinghy, tie up to the dock. Proud of his post-Irma rebuild which includes a new two-story deck, Chef Peter will delight you with some of his unusual dishes as well as the famed Anegada lobster dinner.

Peter, along with his wife, Desne own and run this versatile and unique restaurant. Ranked #1 on Anegada's Trip Advisor. Lunch and dinner are served daily. Happy hour starts at 3:30pm until 5:30pm. Espressos and smoothies are also on the menu to keep tradition with Peter's, well known, "something for everyone style". With 25 years in the business, Peter, who hails from Scotland, brings a lot to the table, so to speak, including a fire-breathing bar tender. There is live pan music on Tuesday and Wednesday and a DJ Monday and Thursday. By season 2019, you should find an additional 20 Mooring Balls that will be free of charge with a dinner reservation. For more information, contact 284-547-0539. Reservations are essential and by 11am if possible. If you have made a reservation earlier in the week, call and confirm upon arrival in the anchorage.

Neptune's Treasure: Brothers Mark and Dean supply fresh fish to a lot of restaurants in the BVI. However, the first stop their fishing boat, ARGUS lll makes is Neptune's Treasure where you can enjoy fresh fish and some of the much sought after bakery delicacies prepared by Mark's wife Pam. Weather permitting, you can dine outdoors. Closed for the summer, they return again the first Monday in November. Mark asks that you not only call for reservations, you place your order at the

Build a Buoyage System and They Will Come

During the late '70s and early 1980s when the charter trade in the BVI was starting to expand, Lowell Wheatley was, as ever, busy developing, planning and rebuilding the Anegada Reef Hotel. About this time the first edition of the *Cruising Guide to the Virgin Islands* was to be published.

Sitting at the bar with Lowell talking about how to get more boats into the anchorage we determined that a reasonable system of markers into the anchorage would certainly encourage sailors to make the passage and perhaps persuade the charter operators to relax the "off limits" approach. With private markers in place a planned approach route, all described in the upcoming guide, we had a plan!

At that same meeting we pulled out a chart and plotted the proposed approach. Then we jumped into Lowell's boat and surveyed the channel into Setting Point to determine where the buoys should be placed. I sent Lowell the proposed chart, he in turn made some changes and eventually between us we got it to press.

Some time later the BVI government placed permanent markers and GPS became mainstream. Now, every time I sail into Anegada, I marvel at the number of yachts sitting at anchor and remember the good old days.

Here's to you, Lowell!

SS

same time. VHF channel 16 or phone, both will get you dinner. Should someone happen to tell you they are closed, a quick call will get you the right answer.

Potter's by the Sea neighbors Anegada Reef a few steps to the east and they don't just serve lobster, fish and the traditional Anegada fare, they are also vegetarian friendly. In addition, if you want to limbo and dance the night away, Potter's serves up some unforgettable fun.

The Lobster Trap moving west, is another of the anchorage's shoreside dining spots. They serve Caribbean food and of course, lobster! Many reviews include glowing positives about their delicious rack of lamb.

Lobster Trap is a sister restaurant to The Anegada Beach Hotel on the north shore operating under the same ownership and transportation between the two is available.

Pomato Point: Serves island fare in a picture beautiful setting, but have no dinghy dock. This is not a problem for diners. If you give them a call, VHF Channel 16 or by phone, they will arrange transportation from Setting Point going to and from the restaurant. Pomato Point is home to a small, one room museum housing artifacts from the Arawak Indian and the Shipwreck Treasury of Finds from some of the 300 shipwrecks that met their tragic fate on the reefs of Anegada.

Prices: To provide an idea of what restaurants charge, you can expect to pay anywhere from $35 for a half Lobster Meal (where served) and $45 to $70 for a whole one depending on size. This is just a general idea as prices may differ from place to place.

Transportation: There are several businesses where you can rent cars, jeeps, Mini Mokes and scooters. This includes the Anegada Reef Hotel, Anjuliena's Scooter Rentals, DW Jeep Rentals, S&K Rentals, VnJ's and Kenny's on the Government Docks. For a general idea of pricing, car rentals range from $65 to $95 at one car rental business. Mini Mokes go for $80 per day including fuel at the Anegada Reef Hotel. Scooters are $45 day. For those who want to leave the driving to someone else, there is the shuttle Safari Bus and Taxi Services available at Potter's, Anegada Reef Hotel and Neptune's. Prices are $12 per person to Cow Wreck Bay and $18 to Loblolly Bay. When arranging transportation, it is advisable to always ask what the rates are before accepting a ride. This will eliminate the possibility of misunderstandings on both ends. Take note that there is only one place to get fuel on the island. Kenneth's Gas Station is just a few steps from Potter's and the Anegada Reef Hotel.

Shopping & Provisioning: Setting Point has begun to expand as a small shopping area with numerous gift stores and a couple of options for provisioning. Lil'Bit Superette and their snack shop, Lil'Bit Taz offers basic provisioning items along with Fun in the Sun mini-mart. Fresh lobster can be purchased at S&K. The Anegada Reef Shop is at the Anegada Reef Hotel, Anjuliena's Gift Shop, VnJ's for gifts, t-shirts and some boutique items, island style.

Exploring Anegada

Heading west from Setting Point and the anchorage, the famed stretch of beaches renown for their incredible, unspoiled beauty begins about here if you are beach walking. If driving, continue around Anegada's westend point, look for the sign to Cow Wreck Beach. This will lead to a narrow, sandy "road" that will take you to the North Shore and Cow Wreck Beach Bar which sits right on the beach with a thatch covered bar and a comfortable place to sit back and enjoy lunch or dinner and an island drink.

A little further to the east is The Anegada Beach Club where they have some very smart, fully contained tents overlooking the sea. The tents are unique and represent the *glamping* experience (glamorous camping). Hang out by the pool, have a drink at the bar, or walk the sand dunes. After this, stay on the same road you came in on. It will wind its way between the beaches and the Salt Ponds. It's an easy and scenic drive offering nature's beauty at its best.

Bones Bight provides a fascinating peak in to the magnificence of the natural. Local lore says to look for another one of Mother Nature's road signs. This one is a Loblolly tree where there is often a

chance to catch a glimpse of the Anegada Rock Iguana. This rare species is said to have a mere 400 remaining worldwide. Caribbean flamingos feed at the Salt Ponds and you never know how many you will see when there. The gloriously Pink Flamingos were, thankfully, reintroduced to the island almost two decades ago. The flamingos arrived in 2002 when the Bermuda Zoo brought 18 birds to the island. The "Iguana Headstart Facility" located in the Settlement where, visitors can enjoy the young iguanas that are being raised in the safety of a controlled environment until they are ready to survive in the wild.

At the airport turnoff take a left to Loblolly Bay, stop at the Big Bamboo to have a cold drink or grab a bite. After you place your order, swim, snorkel or relax in a hammock until it's ready. No formalities here, just good food. Mac's Campground and a Flash of Beauty (which is actually a restaurant) that serves up a lot of island dishes including curries and the BVI famed Roti.

Heading back there is a concrete road to the Settlement, also called the Village or town. It is home to the majority of the 300-person population on the island. There you'll see the fire station, police department, post office, medical clinic, several churches, a restaurant or two, a few grocery stores, a bakery, and some lovely boutiques and gift shops. The iguana "Head Start Facility" is also in the Settlement area.

Fishing & Boat Tours: If angling is your thing, fighting a bonefish in the flats will give you more than a few fishtails to share back home. Alternatively a trip inside the reef for a day of snorkeling and exploration with a knowledgable local guide. The horseshoe reef that surrounds Anegada is rich with sea life. The shipwrecks found along the 18 mile stretch make this a snorkeler's paradise. There are several guides who will take you to the flats by boat and also rent you the needed gear. The boat ride, by itself, is nothing short of fabulous. Several emails have come to our office from visitors wanting to share their very positive experiences with Kelly's Tours (284-544-9661).

ISLAND CONNECTIONS

EMERGENCIES
999 or 911
VISAR (Virgin Island Search and Rescue)
Tel: 767 (SOS), or
+1 284 499 0911
www.visar.org

RESTAURANTS
Anegada Reef Hotel
284-495-8002
www.anegadareef.com
Breakfast, lunch, dinner,
Dinner reservations by 4pm

Anegada Beach Club
Tel: 1-284-346-4005 or
284-340-4455
www.anegadabeachclub.com

The Wonky Dog
Tel: 284-547-0539
www.thewonkydog.com
FB: thewonkydog

Potter's by the Sea
Tel:1 284 341 9769, VHF 16
www.pottersanegada.com
FB: PottersByTheSea

Lobster Trap
Tel: 1 284-346-5055, VHF 16
FB: thelobstertrapbvi
Closed Sept 1- Oct 31

Neptune's Treasure
Tel: 284-345-5436
VHF 16
www.neptunestreasure.com
FB: NeptunesTreasureBVI

Sid's Pomato Point
Tel: 284-441-5565, VHF 16
FB Sids-Pomato-Point-
Restaurant

Whistling Pines
Tel: 284-495-9521

Dotsy's Bakery
Tel: 284-495-9667

Big Bamboo Beach Bar and Restaurant
Tel: 284-346-5850
bigbambooanegada.com
Loblolly Bay on the north
shore

HOTELS
Anegada Reef Hotel
Tel: 284-495-8002, VHF 16
www.anegadareef.com
FB: AnegadaReefHotel

Neptune's Treasure
Tel: 284-345-5436
www.neptunestreasure.com
FB: NeptunesTreasureBVI
Contact about guest cottages

Big Bamboo
Tel: 284-346-5850
bigbambooanegada.com
bigbamboovillas@gmail.com

Anegada Beach Club
Tel: 284-346-4005 or
284-340-4455
anegadabeachclub.com

WATERSPORTS / DIVING
Anegada Beach Club
Tel: 284-346-4005 or
284-340-4455
anegadabeachclub.com

FISHING & BOAT EXCURSIONS
Danny's Bonefishing
Tel: 284-441-6334 or
284-344-1226
dannysbonefishing.com
FB: dannys.bonefishing

Teamwork Charters
Tel: 284-547-6243
FB: teamworkfishing
teamworkfishing@gmail.com

PROVISIONING
Pam's Kitchen
Tel: 284-345-5436

Lil'Bit
Tel: 284-495-9932

CAR / SCOOTER RENTAL / TAXI
Anegada Amazing Rentals
Tel: 284-346-5658 or
284-440-0090
snkamazingrentals.com
FB: anegadascooters

L&H Car & Jeep Rentals
Tel: 284-441-0799
www.picdeer.com/
landhrentals_anegada

Anjuliena's Scooter Rental and Boutique
Tel: 284-544-0958
smithgeorge6089@gmail.com

VnJ's Rentals & Boutique
Tel: 284-494-1522 or
284-545-5644

Jost Van Dyke & Tobago

A large, high island, Jost Van Dyke lies three miles to the northwest of Tortola and becomes visible to yachtsmen sailing from St. Thomas upon entering Pillsbury Sound. With a population of less than 225, the island remains relatively unspoiled. The largest settlement is Great Harbour, which is also a port of entry into the BVI.

Claimed to be named after a Dutch privateer, Joost Van Dyke, the island is known as the birthplace of Dr. John Lettsom, born into a Quaker community on Little Jost Van Dyke in 1744.

Dr. Lettsom (also spelled Lettsome) later returned to his father's native England where he attended medical school and founded the London Medical Society and became a founding member of the Royal Humane Society. A philanthropist, abolitionist and humorist, Dr. Lettsom wrote the following:

I, John Lettsom,
Blisters, bleeds and sweats 'em
If, after that, they please to die,
I, John, lets 'em!

As with many other islands in the region, Jost Van Dyke and the BVI in general saw steady economic decline throughout the 18th century.

From the emancipation era forward, the community of Jost Van Dyke subsisted mainly on small scale fishing and subsistence agriculture. Charcoal making was a practice that began during the plantation era, when strong fires

were vital for sugar and rum production, and charcoal making emerged as a primary industry for the BVI during the post-emancipation years.

Maritime resources were also extremely important historically to the people of Jost Van Dyke, and the island has emerged as a fishing village. The desire for trade and social interaction with nearby islands stimulated the development of seafaring skills. Small, locally constructed sailing vessels like the "Tortola Sloop" flourished in the BVI until about the 1960s when they were replaced with motorized craft.

Waypoints	North	West
BV201	18°26.60'	64°42.75'
BV202	18°25.90'	64°43.05'
BV203	18°26.10'	64°45.00'
BV204	18°26.30'	64°45.80'
BV205	18°26.00'	64°49.50'
BV206	18°26.75'	64°50.00'

Charts
NV Charts: St.Thomas to Anegada: C-14
NIMA: 25641, Imray-Iolaire: A-231
Admiralty Leisure: 5640-5

LITTLE JOST VAN DYKE
DIAMOND CAY, GREEN CAY AND SANDY CAY

Jost Van Dyke

Waypoint: BV201 18°26.60'N 64°42.75'W

Navigation: 23nm from Anegada – 6.7nm from Guana Island (North WP)

Services: Foxy's Taboo (Long Bay): Ice, Restaurant, Bar, Trail to the Bubbly Pool, Moorings, B Line Little Jost Van Dyke Beach Bar and Restaurant

Connected by a shallow channel on the NE extremity of Jost Van Dyke, Little Jost Van Dyke is a small island, approximately 370 feet high, originally the home and estate of Dr. John Lettsome. To the east is the small iconic islet of Green Cay and one mile to the south is Sandy Cay.

From the waypoint (BV201) located between Green Cay and Sandy Cay, traveling to the northwest you will enter Manchineel Bay. On the southeast coast of Little Jost Van Dyke is a delightful

anchorage, in about 12 feet of water where you can stay away from the crowds, or further to the east is the idyllic Green Cay and Sandy Spit which are protected areas and offer National Park Trust moorings for daytime use (with permit).

Traveling to the northwest, the anchorage shown on the chart as East End Harbour, is open to the east/northeast and during the winter months can be choppy.

Nestled between the eastern end of Jost Van Dyke and Little Jost Van Dyke, northwest of Diamond Cay is the Long Bay anchorage known as Diamond Cay,

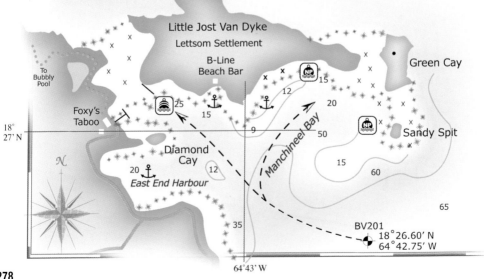

Little Jost Van Dyke

where Foxy's Taboo Bar and Restaurant are located. This is also the access point for a hike to The Bubbly Pool.

Diamond Cay / Long Bay

The approach is straightforward entering from the south and deep water. There is a 12 ft (4 meter) area of light blue water off the SE headland of East End Harbour. Moderate and deep draft vessels should anchor adjacent to the mooring field in 15-30 feet of water on a sandy bottom. Moorings should be paid for ashore at Foxy's Taboo or if reserved in advance, there are six Boatyball orange mooring balls available. If the wind is from the southeast, the anchorage becomes very sloppy and during northerly ground swells the surge can become excessive. Dinghies and smaller powerboats can tie up at the dock, but care should be taken to identify the shoal water extending from the north where the two islands meet.

Ashore

The new temporary building is not quite as large as the original but carries the same Caribbean vibe. Located just north of Diamond Rock on Jost Van Dyke facing east towards Green Cay and Sandy

Spit, this is a fun spot with an open air bar and dining area serving lunch and dinner. The food is excellent and the atmosphere is breezy and light ($15-$30). The marina has depths of 8 to 15 feet and several slips are available. The dinghy dock is to the left as you approach. There are no facilities for garbage disposal here, so please hang on to it until you are somewhere that has garbage bins.

The "Bubbly Pool," a natural pool surrounded by large rocks at the ocean's edge, is about half a mile from the marina. The trail, cleared after Irma, will take you along the beach and over a rocky pathway; reasonable footwear is recommended as flip-flops can be dangerous. At high tide, waves tumble in through a hole in the rocks creating a bubbling salt water pool. During periods of northerly swells, the water rushes in through the opening and surges up the small beach. Hang on to young children and beware of manchineel trees! Ask for directions at the restaurant.

A little further to the east, accessible by dinghy, is the B-Line Beach Bar and Restaurant. Opened in 2014 there is a floating dinghy dock just off the beach which is recommended since the old jetty is dangerous when disembarking crew. The signature drink is "Passion Confusion" and food from the grill is served on weekends. (For those who might remember back to the seventies this was the location of Tony and Jackie Snell's "Last Resort" before it burned down and they moved to Bellamy Cay.)

Little Jost Van Dyke / South Shore

Once again the approach from the south is straightforward. If you are transiting from Diamond Cay, be aware of and identify the shoal area extending from Little Jost Van Dyke to the south. There are two good spots to drop your anchor, the first in about 12-15' of water is just off the shoreline where you will see sandy beach areas separated by two large rocks. The other, further along to the east at the

Bubbly Pool

Green Cay end of the headland allows easier access to Green Cay. Both anchorages should be considered daytime only unless conditions are ideal.

Green Cay/Sandy Spit

Green Cay is the quintessential Caribbean anchorage. Light turquoise water, a small sand island with a few palm trees and no services. It doesn't get better than this! Green Cay and Sandy Spit provide a safe comfortable anchorage in most conditions, but in unsettled weather or during a northerly ground swell, we suggest that

you move to one of the more protected anchorages for overnight.

Anchor on a sandy bottom in 10-15 feet of water. Take the dinghy ashore or swim from the boat. The island is a perfect setting for a picnic.

Sandy Cay

To the southeast of Jost Van Dyke, Sandy Cay is a postcard setting and a perfect daytime stop for swimming and relaxing.

For this reason the anchorage is usually crowded so anticipate company. Sandy Cay is a national park, thanks to the efforts of Laurance Rockefeller, and a botanical tour on the small trail will afford you magnificent views of the surrounding islands.

The anchorage is on the southwest side close to shore, in the lee of the island. There are nine NPS daytime moorings available on the SW shore for permit holders.

Extreme caution should be exercised during winter ground swells as the swell makes its way around both sides of the island, causing waves to break on the beach, making the landing of a dinghy difficult if not disastrous.

LITTLE HARBOUR
(GARNER BAY)

Waypoint: BV202 18°25.90'N 64°43.05'W
Navigation: 3.4nm from Cane Garden Bay; 3nm due north of West End
Services: Restaurants, Moorings, Bars, Ice, Provisions, Water, Fuel, WiFi

Little Harbour, or "Clear Hole" as the locals call it, lies to the east of Great Harbour. Once used as a careenage for island sloops, the local skippers would lay their vessels alongside the beach (where Sidney's Peace and Love stands today), secure a block and tackle from the masthead to the palm trees and careen the boat in order to scrub or repair the bottom. The harbor now caters to the vibrant yacht trade with three restaurants and limited provisioning available. Little Harbour is easy to access and reasonably well protected.

Navigation & Piloting

The entrance to Little Harbour is straightforward and deep. There are no longer any navigation buoys in place so when transiting be mindful of the shoal area extending east from Black Point, stay in the center of the channel. When departing for Green Cay or Little Jost Van Dyke, stay well to the center of the channel to avoid the shoal water extending from the shoreline, just to the south of Abe's, to Gregory Hole Point.

Anchoring & Mooring

The traditional anchorage is in the northwestern end of the bay in 15 feet of water. In recent years, as the number of visiting boats has increased, mooring balls have been laid limiting the available room to lay an anchor. If you are anchoring, pick a spot in the northeastern end of the bay and anchor in 30 feet on hard coral sand. Make sure your anchor is well set before heading for shore.

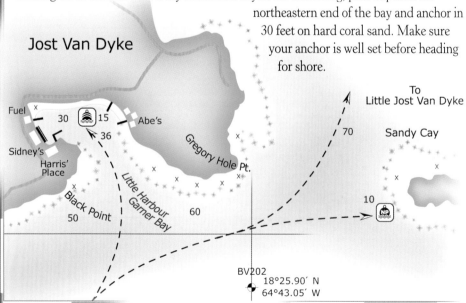

There are 10 mooring balls to the east side of the bay that are controlled by Abe's and another ten white balls to the north and west that are controlled by Cynthia at Harris' Place.

When we were there in June 2019, the mooring pennants were in need of attention but Cynthia assured us that they would be attended to within the next month. There are two yellow mooring balls close to shore, these are private.

Ashore

Little Harbour offers the best of both worlds. The Bay is home to three unique restaurants and a small marina, fringed by nature's design. There is one small exception. A sad reminder of Irma is apparent: from your cockpit looking west, some debris from the storm still clings to the now sparsely vegetated mountainside.

On the western end of the bay is the Little Harbour Marina where you can pick up fuel, water and ice along with some limited provisioning items (VHF 16) or call (284-341-7036). There is 10 feet of water at the head of the dock. Water is $.30 a gallon.

Little Harbour looking south

Tucked up in the western corner of the bay is Harris' Place, open for business with its brightly colored dining room, a work still in progress. Cynthia will greet you with a smile that outshines the island colors she chose to decorate with. Although the rebuild is unfinished (June 2019), Cynthia shares that she is ready and able to host diners with a full menu. She tells us she loves to cook and that is evident as she prepares lobster dinners and a wide variety of island dishes featuring fish, conch, chicken and ribs. The large outdoor dock is not quite completed at the writing of this guide. However, it is well on its way. Open daily for breakfast and dinner, Cynthia is known as the Bushwhacker queen of the BVI. Every night is the "all-you-can-eat lobster night special." Groups of five or more receive a complimentary mooring or round of drinks.

Also on the western end almost next door is Sydney's Peace and Love. Strawberry,

Cruising Guide author and Cynthia from Harris' Place

Boutique at Sydney's Peace and Love

Sydney's daughter, will greet you at the dock and warmly welcome you to the Veranda where island meals are served. The damage to the main part of the building will be repaired along with parts of the bulkhead. Strawberry says they are open for lunch and dinner on the covered spacious patio. Its rear wall was spared by Irma and is filled with names and dates scribbled there by the many patrons who have enjoyed her island cooking and lobster meals for many years. Sydney's still has rebuilding to do, but that doesn't stop the tasty meals from coming out of the kitchen and their little gift shop and boutique from charming you with style. If your party is four or more, the captain eats free. WiFi is available to guests. All restaurants monitor VHF 16.

On the other side of the bay to the east is Abe's by the Sea. Born and raised on Jost Van Dyke, Abe along with his wife Eunicy serve island food; their lobster and ribs are a specialty. In addition, there is a small store where you will be able to get ice, beer, and soft drinks. For taxi service, car or inflatable dinghy rental, Abe's is the place.

Strawberry from Sidney's

Note: To make reservations or contact businesses, VHF channel 16 or phone is suggested. Due to the storm, many phone numbers may not be in service or correct. It does not mean the business isn't open. In some anchorages, going ashore may be the best option.

For those who enjoy hiking, you can walk the road to Great Harbour or East End but for the more ambitious there is a small track that takes you about 1,000 feet up the mountain. For those ambitious enough to make the climb, the views are spectacular – bring water and your camera!

Foxy's Wooden Boat Regatta

GREAT HARBOUR

Jost Van Dyke

Waypoint: BV203 - 18°26.10N 64°45.00'W
Navigation: 5.5 nm from Cane Garden Bay;
4nm from West End; 5.3nm from Durloe Passage,
USVI St. John
Services: Port of Entry BVI, Ice, Garbage disposal,
Provisions, Restaurants, Bars, Shops, Fuel & water
at North Latitude Marina, SUP/Kayak rental, Ferry

This normally sheltered harbor nestled at the foot of 1,000 foot high peaks is a port-of-entry into the BVI and is the largest settlement on the island. On weekends and public holidays, day-trippers and weekend sailors arrive from the USVI and at these times the anchorage can be very crowded so an early arrival is prudent. For those arriving from the USVI and clearing Customs and Immigration it is critical that all passengers remain on the vessel until formalities are complete.

Post Irma, most of the visible impact can be seen ashore, where the mangroves have been decimated leaving areas that heretofore went unseen. In the same way we have to look beyond the surface to see and understand the individual

Ice House

Rudy's Superette

Customs & Immigration

Corsairs

Christine's Bakery

Nature's Basket

Dinghy and Government Dock

Foxy's Bar

Dinghy Dock

Snack Bar

Ferry Dock

Trash

To White Bay

North Latitude Marina

5

6

18

Jost Van Dyke

18° 26.5' N

Dandy Point

35

South Side

Pull & Be Damn Pt.

Dog Hole Pt.

Great Harbour

To White Bay

To Little Harbour

Great Harbour, Jost Van Dyke

hardships that the storm created in her wake. Foxy's dock has been rebuilt, restaurants have been rebuilt or remodeled, debris has been cleared and life on Jost Van Dyke returns to pre-storm normal, leaving the small yellow Methodist church sadly wanting some donations to assist in the rebuilding effort.

Navigation & Piloting

Your approach should be approximately 351°m. On your port side, upon entering the bay, there are two sets of red and green buoys designating a channel for ferries and official government business only. This channel carries a depth of 12 feet. Most pleasure craft head down the middle of the harbor giving the shoreline on either side a reasonable berth. There is a large reef extending out 300 yards from the inner shore-line, be sure to identify the shoal before you reach it. Dinghies can be landed at the dinghy dock located on the west side of the main government dock at the center of the harbor.

Anchoring & Mooring

The layout of the mooring field in Great Harbour tends to make it difficult to find a spot to anchor except to the south and southeast of the bay beyond the mooring balls. There are a

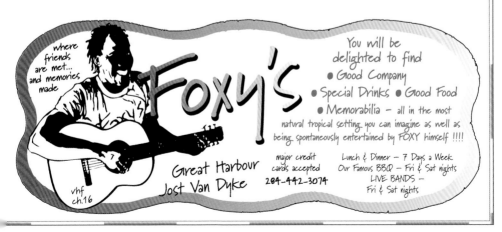

Vinny and Lori from Corsair's

Painkillers, an island favorite

couple of spots close to the shoreline to the east of the moorings in 25ft but the majority of vessels end up in 30-35 ft to the southeast. The holding ground is not brilliant, so make sure your anchor is well set and adequate scope laid out. When the wind moves to south of east, the outer anchorage can get a little choppy. In addition to the available moorings, there are 10 orange Boatyball moorings that can be reserved via the website (www.boatyball.com).

Customs, Immigration & Port Services

Great Harbour is a port of entry with a Customs and Immigration office. Take the dinghy ashore through the break in the reef and head directly for the government dock, in order to avoid shallow coral heads. Small vessels can tie up at the dock in order to complete formalities, there is a dinghy dock on the west side which makes access to the dock easy. The customs officer for Jost Van Dyke is Mark Morris who is located in the two story building at the head of the dock along with Immigration and the police department. Mark Morris is my idea of the perfect customs agent, good natured, businesslike, polite, knowledgable with a good sense of humor. The office will clear vessels in or out of British Virgin Island waters for both Customs and Immigration, however, they cannot give immigration extensions, which must be done at the Road Town Immigration Office. Customs and Immigration are open seven days a week from 8:30am to 4:30pm and are closed briefly to deal with the ferry arrivals and departures.

The ferry dock is located on the western side of the harbor and the dock should be kept clear for inbound and departing vessels. Ferries are available to West End, Tortola on a regular basis departing every 2-3 hours starting at 7am and departing West End about an hour later. A dumpster for garbage is located just to the south of the ferry dock. Do not take garbage bags to the beach area as there are no facilities for disposal.

North Latitude Marina is located just south of the ferry dock and offers diesel, gasoline, water ($0.30 a gal.), and ice in addition to a small convenience store. There is 12 feet of water at the dock and they stand by on VHF 16 daily from 7am to 5pm (9am-5pm on Sunday).

The Jost Van Dyke Health Service is also available for anyone needing assistance.

Ashore

Great Harbour has historically sounded like and has been touted as a fairy tale paradise. For those of you who have been there before, it may not be just as you remember. With this in mind, we can say that paradise has not been lost. There is still a lot going on in and at the harbor. Keep in mind that the island has a very explicit dress code. It's called comfortable! Shorts, tees and flip flops are fine. If you want to jazz it up a bit, that's okay too.

Just above the ferry dock is Sugar and Spice, a snack bar owned and run by Joan Chinnery. Try her empanadas and her roti along with a cold one while you're waiting for the ferry. You can also dinghy over to their floating dock and pick up a

Kenny Chesney with Foxy and his daughter Justine

Love For Love City

Kenny Chesney's Love for Love City Foundation provided support for one of his favorite islands in the wake of Hurricane Irma.

In light of all that has happened since Hurricane Irma tore homes and lives apart, it is no accident that we are standing strong. Foxy's along with many other businesses can thank Kenny Chesney for all he has done to help us. Without his caring and generous involvement, we would not have had our school and clinic up and operating so quickly. He has also helped businesses and private people in putting their lives back together. To list all of the Islands and people he has helped would take more than a book. *Love for Love City* was created to send relief to all of us suffering from the aftermath of the storm. Kenny has sent food, clothing, generators, tools, tarps, dog food, and countless things needed for survival. They came in by the planeload for all storm victims.

The foundation was created so that others can help with their contributions. All proceeds from his new album *Songs for the Saints* will be donated to his own Love for Love City nonprofit Foundation.

Foxy treasures his times singing with Kenny, and we both know our friendship with him will continue on through good times and hard times. Now Kenny is singing for all of us in the islands recovering from Irma. Thank you, Kenny, from all of us on Jost Van Dyke.   ~ Foxy & Tessa Callwood

few rotis to take with you for later on. Joan's son Kendrick often makes the rounds of the anchorage around 7:30am with freshly made empanadas for sale.

At the west end of the beach is Rudy's Superette, well stocked with a sailors "dire necessities" like beer and wine! If you want to refresh your provisions in the way of groceries and produce, Rudy's is still Rudy's but now run by Randy, Rudy's son.

Heading east, you will find Corsair's Beach Bar and Restaurant. Owner, Vinny, is a true chameleon, situated somewhere between Pirates of the Caribbean and Easy Rider. If it's lobster or fish you want, his award winning Chef, Andrew, will show you why Corsair's kitchen has earned its gold stars. If you come to the island and still

want pizza or calzone – yes calzone – "Pizza Dave" has been making pizza and calzones for 30 years along with other italian favorites. New this season is Vinny's salt water BBQ smoker.

Music at Corsair's can be described as, something for everyone. Vinny, through his famed monocle, sees the cup, or in this case, the glass, neither half full or half empty but completely full! Try some Voodoo Juice or an Absinthe at the bar. Whether you stop for drinks, breakfast, lunch, or dinner, Vinny and Lori will make you feel right at home. The dress is, well... just get dressed! It's flip flop casual. WiFi is available and so is Vinny at VHF16 or 284-495-9295.

Next, along your way on the beach is Ali Baba's Restaurant. Serving island fare, prepared by their chef, who came to Jost Van Dyke from the Philippine Islands. Steak and shrimp combo and MahiMahi are features on their menu. They are open for breakfast, lunch and dinner. Souvenirs, hand crafted from wood can also be purchased there. WiFi is free, and you can reach Baba at 284-544-5602.

A & B Bar and Restaurant is open and ready for you to visit for a light lunch, snacks and the occasional dinner. Cool Breeze Bar and Restaurant is open as well serving light lunches and the occasional dinner. The road near the police station that runs perpendicular to the beach will take you to Pinkie's Delight. A stationary food truck is where Pinkie will delight you with her island drinks and dishes.

Jost Van Dyke Scuba have also completely rebuilt the shop post storm and offer scuba lessons and certification in addition to eco-tours and SUP rentals. Call them at 284-443-2222.

At the far eastern end of the beach is the world famous Foxy's Tamarind Bar and Restaurant. Starting to serve food and drink to sailors over 50 years ago, Foxy and wife Tessa came to fame the hard way. It's called hard work and years of it! Today, they are open and sharing as much wild and crazy fun as they have been since day one. Along the way, the needs of the islanders have not been forgotten. Foxy has received numerous awards for dedication and contributions to heritage and tourism in the British Virgin Islands. I guess you could say that he got a stamp of approval from the Queen in the form of an

"OBE". This, by definition, is "Order of the British Empire" from H.M. Queen of England, Elizabeth II.

The Foxhole is another reason to come ashore. The shop carries all kinds of souvenirs, tee shirts and the usual, but the real hook is, it carries the unusual as well. This is one Foxhole you'll want to be in. Specializing in a more upscale choice of island clothing and accessories for men and women, "island sophistication" says it all. Tessa calls it "A Pandora's Box" and has done an excellent job sourcing both interesting and quality merchandise, in addition to all the other "stuff" it takes to create an enticing environment. Annie, the manager does a great job keeping the store ship-shape.

So, what's at Foxy's... sailors, who come from all over the world to have a drink, listen to this Caribbean icon strum his guitar, sing Calypso ballads and tell jokes and stories. One in particular is about getting hijacked on a schooner, only to find Tessa. If you see a large crowd gathering on the beach during the day, it's not a bird! It's not a plane! It's Foxy, himself! He is usually at the bar everyday.

Foxy's hosts the annual Foxy's Wooden Boat Race held in May, as well as their New Years Eve Celebration (although you don't have to wait until then to party at the Tamarind). A New York journalist once wrote that there were only three places in the world to celebrate New Years Eve; Times Square, New York, Trafalgar Square, London and, Foxy's Bar on Jost Van Dyke! This event attracts a crowd that has people anchoring days in advance to secure a place in the harbor.

The restaurant and bar are open for lunch and dinner. Reservations are a good idea if the anchorage is full. At this writing, phones in the islands have been a challenge. Channel 16 on VHF should be fine. However, our best advice – for Foxy's or anywhere – is to go ashore early to be certain they know you're coming for dinner. Tom Warner is the general manager of Foxy's and can generally answer all your questions about the bar and restaurant. Try him at 284-442-3074.

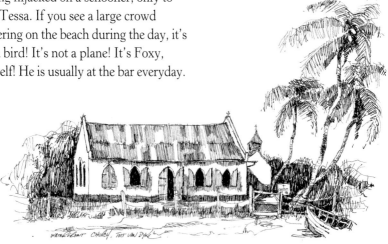

WATERFRONT CHURCH, JOST VAN DYKE

Jost Van Dyke Scuba

Foxy

Foxy's Fox Hole Boutique

White Bay

WHITE BAY

Waypoint: BV204 18°26.30'N 64°45.80'W **Navigation:** 6.1nm Cane Garden Bay; 3.4nm West End

Services: Moorings (Ivan's), Ice, Garbage disposal, Restaurants & bars

White Bay is the westernmost harbor on the south side of the island, aptly named for its beautiful stretch of white sandy beach. White Bay is an excellent anchorage under normal sea conditions. During the winter months however, ocean swells can make it an untenable overnight anchorage, suitable for day stops only. On the weekends, many small craft make their way over from both Tortola and the USVI, often crowding the western end of the anchorage due to the narrow anchorage area inside the reef. Impact from Irma is most noticeable behind the buildings where many of the mangrove trees were torn up.

Navigation & Piloting

Caution: During our last survey, both channels were missing one marker. The middle channel had the red starboard marker in place and the eastern channel had only the green. Skippers should also be aware that the red markers are hard to see in the bright sunlight.

White Bay is a relatively small anchorage with limited maneuvering room once inside the reef, however, there is room for a number of boats if anchored properly. Although there are three entrances through the reef, it is highly recommended that only the middle entrance

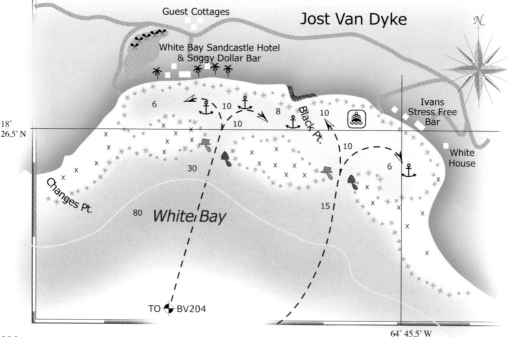

and the eastern entrance be considered since both of these channels are marked.

The middle channel is considered the main channel and once you have visually located the red and green markers proceed through the reef leaving red to starboard on a course of approximately due north. Caution: the red buoy is hard to see due to bleaching by the Caribbean sun.

The eastern pass is also normally marked with red and green buoys (see note above). This entrance is straightforward, but once again, make sure that you have identified the marker before starting your approach.

Anchoring and Mooring

There are no longer any mooring balls available at the western end of the beach. The middle channel will take 10-12 feet of draft. Once inside the reef, anchor either side of the channel in 7-10 feet on a sandy bottom. Do not anchor in or obstruct the channel.

Since the anchorage is narrow, you can swim ashore or if you take the dinghy, pull it well up on the beach and use your dinghy anchor to secure it. It is not recommended that dinghies be landed during a northerly ground swell.

The eastern anchorage is also narrow so tuck yourself up behind the reef either side of the pass and anchor in 8-12 feet of water on a sandy bottom. Do not drop the anchor on coral. There are a few moorings available at the eastern end of the bay, these are on a first come basis and fees should be paid at Ivan's Stress Free Bar.

Ashore

White Bay Sandcastle is a small delightful resort that serves breakfast, lunch and four course gourmet dinners with reservations. The Soggy Dollar Bar is a great spot to swim ashore for a Painkiller and to while away the afternoon in a hammock under a palm tree. The Painkiller, a delicious but potent rum drink was originally invented at the Soggy Dollar Bar (named for the soggy state of dollar bills used to pay for drinks after swimming ashore from an anchored vessel). Next door to the east is the newly built Hendo's Hideout bar and restaurant serving lunch until 6pm in a covered deck environment. Prices range from $18-$28 for lunch and $28-$46 for dinner. Sushi is served on Thursday.

Further to the west along the beach is Sedi's One Love and Coco Lopo. At the eastern end of the bay, Ivan's Stress Free Bar and Restaurant, once lavishly decorated with shells from the beach, was decimated by the hurricane and a temporary structure is now being operated by Ivan's daughter Darlene. If you are planning to walk from east to west or vice versa then we suggest a pair of flip flops as there is a stony pathway around the rocks that needs to be negotiated.

During the winter months when the ground seas are running, consideration should be given to leaving the vessel at Great Harbour and taking a taxi over the hill to White Bay for about $5 a head each way. Years ago we used to see a young man playing a silver triangle at Foxy's bar, and years later we met him again only to find that he still has the silver triangle that he keeps in his taxi. Call Binn at 284-499-8871.

Powercat rendezvous fleet from MarineMax Charters in Great Harbour

Vinny from Corsair's mixing up an Absinthe

Binn Taxi Driver

Donation box at Ali Babas for the yellow Methodist Church

Corsair's new restaurant

GREAT TOBAGO

Waypoint: BV206 18°26.75'N 64°50.00'W
Navigation: 4.5nm White Bay JVD; 7.9nm West End
Services: None
National Parks Trust Protected Area

Great Tobago is the westernmost of the British Virgin Islands, situated approximately 2.5 miles to the west of Jost Van Dyke and 525 feet in elevation. A favorite of divers, the island is remote and exposed. The small anchorage on the west side of the island is large enough to accommodate two vessels only. Generally used as a daytime stop, Great Tobago is unpopulated but home to a large nesting seabird population, protected by The National Parks Trust.

Navigation & Piloting

Approaching Great Tobago, there are three hazards that need to be understood. If your approach from the east takes you to the north of the island, Mercurius Rock lies half a mile to the east and is covered by six feet of water. A better approach is to the south end of the island, sailing close enough to avoid King Rock which is just awash and situated due south of the southwest tip of the island and due east of the northern tip of Little Tobago. Make your approach between Cable Rock, due west of the southwest point and easy to identify, and Great Tobago. The anchorage is a small bay halfway up the western face with a rocky beach landing.

Anchoring & Mooring

Since there is limited room, anchor in 15 feet of water on a sandy bottom. It has been reported that entering the anchorage, there is a submerged rock to starboard about 25 feet from shore with 4-5 feet of water over it.

Ashore

You can hike up the hillside to gain a commanding view of the surrounding islands.

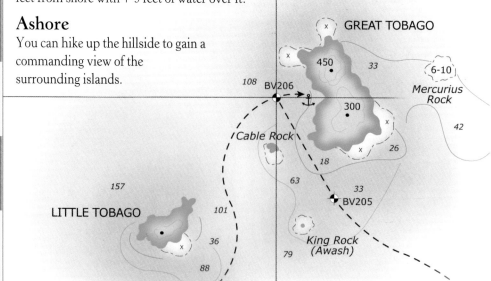

ISLAND CONNECTIONS

EMERGENCIES
999 or 911
VISAR (Virgin Island Search and Rescue)
Tel: 767 (SOS), or
+1 284 499 0911
www.visar.org

GREAT HARBOUR

CUSTOMS & IMMIGRATION
Tel: 284-495-9374 or
284-494-3450, VHF 16

MARINAS
North Latitude Marina
Tel: 284-495-9930, VHF 16
Northlatitudemarina.com
Mon-Sat 7am- 5pm,
Sunday 9am-5pm

FERRIES
New Horizon Ferry
Tel: 284-499-0952 or
284-542-5959
www.newhorizonferry.com
FB: NewHorizonFerry
ServiceLtd, 7am-5pm daily

PROVISIONING
JVD Grocery
Tel: 284-343-6443
www.jvdgrocery.com
8am-8pm daily

Rudy's Marketplace
Tel: 284-340-9282 or
284-340-5771
www.rudysjvd.wixsite.com
FB: rudys.atjvd
M-F 7-7, Sat 8-7, Sun 9-6

RESTAURANTS & BARS
Foxy's Tamarind Bar
Tel: 284-442-3074
www.foxysbvi.com
Lunch, dinner
FB: FoxysBVI (menu/events)

Ali Baba's Restaurant
Phone: 284-544-5602
Reserve dinner early: fresh
fish, roti, shrimp & more

Corsairs
Tel: 284-495-9294
www.corsairsbvi.com
FB: CorsairsBVI (for menu)
Breakfast/brunch, lunch,
dinner. 8:30am-2am daily

A&B Bar & Restaurant
Tel: 284-495-9352
FB: a.and.b.painkiller
Breakfast/lunch/dinner

Rudy's Bar & Restaurant
Tel: 284-340-9282 or
284-340-5771
www.rudysjvd.wixsite.com
FB: rudys.atjvd

SHOPPING
The Foxhole (at Foxy's)
Tel: 284-442-3074
www.foxysbvi.com
Boutique/gift shop, Foxy's
clothing, gear, souvenirs.

WHITE BAY

RESTAURANTS & BARS
Ivan's Stress-Free Bar
Tel: 284 495-9358 or
340-513-1095
ivanscampground.com
FB: ivansstressfreebarjvd

Soggy Dollar/Sandcastle
Tel: 284-495-9888
www.soggydollar.com
FB: soggydollarbarBVI
11:30am-6:30pm

One Love Bar & Grill
Tel: 284-495-9829
FB: One-Love-Bar-and-Grill
onelovebarjvd@yahoo.com

Hendo's Hideout
Tel: 284-340-0074
www.hendoshideout.com
FB: hendoshideoutbvi
Opens at 10am, Sushi Thur

LITTLE HARBOUR

Harris' Place Restaurant
Tel: 284-344-8816
www.Harrisplacejvd.com
FB: @harrisplacejvd
Fresh local seafood entrees
M-W 6-11, T-S 4-12, Su 3-10

Abe's By the Sea
Tel: 284-496-8429
FB: abesrestuarantbvi
Lunch and dinner
Open 11:30am

Sidney's Peace & Love
Tel: 284-346-7838 or
284-344-2160, VHF 16
8am-10pm daily

LITTLE JOST VAN DYKE & DIAMOND CAY

RESTAURANTS
Foxy's Taboo
VHF16
No telephone at this time,
just come ashore

B-Line Beach Bar
Tel: 284-343-3311
FB: blinebeachbar.vi
Serving lunch & dinner daily

THE ANCHORAGES OF THE
UNITED STATES
VIRGIN ISLANDS

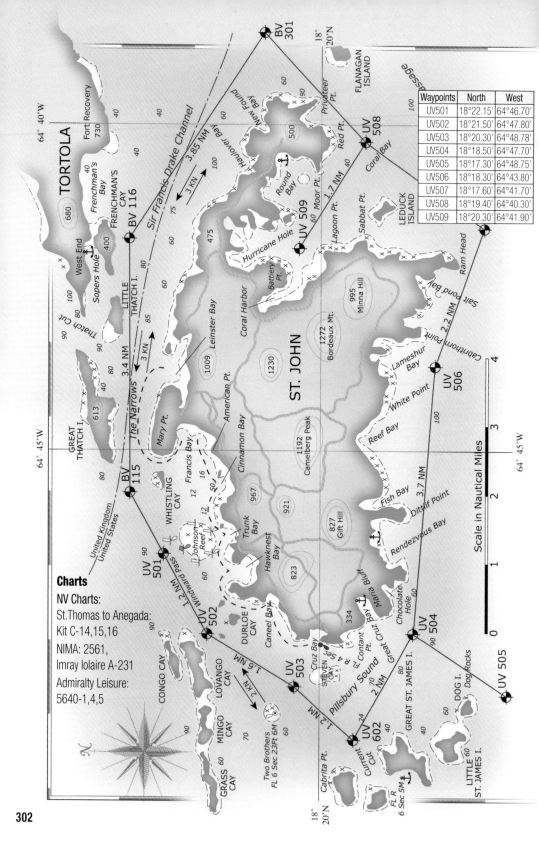

Waypoints	North	West
UV501	18°22.15'	64°46.70'
UV502	18°21.50'	64°47.80'
UV503	18°20.30'	64°48.78'
UV504	18°18.50'	64°47.70'
UV505	18°17.30'	64°48.75'
UV506	18°18.30'	64°43.80'
UV507	18°17.60'	64°41.70'
UV508	18°19.40'	64°40.30'
UV509	18°20.30'	64°41.90'

Charts

NV Charts:

St. Thomas to Anegada:
Kit C-14,15,16

NIMA: 2561,
Imray Iolaire A-231

Admiralty Leisure:
5640-1,4,5

Scale in Nautical Miles

TORTOLA

ST. JOHN

FRANCIS BAY

TRUNK BAY

JOHNSON'S REEF

HAWKSNEST BAY

CANEEL BAY

ST. JOHN

ST. JOHN NORTH COAST BAYS

Two-thirds of this fabulous island is under the auspices of the National Park Service, maintaining its pristine appearance. The Park Service has taken great efforts to provide moorings in most of the anchorages in order to help preserve the underwater reefs and sea beds from the damage of anchors. The Park has stringent guidelines that have helped to keep this island from the abuse of overuse. It is well worth a visit.

There are only a few roads on St. John and most wind up at one or another of the island's gorgeous white sand beaches, framed by the tropical forests of Virgin Islands National Park, which cover more than half the island. Trails wind through the ruins of Danish colonial sugar plantations dating to the 18th century, when sugar, rum and slavery ruled St. John and the rest of the Caribbean. Denmark sold the islands in 1917 for $25 million to the United States and 2017 was the centennial, celebrating 100 years under the US flag.

The town of Cruz Bay is charming with excellent restaurants tucked away and commanding spectacular views. You don't compete with the cruise ships for bargains, but the same duty free status applies here. With the thriving artist community in St. John there are some original and interesting treasures to see and buy. You may even wish to check into villa rentals for your next trip.

It is highly recommended you stop at the National Park Service Headquarters in Cruz Bay for information on the park as a national monument, tours, things to see and regulations. Please read the section on the National Park at the end of this guide before visiting St. John for essential information.

St. John

CRUZ BAY

Waypoint: UV503 -18°20.30'N; 64°48.78'W
Navigation: 6.5nm SW Soper's Hole, BVI;
2.3nm NE Current Cut (Gt. St. James)
Services: U.S. Port of Entry, Ferry service, Island tours, Ice, Water,
Fuel, Provisions
Trails: Lind Point Trail (1.1 miles)

St. John

Cruz Bay, a port of entry, is the main town on St. John
and, without doubt, the best place to clear customs.
Serviced by ferries on an hourly basis, many charterers elect
to leave their vessels anchored under Lind Point and take the
ferry across the sound to Red Hook. Cruz Bay offers
the yachtsman all of the basic services, including banks, post office, grocery
markets, etc. Often crowded, the anchorage, though protected, is
not necessarily a good overnight stop, as the
movement of the ferries tends to make it
uncomfortable. Vessels under
sixty feet may anchor in the
Cruz Bay Creek area
for a maximum of three
hours for the purpose of
clearing customs and
immigration or other
business in Cruz Bay.

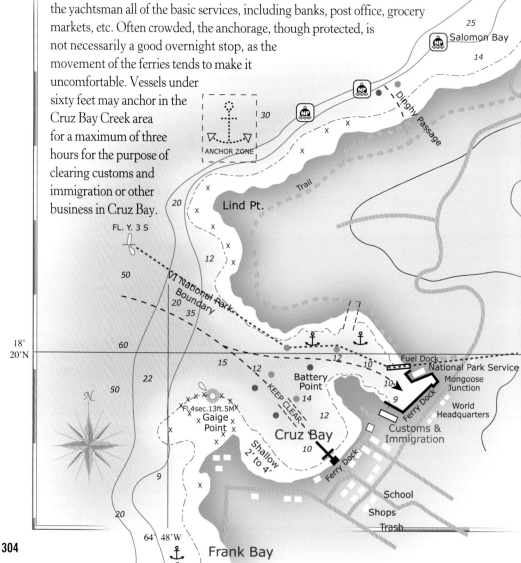

ANCHOR ZONE

30

25

Salomon Bay

14

Dinghy Passage

Trail

Lind Pt.

FL. Y. 3 S

20

12

50

VI National Park
Boundary

20   35

60

18°
20'N

15   12   12   10   Fuel Dock
                                                    National Park Service
22   Battery   10   Mongoose
50   Point   9   Junction
         Fl.4sec.13ft.5M   World
         Gaige   14   Headquarters
         Point   KEEP CLEAR   12
                    Cruz Bay   Customs &
                              10   Immigration
            Shallow
            2' to 4'
9   Ferry Dock
                                        School

20   Shops

64° 48'W   Trash

Frank Bay

8

CRUZ BAY
ST. JOHN
N

NATIONAL
PARK SERVICES
BUILDING

CUSTOMS &
IMMIGRATION

Navigation & Piloting

Approaching Cruz Bay from the north, pass through the Windward Passage (waypoint UV502) or the Durloe Channel leaving Henley and Ramgoat Cay to starboard. Head SW toward the north end of Steven Cay, before turning east into Cruz Bay. A flashing yellow buoy to the west of Lind Point marks the boundary of The National Park. Follow the markers into the inner harbor.

Making your approach from the southwest or Great St. James, it is not recommended to pass between Stephen Cay and St. John, as there are numerous coral heads. Leave Steven Cay to starboard.

The Two Brothers, a set of rocks marked by a flashing yellow at 6 seconds and standing 20 feet above sea level, are always visible in the middle of Pillsbury Sound, and have good water all around. Entering Cruz Bay, there is a reef extending out from Gallows Point to starboard, marked with a 4 second flashing marker 12 feet high. Stay well to the north of it, as it is in very shallow water. There are two marked channels within the harbor, one servicing the ferry dock to starboard, and one servicing the National Park dock and Customs to port.

This is a busy harbor so be aware of ferry traffic at all times.

Sail Paradise

The United States Virgin Islands!

St. Thomas • St. Croix • St. John

usvi-hot-deals.com

NO PASSPORT REQUIRED
FOR U.S. CITIZENS

Scan this QR code
to discover Hot Deals!
Barcode Scanner
App required.

u.s.virgin islands
HOTEL & TOURISM ASSOCIATION

Follow us:

Facebook

Twitter

Anchoring & Mooring

Cruz Bay is a difficult anchorage. Shoal water extends from the marker on the end of the Gallows Point reef about 50 to 60 feet toward the ferry dock and this side (south) of the bay is full of private boats on moorings, making it impossible to anchor. Vessels under 60 feet may anchor in the Cruz Bay Creek area, to the north of Battery Point, for a stated maximum of three hours for the purpose of Customs clearance or other business. Be sure to avoid obstructing both channels or you will incur the wrath of the ferry boat captains. As an alternative, there is a designated NPS anchoring zone just north of Lind Point / Salomon Bay where you can leave the vessel and dinghy around into Cruz Bay. There are also NPS moorings available in this area which are free during the day and $26 per night from 5:30pm. All moorings in Cruz Bay, Great Cruz Bay and Coral Bay are private and subject to stiff fines for unauthorized use. When the weather is calm an alternate anchorage would be Frank Bay to the south of Gaige Point in 9 feet of water. Take care to identify the reef that extends to the southwest from Gaige Point.

There is a public dinghy dock located on the south side of the main ferry pier, it is recommended that you tie the dinghy up short and lock it to the dock with a robust cable as some petty thievery has been reported. An alternative would be to tie up at the National Park Service dock, once again, make sure to secure it.

Ashore

Customs & Immigration: When making an official entry into the U.S. Virgin Islands from a foreign port, the skipper, crew and passengers must all report to Customs and Border Protection with passports and the ship's documents, wearing proper attire (tops, bottoms, and shoes; wearing a bathing suit is not acceptable). The Customs House is on your right in the northern section of the bay known as the Creek. The depth at the dock is 9 feet. Customs

With Permission / Copyright 2012 Geoeye / 2012 Google

and Border Protection is open in Cruz Bay seven days a week from 7am to 5:30pm (suggested arrival no later than 4:30pm). If you arrive before or after those hours, you must remain on your vessel and raise your quarantine flag and report to the authorities when they open. Cruz Bay Customs telephone number is 340-776-6741. You can tie up alongside the dock or take your dinghy. There is a lot of day charter and ferry traffic so try not to get stuck behind a ferry load of passengers arriving from the BVI.

Fuel, Water, Provisions & Garbage:

For fuel, water and ice, the Caneel Bay Marina, across from the Customs and Immigration dock, stands by on VHF 16. This is a concrete jetty and depending on the time of day, it can be both busy and crowded. LP Gas bottles can be filled at Candy's BBQ (ask directions). Her husband Elvis fills propane. It's about a 10-minute walk.

To replenish the galley, there are a couple of options: Starfish Market is open daily 7:30am-9pm, and they do provide provisioning services. (Call them at 340-779-4949.) They sell fresh fruit and vegetables, meats, dairy and all the normal grocery store items. The market also encompasses a full deli for fresh sandwiches and cold cuts. Check out their wine room and the walk-in humidor. Starfish Market has the best selection, but is also the furthest. You can walk there in 10 minutes, but be prepared to take a taxi back to the docks. The Chelsea Drugstore and St. John Hardware are located within the Marketplace complex. Dolphin Market is close to town near the round-about, and there is the Bayside Mini-Market at Meada's Plaza. Garbage should not be deposited in the smaller receptacles which are intended to accommodate litter. Make sure it is in a sealed plastic bag and take it to the dumpster located behind the school a few minutes walk from the ferry dock. For medical emergencies dial 911. There are doctors and clinics in St. John. See our *Island Connections* section at the end of St. John for information on hospitals and clinics.

The National Park Service: One of the first stops you should make ashore is to visit the National Park Service Visitors Center adjacent to the Caneel Bay Marina, across from Customs and Immigration. Open from 9am to 4:30pm daily, they will give you information on the park, moorings, trails and other services. For US visitors over the age of 62, register at the NPS and they will sell you a Parks Pass for $10 which will reduce your mooring fees from $26 to $13 per night.

Jeep Rental & Island Tours: Jeep rentals are readily available from numerous rental agencies. If you know when you will be arriving, it is a good idea to book in advance, otherwise plan to be there as early as possible. Rentals by the day are usually due back that evening, versus the normal 24-hour period. The island is small so the roads are narrow and you will be driving on the left thanks to the British who briefly occupied the islands. The best part however is that the cars themselves are designed to be driven on the right, making for an interesting learning curve and an exciting start to the day. Island tours can be booked with the various taxi drivers or tour operators by the hour or by the day. It is a good idea to have a good picture in your mind as to where you want to go (beach, ruins, tour) and if you want to stop off for a beach swim along the way make sure that your taxi driver understands he/she will be waiting as a lot of the safari bus drivers do not like to wait around. You can also ride the bus all the way to Coral Bay or round trip to anywhere on the island for a very inexpensive fare – a real bargain.

Shopping & Dining: Cruz Bay is a hub of transportation, entertainment, dining

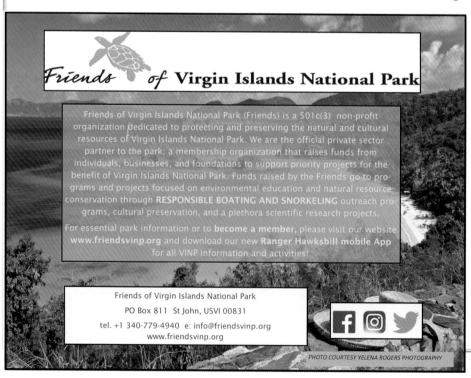

and shopping. St. John is a laid back island and while the extent of the available shopping in no way compares to that of St. Thomas, there are some unique stores, restaurants and boutiques that reflect the unique character of this special Caribbean island. Most of the stores are situated between Wharfside Village to the right of the ferry dock and Mongoose Junction a little further down the road from the National Park Visitors Center a 5 minute walk from the ferry dock. Typical operating hours are 10am-5pm every day of the week.

Mongoose Junction is St. John's premier collection of fashionable shops and restaurants in a unique architectural and tropical setting. The stonework reflects the cultural heritage of the islands and the multilevel structure is charming and inviting. Here you will find a good variety of handcrafted goods, jewelry, accessories and swimwear along with several excellent bars and restaurants. Check out the Sun Dog Café & Gecko Gazebo Bar overlooking the courtyard, it offers an eclectic menu and some refreshing tropical drinks.

Wharfside Village is a unique collection of shops, restaurants, bars, galleries and watersport centers, located at the foot of the ferry dock in the heart of Cruz Bay. Colorful buildings with shutters, framed by flowing bougainvillea connected by tile covered walkways at water's edge provide a great place to wander and stop in for a cold drink while overlooking the harbor. Try a Mango Tango at High Tide Bar & Seafood Grill or try the Waterfront Bistro or upstairs at Vista Mare for some Italian cuisine. Joe's Rum Hut serves a good Mojito with fresh mint and lime juice. Sipping a drink at a waterside bar, looking out over the anchorage and watching the sunset is close to perfect.

The National Park Visitor Center:

One of the first stops you should make when going ashore in Cruz Bay is the National Park Visitors Center opposite the Customs & Immigration building. There is a dinghy dock but it is suggested that you lock the dinghy at all times. There are a number of fascinating displays and videos that are both informative and educational. There are many new rules and regulations that you should be familiar with before spending time sailing and boating in the park: restrictions, mooring fees and payment, garbage disposal and underwater conservation.

There are also numerous free maps that show the various hiking trails, location of ruins and other relevant information. Make sure you pick up an Annaberg ruins self-guided tour map from the National Parks Service center in Cruz Bay since maps are not always available when you get

to the site. If you, or anyone in the party is over 62 and a US citizen or resident then purchase a Parks Pass for $10 which will reduce the nightly mooring fee to $13 (50%). We suggest that you take a number of overnight mooring forms that will allow you to fill them out aboard your vessel versus standing on a floating station using your knee as a table.

Any beach in the USVI can be used by anyone according to USVI law. However, you cannot gain access to that beach by crossing private property, or go beyond the beach onto private property. Some beaches therefore, are accessible only by sea.

See our section on National Parks at the front of this book for many of these important regulations.

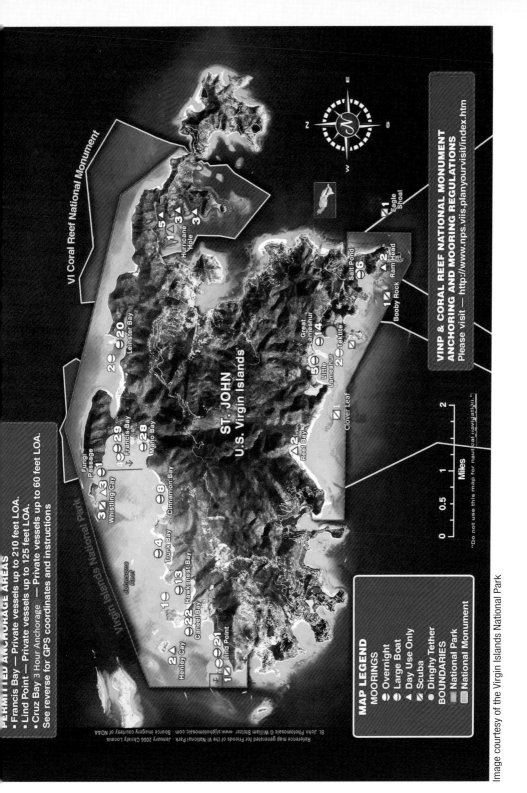

PERMITTED ANCHORAGE AREAS

- Francis Bay — Private vessels up to 210 feet LOA.
- Lind Point — Private vessels up to 125 feet LOA.
- Cruz Bay 3 Hour Anchorage — Private vessels up to 60 feet LOA.
  See reverse for GPS coordinates and instructions

VI Coral Reef National Monument

Virgin Islands National Park

ST. JOHN
U.S. Virgin Islands

Johnsons Reef

Fungi Passage

Whistling Cay

Francis Bay

Maho Bay

Cinnamon Bay

Trunk Bay

Hawksnest Bay

Cancel Bay

Henley Cay

Lind Point

Leinster Bay

Hurricane Hole

Great Lameshur

Little Lameshur

Tektite

Reef Bay

Clover Leaf

Salt Pond

Booby Rock

Ram Head

Eagle Shoal

**VINP & CORAL REEF NATIONAL MONUMENT
ANCHORING AND MOORING REGULATIONS**
Please visit — http://www.nps.viis.planyourvisit/index.htm

MAP LEGEND

MOORINGS
- Overnight
- Large Boat
- Day Use Only
- Scuba
- Dinghy Tether

BOUNDARIES
- National Park
- National Monument

0   0.5   1   2
Miles

"Do not use this map for nautical navigation."

Image courtesy of the Virgin Islands National Park

313

CANEEL BAY
TO HAWKSNEST BAY

Waypoint: UV503 -18°20.30'N; 64°48.78'W
Navigation: 0.6nm NE Cruz Bay; 3.2nm NE Redhook, St.Thomas
Services: Moorings, Caneel Bay Resort & Restaurant
Trails: Lind Point Trail, Salomon Bay Spur, Caneel Hill Trail

St. John

Caneel Bay is the home of the resort of the same name, which is built on the site of an 18th century sugar plantation. The property extends from the east side of the bay, to Turtle Bay, including the Durloe Cays.

Navigation & Piloting

Traveling north and east from Cruz Bay around Lind Point, there is a designated anchoring zone just to the north of the point. Other than Cruz Bay and Francis Bay, this is the only permitted anchoring zone within the park system. Further to the east at Salomon Bay, there is a marked channel for small craft allowing access to the beach and the Lind Point Trail. National Park moorings are available at $26 per night. During the winter months, this anchorage can be rolly and subject to the wakes of high speed ferries passing in the distance.

EASTBOUND

If you are sailing east to Hawksnest or Trunk Bays, care should be taken when negotiating the small channel between the Durloe Cays and Hawksnest Point on St. John. The wind direction can change rapidly around the headland and strong currents (2 knots in either direction) can create a choppy sea. It is prudent to start the motor while negotiating this passage.

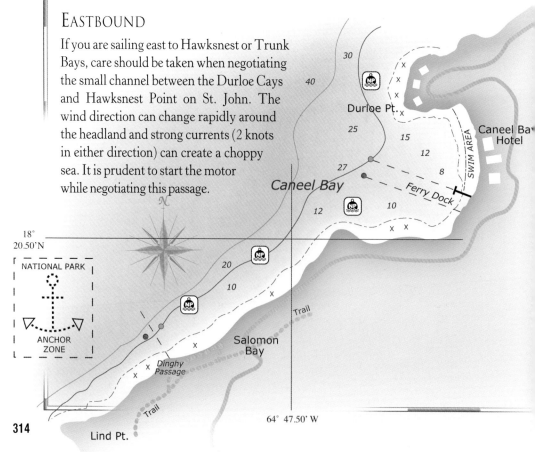

HAWKSNEST BAY

CANEEL BAY

DURLOE CHANNEL

Anchoring & Mooring

Once inside Caneel Bay, there is a marked ferry channel that services the small jetty in the middle of the bay.

Stay outside of the line of buoys off the beach that designates the hotel guest swimming area. There are 22 NPS moorings available to pick up on both sides of the channel and payment is made at the floating pay station by cash or credit card. There is no charge for daytime usage, overnight starts at 5:30pm and the fee is $26.00.

Ashore

During the day, visitors may go ashore via the dinghy dock, where you are requested to utilize a stern anchor. No dinghies are allowed on the beach. Visitors are welcome to visit the old plantation ruins, gift shop and the Beach Terrace but are prohibited from using the hotel as an access point to the rest of the island due to "Homeland Security restrictions." Reservations can be made for lunch and dinner at the charming Caneel Bay Terrace among others, the dress code is resort casual.

There may be times when the hotel must request that outside guests return at another time if the hotel management feels their visitor capacity has been reached. Uniformed hosts and hostesses are stationed throughout the complex to give directions and answer questions.

Snorkeling: Excellent snorkeling is available between Salomon and Honeymoon Bays.

HAWKSNEST BAY

Waypoint: UV501 (Johnson's Reef) - 18°22.15'N; 64°46.70'W
Navigation: 1.5nm NE Caneel Bay; 1.8nm SW Whistling Cay Passage
Services: No pay station (Use Caneel Bay)
Trails: Turtle Point Trail, Peace Hill Trail, Dennis Bay Trail

This lovely, peaceful bay is great for swimming and snorkeling. Hawksnest has 13 NPS moorings plus one large vessel mooring installed for overnight use. No anchoring is allowed. Access to Gibney and Honeymoon Beach is by dinghy. There are two marked dinghy channels. In the winter months when ground seas are running, this anchorage can be uncomfortable.

HAWKSNEST BAY
TRUNK BAY/JOHNSON'S REEF

Waypoint: UV501 (Johnson's Reef) - 18°22.15'N; 64°46.70'W
Navigation: 1.3nm SW Whistling Cay Passage
Services: NPS Moorings, Underwater trail
Trails: Peace Hill, Dennis Bay

St. John

HAWKSNEST BAY
Navigation & Piloting

Approaching from the southwest via Durloe Channel, identify Hawksnest Rock to the north of Hawksnest Point before making your turn into the anchorage.

If your approach is from the north, special note should be taken of the buoyage system around Johnson's Reef. If your transit is south of the reef, you will be leaving the yellow buoy "JC" marking the southern extremity to starboard.

Johnson's Reef is a large reef a half mile to the north of Trunk Bay. Although well marked, the reef continues to claim its share of wrecks due to negligence. The reef is marked at the northern end by a green flashing (JR-1) buoy, further north

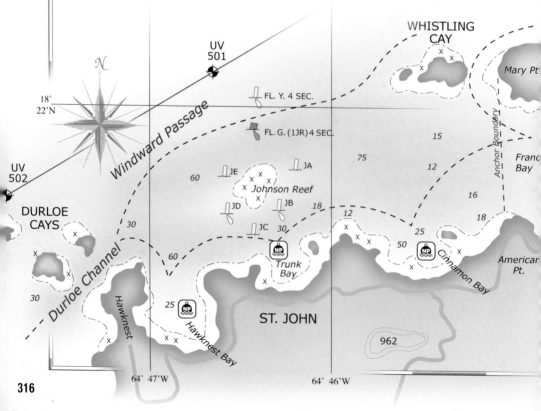

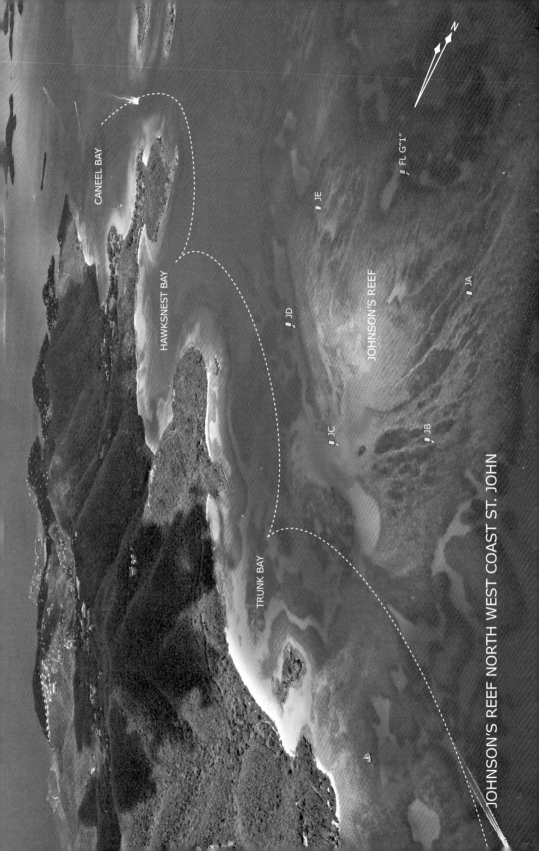

CANEEL BAY

HAWKSNEST BAY

TRUNK BAY

JOHNSON'S REEF

JE

JD

JC

JB

JA

FL G"1"

N

JOHNSON'S REEF NORTH WEST COAST ST. JOHN

Trunk Bay

is a yellow 4 sec fl. National Park boundary buoy, marking the northern extremity of the National Park. The reef is surrounded by an additional five yellow buoys marked JA-JD, three of which are flashing. Do not go between them. If sailing south of the reef, identify the southernmost (JC) marker. Care should be taken to give the reef a wide berth.

TRUNK BAY

One of the more spectacular beaches in the Virgin Islands, Trunk Bay is the site of an underwater snorkel around Trunk Cay, a small islet about 48 feet high. During the winter months or when a ground sea is running, it is not recommended as an overnight mooring area because of the bad swell. There are several NPS moorings available.

Navigation

The approach to Trunk Bay is straightforward with the exception of Johnson's Reef, as previously noted. If approaching from the west, there is a small cay (Perkins Cay) north of the headland to watch for. When departing to the east, you can proceed between Trunk Cay and the yellow marker (JC) marking the southern tip of Johnson's Reef, taking care to stay at least 200 yards off the shoreline. When a heavy ground swell is running, there will be considerable surface action and it is recommended to go around the outside, once again giving the reef a good offing.

Anchoring & Mooring

There will be a line of marker buoys off the beach, which indicates the swimming area. Dinghies going ashore must use the channel marked with red and green buoys toward the western end of the beach. A field of National Park moorings are available on a first come basis (payment ashore at the kiosk).

During ground seas, the surf on the beach can make the landing of dinghies a difficult, if not a dangerous, task.

Ashore

The National Park Service maintains an underwater snorkel trail at Trunk Bay. Picnic grounds and facilities are also maintained by the Park Service and snacks and cold drinks are available.

CINNAMON BAY

Navigation: 0.7nm E Trunk Cay
Services: NPS Moorings, Restaurant, Good snorkeling, General store
Trails: Cinnamon Bay Loop Trail, Cinnamon Bay Trail, America Hill Spur Trail

The site of the National Park Campground, Cinnamon Bay provides a good daytime spot to pick up a mooring for lunch and a snorkel. Being exposed, it can be uncomfortable as an overnight anchorage and largely untenable during northeast ground seas. The NPS has provided 8 mooring buoys for day or overnight use. To the east end of the bay is Cinnamon Cay. A reef extends to the southwest and is marked by private buoys. A dinghy landing area is provided by the National Park Service building.

Accommodations at the campground include cottages, tents, and bare sites. The watersports center offers snorkel gear and beach chairs for rent, as well as diving, sailing and windsurfing. There are also two short trails (0.5 to 1.5 miles) that are well sign-posted and intertwine, offering great views of the coastline and the ruins of an old sugar mill. There is a restaurant called T'ree Lizards on the terrace of the Cinnamon Bay Campground that serves American/

Caribbean cuisine for breakfast (8:30-10am), lunch (11:30am-2pm) and dinner (5:30-8pm). Their menu includes vegetarian selections as well as selections from the bar. Hours are seasonal so they ask that you please check with the front desk for current hours of operation.

The General Store, also found on the terrace, carries essential groceries and toiletries. From the beach, take the path to the left of the watersports center to find the Front Desk, the General Store, and the T'ree Lizards Restaurant.

MAHO BAY

Navigation: 0.6nm East of Cinnamon Cay
Services: 28 NPS Moorings and kiosk, Snorkeling
Trails: Maho Bay Goat Trail, Francis Bay Trail, Maria Hope Trail

To the northeast of American Point (525 feet high) and less than 0.5nm from the Fungi Passage, between Whistling Cay and. Mary Point is Maho Bay, a delightful, well protected anchorage fringed with white sand. The head of the bay is shoal. To the east is Maho Point marking the northeast extremity of the bay. There are 28 moorings

provided for day or night use. The Maho Bay Camp is now closed along with the service businesses associated with it. The land was sold to a private buyer and although an effort was made by the Parks Trust to secure it in order to upgrade the infrastructure and reopen the campground, they were unable to come to terms. We further understand that the new owner will be building a private estate on the property. Let us hope that his vision for this site maintains the natural state of Maho Bay. Use the marked dinghy passage when coming ashore. During the winter months during northerly ground seas it is recommended that you move across to Francis Bay under Mary Point. Dinghies should be landed on the beach via the marked channel.

FRANCIS BAY

Waypoint: UV501 (Johnson's Reef) - 18°22.15'N; 64°46.70'W
Navigation: 3.7nm NE Cruz Bay
Services: 29 NPS Moorings plus 4 large vessel moorings/ Dinghy tether
Trails: Francis Bay Trail, Leinster Bay Road, Leinster Bay Trail

Located on the northern shore of St. John, Francis Bay is the large bay, extending to the very southeast of Whistling Cay. Protected from the north by Mary Point, Francis Bay is fairly deep (50 feet) until close to shore where it shelves to 15 feet.

Navigation

If you are making your approach from the west, you will be rounding Johnson's Reef. Favor the northern end leaving the large green buoy to starboard. There is also a channel between Trunk Cay, and

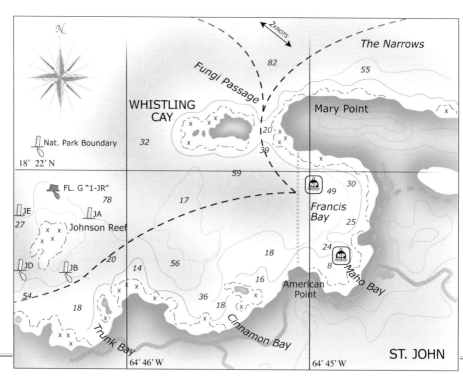

the yellow buoy "JC" (leave to port or north). If you are approaching from the north, there is plenty of water through the Fungi Passage that lies between Mary Point on St. John and Whistling Cay. A small shoal area extends south from Whistling Cay, where the decaying ruins of an old customs house can still be seen.

Anchoring & Mooring

This bay is the only bay in the National Park that allows yachts from 125 - 210 feet to anchor following the NPS guidelines.

All vessels over 125 feet and less than 210 feet in length must anchor in sand at depths of 50 feet or greater, in Francis Bay, at least 200 feet shoreward of a line from Mary Point to America Point according to NPS regulations. Yachts 60 feet or under in length may pick up a NPS mooring. There are 29 moorings provided in Francis Bay along with a floating kiosk for payment.

When the wind is light, it may get buggy if you are close to shore. A small sandbar lies in the northeastern corner. Stay outside the buoys designating the swimming area.

Ashore

For those who feel like taking a healthy walk, the National Park Service maintains a trail (Francis Bay Trail) that extends from the picnic site to an abandoned plantation house. From there you can follow the road to the Annaberg Ruins and the Annaberg Trail. The National Park Service maintains garbage facilities ashore.

Departing

If you are heading east, you will find yourself in the Narrows with the wind and current against you. Many of the local skippers prefer to lay a tack toward Jost Van Dyke, and then tack back through the cut between Great Thatch and Tortola, rather than fighting the Narrows with its strong adverse currents.

TRUNK BAY

CINNAMON BAY

MAHO BAY

FRANCIS BAY

ST. JOHN NORTH WEST COAST BAYS

LEINSTER BAY

St. John

Waypoint: BV116 (Frenchman's Cay) - 18°22.70'N; 64°41.90'W

Navigation: 1.7nm east of Fungi Passage; 2.1nm SSW Soper's Hole

Services: 20 NPS Moorings plus 4 large vessel moorings / Dinghy tether, Snorkeling, Annaberg Ruins

Trails: Annaberg Trails, Johnny Horn Trail

Located on the north coast of St. John, Leinster Bay lies directly to the south of the westernmost tip of Little Thatch. The bay is well protected and quite comfortable.

Navigation & Piloting

Leinster Bay is open and straightforward whether your approach is from the west or east. Approaching from the east, leaving Waterlemon Cay and the marked restricted area to the west of Waterlemon Cay to port; work yourself up into the eastern end of the bay, known as Waterlemon Bay. Transit between Waterlemon Cay and Leinster Point on St. John is not allowed.

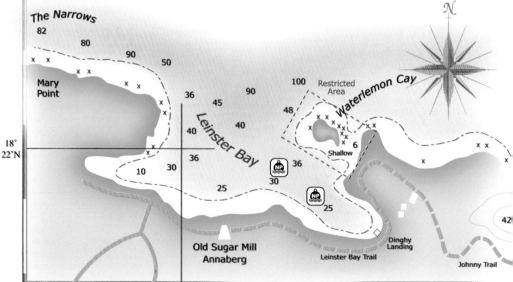

The Narrows

82

80

90

50

x x

x x

Mary Point

x x

36

45

90

100 Restricted Area

Waterlemon Cay

N

48

Leinster Bay

40

40

36

10

30

25

36

30

NP 36

30

Shallow

6

x x

x x

18° 22'N

x x

NP 25

25

42

Old Sugar Mill Annaberg

Leinster Bay Trail

Dinghy Landing

Johnny Trail

64° 44' W

ANNABERG PLANTATION RUINS

MOORINGS

NP

NP

Anchoring & Mooring

Leinster Bay has 20 overnight moorings and a floating kiosk for payment provided by the National Park Service.

As is the case throughout the National Park system, anchoring is not allowed because of the impact to the sea bed over time.

Ashore

Dinghies are not permitted to land on Waterlemon Cay. Dinghy moorings are provided just inside the restricted area. There is no ideal dinghy landing area to the southwest of the anchorage and skippers are encouraged to land their dinghies on the beach to the east, pull them up and secure them. From here it is a short hike back along the shoreline trail to the access road to the ruins of the Annaberg Sugar Mill, which have been restored by the Park Service.

The Leinster Bay Trail follows the perimeter of the shoreline west to the ruins at Annaberg or east to the ruins of the Leinster Bay Plantation, then up to the Old Guard House on Leinster Point, continuing on to meet the Johnny Trail that snakes its way all the way to Coral Bay.

LEINSTER BAY

The Ruins of the Annaberg Plantation

Years before the United States purchased the US Virgin Islands from Denmark in 1917, sugar cane was the raison d'être for plantation life on St. John. Above the anchorage at Leinster Bay, the Annaberg ruins offer a brief insight into the island's history. Walk around the stone-and-coral remains of the old slave quarters, windmill and horsemill used to extract the juice from the sugar cane. Close your eyes and conjure up the sweet heavy scent of crushed cane, molasses and rum. If your timing is right, you will detect the aroma of fresh bread baking; follow your nose to the kitchen and you might be lucky enough to taste a slice of "dumb bread" as it comes out of the traditional oven. Wandering through this historic site it's easy to see what led to the slave revolt against the plantation owners in 1733. It was thwarted, but in 1848 a second uprising heralded the end of slavery and the economic collapse of the sugar plantations. Cultural demonstrations, including baking "dumb bread" take place Tuesday through Friday from 10 a.m. to 2 p.m. In August to November the demonstration also includes subsistence gardening.

Miss Olivia

Wind Mill and Horse Mill – St. Croix

Cane crushing machinery – St. Croix

Ruins at Cinnamon Bay

Sugar Cane Production

The hillsides above the plantation were cleared and terraced. Sugar cane grew in rows, an even carpet about six feet high. Given the steep hills and labor intensive work, slave labor was the only way the plantations could make a profit. The cane was taken to the mill where it was crushed between rollers, the juice flowing downhill in wooden troughs to the boiling room. Windmills could produce more juice than the horse mill and required less labor. The boiling room was intensely hot with steam rising from the huge cauldrons. Slaves ladled the cane juice from kettle to kettle, gradually concentrating and purifying the boiling liquid. They then poured the juice into flat pans where it cooled and crystallized into sugar.

Coral Bay
Coral Harbor, Round Bay, Hurricane Hole

St. John

Waypoint: UV508 (Coral Bay) - 18°19.40'N; 64°40.30'W
Navigation: 9.7nm E Cruz Bay; 7.5nm SE Leinster Bay
Services: Coral Harbor: Provisions, Chandlery, Bars, Restaurants, Trails

Comprised of a series of bays, coves, and fingers of land, Coral Bay contains Coral Harbor, Hurricane Hole and Round Bay. They are located on the southeast corner of St. John and are generally open to the southeast. Hurricane Hole is now part of the Coral Reef National Monument and anchoring is strictly prohibited. However, the Park Service maintains 8 moorings for day use only – overnight use is prohibited. Hurricane Hole and the Coral Reef National

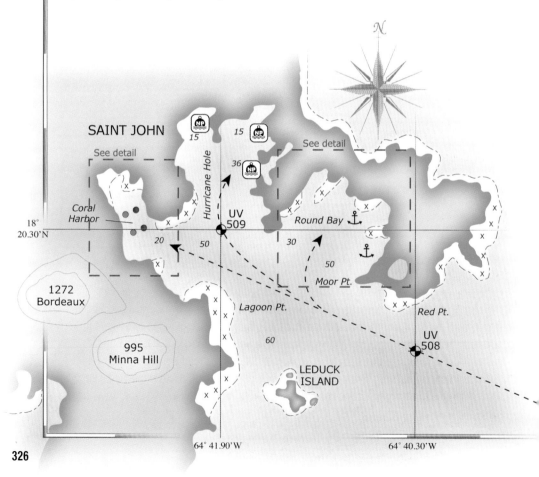

Coral Bay – Looking East

Monument are a no-take zone, so fishing, and collecting are not permitted. At the time of the slave days, when the sugar mills were at their peak, Coral Harbor was the main anchorage on St. John. There are some interesting ruins still in existence.

Navigation & Piloting

If you are approaching from the north or east or northeast, the route is straightforward. Leave Flanagan's Island to port and proceed to waypoint UV508 or make your entry into the bay midway between Red Point on St. John and Leduck Island (85 feet high) to the south. It is wise to give all headlands in this area a wide berth as most have rocks and coral extending out from them.

Approaching from the south or west, care must be exercised to avoid Eagle Shoal, situated about 0.7 nm south of Leduck Island. The shoal is very difficult to see and has about 2 feet of water over it. When rounding Ram's Head, it is possible to hug the shoreline, passing midway between Sabbat Point and Leduck Island via the Sabbat Channel in 50 feet of water, however, given the fact that this route puts you on a lee shore, the more prudent route is to stay south of a line drawn between Ram's Head and Water Point on the northern tip of Norman Island until Leduck Island bears northwest. Then enter Coral Bay midway between Leduck Island and Red Point.

ROUND BAY

Waypoint: UV508 (Coral Bay) - 18°19.40'N; 64°40.30'W

Navigation: 1.8nm E Coral Harbor

Services: Floating taco bar

St. John

Round Bay is really a series of smaller bays comprised of Long Bay, Hansen Bay and Elk Bay. Open to the south, the anchorages at times can be rolly and uncomfortable. The most protected of the bays is Hansen Bay, which, when tucked in behind and to the north of Pelican Rock makes a delightful anchorage.

Navigation & Piloting

Approaching Coral Bay from the southwest between Red Point to the north and Leduck Island to the south, you will round Moor Point (Long Point) that extends to the west. Long Bay extends north from the point and you can anchor in 10-15 feet of water on a shell bottom. We have always found this bay uncomfortable as it is exposed to the south and the surge tends to find its way around the point. Continuing north to Hansen Bay, do not pass between the shore and Pelican Rock. Leave Pelican Rock (7 feet high) to starboard and anchor to the north of the rock in 25 feet of water on a grassy bottom. Anchored up in the northeast corner of the bay is the Lime-Out, a floating lime colored taco bar where you are served in the water on a bar just above water level. It is recommended that you kayak or SUP over.

Further to the north is Limetree Cove and Elk Bay. Both are with within the National Park boundary and fairly exposed.

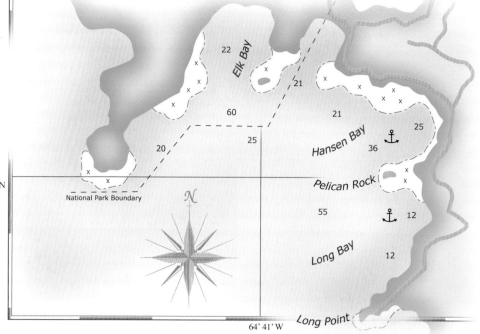

CORAL HARBOR

HURRICANE HOLE

ROUND BAY

LONG PT

ED PT

PRIVATEER PT

N

CORAL BAY ST. JOHN

Hansen Bay, St. John

PELICAN ROCK

HURRICANE HOLE

Hurricane Hole is now part of the Coral Reef National Monument and anchoring is strictly prohibited. However, the Park Service maintains eight moorings for day use only, overnight use is prohibited, for vessels not exceeding 60 feet (length on deck).

Navigation & Piloting

Departing Round Bay and heading toward Hurricane Hole, you will be leaving Turner Point to starboard, there is a small reef that extends to the southeast so allow a reasonable offing as you round the point. Working your way up into Hurricane Hole, the depth will be around 60 feet and the shoreline lined with thick mangrove growth. Water Creek is the first finger that opens to the northeast with a secondary bay to starboard that is about as protected as you can be. The depth is 15 to 20 feet.

Further north is Otter Creek (15 feet) and Princess Bay (22 feet) heading off to the northeast. Bork Creek (18 feet) is at the head of the bay to the northwest. All of these bays provide excellent protection.

Hurricane protection is available by application from the Park Service. Applications usually have to be submitted by the end of May to ensure a preset location. It is not permitted to tie to the mangroves.

ROUND BAY

CORAL HARBOR

HURRICANE HOLE

CORAL BAY | HURRICANE HOLE   N

Lime Out Taco Bar, Round Bay

CORAL HARBOR

Waypoint: UV509 (Hurricane Hole) - 18°20.30'N; 64°41.90'W

Navigation: 3.4nm N Ram's Head; 2.2nm NW Moor Point (Long Point)

Services: Provisions, Chandlery, Bars, Restaurants, Gift stores

Trails: Johnny Horn, Brown Bay Trail

St. John

Coral Bay historically was the center of plantation life in the early 18th century. It still bustles with the sailors who anchor in the bay, and many of them flock to Skinny Legs for a libation or two. Coral Harbor in particular has a truly laid-back character reflecting the iconoclastic nature of the inhabitants, craftsmen and artists preferring to be perched on the other side of the great divide of the bustling town of Cruz Bay. The anchorage is open to the southwest.

Navigation & Piloting

The entrance to Coral Harbor is straightforward but narrow. The anchorage is usually crowded with cruisers and private moorings, which makes it difficult to find room to anchor. Stay mid-channel until the stone house on the eastern side of the bay bears northeast. The channel is marked by two sets of red and green buoys that are privately maintained. You should then be able to anchor in 10-15 feet of water. Keep the channel clear for fishing boats, and do not pick up the private moorings you will see here. Ashore there is a small dinghy landing area, which usually reflects the high density of the anchorage.

Coral Bay

Skinny Legs

Dinghy Dock

10   10

390

20

Harbor Pt.

18

Coral Harbor

18°
24.30'N

18

35

Sanders Bay   10

N

Johnson Bay

CORAL HARBOR ST. JOHN

Ashore

There is no Customs service at Coral Harbor. There are a number of buildings left over from slavery days, including the Moravian Mission and the ruins of an old sugar mill and a fort. Coral Harbor has become the place to eat in St. John.

Try Skinny Legs Bar & Grill, a funky laid back store/restaurant which is the local hang-out with good burgers and good music. Opens at 11am. For a different experience with outdoor dining, try Aqua Bistro for a casual seafood meal, open for lunch and dinner 11am - 9pm. Provisioning is available from The Dolphin Market, in the Cocoloba Center or Love City Market who have a reputation for friendly service. Further along the road to the south is the Calabash Market in Johnson Bay. For retail therapy, check in at The Jolly Dog for clothes, gifts and souvenirs or Pottery in Paradise. There are no ATM's in Coral Harbor.

Coral Bay Marine monitors VHF 16 from 9am to 5pm Monday through Friday and 9am to 1pm on Saturday. Sunday they are closed. They provide engine repairs, sail repairs, ice and miscellaneous items.

Coral Harbor is home to some wonderfully eccentric and dedicated cruising sorts. It is considered more of a haven from the tourists, rather than a tourist destination.

THE SOUTH COAST BAYS
SALT POND BAY & LAMESHUR BAYS

St. John

Just a half mile beyond the point of Ram's Head, there are a number of bays, less frequently visited by the cruising yachtsman. We have listed below several of these anchorages, along with any pertinent information. In the south bays no anchoring is permitted by the National Park Service, however, there are some moorings available to pick up that are maintained by the Park Service.

SALT POND BAY

Waypoint: UV507 (Ram's Head) - 18°17.60'N; 64°41.70'W
Navigation: 0.5nm NW Rams Head
Services: 6 NPS Moorings / Kiosk Ashore
Trails: Ramshead Trail, Drunk Bay Trail, Salt Pond Bay Trail

When the weather is settled, Salt Pond Bay is an excellent spot to pick up an NPS mooring. It is easy to enter, although there are rocks awash at the entrance. You can pass on either side of them; however, there is more room if you leave them to starboard. Both channels have a minimum of 12 feet of water.

When approaching and leaving Salt Pond Bay, Booby Rock is easy to see (35 feet) with good water all around to the north and a small reef extending to the south-southwest. Anchoring is forbidden. The snorkeling around this anchorage is excellent.

Yawzi Point   10

15

18

30

25

Little Lameshur Bay

Great Lameshur Bay

25

ST JOHN
South Coast Bays

12

25

Cabrithorn Point

18°
18.30'N

70

60

N

Salt Pond Bay

31

Booby Rock   25

20

Rams Head

64° 43' W

GREAT LAMESHUR BAY

LITTLE LAMESHUR BAY

LAMESHUR BAYS ST. JOHN

There are several trails (see list above), varying from 0.25 to 1.4 miles long, that can be accessed from this anchorage.

A word of caution is that this bay has been subject to some petty thievery. Sunbathers, rental cars and boats all seem to be fair game.

GREAT & LITTLE LAMESHUR BAY

Waypoint: UV506 (Lameshur Bay) – 18°18.30'N; 64°43.80'W

Navigation: 1.5nm NW Ram's Head; 5.1nm SE Cruz Bay

Services: Great Lameshur 14 NPS Moorings plus 2 large vessel moorings / Kiosk Ashore; Little Lameshur 5 NPS moorings

Trails: Lameshur Bay Trail, Yawzi Point Trail, Europa Bay Trail

Making your approach from Ram's Head to the southeast, stay well to the south of Cabrithorn Point as there is a reef that extends to the south. Once past the point, turn northeast toward Yawzi Point that separates the two bays. Be aware that shoal water extends southwest from Yawzi Point so do not cut the point close transiting from one bay to the other. When entering either side, favor the middle of the channel.

Great Lameshur Bay carries 15 feet almost all the way to the shoreline and Little Lameshur has 10 feet of depth.

GREAT LAMESHUR BAY

Another well protected bay, Great Lameshur Bay is easy to gain access to. Once inside, pick up a Park Service mooring. Anchoring is forbidden.

LITTLE LAMESHUR BAY

To the west of Great Lameshur, Little Lameshur offers good protection except when the wind is from the south. This is another bay with restricted anchoring. Pick up a mooring and head for the water. Snorkeling here is excellent.

EMERGENCIES
At sea call for mayday on
Channel 16
Ashore dial 911
Supervisory Ranger
Tel: 340-776-6451

Ambulance/EMT
Tel: 340-776-6222

Emergency Clinic
Tel: 340-693-8900

CANEEL BAY
Caneel Bay Resort
Tel: 340-776-6111 or
www.caneelbay.com
Note: Currently closed
for re-building. No
reservations accepted
through the end of 2020.

**Friends of Virgin
Islands National Park**
Tel: 340-779-4940
www.friendsvinp.org

CINNAMON BAY
**Cinnamon Bay
Campground**
Tel: 669-999-8784
www.cinnamonbay.com
Note: To re-open for the
2020-2021 season

National Park Service
Tel: 340-776-6201
www.nps.gov/viis/
index.htm

CORAL BAY
PROVISIONS
Love City Market
Tel: 340-643-0010
Open 6am-10pm

Dolphin Market
Tel: 340-776-5005
Open 7am-10pm

RESTAURANTS
Lime Out VI
(Floating Bar)
Tel: 340-643-5333

Skinny Legs
Nightly band, serves
burgers, hot dogs, salads
Open 11am-9pm
Tel: 340-779-4982
www.skinnylegs.com

Aqua Bistro
Tel: 340-776-5336
aquabistrostjohn.com

SERVICES
**Connections East
Business Services**
Telephone, mail,
computer usage, etc.
Coral Bay
Tel: 340-776-6922
connectionsstjohn.com

SHOPS
Now & Zen Shop
Clothing and more
Tel: 340-714-1088

CRUZ BAY

Customs and Border Control
Tel: 340-776-6741
7am-6pm 7 days a week

Myrah Keating Smith Community Health Ctr.
24-hour Emergency Services
Tel: 340-693-8900

AMBULANCE
Tel: 911
Cell phone: 340-776-9110 or 340-776-6222

POLICE
Tel: 340-693-8880

Virgin Islands National Park Service
Visitors Center
Open from 8am-4:30 pm
Tel: 340-776-6201,
ext. 238
www.nps.com/viig

PROVISIONS
Starfish Market
Tel: 340-779-4949
Online ordering available
www.starfishmarket.com

Dolphin Market
Tel: 340-776-5328
Open 7am-11pm

PROFESSIONAL GUIDES
Virgin Island Ecotours
Professional guides
Hike or paddle
Tel: 340-779-2155
www.viecotours.com

RESTAURANTS
The Lime Inn
Tel: 340-776-6425

There are many restaurants in Cruz Bay, but this will get you started if you want a night on the town!
www.mongoosejunction
stjohn.com

SERVICES
Connections West Business Services
Telephone, mail, computer usage, etc.
Tel: 340-776-6922
connectionsstjohn.com

US Virgin Islands Hotel & Tourism Association
St. Thomas, St. Croix, St. John
www.usvi-hot-deals.com

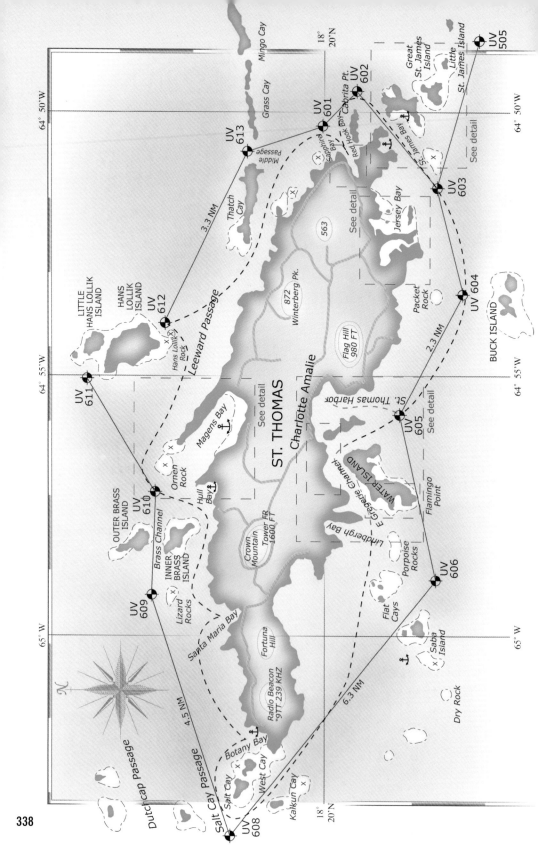

338

St. Thomas

Charts
NV Charts:
St.Thomas to Anegada:
Kit C-14,14A,16
NIMA 2561,
Imray Iolaire A-231
Admiralty Leisure:
5640-1,4,10

Waypoints	North	West
UV601	18°20.00'	64°50.00'
UV602	18°19.30'	64°49.60'
UV603	18°18.20'	64°51.30'
UV604	18°17.60'	64°53.40'
UV605	18°18.60'	64°55.60'
UV606	18°18.10'	64°59.00'
UV607	18°16.80'	65°06.30'
UV608	18°22.00'	65°04.20'
UV609	18°23.40'	64°59.65'
UV610	18°23.40'	64°57.50'
UV611	18°24.75'	64°55.00'
UV612	18°23.40'	64°53.70'
UV613	18°21.50'	64°50.70'

A Brief History

St. Thomas was made a free port in 1815 and in the years following it became a shipping center and distributing point for the West Indies. Charlotte Amalie flourished commercially. A large part of all West Indian trade was channeled through the harbor. The population and atmosphere was very cosmopolitan, particularly in comparison to its sister island of St. Croix where plantation life was the norm. It is on St. Croix that a slave revolt in 1848 prompted the abolition of slavery in the Danish West Indies.

With the increase of steamships in the 1840s, St. Thomas continued forward by becoming a coaling station for ships running between South and North America. Shipping lines made Charlotte Amalie their headquarters. Later advancements in steam and political climate made it possible for Spanish and English islands to import directly from producers, therefore skipping St. Thomas. By the 1860s, the end of prosperity loomed on the horizon. Coaling however, would continue until about 1935.

In the late 1800s through early 1900s, several major natural disasters including hurricanes, fires and a tsunami left Charlotte Amalie wanting for major rebuilding. On St. Croix, plantations were suffering with labor issues and low market prices on sugar. The Danish West Indies became more and more dependent on Denmark and its treasury during these difficult times.

Negotiations between the United States and Denmark were initiated on several occasions between 1865 and 1917 when the final deal was struck and the United States bought the Danish West Indies for $25 million.

The United States flag was hoisted on the three "Virgin Islands of America" on the 31st of March 1917.

St. Thomas Harbor and the town of Charlotte Amalie

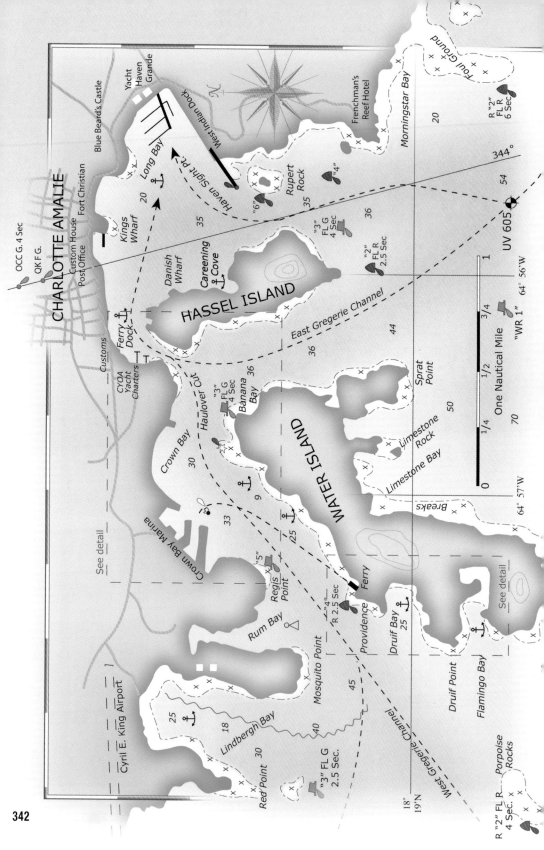

CHARLOTTE AMALIE

OCC. G. 4 Sec

QK F.G.

Blue Beard's Castle

Fort Christian

Custom House

Post Office

Customs

Yacht Haven Grande

West Indian Dock

Long Bay

Haven Sight Pt.

Kings Wharf

Danish Wharf

Careening Cove

20

35

"6"

Rupert Rock

35

"4"

"4"

Frenchman's Reef Hotel

Morningstar Bay

20

Foul Ground

R "2" FL R 6 Sec

54

344°

UV 605

64° 56'W

"3" FL G 4 Sec

36

"2" FL R 2.5 Sec

HASSEL ISLAND

East Gregerie Channel

36

44

"WR 1"

Sprat Point

50

Limestone Rock

Limestone Bay

Breaks

70

64° 57'W

One Nautical Mile

0   1/4   1/2   3/4   1

Ferry Dock

CYOA Yacht Charters

"3" FL G 4 Sec

Banana Bay

36

Haulover Cut

Crown Bay

30

33

Crown Bay Marina

9

25

"5"

Regis Point

Rum Bay

"4" R 2.5 Sec

Providence

Ferry

Druif Bay

25

WATER ISLAND

Druif Point

See detail

Flamingo Bay

See detail

Cyril E. King Airport

Mosquito Point

45

Lindbergh Bay

18

40

25

Red Point

30

"3" FL G 2.5 Sec

West Gregerie Channel

18° 19'N

R "2" FL R 4 Sec.

Porpoise Rocks

342

St. Thomas Harbor

Named after a Danish Queen, Charlotte Amalie is the capital city of the U.S. Virgin Islands and historically a major seaport. Used extensively over the centuries as a haunt of pirates and privateers, St. Thomas was declared a free port by the Danes thus enabling the sale of goods, livestock and ships acquired in honest trade or under the flag of piracy.

The town still has many of the original Danish buildings and mansions on the hillside overlooking the harbor. Picturesque alleys and stairways will lead you from large mansions to traditional West Indian houses surrounded by gardens.

Sheltered in all weather, St. Thomas Harbor tends to have a surge, especially when the wind moves around to the south, making it uncomfortable for small boats. Since it is a commercial harbor, swimming is not recommended.

Approaches

There are three approaches to Charlotte Amalie and St. Thomas Harbor. If your approach is from the west you will be using the West Gregerie Channel. Leaving Water Island to starboard and Crown Bay Marina to port then on through Haulover Cut into the main harbor.

Approaching from the east, via Current Cut and St. James Bay; leave the exposed rocks (Cow and Calf) west of the cut to port (waypoint UV603). You will pass the red nun buoy (#2) marking the southern end of Packet Rock (waypoint UV604), which lies approximately one mile due north of the easily distinguishable Buck Island (115 feet).

At the mouth of the harbor a red buoy "R2" marks the shoal ground that extends south from Morningstar Bay under the recognizable Frenchman's Reef Hotel. To the west is the green flashing 4 sec. buoy (WR1).

From here you can approach the harbor via the main commercial channel to the north, or if proceeding on to Frenchtown, Crown Bay Marina or Water Island then via the East Gregerie Channel to the northeast leaving Hassel Island to starboard.

St. Thomas Harbor & Yacht Haven Grande

Navigation & Pilotage

From waypoint UV605 head 370°m toward the red ("4"fl. 4 sec.) and green ("3" fl. 4 sec.) markers. Continue in on the same course and you will pass red marker ("6" fl. 4 sec.) marking the western extremity of Rupert Rocks. There is also flashing red on the western end of the West Indian dock (cruise ship). Leaving them to starboard, you can head directly for the anchorage.

There is also a range that brings you into the harbor. From a point west of the red buoy ("2" fl. 6 sec.) at the entrance, the range aligns two green lights on Berg Hill,

ST. THOMAS HARBOR

one at 300 feet the other at 200 feet. The range is 344° (358°m).

Once inside the harbor, you will note several buoys off the West Indian dock. These designate the turning area for the many cruise ships that come and go on a daily basis and the anchorage lies to northeast of them. Yacht Haven Grande is at the head of the harbor at the foot of the cruise ship dock.

Vessels wishing to clear Customs and Immigration, or anchor/moor in close proximity to the arriving and departing ferries should head for the Frenchtown

anchorage located in the far western end of the harbor, north of Hassel Island just inside of Haulover Cut. Moorings may be available from CYOA Yacht Charters who monitor VHF 16.

Anchoring & Mooring

The traditional anchorage for yachts in St. Thomas is off the Yacht Haven Grande Marina complex. Take care not to foul any of the private moorings that have been placed by the charter yachts operating out of the harbor. It is not recommended to tie up to the quay in Charlotte Amalie, as the surge is both dangerous and uncomfortable.

Customs & Immigration

Customs clearance can be carried out wharf-side at the ferry dock at the west end of the harbor; the hours are from 8am to noon and 1pm to 5pm, Monday through Saturday. Sundays the hours are from 10am to 6pm. The telephone number is 340-774-6755. If you are planning on staying at the marina you may also clear in at the Yacht Haven Grande seven days a week by appointment with 48 hours notice. Their telephone number is 340-774-9500. Cruisers planning to stay on the east end of St. Thomas may find it easier to clear in at Cruz Bay, St. John. Open 7am to 5:30pm seven days a week. They do not monitor the VHF radio.

When clearing at Customs, bear in mind the dress code ashore calls for shirts and shoes, as wearing just bathing suits is deemed generally inappropriate.

US Virgin Island Customs and Border Control law requires that all people onboard must accompany the skipper while clearing. Non US citizens or residents arriving by private or chartered boat must have a visa and passport in order to clear into the US. US citizens must have a passport to check in to the US Virgin Islands from other countries, including the British Virgin Islands. US resident aliens must have a green-card. For questions call Immigration at 340-774-4279.

YACHT HAVEN GRANDE

Yacht Haven Grande is situated in Long Bay, near the cruise ship docks. This state of the art marina has 5,200 linear feet of dock designed for luxury yachts and can accommodate mega-yachts over 600 feet in length with a depth of 18 feet and a beam of 54 feet. High speed fueling is from a pedestal right at your slip – no need to move to a fuel dock. Also provided are cable television, telephone service, and WiFi throughout the marina complex. They will also dispose of oil, black water etc. Fuel hours are 8am to 5pm in season and 8am to 4pm off season.

The marina complex has everything you need including an ATM, fine dining (The Blue Eleven has recently reopened and although expensive the food is excellent). For provisioning, Moe's Market has recently opened a branch near the marina office, with an excellent selection including wine and liquor. Laundry services, ship's chandlery, florist and a well equipped gym are available in addition to an upscale group of shops and boutiques at duty free prices.

If you need some time off the boat, relax in the pool, use the tennis courts, or hone your skills on the putting green. Yacht Haven Grande has included some fantastic condominiums in their complex if you want to stay and live the dream!

Security is a priority in the marina complex. Your personal safety and the security of your vessel will be assured. The marina can be reached on VHF channel 16/10 or 340-774-9500.

YACHT HAVEN GRANDE

Nearby, within walking distance are a number of helpful shops such as Pueblo Supermarket, bank, car rentals and more. You will also come across various restaurants, bars and fast food for those craving a burger and fries.

Near Yacht Haven Grande is a tramway that will carry you to the top of Flag Hill to Paradise Point, presenting incredible vistas of Charlotte Amalie and the harbor. You can get a variety of tropical drinks and food as you gaze out on this spectacular view, as well as finding some interesting things to buy to remind you of your trip. Don't forget your camera!

A short walk from the marina brings you to Havensight Shopping Mall full of gift shops like A.H. Riise, Royal Caribbean and Little Switzerland, and a collection of glamorous jewelry shops like Cardow, and Amsterdam Sauer. Many other shops of all descriptions provide for more than a few hours of shopping gluttony!

HASSEL ISLAND (VIRGIN ISLAND NATIONAL PARK)

Hassel Island, just minutes from the Charlotte Amalie waterfront, is under the domain of the National Park Service. You can still see some 18th and 19th century British fortifications from the Napoleonic Wars, as well as some private homes and the ruins of an old shipyard visible at the north end of the island. The shipyard is under restoration.

The park has a limited trail system at this time, amongst the cactus and orchids. Green iguanas can be spotted from time to time. There is a small anchorage in the Careening Cove on the eastern side of the island, often full of local boats . There is 15 feet on a hard sand bottom.

FRENCHTOWN/HAULOVER CUT

Navigation: 0.8nm NW Main Harbor Entrance
Services: Marina, Moorings, Slips, Garbage, Showers, and Restaurants

Frenchtown Marina, near the ferry dock in the far western section of St. Thomas Harbor, is the base for the CYOA Yacht Charters and their fleet of power and sailboats. The marina is open from 8am to 5pm daily and monitors VHF 16. The water is from 6 feet to 18 feet deep and they can accommodate vessels from 30 to 150 feet long, stern to the dock. Water, electricity, showers and garbage drop off are all available. Moorings just off the marina can be picked up and paid for at the marina.

Frenchtown is quaint, steeped in history and is home to some really great restaurants such as Hook Line and Sinker, Oceana, Craig and Sally's, and the Frenchtown Deli. It is worth the stop for that alone! Frenchtown is also a convenient spot to get to the ferry terminal if you are planning to go to St. John or the British Virgin Islands, or it is only a very short walk to the Main Street shops and restaurants.

HAULOVER CUT

Traveling west from Frenchtown you will pass through the Haulover Cut in 12 feet (3.6 meters) of water. The high speed ferry traffic uses this channel and therefore extreme caution should be exercised and a sharp lookout for traffic. There are no lights or markers, but the reef on both sides at the western end is easy to see.

Frenchtown Marina

CUSTOMS

CROWN BAY
MARINA

HAULOVER CUT

WATER ISLAND

EAST GREGERIE CHANNEL

HASSEL ISLAND

ST. THOMAS HARBOR LOOKING WEST

ASHORE IN CHARLOTTE AMALIE

Main Street, or Dronningens Gade (which means Queen Street) with its Danish buildings and stone alleys, is laced with shops and restaurants. Known as a free port, St. Thomas bustles with shoppers from the cruise ships, and visitors from all parts of the Caribbean and many other parts of the world.

US citizens are allowed a $1600 duty-free exemption on imports purchased in the USVI. Excellent values can be found on such luxury items as perfumes, camera gear, liquor, jewelry and other treasures.

Charlotte Amalie has many historical buildings steeped in a myriad of cultures. A tour of the town will take you through many fascinating labyrinths of old stone buildings and wooden houses.

Across Tolbod Gade from the brightly colored Vendors Plaza is the office of the VI Government Visitors Bureau and the Native Arts and Crafts Cooperative. This was once the old Customs building and is a good place to get your bearings before shopping. They

Main Street (Dronningens Gade)

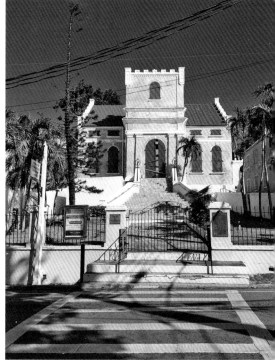

are very helpful. Emancipation Park, named for the freed slaves, borders the vendors market on the seaside of the park. You can easily find it by looking for the rainbow of umbrellas with vendors selling local handicrafts and assorted other mementos. Next to the park, Fort Christian, now a museum, is the oldest building in St. Thomas, having been built in the 1600s.

Market Square, just west of the busy shopping district of Main Street, was a slave market in earlier days, and later became a market for local farmers. Note the wrought iron roof, which came from a European railway station at the turn of the century.

The second oldest synagogue in the United States is located on Crystal Gade. The sand floors in the synagogue are characteristic of Sephardic Carib synagogues.

On Norre Gade stands the Frederick Lutheran Church, the official church of the Danish Virgin Islands. It was rebuilt in 1826 after a fire. You may visit the church Monday through Saturday from 8am to 5pm and on Sunday from 8am to noon.

Above Main Street, the Governor's House and other government buildings are painted with traditional bright red roofs to be easily spotted from sea. This lovely building has housed both the governor's residence as well as his offices. The spacious second floor reception room can be viewed by appointment.

Bluebeard's Castle tower guarded the harbor and the Danish settlers, with the help of Fort Christian and Blackbeard. The hotel and grounds command an excellent view of the entire harbor.

CROWN BAY MARINA

Navigation: 1.75nm west of Haulover Cut
Services: Fuel, Water, Provisions, Restaurant, Pump-out, WiFi, Car rental

St. Thomas

Navigation

Located immediately west of the historic Charlotte Amalie Harbor and Hassel Island and north of Water Island, Crown Bay lies within the area known as Subbase. Yachts may approach via either West Gregerie Channel or East Gregerie Channel; both of which are well marked, as is the reef extending northward from Water Island. While in Gregerie Channel, yachtsmen may approach Crown Bay Marina by leaving the cruise ship dolphin piling to port. The signed entrance to the marina is immediately north of the northernmost cruise ship dock. The tall Puma sign on the fuel dock marks the entrance to the marina.

Upon entering, the marina's 315 foot fuel dock with high volume pumps lies hard to starboard and is open from 8am to 5pm daily. Water, diesel, gasoline and a pump-out station are available. There is ample maneuvering room inside the turning basis with a controlled depth of 20 feet. The wet slips have a depth of 15 feet. The marina monitors VHF channel 16 or call 340-774-2255. Dinghies can be landed in the southwest corner (12 foot maximum).

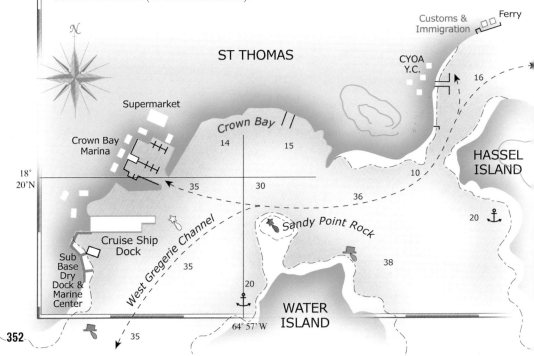

Ashore

Situated on four acres of landscaped grounds, the facilities at Crown Bay Marina are exceptional. There are 99 slips available ranging from 25 to 200 feet, including 16 alongside and stern-to-berths catering to megayachts up to 200 feet in length.

The slips have metered power, water, satellite TV service and WiFi high speed broadband internet service. The marina office is open from 8am to 5pm and provides on-site security, specialized ship's agent service for port clearance and wire transfer banking assistance. Crown Bay Marina is in close proximity to the airport. A garbage dumpster is located to the left of the office.

Dockside retail shops include Island Marine Outfitters, a fully stocked marine chandlery. The Gourmet Gallery has closed and therefore provisions can be purchased at Pueblo Supermarket which is a five minute walk from the marina. We are given to understand that Moe's Market will be opening another store somewhere in the vicinity but there is no confirmation at press time. The Tickles Dockside Pub, with a casual atmosphere is open daily serving dinner until 10pm with the bat staying open for late night drinks.

Your Choice Laundry offers self-service washers and dryers or laundry can be dropped off for full service. If the turn-around time is critical then an appointment should be made.

Phoenix Visions hair salon can help tame that wind-blown hair look offering a full range of services for both men and women.

Mail Stop can assist with mail, courier service, mail boxes, notary services, photocopying and more. Yacht captains and owners without Caribbean

bank accounts are able to transfer money via the marina account to facilitate with emergency funds.

The Water Island Ferry Service provides several round-trip runs daily between the marina and Water Island. Check with the operators for schedules and fares.

More and more luxury yachts today are utilizing the services of United Yacht Transport to facilitate the movement of yachts to and from the Caribbean region. Crown Bay Marina's close proximity to the United Yacht Transport staging area is advantageous for yachtsmen utilizing UYT which ferries dozens of luxury yachts across the Atlantic in dry-dock cradles secured to the deck.

CROWN BAY MARINA

THE SUBBASE/ DRY DOCKS & MARINE CENTER

The area known locally as the Subbase and originally developed during World War I as a submarine base, underwent further expansion and development in 1941 as America contemplated its future role in the expanding hostilities in Europe and the requirements of a two ocean Navy. The deep water channel known as the Gregerie Channel provided an ideal location for a submarine base and bunkering for deep draft vessels. These developments were completed in concert with the development of the airport, which at that time was known as Bourne Field and Lindbergh Bay as a base for seaplanes.

In the early 1980s a couple, Gene and Mary Kral, moved their fledgling business from Yacht Haven, the site of today's Yacht Haven Grande, to Subbase and over time developed a complete marine center that incorporates alliances with many major marine service providers.

Today, Subbase Dry Dock, Inc. has both a 1200 ton and a 400 ton dry dock system that allows them to provide services for both vessels up to 220 ft in length, and local ferry services. They also have a 100 ton crane. Call them at 340-776-2078.

Island Rigging and Offshore Marine are all located in the marine center. They are open from 8am to 5pm Monday through Friday and on Saturday as needed. Contact information for these marine businesses is located on the *Island Connections* pages.

WATER ISLAND

Water Island gets its name from the fact that it was one of the few places in the Caribbean with fresh water ponds where sailing vessels could replenish their fresh water casks. Both the pirates and merchantmen were accustomed to coming to Water Island for water.

It is known that the pirates used to anchor in its bays out of range of the guns of the Danish Fort on St. Thomas and lie in wait for merchant vessels that were entering or leaving the port of St. Thomas.

Water Island is 2.5 miles long and 0.5 miles wide. It can be reached via the ferry that leaves from Crown Bay Marina on St. Thomas. Water Island divides the east and west Gregerie Channels. On the southernmost part of the island is an old lookout tower on the top of Flamingo Hill.

From Haulover Cut, transiting to the southwest along the West Gregerie Channel, Sandy Point Rock, marking the northern point of Water Island, will be seen to port standing 15 feet above water level. South of the point is Ruyter Bay and there are usually numerous cruising yachts anchored here in 15-20 feet of water. Further to the south is Elephant Bay, where once again yachts can be seen at anchor. This is a popular anchorage due to its close proximity to Crown Bay Marina.

R '4' FL R 2 1/2 Sec.

47 Providence Pt.

40

Druif Bay
(Honeymoon Bay)   10

47

WATER ISLAND

18°
19'N

60

58

Flamingo Bay   16

30   30

235
Flamingo Hill

64° 57'60 W   Flamingo Pt.

Honeymoon (Druif) Bay

Navigation: 1.5nm SW of Haulover Cut, West Gregerie Channel
Services: Restaurants, Ferry to Crown Bay

Just south of Providence Point, Honeymoon Bay, or Druif Bay, is a favorite anchorage with local sailors and the beautiful white sand beach attracts day-trippers from St. Thomas. The anchorage can be a little rolly at times but is well protected and provides a wonderful backdrop at night of the lights on St. Thomas. The anchorage has a sandy bottom in 15 to 20 feet of water. Good snorkeling can be found along the southern shore. Dinghies should be landed on the right side of the beach adjacent to Dinghy's Beach Bar & Grill and watersports rental. The designated swimming area is well marked.

Flamingo Bay (Water Island)

Navigation: 0.5nm south of Honeymoon Bay
Services: None

Flamingo Bay is situated at the southwest end of Water Island. When the wind works its way round to the south, the anchorage can be subject to a surge and therefore not suitable for an overnight anchorage. The inner harbor is shallow and therefore suitable only for small boat traffic. The outer harbor is fairly deep and under normal conditions you can tuck yourself up in the northeast corner and drop the hook in 15 to 20 feet on a sandy bottom. The island is privately owned and therefore consideration should be shown to the homeowners ashore.

Lindbergh Bay (St. Thomas)

Navigation: 2.3nm west of Haulover Cut
Services: Restaurant

Lindbergh Bay, situated east of the terminal and south of the runway at the Cyril E. King Airport is a pleasant bay with no obstructions. At the mouth, depths are about 30 feet, gradually reducing to 15 feet inside the bay. A beautiful beach lines the inner bay and the adjacent hotel provides beach services. Lindbergh Bay is open to the south and the occasional sea swell makes its way into the anchorage. Being so close to the airport you will also have to contend with the noise of jet traffic during the day. A submerged cable runs up the east side of the bay, so when anchoring favor the west and center of the bay.

Departing from Lindbergh Bay for the west, make sure that you continue out to the green marker #3 before making your turn to starboard in order to avoid the shoal area south of Red Point.

WATER ISLAND

CYRIL E. KING
AIRPORT

MOSQUITO PT.

LINDBERGH BAY

RED PT.

Westward Bound

Heading west from Lindbergh Bay and the green marker #3 you will pass to the north of Flat Cays, a small group of rocks surrounded by reef, they are easy to see. To the north tucked up behind the head of the airport runway, is Brewer's Bay. The anchorage is seldom crowded and although close to the airport is surprisingly peaceful. Anchor in about 20 feet of water on a sandy bottom.

Heading toward waypoint UV608 (Salt Cay Passage) located just west of the tip of Salt Cay, the recommended route is to leave Saltwater Money Rock and Kalkun Cay to port with West Cay and Salt Cay to starboard. Do not attempt to pass between the western extremity of St. Thomas and West Cay named Big Current Hole. Although there is seven feet of water, the narrow channel is best negotiated by those with local knowledge.

From waypoint UV608 you will be heading west toward Puerto Rico or turning northeast toward waypoint UV609 (Lizard Rock) to explore the north shore bays of St. Thomas.

BOTANY BAY
(WEST END OF ST. THOMAS)

Waypoint: UV608 (Salt Cay Passage) 18°22.00'N; 65°04.20'W

Navigation: 6.5nm NW of St. Thomas Harbor: 1.5nm SE Salt Cay

Services: None

Less than 1.5 miles SE of Salt Cay on the northwestern tip of St. Thomas is a delightful anchorage known as Botany Bay. The bay itself is separated into two smaller bays by a point of land that has some coral heads extending to the west. Although the various charts mark these bays differently, for the purpose of this document we will assume Botany Bay to be the anchorage to the south of the point separating the two bays. The bay to the north of the small point and directly south

of Botany Point is also a suitable anchorage; however there is a ledge of patch coral that extends across the entire bay.

Although suitable as an overnight in settled weather, during times when the northeast trade winds are at their peak, or a NE swell is present, these anchorages should be treated with extreme caution.

Approaching from the west, after rounding Salt Cay (waypoint UV 608), continue east until you can identify Botany Point and Sandy Bay to the south, then proceed due south. The recommended anchorage would be in 15-20 feet of water on a sandy bottom. At the time of the last survey no services were available, however it should be noted that development has been is underway for some time and therefore changes should be anticipated.

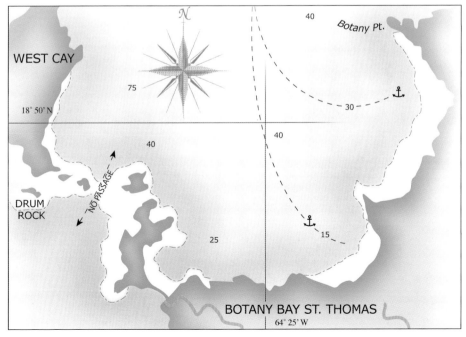

BOTANY BAY ST. THOMAS
64° 25' W

BENNER BAY
(THE LAGOON)

Waypoint: UV603a (Jersey Bay) 18°18.50'N; 64°51.50'W
Navigation: 5.5nm east of St.Thomas Harbor
Services: Full service marinas, Repair, Travel lift, Chandlery, Provisions, Restaurants

Benner Bay, locally known as The Lagoon, is probably the most protected anchorage for small craft on the island. There are several marinas and services available once inside. Yachts drawing up to five feet have access to the Lagoon, yachts drawing over 5 feet should enter on a high tide. Independent Boatyard monitors VHF 16.

Navigation & Pilotage

When making your approach into Jersey Bay and The Lagoon, from the west, it is imperative that you not confuse it with the tricky "false entrance" to the west of Red Point. As its name implies, there appears to be a direct passage when approaching from

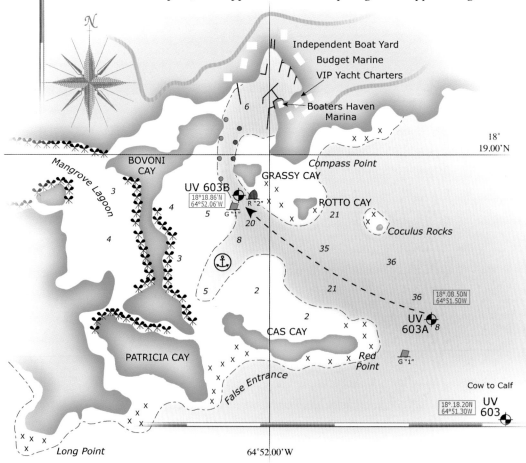

NO PASSAGE

FALSE ENTRANCE

RED POINT

I G"I"

UV603A

COCULUS ROCKS

UV603B

N

THE LAGOON | BENNER BAY

the south or west, and boats at anchor can be seen at the head of the bay, but beware, there is a reef extending all the way across the "false entrance." A good rule of thumb would be to say: if you can't see a green "1" buoy on the port side of the channel, marking the eastern end of Cas Cay (Red Point), don't go in! That being said, the channel into The Lagoon is well marked and provides no problems once you have identified Rotto Cay and its relationship to other landmarks.

Approaching from the east from Current Cut, you will see a set of rocks named Cow and Calf (north of Deck Point), leaving them to port you will be able to identify the green "1" buoy. Waypoint UV603a marks the approach to the channel and a shallow (7 feet) spot east of the green buoy.

Leaving the green "1" buoy on the tip of Cas Cay to port, and Coculus Rocks to starboard, proceed to Grassy Cay (waypoint UV603b). You will see a green buoy on your port hand and red nun marking the southern tip of Grassy Cay. Leave it to starboard. Take Grassy Cay to starboard by 25 feet, and round the red buoy on the northwest side. Leave the anchored boats to port and follow the channel. The channel is marked with red and green buoys and is easily followed leaving the red nuns to starboard when entering from the sea.

Ashore

Independent Boatyard and Marina provide a full-service boat yard, complete with a 50-ton travel lift and a 10-ton crane. The boat yard maintains contractors to accommodate boats requiring services, including: Island Marine Outboards, Bruce Merced's Marine Repair, Benner Bay Marine (outboard repairs), Carpentry Plus, Dave Gott Refrigeration, Mike Sheen's Fiberglass Shop and Tim Peck Enterprises (Awlgrip work). The marina includes 85 slips, with full services for both transients and live-aboards. The depth is 6.5 feet. Daily hours are from 8am to 5pm.

Budget Marine offers one of the largest inventories of any chandlery on St. Thomas. The knowledgeable staff are very helpful. They can also help with special orders which they can expedite from the substantial inventory of their very large St. Maarten flagship store. Call or email ahead and they will set your order aside. Budget Marine St. Thomas is open seven days a week, Monday to Saturday 8am-5pm, and Sunday 9am-2pm.

Compass Point Marina

Adjacent to Independent Boatyard is Caribbean Inflatables. They can service life rafts and sell and repair inflatable boats, along with selling emergency gear. They are open from 8:30am to 5pm.

Compass Point Marina, across the Lagoon, has over 100 slips and will accommodate boats up to 60 feet with a max 19 feet beam and six-foot draft. The marina provides electricity, water, showers, storage, marine services and a public dinghy dock on the southeast side of the marina. Skippers should contact the marina at (340)-775-6144 to make a reservation. The marina is conveniently close to restaurants and shops including The Dive Bar which serves a great hamburger. Cash only!

Compass Point is also the home to Virgin Island Charters who operate a new fleet of catamarans and monohulls. Kristi and John are the owner/operators and can be reached at 340-776-8492 VHF16 (www. virginislandyachtcharters.com). There are also numerous other marine service businesses located at Compass Point.

Pirate's Cove Marina has 24 slips with depths from 3 to 7 feet. The marina primarily rents slips on a yearly basis. They sell gas and diesel, provide water, ice, and electricity, and they also have internet access.

You can purchase provisions from the General Store and items from the Pirate's Cove Gift Shop and Boutique. The Pirate's Cove Bar and Grill is a casual, breezy spot for breakfast, lunch and dinner daily. The marina monitors VHF 16.

BENNER BAY

Nazareth Bay (Jersey Bay)

Nazareth Bay or Secret Harbor as it is also known is tucked away in the northeast corner of Jersey Bay and can be a pleasant anchorage in settled weather. The approach from the south is straightforward from waypoint UV603 (Cow and Calf 18°20.00'N; 64°51.30'W), proceed due north leaving Coculas Rocks to port. Approaching from the east, head towards the entrance to the Lagoon and look for the white buildings of Secret Harbour Beach Hotel on the right.

The east side of the bay is full of coral heads, so head to the west side and anchor in about 20 feet of water. Do not use the moorings, as they are private.

Do not attempt to bring your boat in to the dock, as it is extremely shallow. You may tie your dinghy up to the hotel dock. The dock to the right of the hotel dock is private.

Ashore

The Blue Moon Café and Aqua Action Dive Center are located on the property of the Secret Harbour Beach Hotel. The restaurant, with a stunning view of the sea, is open daily and serves breakfast lunch and dinner with reservations.

Cowpet Bay

Navigation: 6nm east of St. Thomas Harbor; 0.25nm east of Current Cut
Services: Restaurants

Cowpet Bay, located in the northwest region of St. James Bay and just to the west of Current Cut, is home to the St. Thomas Yacht Club. Much of the bay is occupied with member moorings, which makes this a difficult choice for an anchorage. When the wind is from the south the bay can get quite choppy, exacerbated at times by the wash from fast moving ferry traffic to and from St. John via Current Cut.

If room to anchor can be found without fouling the surrounding moorings, you will be in 15-18 feet on a sandy bottom.

Ashore

Cowpet Bay is the home of the St. Thomas Yacht Club on the western end of the bay. Moorings and the dock are reserved for yacht club members only. The anchorage can be quite crowded at times.

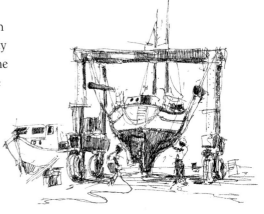

Pizza Pi – Christmas Cove

American Yacht Harbor

American Yacht Harbor

CURRENT CUT/CHRISTMAS COVE
(GREAT ST. JAMES ISLAND)

St. Thomas

Waypoint: UV602 (Cabrita Point) 18°19.30'N; 64°49.60'W
Navigation: 2.4nm SW Cruz Bay
Services: Moorings, Pizza Pi

Navigation & Pilotage

Current Rock "4" sits astride the channel, easily identified at 20 feet above sea level and marked with a flashing 6 sec. light. The easternmost channel is recommended, although the west channel can carry 8 feet but is narrow and fringed with coral.

As the name implies, there can be a strong current of up to 4 knots running in either direction depending upon the tide. If approaching from the west start your engine in advance, as the island of Great St. James tends to blanket the wind. The Cow and Calf, a group of rocks awash to the southwest of Current Cut, are easy to see.

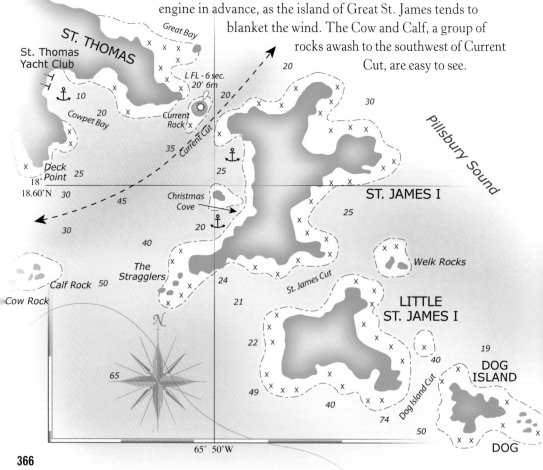

GREAT ST. JAMES

CHRISTMAS COVE

Christmas Cove is to the east of the cut and sheltered in the lee of Great St. James. Making your approach to Christmas Cove, you will notice it is divided north/south by Fish Cay. There is a reef extending from the Cay southeast toward the shoreline of St. James. Although there is 6 feet of water between the shore and the cay, it is recommended that you transit via the west end of Fish Cay.

Anchoring & Mooring

Anchor on either side of Fish Cay in 15 feet of water. Do not anchor too far out as the wind tends to become erratic. Do not pass between Fish Cay and the shore. If anchoring to the north of Fish Cay, ensure that you are anchored close enough to the shore in order to be out of the current flow. There are a number of mooring balls available free of charge that were installed as part of a grant program to Fisheries & Natural Resources Department. They are reported to have been serviced by the DNR post hurricane,

but it is strongly suggested that the mooring ground tackle is visually checked before overnighting. The DNR indicate that once permanent funding is established they will be serviced on a regular basis.

Ashore

There is good snorkeling toward the southern tip of the island. When the weather is calm, take the dinghy and explore the waters and reefs around the south end of St. James Island. When diving and snorkeling in this area always be mindful of the current and ferry traffic.

During the season, November to mid-June, Pizza Pi will be anchored off of Fish Cay serving pizzas to both anchored yachts and day-trippers on smaller powerboats. Pull up to the stern of the boat with your dinghy and place your order. We renamed their 16" pizza the 50+ (assuming it to be 50.26" in circumference). Prices are $19-$30.

RED HOOK BAY (VESSUP BAY)

Waypoint: UV601 (Red Hook) 18°20.00'N; 64°50.00'W

Navigation: 2.1nm NW Current Cut; 3nm E Cruz Bay

Services: Full service Marina, Provisioning, ATM, Dive shop, Restaurants, Ferry service, Urgent Care Center, 30 mins to airport

St. Thomas

Just to the north and west of Cabrita Point on the eastern end of St. Thomas, Red Hook Bay is a busy harbor with ferries departing for Cruz Bay, St. John on the hour. Vessup Bay is the inner bay and home of the American Yacht Harbor, an IGY marina on the north side, providing yachtsmen with full marine services. Vessup Point Marina to the south is derilect and plans to rebuild are still in discussion. Because of its exposure to the east, Red Hook is often a choppy anchorage with limited space to anchor in the inner bay.

Navigation & Pilotage

From the south, once around Cabrita Point, Green Marker "1" (UV602), follow the coastline around to the west but favor the middle of the channel. There is a buoyed ferry channel to the north of the bay, but most private vessels make their approach just to the south of the buoys in 12 feet of water. Keep an eye out for ferry traffic and stay out of its way. The marina monitors VHF channel 16/11 (Tel: 340-775-6454).

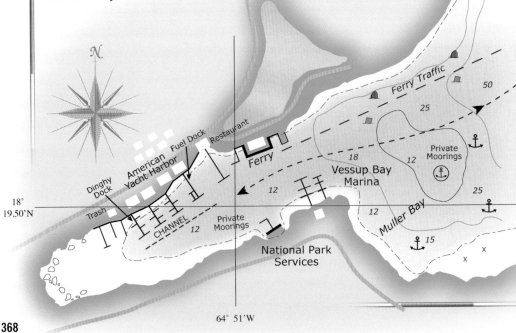

64° 51'W

RED HOOK BAY

Anchoring & Mooring

As there are numerous private moorings and a considerable amount of ferry and other traffic within Vessup Bay, it is virtually impossible to find a place to anchor. A more favorable anchorage for yachts can be found at Muller Bay on the southern side of Red Hook. That being said there are still numerous private moorings and care should be taken when laying an anchor (15-20 feet) not to foul a vacant mooring. The further you can get up to the southern shoreline the more comfortable you will be and away from ferry traffic. Island Yacht Charters maintains numerous moorings in this area but these should be considered private.

If you are looking for a slip or taking on fuel or water, the unique architecture of American Yacht Harbor will be evident to starboard. Don't go too deep into the bay, as it shoals off rapidly past the last set of docks and there is a "hump" just off the end of D dock. The marina monitors VHF 16/11.

Ashore

American Yacht Harbor is part of the International Global Yachts (IGY) group of luxury marinas. It has far more than just the basic marina amenities. This includes dockage, ice, water, showers, fuel, electricity, cable TV, and free WiFi. The marina can accommodate vessels up to 110 feet in length with a 10 foot draft and a 30 foot beam. Mail, telephone, fax and internet services are also provided at the marina office. The dinghy dock is located at the base of C dock where you will also find the garbage facilities.

The large marina complex and adjacent business centers include a shopping village, with convenient stores and businesses; marine chandlery, charter and water-sports rentals, banks, laundry services, movie rentals and a host of gift shops and boutiques. There are numerous restaurants both in the marina and within a few minutes walking distance. Catch a sunset at Island Time Pub.

For provisioning, Moe's Fresh Market is right across from the marina and very well stocked with fresh produce, meats, poultry, wines and bakery items. Other services include: Harbor Laundry, Red Hook Dive Center, First Bank, Island Marine Outfitters, Neptune's Fishing Supplies, Red Hook Video and Rhiannon's Unique Gifts. Several sport fishing charters, powerboat rentals and sailing charters are based here including Island Yacht Charters. American Yacht Harbor hosts some very well-known billfish tournaments and is located across from the Virgin Islands Game Fishing Club.

The ferry to St. John leaves from the Red Hook East End terminal hourly, and ferries to and from the British Virgin Islands stop here as well. Rental cars and taxis are readily available.

On the southern part of the bay, across from American Yacht Harbor, is the Vessup Point Marina. The docks and bulkhead were severely damaged in a hurricane some years ago and complications have prevented necessary upgrades. This marina should be considered derelict. Further into the bay is the National Park dock. Even if it looks like a perfect place to put your boat, don't do it!

Coki Point around the corner from Red Hook is the home of Coral World Marine Park. Situated on four beautifully landscaped acres, this marine park offers incredible views of the ocean coral reef life twenty feet below the sea through a unique underwater observatory. Feedings for the fish and the sharks are scheduled throughout the day. The park is complete with a gift shop, dive shop, and restaurant. It is well worth a visit.

SAPPHIRE BAY MARINA

St. Thomas

Waypoint: UV601 (Red Hook) 18°20.00'N; 64°50.00'W
Navigation: 2.9nm east of Cruz Bay
Services: Marina, Water, and Restaurants

To the north of Red Hook Bay and the American Yacht Harbor is the Sapphire Bay Marina, a part of the Sapphire Bay Resort complex. The marina has 67 slips, water, electricity and fresh water showers. The depth is 10 feet. ATM and car rentals are available. The entrance is narrow and the marina is generally full of local boats. Call ahead on VHF 16 for slip availability.

Navigation & Piloting

Approaching from the northeast, leave Shark Island to starboard and head for the southern end of Red Bay under Red Hook Hill. There is a set of red and green buoys marking the channel entrance and the extremity of the reef on the port side. The marina entrance is narrow and you will be making a 90-degree starboard turn once inside the breakwater.

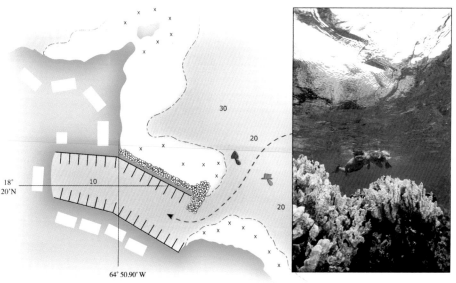

THE LEEWARD PASSAGE/ NORTH COAST

Many of the anchorages along the north coast could be subject to the NE swell when the trade winds are heavy. In fair settled weather, there are some beautiful anchorages to explore.

Traveling northwest via the Leeward Passage from Pillsbury Sound, there is generally a 1 to 2 knot current that flows either to the NW or to the SE. There are two obstructions that skippers should note; Shark Island, northeast of Prettyklip Point and SE of Cabes Point. The second is Turtleback Rock that lies between Coki Point to the NW and Cables Point to the SE. Favor the Thatch Cay side of the channel until you are past Coki Point. Favor Lee Point on the western end of Thatch Cay as there are two small inshore reef areas around the points of Sunsi and Mandal Hill. From here you have clear water to Hans Lollik Island or to Picara Point. Both have obstructions. Hans Lollik Rock at the southern extremity of the island is awash. Picara Point has a reef that extends north from the point some 30 yards so give it a wide berth. Ornen Rock is an unmarked hazard 0.5nm northeast of Picara Point. Yachts traveling into Magen's Bay can round Picara Point in 50 feet of water, however those that are heading to the Brass Channel between Inner and Outer Brass Islands should exercise caution.

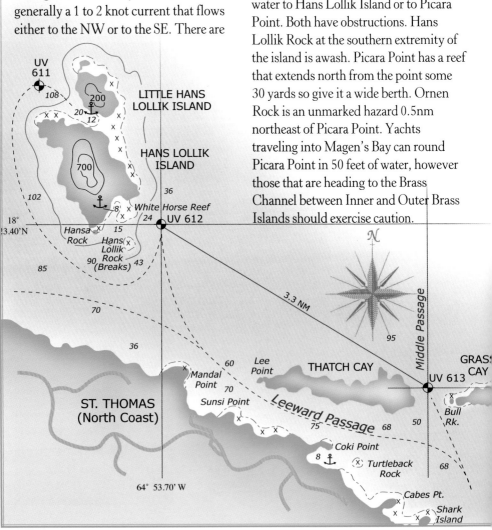

Hans Lollik Islands

Waypoint: UV612 (Hans Lollik) 18°23.40'N; 64°53.70'W;

UV611 (Little Hans Lollik) 18°24.75'N; 64°55.00'W

Navigation: 5nm NW Red Hook Bay

Services: None, but good snorkeling

Both of the anchorages on Hans Lollik Island are considered day anchorages only, except in very light weather. During the winter months when the trade winds are at their heaviest and there is a NE swell present, we recommend extreme caution.

There are two possible anchorages, one at the southern end of Hans Lollik, known as Coconut Bay and exposed to the east. The other, approached from the west, is south of Little Hans Lollik behind the reef that connects the two islands.

Navigation & Piloting

Approaching from the east to waypoint UV612 there are three obstructions. Hans Lollik Rock will be to the southwest. This rock is awash and will be breaking in a swell. To the northwest is Whitehorseface Reef and to the west is Hansa Rock. Assuming weather is calm, anchor in 15 feet on a sandy bottom. Smaller, shallow-draft vessels can make their way inside the reef to Coconut Beach.

Approaching from the west via waypoint UV611 head for the south end of Little Hans Lollik and work your way into the saddle between the two islands. Anchor in 15 feet of water to the west of the reef between the two islands.

HANS LOLLIK

PELICAN CAY

LITTLE HANS LOLLIK

HANS LOLLIK

MAGEN'S BAY & HULL BAY

St. Thomas

Waypoint: UV610 (Ornen Rock) 18°23.40'N; 64°57.50'W
Navigation: 8nm NW Pillsbury Sound
Services: Moorings, Restaurant, Gift shop

A deep bay on the north coast of St. Thomas, Magen's Bay is 1.5 miles deep and 0.5 miles wide. To the east is a beautiful beach that logically attracts many daily visitors from the cruise ships berthing daily in Charlotte Amalie on the south side. To the north of the bay is a long tongue of land extending to the NW that ends at Picara Point. To the west is Tropaco Point looking out toward the Brass Islands. During periods of heavy ground swell, Magen's Bay can be rolly and uncomfortable.

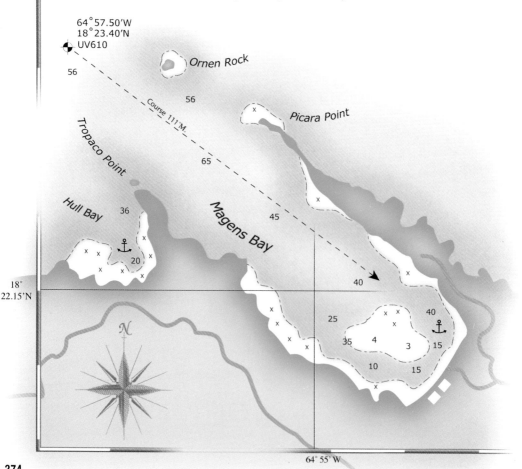

MAGENS BAY

TROPACO POINT

HULL BAY

Navigation & Piloting

Approaching Magen's Bay from the east and Picara Point, care should be taken to keep a minimum of 50 yards off the point, as there is a reef that extends to the north and during the winter months the seas can be very confused in this area. Further to the northwest (0.5nm) is the unmarked Ornen Rock.

Approaching from the Brass Channel between the two islands, and waypoint UV610 leaving Ornen Rock to port, steer 111° magnetic, which will bring you to the anchorage near the head of the bay in 30-35 feet of water.

Anchoring

At the southwestern end of the bay there is a shoal with about 3-4 feet of water over it. There is deep water all around but the safe approach is to head for the anchorage up in the northeast section of the bay in 30-35 feet of water on a sandy bottom.

Ashore

Magen's Bay Beach, under the auspices of the Magen's Bay Authority, is arguably one of the most beautiful and popular beaches in St. Thomas. Try to visit either before or after the cruise ship passengers are there! There are bathroom facilities, a snack bar and a gift shop.

A nominal entrance fee is collected for those arriving by land. The prices are determined by whether you are a local resident or a visitor. The fee is only charged if you enter the beach by road; anchoring and coming ashore is free. The fee helps to keep the grounds and beach clean and maintained.

Hull Bay

Navigation: 0.8nm SE Boulder Point (Inner Brass Is.)
Services: Restaurant, Dive Shop

When the weather is calm, Hull Bay is a delightful small anchorage under Tropaco Point. Caution is recommended since there are coral reefs to the SW and at the head of the bay.

From Boulder Point, off the southern end of Inner Brass Island, head for Tropaco Point before turning to the SE and paralleling the coastline into the anchorage. Anchor in 25 feet of water on a sand bottom.

Ashore

This lovely bay is often frequented by local fishermen, many of whom are descendants of the French settlers who escaped to St. Thomas over 200 years ago. Their small fishing boats are anchored in the bay and their fishing nets are often drying on the trees. The bay is tranquil and shady – a good place to relax with a book or just watch the fishermen and do nothing at all.

Ashore you will find a casual restaurant/bar, the Hull Bay Hideaway, who specialize in fresh fish dishes. They have a dart room, pool table, computer with internet and a television for watching those sports games you thought you would have to miss.

The restaurant is open from 10am to 10pm on weekdays and 10am to 11pm on weekends.

TROPACO PT.

18   ⚓   15

Hull Bay, St. Thomas

THE SPANISH VIRGINS

Sailing west to the Spanish Virgins is usually a broad reach or a run, depending upon departure point, wind direction and intended destination. The Antilles north equatorial current flows in a westerly or northwesterly direction at 0.5-1.5 knots. Departing from St. Thomas, you will have to plan on clearing Customs in Culebra since St. Thomas is a free port. Your route should take you either to the north of Isla Culebrita (WP 18°20.0N, 65°14.0W) where you will make your entrance to Culebra via the channel west of Culebrita and northeast of Culebra, or to the south around Grampus Banks to the red buoy Fl. R 4 sec. '2' (WP 18°40.30N, 65°12.50W). The distance is 10-15 nautical miles depending whether you are departing from WP UV608 by Salt

Cay or WP UV606 east of Saba Island. It should also be noted that when it is blowing hard, the sea can pile up on the Grampus Banks making it quite choppy.

Depart St. Thomas early enough to get you there while the sun is still overhead, since the navigation around the reefs will require good light. Plan on spending your first night at Dakity Harbor, behind the reef entrance to Ensenada Honda. The following morning you can proceed to the head of Ensenada Honda to clear in at Dewey.

Since the return trip to the Virgin Islands will be upwind and against the current, consideration should be given to sailing from Culebra or Vieques to St. Croix (44 nautical miles) for some exploration before reaching back to the US or British Virgin Islands.

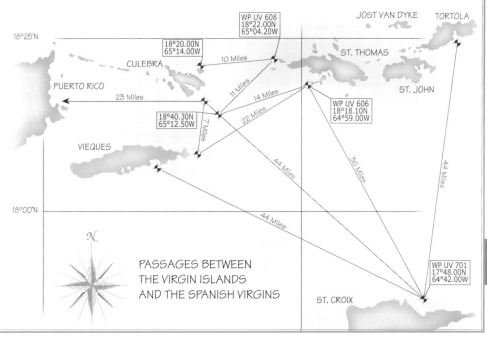

PASSAGES BETWEEN THE VIRGIN ISLANDS AND THE SPANISH VIRGINS

COWPET BAY

RESTAURANTS
St. Thomas Yacht Club
Tel: 340-775-6320
www.styc.net

CROWN BAY

MARINAS
Crown Bay Marina
Tel: 340-774-2255
www.crownbay.com
VHF channels 16 and 11

BUSINESS SERVICES
Mail Stop
Tel: 340-776-4324
M-F 8am-5pm,
Sat 9am-1pm
www.mailstopvi.com

CHANDLERIES
Island Marine Outfitters
Tel: 340-714-5311
Ship's chandlery

LAUNDRY
Your Choice Laundry
Tel: 340-715-3277

RESTAURANTS
Tickles Dockside Pub
Tel: 340-776-1595
7am-midnight
ticklesdocksidepub.com

CROWN BAY & SUB BASE

BOAT SERVICES
Subbase Dry Docks and Shipyard
1200-ton dry dock
Machining and fabrication, paint, fiberglass, rigging, engine services
Tel: 340-776-2078
www.subbasedrydock.com

Island Rigging & Hydraulics Inc
Tel: 340-774-6833
www.offshorevi.com

Offshore Marine
Inflatables, diesel engines, outboard engines
Tel: 340-776-5432
www.offshorevi.com

FRENCHTOWN

CHARTER COMPANY
CYOA
Tel: 340-777-9690
800-944-2962
www.cyoacharters.com

RESTAURANTS
Bella Blu
Small restaurant with delicious Mediterranean food
Tel: 340-774-4349
www.bellabludining.com

The Twisted Cork Café
Tel: 340-775-2675
thetwistedcorkcafe.com

Frenchtown Deli
Open Monday through Friday from 7am to 8pm
Tel: 340-776-7211

Hook, Line and Sinker
Tel: 340-776-9708
Lovely restaurant with a harbor view; serving lunch, dinner and Sunday brunch
hooklineandsinkervi.com

Oceana Restaurant and Wine Bar
Tel: 340-774-4262
Located in Villa Olga
Seafood menu, great wine bar
www.oceanavi.com

HULL BAY

RESTAURANTS
Hull Bay Hideaway Restaurant & Bar
Tel: 340-690-5607
hullbayhideaway.com

THE LAGOON

CHARTER COMPANY
Virgin Island Yacht Charters
Tel: 340-776-8492
virginislandyachtcharters.com

MARINAS
Compass Point Marina
Electricity, water, pump out station
Tel: 340-775-6144
compasspointmarina.com

ISLAND CONNECTIONS

Independent Boatyard and Marina
Tel: 340-473-9423
VHF channel 16
Water, electricity and pump-out station
Haul out facility with repair facilities
www.ibyvi.com

Saga Haven Marina
Tel: 340-775-0520
Water, fuel, electricity, small shop
www.sagahaven.com

CHANDLERY
Budget Marine
Tel: 340-779-2219
www.budgetmarine.com

FIBERGLASS SHOP
Mike Sheen, Boat Repair
Tel: 340-714-1884

YACHT CARPENTRY P LUS
Jeff Hart
Tel: 340-775-9255

MACHINE SHOP
Bruce Merced
Tel: 340-513-0671

MAGEN'S BAY

INFORMATION SOURCE
Magen's Bay Authority
Tel: 340-777-6300
magensbayauthority.com

REDHOOK

MARINAS
IGY American Yacht Harbor
Tel: 340-775-6454
VHF channel 16
All amenities
www.igy-american yachtharbor.com

CHANDLERY
Island Marine Outfitters
Tel: 340-775-6621

CHARTER COMPANY
Virgin Island Yacht Charters
Tel: 340-776-8492
www.virginisland yachtcharters.com

DIVING
Red Hook Dive Center
(formerly Chris Sawyer's)
Tel: 340-777-3483
redhookdivecenter.com

LAUNDRY
Harbor Laundromat
Tel: 340-714-7672

BANKING
First Bank VI
Tel: 340-775-5650
24 hour ATM
www.1firstbank.com

RESTAURANTS
Island Time Pub
Pizza
Tel: 340-774-2929

Caribbean Saloon Steakhouse & Bar
Tel: 340-775-7060
Casual steakhouse
www.caribbeansaloon.com

Duffy's Love Shack
Tel: 340-779-2080
duffysloveshack.com
Open 11:30am-2am
Across the street from the marina
www.duffysloveshack.com

PROVISIONS
Moe's Fresh Market
Tel: 340-693-0254
www.moesvi.com
Open 7 days a week, 7am -9 pm

Cost-U-Less
Tel: 340-777-3570
M-F 8am-9pm
Sat 9am-9pm
Sun 9am-7pm
www.costuless.com

ST. CROIX

Charts

NV Charts: Virgin Islands Kit C-17
NIMA: 2561, Imray Iolaire A-23, A234
Admiralty Leisure: 5640-11, 11A,11B,12

St. Croix lies in splendid isolation 40 miles south of the other Virgin Islands. It is surrounded by the largest island barrier reef system in the Caribbean, and thus has fantastic diving. Rich in history and natural beauty and much less crowded than the other U.S. Virgins, it's definitely worth the trip. The blue water passage takes you over the deep Virgin Island Trough. Allow at least three days – one to get there, one to tour and one to return. Better yet, stay a while. St. Croix is the largest Virgin, more than twice the size of St. Thomas or Tortola. Flatter and more fertile than most islands, it was known as The Garden Spot of the Caribbean during the colonial centuries and it is still relatively unspoiled and undeveloped. There are two charming towns, Christiansted and Frederiksted, and friendly vibes that make the island feel like home. Many cruisers who dropped anchor for a short visit have become permanent residents of St. Croix.

Hams Bluff

UV 707

Frederiksted

See detail

Long Point

Southwest Anchorage

Southwest S

64° 55'W   64° 50'W

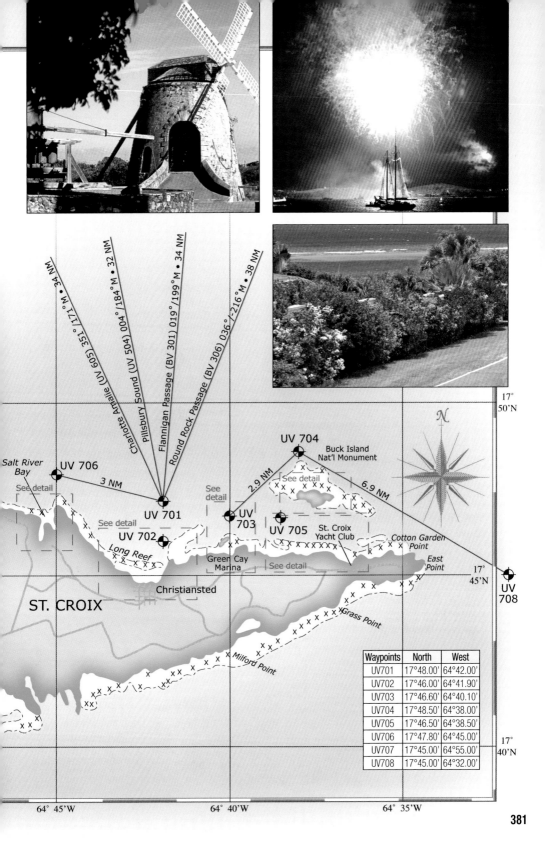

Charlotte Amalie (UV 605) 351° / 171° M • 34 NM
Pillsbury Sound (UV 504) 004° / 184° M • 32 NM
Flannigan Passage (BV 301) 019° / 199° M • 34 NM
Round Rock Passage (BV 306) 036° / 216° M • 38 NM

17°
50'N

N

UV 704
Buck Island
Nat'l Monument

Salt River
Bay

UV 706

See detail

3 NM

UV 701

2.9 NM

See
detail

UV
703

See detail

UV 702

UV 705

6.9 NM

St. Croix
Yacht Club

Cotton Garden
Point

See detail

Long Reef

Green Cay
Marina

See detail

East
Point

17°
45'N

UV
708

Christiansted

ST. CROIX

Grass Point

Milford Point

Waypoints	North	West
UV701	17°48.00'	64°42.00'
UV702	17°46.00'	64°41.90'
UV703	17°46.60'	64°40.10'
UV704	17°48.50'	64°38.00'
UV705	17°46.50'	64°38.50'
UV706	17°47.80'	64°45.00'
UV707	17°45.00'	64°55.00'
UV708	17°45.00'	64°32.00'

17°
40'N

64° 45'W

64° 40'W

64° 35'W

CHRISTIANSTED

St. Croix

Waypoint: UV702 (17°46.00'N; 64°41.90'W)
Navigation: 38nm SSW Round Rock Passage
Services: Full service marina, Travel lift (300 ton),
Chandlery, Provisioning, Island tours

Christiansted is considered by many the most beautiful town in the Caribbean. Formerly the capital of the Danish West Indies, it looks much the same today as it did in colonial days. Entering the harbor is a visual treat, as beautiful old buildings in a bouquet of pastel colors line the waterfront. The harbor is protected by Long Reef to the west and Scotch Bank to the east, the controlling depth is 16 feet.

Navigation & Pilotage

If you are arriving from the other Virgin Islands, try to depart from either the eastern end of St. John or Norman Island in the BVI to gain a close or beam reach. Leave early, no later than 8:00 am, to ensure you enter Christiansted Harbor, which is well-marked, in daylight. If the weather is clear you can see St. Croix from St. Thomas and Tortola. If not, you won't be able to see the hills until you are two hours out. Allow for a westerly 0.5 knot current. If you lay your course for the eastern end of the island you can alter as you near the island. The saddle formed by Lang Peak and Recovery Hill makes an easy landmark. Head for a point midway between them until you pick up the radio tower on Fort Louise Augusta. Pass the first green buoy (#1) to port, then line up the radio tower between the channel markers. This should be approximately 164° True. Long Reef, which extends across the harbor (and offers good diving), will be seen breaking to starboard. On your port hand is Scotch Bank and, although the charts indicate that parts of it are covered with adequate water, it is wise to stay clear whenever there is a sea running, as it breaks in a ground swell.

Although the entrance to Christiansted Harbor is well buoyed, note that Round Reef, which lies to the west of Fort Louise Augusta and is clearly visible, is a major navigational hazard. There are channels on either side of it but local cruisers recommend taking the "schooner channel" to port, which carries 10 feet. Round Reef is marked at the northeastern end by a striped (green/red) mid-channel flashing marker "RR". If you are taking the Schooner Channel, leave this mark to starboard and your second buoy will be green #5 which you will leave to port.

Anchoring & Mooring

The anchorage in the lee of Protestant Cay is quite crowded with the permanent moorings of cruisers who call this home and seaplanes coming and going to

UV
702

17°46.00'N
64°41.90'W

15 Scotch Bank

17°
46' N

4

Range 164°

500

8

'1' FL G 2 Sec.

18

80

'3'
'4' FL G 4 Sec.

45 12

To Green Cay
and Buck Is

'6' 12

Barracuda
Ground

12

17°
45.50' N

'8'

LONG REEF

'7'
FL G 4 Sec. 15 Ft. 4M

40

18 40
FL R 2 Sec. '9'

"RR"
FL (2+1) G

12

'11'
Round Reef

'5'

Fort Louise Augusta

'12'

'6'

FL R 4 Sec.

30

'8' 12 '7'

'2'

'10'

12 '9'

Altona
Lagoon

'1'

40

'11'

Fishing
Dock

3

12

'13'

'14'

PROTESTANT
CAY

20

17°
45' N

'15'

Iso.
6sec.93ft.8M

8

St. Croix Marine

Altona
Hill
120' FT

10

18

Customs

Mt. Welcome
125' FT

Fort
Christian

18

ST. CROIX

PROTESTANT CAY

SHOAL

LONG REEF

FL R

GR BUOY

GR BUOY

R

ROUND REEF

GR BUOY

RR
GR BUOY

RED 'G'
NUN BUOY

FL G 7

G5

TOWER

G7

G9

G11

ST. CROIX MARINA

FISHING DOCK

FORT LOUISE AUGUSTA

ALTONA LAGOON

St. Thomas and San Juan from the Seaborne base at the west end of town. Visiting yachts are asked to go to the east side of the harbor, where you can anchor west of St. Croix Marine or further to the northeast under the point off Altona Lagoon adjacent to the channel. The holding ground is good and there are some moorings in this area that were placed by the government several years ago, under a special grant to accommodate transient yachts. According to Mr. Howard Forbes Snr. of the Department of Planning and Natural Resources, the moorings were due to be serviced prior to the hurricane but funding was reallocated. He strongly advises skippers to drop an anchor as he considers them unsafe. If you do pick up a mooring you do so at your own risk, there is no charge, but someone needs to dive and check the ground tackle. Mr.Forbes

indicates that funding for the project is in the works but does not expect anything to happen by the 2019/20 season. The Department of Natural Resources (DPNR) can be reached at (340) 773-5774.

Altona Lagoon is a public beach and fishing area, do not tie your dinghy to the fishing dock but go to St. Croix Marine, where there is a dinghy dock at the end of Dock C.

Ashore

Vessels sailing from the BVI or other foreign ports must clear Customs and Immigration at the Gallows Bay Harbor Dock located just west of St. Croix Marine. If your boat is registered in the U.S. you can report your arrival between 8:00am and 4:30pm at 340-773-1011. Foreigners (non US) must visit in person, with passport and visa. After hours, weekends and holidays call 340-778-0216.

CHRISTIANSTED

There's a lot happening on this quiet island. If you'd like to see what's going on, pick up *St. Croix This Week*, a free tourist magazine with just about everything there is to know about the island and a calendar of events. A comprehensive website is gotostcroix.com and stcroixlime.com.

If you're here in the winter months you will probably see the beautiful Roseway at the dock or in nearby waters. A National Historic Landmark schooner, she is the home of the World Ocean School, introducing local middle school students to the wonders of sailing by day and offering short cruises at sunset.

The St.Croix Marine Center, a full service marina and boatyard, is just east of the Customs dock. Under new ownership, the Marine Center specializes in sales, restoration, refits and repairs. The marina offers transient and permanent dockage with 44 slips and can accommodate vessels up to 150 feet with drafts up to 10 feet. Fuel, ice and water are available along with marina wide WiFi coverage and an onsite restaurant. The staff are friendly and knowledgable and are happy to assist with transportation and the logistics and delivery associated with provisioning services. The fully stocked chandlery is also a sales and service dealer for Evinrude and are open from 8am to 5pm Monday through Saturday. VHF 16 or call (340) 773-0289.

The boatyard offers long and short term storage and the 60 ton Travelift is capable of hauling both monohulls and catamarans with beams of up to 18 feet. Welding, fiberglass repair, painting and carpentry services are available from a knowledgable staff of experienced technicians.

The Marine Center is also close to the ferry dock that services the QEIV ferry to St.Thomas on a daily schedule.

With Permission / US Geological Survey / Copyright 2012 Google

Christiansted Fort

Christiansted

A boardwalk lined with small hotels, restaurant/bars and shops runs along the entire waterfront, from the seaplane terminal to the town wharf and fort area. (Plans call for continuing the boardwalk all the way to Gallows Bay.) You can tie your dinghy up anywhere along the boardwalk and hit the watering holes or walk to town. Angry Nate's and the Fort Christian Brew Pub are boater hang-outs. Nate's is known for its fresh seafood and the pub hosts crab races Monday during happy hour. On Protestant Cay in the middle of the harbor you'll find Hotel on the Cay. Its Harbormaster Beach Club has a beach barbecue and local music Sunday afternoons and Tuesday nights. In town there are several remarkably good restaurants. So if a gourmet dinner is on the agenda, we suggest either Balter, 40 Strand Street (characterized as simple elegance with happy hour $2-off wine by the glass, $4 beers), or Zion, a farm to table restaurant serving Caribbean and seafood cuisine (vegetarian friendly). Open Tuesday through Sunday 5pm -9pm.

The Town of Christiansted

This gem of a town was built early in the Danish era (1733-1917). Basically neoclassic, the stately architecture was gracefully adapted to the tropics, with arched arcades to protect pedestrians from the sun and rain. The outskirts of town have deteriorated, but restorations are underway.

The Christiansted National Historic Site preserves the wharf area and surrounding buildings much as they were in Danish times. Five yellow buildings are administered by the National Park Service: the imposing Fort Christiansvaern, complete with cannons and dungeons; the Steeple Building, the first church on the island; the Scale House, where merchants weighed their produce before shipping it abroad and where you can find a visitors' center with tourist information; the old Customs House; and the Danish West India & Guinea Company Warehouse, where slaves were auctioned in the courtyard. A museum dedicated to the history of the slave trade is planned for this building. A short way up King Street are two other historic landmarks, imposing Government House, which once was the seat of government and boasts a lovely ballroom upstairs, and the pretty Lutheran Church.

The heart of town is a triangle bound by the waterfront, Queen Street and King Cross Street. Here you can do your duty free shopping in a pleasant, laid back ambiance of charming and uncrowded stores. There are a few really interesting

gift shops featuring tropical items and one that carries only locally made arts and crafts called Many Hands. Jewelry stores are abundant but most of them are small and personal, with the designer on the premises. This island is famous for its bracelets, most notably "the St. Croix Hook" originated by Sonya and copied by everyone else and "The Crucian Bracelet" by Crucian Gold. IB Designs and other local jewelers, specialize in incorporating chaney, bits of broken old china found on the ground, into their designs. There is also a number of attractive boutiques selling island fashions. The V.I. Tourism Bureau is in Government House.

The island is home to many artists, and Christiansted has numerous galleries.

You can visit them all in one evening during Art Thursdays, the third Thursday of each month except in summer. Four nights a year you can join a terrific town party called Jump Up, when the streets are full of bands, vendors and moko jumbies (stilt dancers), and the shops and restaurants offer special sales. They happen on the Friday night of a special weekend: Thanksgiving, Valentine's Day, a triathlon the first weekend in May, and July 4, in honor of founding father Alexander Hamilton, who spent his boyhood here.

The St. Croix Ironman 70.3 Triathlon draws hundreds of international athletes the first Sunday in May every year. The historic wharf area is the hub of the action, starting at dawn. Other major events in Christiansted include the St. Patrick's Day Parade on the Saturday closest to March 17, complete with water balloons and plenty of green beer. And if you're here any time around the Christmas holidays you can catch some of the action of the Crucian Christmas Festival, which starts in early December and continues past Three Kings Day, January 6. This is the St. Croix version of Carnival and, although most of the major events take place in Frederiksted, there are several others in and around Christiansted.

Island Tour

This beautiful and gentle island is one you will want to drive around in a rental car or tour bus. It doesn't have the precipitous hills and intimidating turns of the other Virgins, but it does have endless beautiful vistas and numerous points of historical or natural interest. Just remember to drive on the left.

St. Croix has been under seven flags, most notably Denmark, which ruled for almost 200 years and divided the island into 375 plantations of about 150 acres each. Sugar cane was the dominant crop. The Danes left a stunning architectural legacy, and the countryside is full of restorations and ruins of the plantation era: greathouses, slave quarters, rum factories and many hurricane-proof windmills, where the sugar cane was ground. They are known locally as sugar mills.

The island is 28 miles long by 7 miles at its widest point. Topographically diverse, it is close to desert on the east end and almost rainforest in the west. In between are mountains and valleys and, on the south shore, miles of grasslands grazed by Senepols, a breed of cattle developed by St. Croix ranchers.

A good way to see most of the island and its highlights within a day is to make a circle tour. If you start in Christiansted and head east on Route 82, you will pass the lovely old Buccaneer Hotel; Tamarind Reef Resort with Green Cay Marina; Southgate Coastal Reserve, a bird haven owned by the St. Croix Environmental Association; the St. Croix Yacht Club; Cramer Park, a public beach with picnic facilities; and an 82-foot dish antenna, part of the Very Long Baseline Array of the National Radio Astronomy Observatory.

The island to the north is Buck Island Reef National Monument, a popular

sailing and snorkeling destination. Stop at Point Udall, the easternmost point of the U.S., where there is a monument to the millennium. It overlooks beautiful bays on both sides. To the south are Jacks and Isaacs Bays, acquired by The Nature Conservancy as a preserve.

Continuing along the south shore on Route 60, you will see the Divi Carina Bay Resort and across the road its casino. Turn left on 624 and left again on 62 and pass miles of cattle ranches. Go left on 68 where you will see the now non-operational Hovensa Refinery, once the largest in the western hemisphere. It declared bankruptcy and closed in 2012. In 2016 it was bought by Limetree Bay Terminals who initially are using only the oil storage facilities. Further to the west you will see St. Croix Renaissance Park, a huge environmentally-oriented industrial and business park on the site

of the old Alcoa Alumina plant. The huge complex near the road is the new headquarters and distillery of Diageo's Captain Morgan Rum.

This road will deliver you to Route 66, the Melvin Evans Highway, the only four-lane road on the island. You'll pass the airport off to your left. (Route 64 is a U-shaped road that skirts the airport, first as East Airport Road and later as West Airport Road). Go right at the latter and you're soon at the Cruzan Rum Distillery, for generations a family-run business on the site of an old plantation, where you can tour the factory in half an hour and sample one of their famous flavors. Make a slight departure from your circle tour by turning right on 70 (Queen Mary Highway, also known as Centerline Road) to see St. George Village Botanical Garden, where an excellent collection of native plants and ornamentals is displayed among relics of the pre-Columbian and colonial periods. Back on 70, head west to Whim Museum, a restored sugar plantation. Both the Botanical Garden and Whim Museum are worth touring, and both have attractive gift shops. They are the island's major tourist attractions and both hold numerous popular events during the year – chamber music concerts and Ruins Rambles at Whim; an art exhibit, Christmas gala, moonlight garden walks and a mango festival at the Garden. Also on this road is a KMart, the island's only department store.

Follow 70 into the quaint town of Frederiksted. This is a good stop for lunch and a swim at Coconuts or Rythms at Rainbow Beach or the Beach Side Café south of town. In town, check out Polly's bistro-style restaurant on Strand Street for healthy sandwiches and salads with local produce or Blue Moon. Strand Street is on the beautiful waterfront, site of the impressive Caribbean Museum Center for the Arts, and on cruise ship days, the town is hopping with lots of street vendors selling clothing, jewelry, artwork and local fare. At the north end is Fort Frederik where, on July 3, 1848, thanks to progressive governor Peter von Sholten and non-violent slave leader Buddhoe, the slaves of the Danish West Indies were emancipated peacefully. Frederiksted is thus known as Freedom City.

If you like paddle boarding, the first beach north of town is where Teres Veho rents boards. The water here is flat and great for beginners.

When you leave the town head north on 63 and take the second turn to the right,

Mahogany Road (Route 76). This takes you through the tropical forest where you will pass the Lawaetz Museum, a charming old farmhouse built by Danish settlers whose descendants still live on the island; St. Croix LEAP, a woodworking shop using fallen trees; the turnoff to Mount Victory, an eco-camp, and Ridge to Reef Farm, a sustainable farm institution, two bright stars in the island's growing eco-tourism field; and the Domino Club, a thatch-roofed bar featuring beer-drinking pigs. Turn left on 69, which takes you past the beautiful Carambola Golf Course designed by Robert Trent Jones (one of three golf courses on the island), then down The Beast, a monstrous hill triathletes ride their bikes up in the half Ironman competition every May.

You are now back on the north shore. Carambola Hotel is to the left and Route 80 to the right, which takes you past Cane Bay with its famous dive site, the Wall, and a few pleasantly laid-back waterfront bar/restaurants; and Salt River Bay National Historical Park and Ecological Preserve, the only place on U.S. soil where a Columbus party landed and the site of his first hostile encounter with indigenous people. The Salt River Marina is located here. When you reach the end of 80, turn left on 75 and follow it back into Christiansted. You will enter town at Sunday Market Square, a restored block that looks as it did when the slaves gathered there on their day off to visit and buy and sell their own produce and handiwork.

BUCK ISLAND REEF NATIONAL MONUMENT

St. Croix

Waypoint: UV703 (Green Cay) 17°46.60'N, 64°40.10'W
Navigation: 4.6 nm NE Christiansted Harbor
Services: Moorings, Underwater trail

This is the only offshore sailing destination from St. Croix, but it's so good the locals go back time after time. Several charter boats are National Park Service concessionaires and make day and half-day runs. A small, uninhabited island about a mile off the northeast shore, Buck Island has a gorgeous beach on one end and a snorkeling trail on the other. You're likely to see sea turtles and sting rays here, as well as plentiful reef fish. Schools of Blue Tang abound, swimming through the underwater coral garden and its grottos. The trail has underwater signs guiding snorkelers through the reef and identifying the fish and coral, and there are a couple of floats to rest on so that you won't be tempted to touch the coral. The boundary of the National Monument was expanded in 2001, adding over 18,000 acres of submerged lands to the park. Fishing is prohibited.

Navigation & Pilotage

Departing Christiansted Harbor, there are two options; the first takes you to the west of Scotch Bank, leave the same way you came in until you reach the green sea buoy (#1). Then continue north to waypoint UV701 (1.9nm) marking the central navigation point for the island, then proceed east for 4 miles heading for the prominent point on the south end of Buck Island. An alternate shorter route via the Scotch Bank Channel (12ft) is to proceed north out of the harbor to buoy G7 (15 feet high) just due north of Fort Louise Augusta, leaving it to starboard. Do not go further inshore, as there are two shoal areas. On an approximate bearing of 076°m (4.2nm) leave Green Cay to starboard and head for the white beach on the western end of Buck Island. There are two white buoys that mark the extremities of the park's western patch reef area. If you want to go to the snorkeling trail, proceed eastward along the south shore of the island, keeping the white buoy to port, until you see green and red buoys marking the entrance through the reef into the lagoon. Follow the lagoon passage to the eastern end of the island and pick up one of the Park Service moorings. Depth inside the lagoon varies, averaging only 6 feet. Stay in the middle to avoid shoal areas.

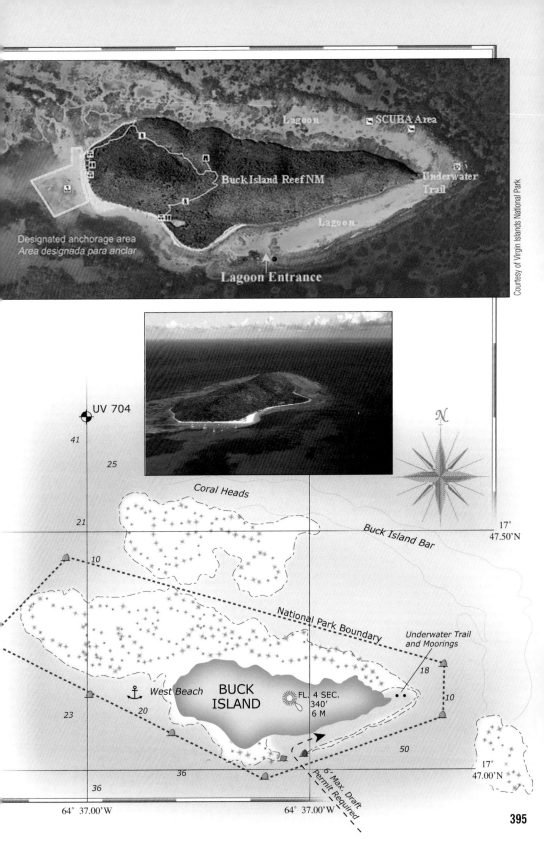

Courtesy of Virgin Islands National Park

Lagoon

SCUBA Area

Buck Island Reef NM

Underwater Trail

Lagoon

Designated anchorage area
Area designada para anclar

Lagoon Entrance

UV 704

41

25

Coral Heads

21

Buck Island Bar

17°
47.50'N

10

National Park Boundary

Underwater Trail
and Moorings

18

West Beach   BUCK
ISLAND

FL. 4 SEC.
340'
6 M

10

23   20

50

17°
47.00'N

36

36

6' Max. Draft
Permit Required

64° 37.00'W   64° 37.00'W

395

Anchoring & Mooring

There is no anchoring inside the reef. At the underwater trail you're welcome to pick up one of the Park Service moorings for day use only. For the time being anchoring is allowed at the designated area off West Beach. Boaters are requested to obtain a permit (good for one year) from the National Park Service office near the wharf in Christiansted or call 340-773-1460. You can anchor anywhere off the beach in about 15 feet of water in deep sand. Please avoid sea grass areas!

Ashore

Buck Island is a nesting site for four species of endangered or threatened sea turtles. If you anchor overnight between June and December, you are not allowed ashore between sunset and sunrise, and bright lights and loud noise are not permitted. You may see monitors and researchers at work ashore.

There are two picnic areas on Buck Island with pit toilets, picnic tables and barbecue grills, a pavilion east of the small pier on the south shore and one without shelter on the western end. Visit the information kiosk located at each picnic area for park guidelines and information. An overland hiking trail provides a 45-minute walk from beach to beach with a stop at the north side reef overlook. Avoid contact with any plants on the island as many will burn or cause an allergic reaction. There is no collecting permitted in the park.

EAST END MARINE PARK

The entire eastern tip of St. Croix has been designated a marine park to protect and replenish corals and fish by regulating boating, diving and fishing within its boundaries, from Chenay Bay on the north to Great Pond on the south. The local government has placed some single point moorings along the north shore for day use only. Look for 16" yellow mooring balls.

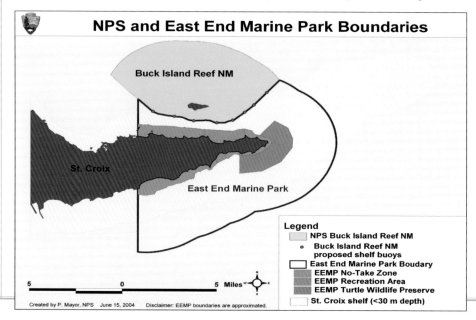

NPS and East End Marine Park Boundaries

Buck Island Reef NM

St. Croix

East End Marine Park

Legend
- NPS Buck Island Reef NM
- Buck Island Reef NM proposed shelf buoys
- East End Marine Park Boudary
- EEMP No-Take Zone
- EEMP Recreation Area
- EEMP Turtle Wildlife Preserve
- St. Croix shelf (<30 m depth)

5   0   5 Miles

Created by P. Mayor, NPS   June 15, 2004   Disclaimer: EEMP boundaries are approximated.

GREEN CAY MARINA

St. Croix

Waypoint: UV703 (Scotch Bank) 17°46.60'N, 64°40.10'W

Navigation: 3nm E of Christiansted Harbor

Services: Marina slips, Fuel, Laundry, Showers, Restaurants, Bar, Hotel, WiFi, Pump-out station, Car rental, Boater's lounge, Day Sailing to Buck Island, Mailboxes, Fitness center

Green Cay Marina is a full service, customer friendly, well protected marina on St. Croix's northern coast east of Christiansted and just south of Green Cay, a small nature preserve. This marina has survived two hurricanes virtually intact and slips are available during hurricane season on a 3-month contract basis. It should be approached from the western side of Buck Island. Look for the yellow buildings with white roofs of Tamarind Reef Resort. The resort and marina are part of the same complex. Visiting yachts enjoy resort privileges including tennis, swimming pool, beach, paddle boards, kayaks, spa and more. The marina manager, Steve Kuntzler, is a customer focused manager and offers several attractive rate offerings for short and long term stays.

Navigation & Pilotage

From the north, or waypoint UV703, leave Green Cay to port and head for the rock jetties. There is a shallow area (7-8') just inside the jetty to port so stay in the middle of the channel (12'). The marina monitors VHF 16 and tel: 340-718-1453. If you call ahead, the dock-master will meet you at the fuel dock and lead you to a slip. Depths are between 8-12 feet. Marina hours are 8am-5pm weekdays and 8am-4pm weekends and holidays. Fuel is available seven days a week. WiFi is free.

Ashore

The marina is well kept and has all the amenities including showers, laundry, water, electricity, pump-out, 24-hour security, fuel and ice, in addition to the 39-room luxury, beachfront resort, beach, tennis courts, kayaks, snorkels, pools and day spa, there are two restaurants, a casual open-air spot (Deep End) on the waterfront and an air-conditioned fine dining establishment (Galleon) overlooking the marina.

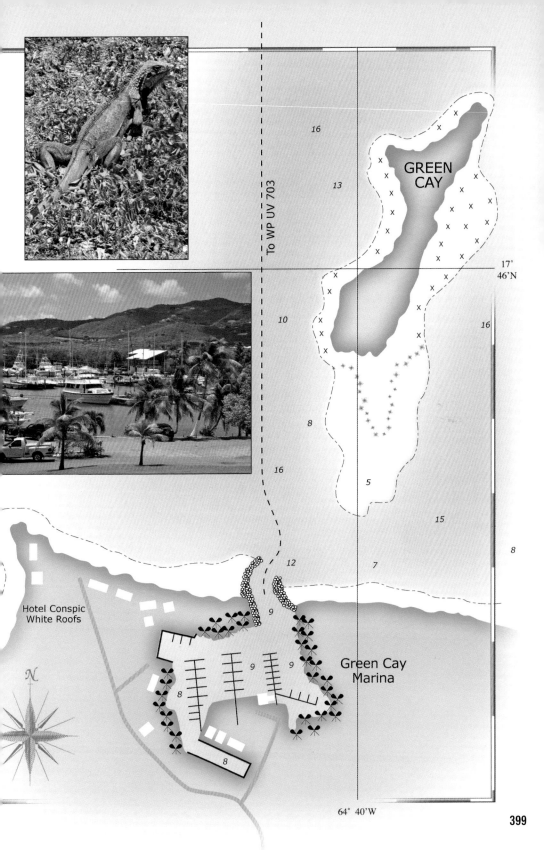

16

To WP UV 703

GREEN
CAY

13

x x x
x x
x x x
x x x
x x x
x x
x x x

17°
46'N

10

x
x x
x x
x x
x

16

8

*
*
*
*
*
*

5

15

16

Hotel Conspic
White Roofs

12

7

8

9

9   9

Green Cay
Marina

N

8

8

64° 40'W

ST. CROIX YACHT CLUB/TEAGUE BAY

Waypoint: UV705 (Coakley Bay) 17°46.50'N, 64°38.50'W
Navigation: 5.2nm E Christiansted Harbor (3.2nm to reef entrance)
Services: Water, Restaurant, Bar, Showers

St. Croix

Navigation and Pilotage

Teague Bay (also marked on the charts as Tague Bay) is 2.5 miles SSW of Buck Island, protected to the north by a continuous reef. Enter from the west at the Coakley Bay Cut where you will see a lighted green marker (Fl.G.4 sec. 15 feet). Leave the marker to port, head well into the bay towards the windmill, then head east, favoring the shore side. The entrance is good for 12 foot depths. The passage is narrow and the prudent skipper will post a lookout on the bow to watch for coral heads. Another opening in the reef, the Cotton Valley Cut, is not recommended except for those with local knowledge as the buoys are privately maintained and there are patch reefs inside the cut. The distance from Coakley Cut to the Yacht Club is approximately 2.7 miles.

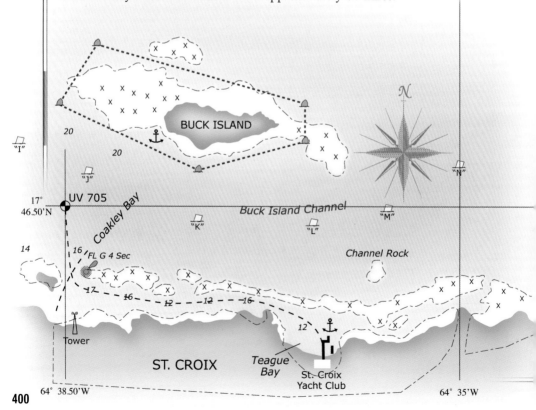

Anchoring

Enter the Yacht Club basin between red and green buoys at coordinates 17°45' 27.7" N, 64°36' 13.3" W. Anchor west of the mooring field or call the club on VHF 16 or 340-773-9531. Slips are rarely available (except in an emergency) and there are no guest moorings. Keep the channel clear to the club dock. You can tie up your dinghy on the main dock or at a small dinghy dock to the east, both available for a fee.

Ashore

The St. Croix Yacht Club extends a friendly welcome to visiting yachts. Reciprocal use is offered to members of recognized yacht clubs, and others may request a guest pass.

The Club is open Wednesday through Sunday and some holidays. Showers are available, ice may be purchased and garbage may be left in the on-site dumpster. However, no fuel, laundry or provisions are available.

The Club has a bar and restaurant and a full social calendar, with happy hour every Friday and a five-course dinner (by reservation) on Wednesdays. There is an active children's program and frequent races for adults and/or children on weekends. After 16 years hosting the St. Croix International Regatta, it continues to attract yachts from all over the Caribbean.

A short dinghy ride from the Yacht Club is the restaurant Duggan's Reef (340-773-9800), a waterfront restaurant specializing in seafood and open every night for dinner and Sundays for brunch. Ziggy's Island Market convenience store is located 2 miles to the west. Tel: 340-773-8382.

ST. CROIX YACHT CLUB/TEAGUE BAY

SALT RIVER
NATIONAL HISTORICAL PARK AND ECOLOGICAL PRESERVE

St. Croix

Waypoint: UV706 (White Horse Rock) 17°47.80'N, 64°45.00'W

Navigation: 3.5nm west of Christiansted Harbor (Caution - Local knowledge required)

Services: Marina, Water, Garbage disposal, Dive tours, Kayak rental, Bioluminescence

Salt River Bay and all the adjacent land surrounding it has been designated a National Park. Ecologically, the bay, with its mangrove forests and sea grass beds, is the heart of a still healthy chain of ecosystems. Historically, this is the only documented Columbus landing site on U.S. soil, and it wasn't a pleasant experience. His armed men went ashore looking for water and were confronted by a canoe full of Carib Indians with bows and arrows. In the altercation that followed, each side had one fatality and all the remaining Indians were taken as slaves.

The Park is managed jointly by the National Park Service and the V.I. Government. In 2004 it acquired the large white house on the western point as a Visitor's Contact Station. On the eastern point work has started on the campus of a Marine Education and Research Center that is slated for construction this decade. A project of the Joint Institute for Caribbean Marine Studies, a collective of three universities – North Carolina, the Virgin Islands and South Carolina – it is intended to incorporate the latest green technologies in a design chosen from a competition among architecture and engineering students.

Navigation & Pilotage

Salt River Bay is in the middle of the island on the north shore. It is a very safe anchorage and a popular hurricane hole but is suitable for shallow draft only, a maximum of 5'10" (1.7 meters) can be carried over the inner sand bar. Local knowledge is advised to enter, as the channel through the reef is narrow, its navigation marker is privately maintained and sandbanks extend from both sides of the bay. Use of your engine and your depth sounder is advised. Some distance

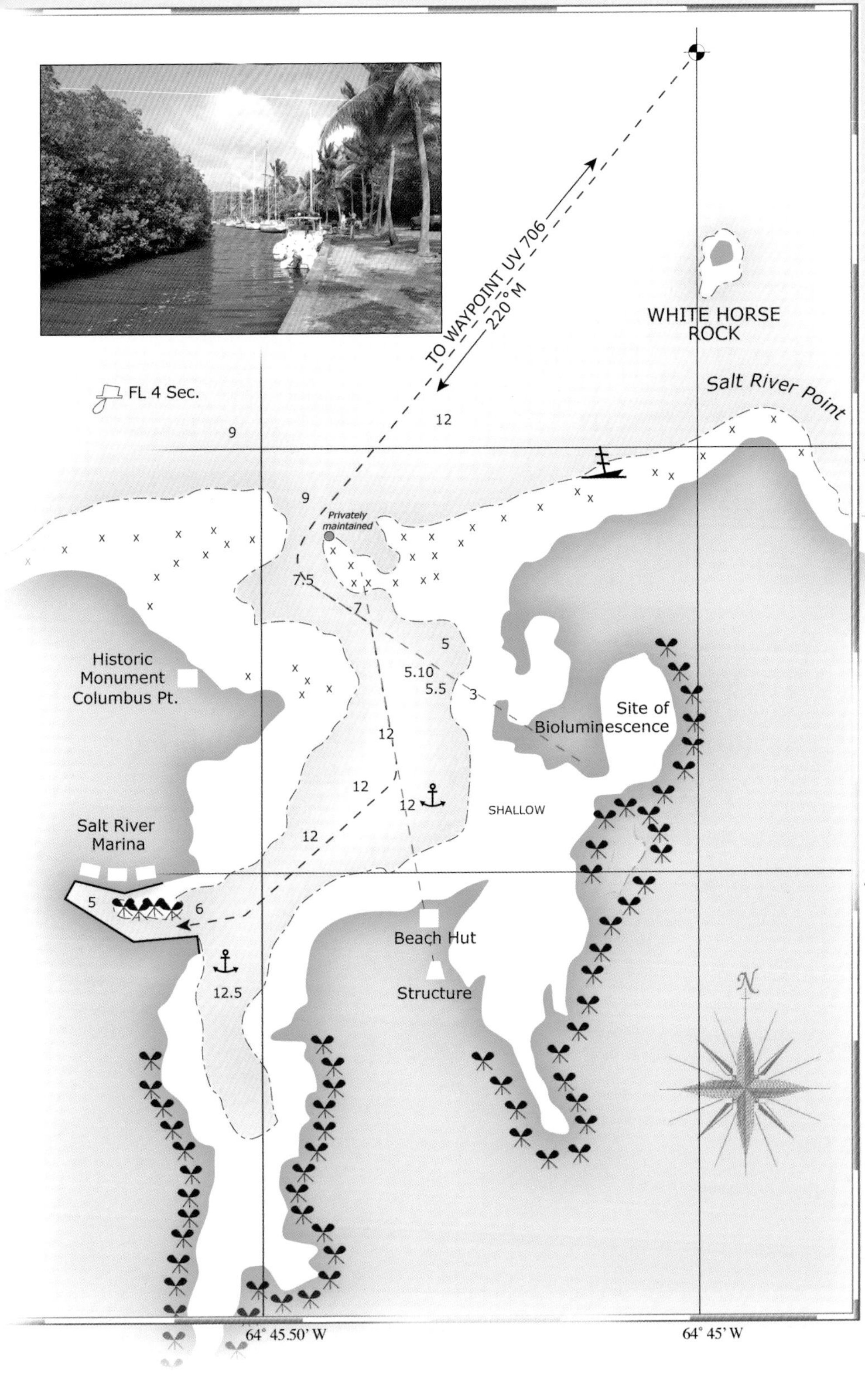

FL 4 Sec.

TO WAYPOINT UV 706
220 M

WHITE HORSE ROCK

Salt River Point

17° 47' N

9

12

9

Privately maintained

7.5

7

5

5.10

5.5

3

Historic Monument Columbus Pt.

Site of Bioluminescence

12

12

12

12

SHALLOW

Salt River Marina

5

6

17° 46.50' N

12.5

Beach Hut

Structure

N

64° 45.50' W

64° 45' W

west of the reef entrance, you will see a tall marker. This is a scientific device monitoring various physical attributes of the reef. It is part of a NOAA project called CREWS (Coral Reef Early Warning System).

Approaching Salt River Bay from the east leave White Horse Rock to port. The rock marks the northern extremity of Salt River Point. From waypoint UV705 (north of White Horse Rock), a course of 220°m will bring you to the entrance to the bay. The reef extends from Salt River Point west across the entire bay towards Columbus Landing and Barrons Bluff further to the west. The narrow entrance into the bay is marked by a privately maintained green buoy that is only anchored by a weight on the seabed. Do not rely on it being on station. Leaving the green marker to port, follow the reef around to port (until the green buoy at the entrance behind you is abeam); turn southeast until you can see a spire roof on the shore to the south. As soon as you can align the spire with a beach shack in front of it, turn toward it and continue toward that range into the anchorage. Compass bearing 180°m should get you safely between the sand bars. Although the sand bars are constantly shifting it was reported to be able to carry 5'10'' (1.7 meters) maximum as of May 2019. As soon as you are past the sandbar the depth will increase rapidly. Salt River Marina monitors VHF 16, if you need assistance.

The entrance to the marina is via a narrow channel on the western side of the bay. A sea wall marks the southern side and a mangrove islet will be evident to the north. Do not enter the marina channel without calling the marina first, the marina is small and maneuvering room is very tight once inside.

Anchoring & Mooring

You may anchor anywhere you find sufficient water except in the marina channel. You can leave your dinghy at the

Salt River Bay

marina. There is a dinghy dock near the kayak shop. The outer bay can be subject to wave action that works its way over the reef, if you are staying aboard the vessel you will want to move deeper into the bay.

Ashore

Salt River Marina is a small and homey facility tucked into a very protected basin on the west side of the bay. This is a perfect hurricane hole, but as such can be hot and buggy. Space is limited and advance notice is recommended. The marina is open 7 days a week and monitors VHF 16 or 340-778-9650 during daylight hours. All services are available to dockside customers, with fuel requiring 24-hour notice. Flyer's Bar & Grill is a lively spot within the marina complex open 12pm-9pm Tuesday-Saturday. tel: 340-772-32222. Dive tours to the Salt River Canyon, one of the best dive sites in the Caribbean can be booked through several companies with pick-ups at the marina. Kayaks can be rented for touring the mangrove-fringed fingers of the bay including evening tours to visit the bay to the east famous for its bioluminescence. Gold Coast Yachts custom designs and builds 40 to 80 foot catamarans on the property. Otherwise, Salt River is not convenient to shore-based services, but taxis can be called and rides to town can be arranged.

SALT RIVER

FREDERIKSTED

Waypoint: UV707 (West point) 17°45.0'N, 64°55.0'W
Navigation: 3.5nm South of Ham's Bluff (NW point)
Services: Provisions, Restaurants, Bars, Garbage disposal

Frederiksted, located on the west coast, is an open roadstead, protected from the prevailing trade winds, but can be dangerous in westerlies, which are extremely rare.

Frederiksted is a quaint, charming and laid-back town with a mixture of Danish Colonial and Victorian architecture framed by beautiful parks along the waterfront. There is an ongoing restoration program evident in Frederiksted as many of the original buildings are painted and renovated in support of the tourism industry. At this time there is no marina in Frederiksted and therefore water and fuel are not available except via dinghy and jerry-cans.

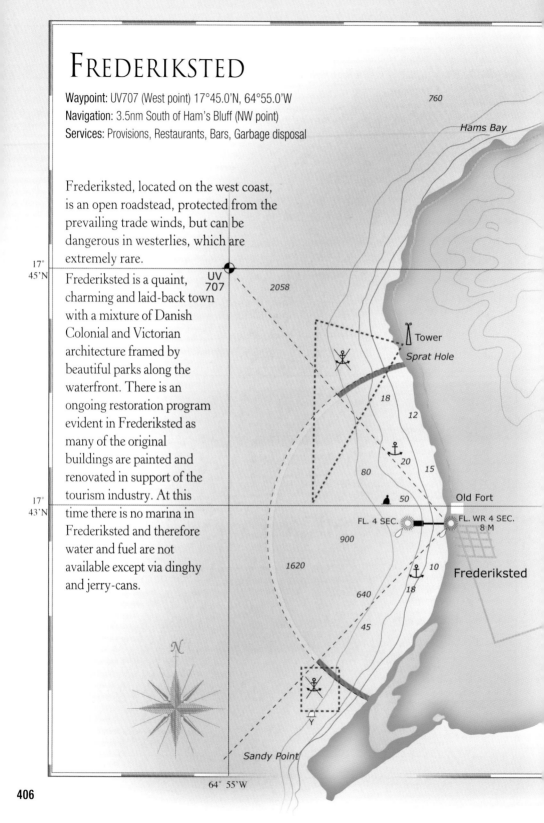

Navigation & Piloting

Frederiksted makes a good landfall when sailing from The Spanish Virgin Islands to the west or the Dutch ABC islands to the south. Approaching from the south, give Sandy Point (the SW extremity of St. Croix) a wide berth. A red buoy (R2) at 17°39.40'N – 64°54.37'W is in 60 feet of water outside a shifting sandbar. Approaching from the north you can hug the shore closely at Ham's Bluff on the NW corner of the island, but once around the point stay about 100 yards offshore of the west coast to avoid shoals. At the red destroyer-mooring ball you can head east to the beach and run close to the beach on into Frederiksted.

Anchoring & Mooring

South of the cruise ship pier the holding is poor with a thin layer of sand over rock. Holding is better on the north side of the

pier and improves as you head north along the beach. Do not anchor within 500 feet of the cruise ship dock. The anchorage along the beach away from town is usually quiet but can be rolly if northerly swells are running. Dinghies can be landed on any stretch of the beach or at low docks either side of the cruise ship pier. The prudent skipper will exercise caution leaving the dinghy as some petty theft has been noted in this area.

Ashore

Frederiksted has a long and storied history. The town was established in 1751 and it was originally protected by Fort Frederik, which dates back to 1700. Today, the fort houses a museum. Locals often refer to Frederiksted as "Freedom City" because it is the site where then Governor General Peter Van Scholten read the proclamation abolishing slavery in 1848.

The town was destroyed by fire in 1878 as a result of a labor revolt. It was later restored during the Victorian era, which is why it now has such lovely blend of "gingerbread" Victorian and Dutch Colonial architecture. The town retains its original seven street by seven street city design.

A visit to Frederiksted will allow you to see several historic buildings including St. Patrick's Catholic Church, which was built in the 1840s, along with its primary school, the Customs House, the 19th Century Apothecary, as well as many other historic buildings. Unfortunately, many of these have fallen into disrepair

due to several major hurricanes and the passing of time.

This small town has all the basics: a post office, banks, drug store, laundry services, small grocery stores and clothing shops, a barber shop, dive shop and coffee shop. It also has some very special attractions notably the Caribbean Museum Center for the Arts, the Crucian Christmas Festival, a loud, colorful and boozy event, and every third Friday of the month Sunset Jazz, a free concert featuring excellent musicians that brings out a diverse family crowd.

Several restaurants are worth mentioning such as the Blue Moon Restaurant on the waterfront on historic Strand Street. They have live jazz on Friday nights and at Sunday Brunch. There is also the Beachside Café at Sand Castle on the Beach for something more casual and try Polly's by the pier on Strand Street and The Lost Dog Pub serving Italian American fare. Rhythms at Rainbow Beach serve burgers, wings, salad and fish.

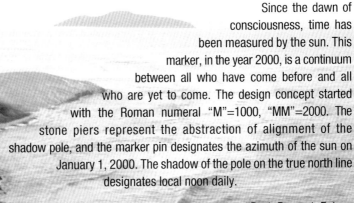

A Millennium Vision

January 1, 2000

Since the dawn of consciousness, time has been measured by the sun. This marker, in the year 2000, is a continuum between all who have come before and all who are yet to come. The design concept started with the Roman numeral "M"=1000, "MM"=2000. The stone piers represent the abstraction of alignment of the shadow pole, and the marker pin designates the azimuth of the sun on January 1, 2000. The shadow of the pole on the true north line designates local noon daily.

"Past, Present, Future:
A Millennium Vision"

The Millennium Monument, East End, St. Croix

CHRISTIANSTED

AUTO RENTAL
Olympic Rent-A-Car
Tel: 340-718-3000
www.olympicstcroix.com

BANKS
Popular
Tel: 340-693-2935
www.popular.vi

Bank of St. Croix
Tel: 340-773-8500
www.bankofstcroix.com

First Bank
Tel: 340-773-0440
www.1firstbank.com

ScotiaBank
Tel: 340-778-5350
www.scotiabank.com

DIVE SHOPS
Cane Bay Dive Shop
Tel: 340-718-9913
www.canebayscuba.com

Dive Experience
Tel: 340-773-3307
www.divexp.com

SCUBA: St. Croix
Ultimate Bluewater
Adventures
Tel: 340-773-5994
www.stcroixscuba.com

N2theBlue
Scuba Diving
Tel: 340-772-3483
www.n2theblue.com

Sweet Bottom Dive
Center
Tel: 340-773-3483
sweetbottomdive.com

ELECTRONICS
Mike's Electronics
Warehouse
Tel: 340-778-6655

Radio Shack
Tel: 340-778-5667

SHOPPING
Purple Papaya
Tel: 340-713-9412

From the Gecko
Boutique
Tel: 340-778-9433
www.fromthegecko.com

Sonya Ltd
Tel: 877-766-9284
The creator of the original
St. Croix Hook Bracelet
www.sonyaltdstore.com

IB Designs Jewelry
Tel: 340-773-4322
www.islandboydesigns.com

Island Tribe
of St. Croix
Tel: 340-719-0936
islandtribestcroix.com
Batik dresses

Many Hands Gallery
Tel: 340-773-1990
www.manyhands.com

Violette's Boutique
Cosmetics, perfumes
Tel: 340-773-2148

LIQUOR, BEER, WINE
Baci Duty Free
Tel: 340-773-5040
www.bacidutyfree.com

Crucian Cellar &
Specialty Shop
Tel: 340-713-9163

S&B Liquor
Tel: 340-772-3934

LAUNDRY SERVICES
Tropical Cleaners
Tel: 340-773-3635

Sadi's Laundry
Tel: 340-772-5000

La Reine Laundry
Tel: 340-778-2801

EMERGENCY/MEDICAL
Ambulance/Fire/Police
Tel: 911

Acute Alternative
Medical Group
Tel: 340-772-2883
Urgent care center

Gov. Juan F. Luis
Hospital
Tel: 340-778-6311
www.jflsvi.org

Rodney A. Fabio, Jr., DDS
Tel: 340-778-6900
Dentist

Daniel T. Kenses, DDS
Tel: 340-692-9770
Dentist

Denise Colbert, DDS
Tel: 340-719-9991
Orthodontist

LODGING
Tamarind Reef Resort, Spa & Marina
Tel: 340-718-4455
tamarindreefresort.com

Holger Danske
Tel: 340-773-3600
www.holgerhotel.com

Buccaneer Hotel
Tel: 340-712-2100
www.thebuccaneer.com

Carrington's Inn
Tel: 340-713-0508
www.carringtonsinn.com

Chenay Bay Beach Resort
Tel: 340-201-1309
www.chenaybay.com

Hotel on the Cay
Tel: 340-773-2035
www.hotelonthecay.com

King Christian Hotel
Tel: 340-692-6330
hotelkingchristian.com

PROVISIONS
Cost U Less
Tel: 340-719-4442

Food Town Supermarket
Tel: 340-718-9990
www.foodtownvi.com

Plaza Extra East
Tel: 340-778-6240

Pueblo Supermarket
Tel: 340-778-0584

MARINA
St. Croix Marine Center
Tel: 340-773-0289
stcroixmarinecenter.com

RESTAURANTS
Dashi
Tel: 340-773-6911
Excellent sushi and Vietnamese specials served in a quaint courtyard – often with live music
www.dashisushi.com

Galangal
Tel: 340-773-0076
A new Thai restaurant near the wharf, open every night but Sunday.
www.galangalstx.com

Balters
Tel: 340-719-5896
Fine cuisine in a simple sophisticated setting
www.balterstx.com

Luncheria
Tel: 340-773-4247
Moderately priced Mexican food in a casual outdoor setting. Open 11am-9pm daily except Sunday.

Rumrunners
Tel: 340-773-6585
Right on Christiansted Harbor, this restaurant serves three meals a day, seven days a week.
rumrunnersstcroix.com

Savant
Tel: 340-713-8666
Dine in or out every evening but Sunday on a fusion of Thai, Mexican and Caribbean cuisines. Reservations suggested.
www.savantstx.com

SAILMAKERS/REPAIRS
**Wesco Awning &
Marine Canvas**
Tel: 340-778-9446
www.wescoawning.com

Wilson's Cruzan Canvas
Tel: 340-773-0694
www.doylecaribbean.com/
locations/usvi.html

MARINE REPAIR & SUPPLIES
St. Croix Marine Center
Tel: 340-773-0289
www.stcroixmarine.com

**Blue Mountain
Purified Water**
Tel: 340-778-6177

TAXI
Antilles Taxi Service
Tel: 340-773-5020

St. Croix Taxi
Tel: 340-778-1088
www.stcroixtaxi.com

FREDERIKSTED

AUTO RENTAL
Avis Rent-A-Car
Tel: 340-778-9355

Budget Rent-A-Car
Tel: 340-778-9636

Centerline Car Rental
Tel: 340-713-0550

Hertz Rent-A-Car
Tel: 340-778-9744

BANKS
First Bank
Tel: 340-773-0440
www.1firstbank.com

ScotiaBank
Tel: 340-778-5350
www.scotiabank.com

DIVE SHOP
**Cane Bay Dive Shop
West**
Tel: 340-718-9913
www.canebayscuba.com

LODGING
Frederiksted Hotel
Tel: 340-772-0500

The Fred
Boutique hotel and
restaurant on the beach
Tel: 340-777-3733

**Sandcastle on the
Beach**
Tel: 340-772-1205
www.sandcastleonthe
beach.com

PROVISIONS
**Stop & Shop
Supermarket**
Tel: 340-692-2771

Supersave Supermarket
Tel: 340-772-3030

RESTAURANTS
Beachside Café
Tel: 340-772-1266
At Sand Castle on the
Beach Hotel south of
Frederiksted, serving
lunch/brunch and
dinner. Live jazz Sat
nights. Reservations
recommended.
www.beachsidecafeatsand
castleonthebeach.com

Lost Dog Pub
Tel: 340-772-3526

Polly's at the Pier
Tel: 340-719-9434
A waterfront neighborhood
café in downtown
Frederiksted serving
breakfast and lunch 7 days
a week. On Strand Street
across from the cruise ship
pier. Organic, gluten-free,
and vegetarian options.

**Rhythms at
Rainbow Beach**
Tel: 340-772-0002
www.rainbowbeachstx.com

Turtles Deli
Tel: 340-772-3676
A unique deli and coffee
shop, with gourmet
sandwiches served on
homemade bread in a
setting right on the beach.
Mon-Sat 8:30am-5:30pm
www.turtlesdeli.com

ISLAND CONNECTIONS

GREEN CAY

LODGING
Tamarind Reef Resort
Tel: 340-718-4455
tamarindreefresort.com

MARINA
Green Cay Marina
Tel: 340-718-1453
VHF channel 16
tamarindreefresort.com

RESTAURANTS
Cheeseburgers in America's Paradise
Tel: 340-718-1118
Near Green Cay Marina. A popular, friendly spot serving lunch and dinner every day from 11am to 9:30pm.

Deep End Bar
Tel: 340-718-7071
Green Cay Marina/ Tamarind Reef Resort complex. Casual open-air restaurant, breakfast, lunch & dinner daily
www.newdeepend.com

SALT RIVER

RESTAURANTS
Flyer's Bar & Grill
Tel: 340-772-3222
12-9pm Tues.-Sat.

DIVE SHOP AND WATERSPORTS
Kayak Caribbean Adventure Tours
Tel: 340-778-1522
www.stcroixkayak.com

Cane Bay Dive Shop
Tel: 340-773-9913
www.canebayscuba.com

LODGING
Carambola Beach Resort
Tel: 340-778-3800
carambolabeach.com

The Waves at Cane Bay
Tel: 340-718-1815
www.thewavescanebay.com

MARINA
Salt River Marina
Tel: 340-778-9650
www.saltrivermarina.com

TEAGUE BAY

St. Croix Yacht Club
Tel: 340-773-9531
www.stcroixyc.com

LODGING
Divi Carina Bay Resort & Casino
Tel: 340-773-9700
www.carinabay.com

PROVISIONS
Ziggy's Island Market
Tel: 340-773-8382
Convenience items, a kitchen specializing in BBQ and island specialties, and the Libation Station bar with scenic deck seating
www.ziggysmarket.com

AFTER THE STORM

Hurricane Irma

Hurricane Irma was a huge news story to most of the world. Days and nights of media coverage turned into weeks of the same. Then, as quickly as this storm tore though the island chain and subsequent areas, updates and stories began to fade from media letting Irma take its place in meteorological history. Although Category 6 is nowhere on the "Saffir-Simpson Hurricane Wind Scale," Irma's winds were recorded to have reached 215 mph, and even higher inside tornadoes that hung on the outside of the eye of the storm. Tearing through the island chain like the witch of all winds, she was the most powerful Atlantic Hurricane ever recorded. Irma left at least 80% of buildings damaged or totally destroyed with one exception. Anegada, an out lying island in the chain, though hit very badly, was spared the worst of the storm's wrath.

Paraquita Bay, Tortola – before and after Hurricane Irma, September 2017

Getting Through & Getting On

These loved islands – long home to a burgeoning yacht charter industry, with countless businesses revolving around sailors and yachtsmen – took toll of the storm's destruction. This involved an equation whose principal numbers have dollar signs – many from the charter boats, a major source of jobs and income. Few boats survived the storm intact. Many lay in different stages of ruin clustered along beaches, shorelines, and even on the other side of roads parallel to the bays.

In the year following the storms devastation, yacht charter companies – knowing how much income was generated by their presence – were quick to clean up, repair docks, and refurbish fleets. Although the storms rearranged much of the scenery, leaving mountainsides more brown than green, trees missing, skeletons of what were homes and debris clinging to rocky slopes; the beautiful waters did not change. In a show of sheer courage and ingenuity, beach bars and restaurants set up to accommodate the much welcome sailors. In many cases, they were temporary or temporarily repaired structures. However, in spite of all of the challenges, food and music coming out of these sea-washed walls was no less than excellent. Scenery may have changed, but sailing has not.

Seeing the islands right after the storm had a shock value that was off the charts. Seeing the landscape today, it is hard to believe that two years ago, buildings lay in piles of rubble. Cars and boats were literally picked up by the winds and moved improbable distances

from where they stood. Roofs were ripped from buildings and homes and literally flew so far no one could believe what they were looking at. People stood, helpless and hopeless amidst the piles and pieces of their broken, destroyed homes. A lot of islanders say, had the storm hit during the dark hours, many more than 4 lives would have been lost. The widespread destruction and fatal blows to the infrastructure and all of the islands was like something you'd think

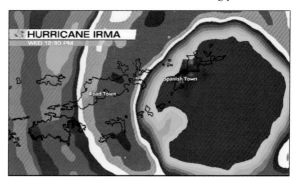

AFTER THE STORM

Virgin Gorda Yacht Harbour

Bitter End North Sound

was the aftermath of a nuclear bomb. Yes! It was that bad, only to be followed by Maria, the second category 5 storm to lash the islands in two weeks. They say a picture is worth a thousand words.

Today, the cleanup and rebuild, though far from complete, is a world away from what it was two years ago, even one year ago. Roads are cleared, supermarkets are open and many restaurants and pubs, if not yet ready are about to open their doors to you and a fresh season for sailing, dining and having fun. Most of the mainstream charter companies are back and have been sending out happy sailors and booking the 2019-20 season. What can you expect on your return post storms? You can expect unspoiled sailing in the bluest of waters, still famed to be some of the best in the world.

After such a litany of monumental tragedy and roadblocks, you might think you will find scowling faces. In reality, there are always a few, but overall, smiles greet you everywhere. Islanders recognize that although they may have lost all of their material possessions, they have their lives to be thankful for. We, who love sailing and love the islands are thankful for their strength and determination in rebuilding paradise.

Soper's Hole West End, Tortola

It Takes a Village

Laid back Jost Van Dyke, laid down by Irma, survived almost indescribable devastation. The destruction on this tiny island cannot be explained in words. Buildings reduced to rubble, debris blown every where, no power, no water and at first, no way to communicate. For those who remember way back when Foxy's was the only beach bar on the island (and

probably, the grandfather of all that came later) it seemed only natural that his Tamarind Bar and Restaurant would become the command center as well as a lifeline for Jost Van Dyke's beleaguered and confused residents. The storm hit hard and long, the calm of the eye lulling some in to thinking the worst was over, but the back end of this force took the largest toll.

Though the roof over Foxy's bar was badly damaged, it was a place where food was prepared and shared. Thankfully there were a few generators on the island and at Foxy's. The first week, that was the only

power available until more were brought in. What food they or anyone else on the island had was stretched to feed everyone. These days, Tessa, Foxy's wife, kind of grimaces at the thought of french fries. She explained that after the storm, the food from all of the bars on the beach was pooled. That included 50 large commercial boxes of fries that became a frequent part of a very meager menu during week one.

Going there today, it's hard to believe that two years ago, mountain sides were stripped almost bare, trees were not only torn from the ground, bark was peeled from their trunks and most all that stood, whether created by nature or built by man, was mortally damaged or destroyed. Along with things lost, a coconut tree had fallen on the roof of Tessa's office, it housed more than 50 years of memorabilia. Along with family photos and much more, she and almost everyone on the island now have to rely on the scrapbooks in their own

Tessa and Foxy

memories. Today the iconic "Foxy's" is back in full 3D party mode. 3D is Dine, Drink and Dance in whatever order you like.

Ali Baba's is open, but only after a long, hard push to overcome the storm's wrath. Off island when it hit, Baba was a long way from what has been home since being brought to the island at the tender age of 5. Unable to get a flight back for several weeks, he didn't know what was going on. He finally returned only to find "a broken down Ali Baba" and confesses "it was really scary seeing this pile of just stuff." He went on to say that "it was work, work, and more work and the next day it looked as if nothing had been done." He and Urinthia, wife/co-owner of the restaurant and bar, struggled to rebuild their businesses and lives with grit and faith.

Corsair's saw the storm destroy their building leaving nothing to salvage. Owner, Vinny says there was just one option for him, to finish the job Irma started and level what she left. Off island when the storm hit, about a week later he was able to return. "Everyone," Vinny said, "was walking around trying to do something... a head count was being taken and all I can say is, "thank God for life, what else can you do?" Vinny explains what it felt like to see his place bulldozed and was happy when, girlfriend, Lori jumped in with her talents to help redesign the building. They are open and ready to serve you three great meals a day.

If you wander toward the west end of the beach toward the Ferry Dock, on your right, you'll see a little snack shop run by a courageous little lady, Joan. Joan's son shared an after the storm story with us that spoke to the dedication many visitors have to the islands. Post Irma, Joan's kitchen was minimal. She was asked to cook dinner for a family who was visiting

Dinghy dock, Cane Garden Bay

Jost Van Dyke. She apologized, explaining that it would take a long time as she had only one burner to cook on. The people gave her a go, were patient and dinner was great. Several weeks later, there was a package for her at the dock. She was going to pick it up and advised she would need help. To her surprise, the big box she went to pick up was a 4 burner stove and oven. The sender... the family who had patiently waited for the dinner she had cooked on one burner.

When asking different people on the island what it was like for them after Irma, they all, in one way or another, said the same thing. It was hard coming to terms that this was real and not just a bad dream. It was, in fact, a living nightmare and it was, teamwork sharing and caring that made recovery start to happen.

"First I'd like to thank Cruising Guides for their quest in getting the best and most accurate information available to their audience.

Without hesitation I express sincere gratitude to the RDA's Deputy Director in the Programme Strategy Department, Mr. Matthew Waterfield for his tireless support in responding to countless inquiries regarding the progress of existing projects as well as future plans with the government. The teamwork here has been wonderful. Last, but certainly not least, we continue to welcome sailors and visitors to the Virgin Islands and thank you all for your loyalty and support."

~ Colene A. Penn, Head of Communications,
Recovery and Development Agency (RDA)

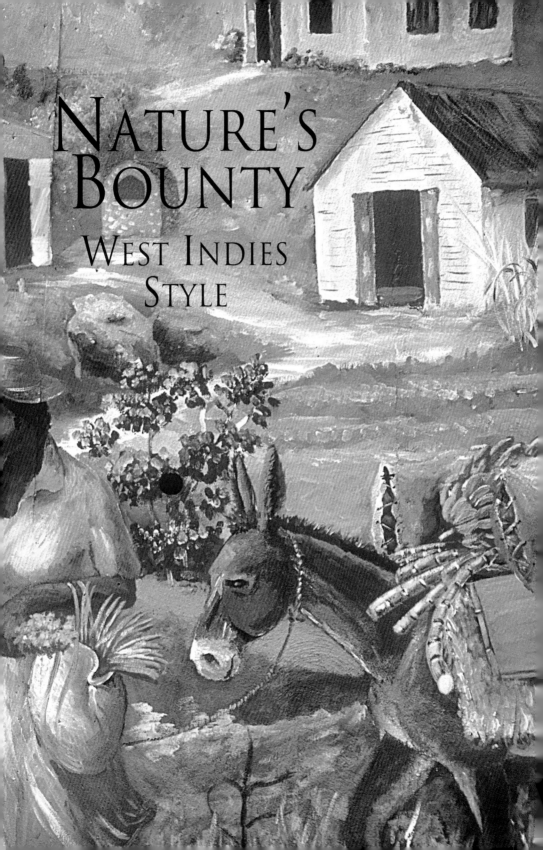

Nature's Bounty

West Indies Style

Fabulous Island Fruits & Vegetables

A collection of some of the most delicious tropical produce to be found in the Virgin Islands.

Sugar Apple

A favorite throughout the islands, the sugar apple looks like it wears a coat of armor! Actually when ripe, it breaks open easily and the delicious, custard-like interior can be scooped out by the spoonful or by eating it by the mouthful, taking care to spit out the shiny seeds inside. It is well worth the effort, as the inside is sweet, with a wonderful sort of soft texture.

Guava

This colorful fruit is used for making jams, jellies, and is scrumptious in pies and tarts. The guava is a small, usually round fruit that grows on a tree. The skin is green to yellow-green, and pulp inside is pink or peach to an almost red colour, with lines of seeds. Guava ice cream is a delicacy not to be missed.

Passion Fruit

Despite the connotation of the name, this fruit may be rather baffling to the first time taster. It is actually quite unattractive with a tough, wrinkly, brownish skin and is about the size of a lemon. The interior has a yellow green jellyish pulp with edible brown seeds. When the seeds are removed, the passion fruit essence is used to flavor exotic drinks, ices, tarts and pies, becoming an interesting, perfumey addition to many recipes.

Genip

Looking like a bunch of green grapes, these small, round fruits are a bit more challenging to eat! First the somewhat tough skin encasing the pulp must be pulled off (usually with your teeth). Once the skin is gone, the inside is yours to tug the sweet, sometimes tart pulp from the rather large pit. Although not easy fruits to eat, genips can keep you busy for quite awhile!

Ugli Fruit

Resembling an ugly version of a grapefruit the ugli fruit is light green to a yellowy orange colour, and can be the size of an orange to the size of a large grapefruit. Succulent and dripping with juice it is best eaten the same way as a grapefruit or an orange (the skin is easily peeled). If you have an opportunity to try this wondrous fruit, be sure to enjoy its blessings.

Tamarind

Growing from large, lovely shade trees are the pods of the tamarind tree. Used in many sauces such as Worcestershire, chutney, and piccalilli, tamarind is also used for sweet candies, and jams. One has to develop a taste for this often tart fruit, but, once acquired, it is hard to stop the attachment. To eat you must first crack open the pod, remove the threads and then consume the sticky paste attached to the large seeds.

Papaya

Growing from a tall, slender umbrella-shaped tree, the fabulous "paw-paw" varies from an eggplant shape to an oval or round shape. The colors vary from a green to orange or yellow, but the fruits must be tested by squeezing to ascertain whether it is ripe or not. The texture of the lovely orange, melon like interior of the fruit is almost as heavenly as the taste, especially when sprinkled with a bit of fresh lime. Green papaya still hard to the squeeze, is used as a cooked vegetable in many delectable recipes.

Sapodilla

About the size of a medium apple, the sapodilla should be eaten only when very ripe and almost mushy like a plum. The skin is a pale tan or beige colour with shiny black seeds inside that should not be eaten. This fruit is used in making many dessert dishes, and is delicious when eaten with other fruits in a fruit salad.

Soursop

A very unlikely looking delicacy this fruit is large (often weighing several pounds), with a green, spiny exterior. The shape is like that of a large pine cone irregularly formed. Only very few are eaten fresh, as most are used in flavoring other dishes with it's sweet fragrance, like soursop ice cream, or in tropical fruit drinks with a healthy measure of rum!

Mango

The mango grows from a large, leafy tree that during mango season becomes heavily laden with its scented fruit. Mangos come in many varieties, but are usually best eaten at the beach, where one can jump into the sea to clean off the delicious stickiness. Grafted mangos are less fibrous, and when peeled are a delight. One may see children and adults sucking on mangos to extract the juicy, orange flesh from the fibers and bulky seed in the middle.

Breadfruit

The breadfruit tree is a common sight on many Caribbean islands. Mature fruits have dimpled green skins and grow to 6 inches or larger in clusters on magnificent trees of up to 60 feet in height with huge, long-fingered leaves. Inside, the soft, fleshy fruits are yellowish-brown to white in color and rich in carbohydrates and vitamins A, B and C. Breadfruit can be cooked as a starchy vegetable side dish or in breadfruit breads, puddings and pies. Try it baked with salt, pepper and butter.

Christophene

The pear-shaped christophene originated in Mexico where it is known as chayote, and is a member of the gourd family. It can be eaten raw or cooked and is crisp, juicy and nutty flavored, with a taste like fresh, young squash. Large christophenes may be stuffed with a mixture of bread crumbs, meat, cheese, onions, herbs and seasonings and broiled or baked.

Dasheen

This versatile plant grows to a height of four to six feet. The large, handsome, arrow-shaped leaves, sometimes called elephant ears, are similar to spinach. The young, tender leaves are used in callaloo soup, while the tubers, shown here, are generally stubby and similar in size to potatoes. Also called cocoyam, taro, eddo and kalo, the dasheen tubers are usually boiled, roasted or baked and eaten like potatoes.

Aubergine

This egg-shaped member of the nightshade family is a common plant throughout the Caribbean, as it relies on the warm climate and plentiful rain supply to support its growth. The large, glossy fruits are known by various other names, including Chinese eggplant, Jew's apple, egg fruit, melongene, garden egg and mad apple. The skin colors range from dark purple to mottled purple and white. Served as a vegetable, the ripe aubergines may be cubed and boiled or cut into strips or slices, battered and fried. Comprised of over 90 percent water, aubergines are low in both calories and nutritional value.

SUGAR KINGS, RUM, PIRATES & THE ROYAL NAVY

On his second voyage to the West Indies in 1493, Christopher Columbus brought sugar cane, where it flourished in the tropical environment and within a decade it was being cultivated on Hispaniola (now Haiti and the Dominican Republic). From there, the Spanish developed sugar plantations in both Jamaica and Puerto Rico. Eager to participate in the vast potential for trade in the region, the major powers of Europe raced to establish colonies within the Americas.

It is commonly understood that the first distillation of rum took place on the plantations of the Caribbean region, where it was discovered that molasses could be fermented into an alcohol known as rum. As the demand for sugar in Europe increased, the plantations throughout the Caribbean became larger, which in turn increased the demand for labor as the burden of manning plantations fell to thousands of enslaved Africans.

Pirates and Privateers throughout the Caribbean, preyed upon merchant shipping passing through the area on their way back to Europe and North America laden with gold and with holds full of rum. Logically the rum, an inexpensive commodity throughout the Caribbean, became synonymous with pirates, no doubt popularized by literature such as Robert Louis Stevenson's Treasure Island. Rum would often be the downfall of many pirate crews where, unlike navy and merchant ships of the time where the purser measured out the daily rum ration, a democratically run pirate ship, with its less than robust code of discipline, often led to a complacent disregard for sobriety.

When the British fleet captured the island of Jamaica in 1655, the availability of local rum prompted the Royal Navy to exchange each seaman's daily tot of French brandy to rum. It is commonly thought that this practice of having spirits aboard originated because fresh water aboard vessels traveling long distances would become stale quickly, and the addition of a small amount of brandy or rum made it more palatable and helped kill the algae. The tradition of the 'tot' gives platform to the legend of the origins of the term 'Nelson's Blood.' Subsequent to the death of Admiral Nelson at the conclusion of the battle of Trafalgar, his body was ordered to be preserved in a barrel of rum in order to be shipped back to England. Upon arrival the barrel was found to be dry and after the body was removed it was found that several holes had been drilled in the bottom and the rum drained, and no doubt consumed by the battle worn sailors; hence the terms "Nelson's Blood" and "Tapping the Admiral."

THE PERFECT VIRGIN ISLAND RUM DRINK?

It is hard to say for sure but intense surveys remain an ongoing part of our research each year, in an effort to discover the perfect sailors drink in paradise. From the remote beach bars on Anegada to the laid back island of Jost Van Dyke and the sheltered coves of Gorda Sound, we bring you a selection of our favorite recipes to make aboard while conducting your own research.

CARIBBEAN RUM PUNCH

(serves 2)
0.5 oz. fresh lime juice
4 oz. orange juice
4 oz. pineapple juice
1.5 oz. Pusser's rum
(or other dark rum)
1.5 oz. light rum
A little grenadine for color

Mix ingredients together, pour over ice, sprinkle with nutmeg, and garnish with an orange slice and a cherry.

THE ISLAND MOJITO

1.5 oz good quality light rum
Club soda
12 mint leaves
½ lime
2 tbsp simple syrup

Muddle the fresh mint leaves and the juice of ½ a lime. Cover with 2 tbsp. of simple syrup and top with ice. Add 1.5 oz of light rum and top with club soda. Stir well and garnish with a wedge of lime and mint leaves. Add a stick of sugar cane if available.

THE DARK 'N STORMY

1.5 oz. Pusser's Rum
(or other dark rum)
Ginger beer
Fill a tall glass with ice cubes, add 4 oz ginger beer, add rum, and garnish with a slice of fresh lime

*Try them all,
and let us know
your favorite!*

THE PAINKILLER

4 oz. pineapple juice
1 oz. orange juice
1 oz. Coco Lopez cream of coconut
2-4 oz. Pusser's
(or other dark rum... depending upon your stamina)
Grated nutmeg

Combine all ingredients and shake vigorously. Pour into a tall glass with ice cubes and sprinkle with fresh nutmeg.

SEX ON DE BEACH CARIBBEAN STYLE

1.5 oz. coconut rum
0.5 oz spiced rum
1 oz. peach schnapps
2 oz. cranberry juice
2 oz. pineapple juice

Combine ingredients with ice, shake vigorously until frothy, and pour into tall glass over ice. Garnish with orange slice and cherry.

ABOUT THE AUTHOR

The genesis of *The Cruising Guide to the Virgin Islands* started in New York in the late '60s when Simon and then-partner, decided they would blend their respective skills to develop informational/photographic publications based upon their intended sailing adventures. At the time, Simon, a native of the UK, was an aspiring member of the Madison Avenue advertising world. They acquired a classic 1936 John Alden cutter, and after a good deal of preparation, consternation, and trepidation set sail for the warmer waters of the Caribbean. Weather is capricious; older wooden boats more so.

The loss of a rig became serendipitous when, awaiting a new mast, they became maritime residents of West End, Tortola. During this extended stay, Simon discovered that a new fledgling industry was starting to develop. A career in international marketing was swiftly traded for a management position in a new charter fleet where he was ideally positioned to listen to the concerns of sailors from around the world discovering the delights and challenges of Caribbean cruising.

Some years later and back in the USA, the first edition of *The Cruising Guide to the Virgin Islands* was published in 1982. Contemporaneously, he joined The Moorings as VP Sales and Marketing where he remained for 15 years, the latter five as CEO as the company grew in size from twenty yachts and one base location to an international company with over twenty-five base locations across the world.

The Scotts have been writing the *Cruising Guide to the Virgin Islands* for 38 years, in addition to running Cruising Guide Publications which also publishes other popular cruising titles that span the islands of the Caribbean from the Virgin's down through the Leeward and Windward Islands to Grenada in the south. The BVI was their first home, and as the saying goes "home is where the heart is." Their personal boat, a Cambria 44 *(Toad Hall)* has been a familiar profile in Caribbean waters. Regrettably she was also a victim of Hurricane Irma along with so many others and so much property throughout the islands. Another boat is on the horizon, but in the meantime, chartering provides access to the places and people that are the focus of the guide. The offices of Cruising Guide Publications are located in Florida, USA, where they can be reached with updates and suggestions for improvement.

info@cruisingguides.com

ADVERTISERS DIRECTORY

ANCHORAGES